WILLIAM LLOYD GARRISON.

A.W. Elson & Co. Boston

Wm. Lloyd Garrison
1874.

MY COUNTRY IS THE WORLD:
MY COUNTRYMEN ARE ALL MANKIND.

WILLIAM LLOYD GARRISON

1805-1879

THE STORY OF HIS LIFE

TOLD BY HIS CHILDREN

VOLUME IV. 1861-1879

NEW-YORK: THE CENTURY CO.
1889

LIST OF ILLUSTRATIONS.

Vol. IV.

TABLE OF CONTENTS.

VOL. IV.

THE END.

(1861-1879.)

WILLIAM LLOYD GARRISON.

CHAPTER I.

"No Union with NON-Slaveholders!"—1861.

"TO me," wrote George Thompson to Mr. Garrison, on hearing of Lincoln's election, "it seems that the triumph just achieved has placed the cause in a new, a critical, and a trying position; demanding (if it be possible) additional vigilance, inflexible steadfastness to fundamental moral principles, and unrelaxed energy in the employment of anti-slavery means. You have now to grapple with the new doctrine of Republican *conservatism*, and will be called to contend with those in power who, having gained their object by the assistance derived from the abolition ranks, will use their power to repress, if not to punish, the spread of the true gospel of freedom. You have now to make genuine converts of those who have as yet only been baptized into the faith of non-extension, and whose zeal in that direction is mere *white-man-ism*. Forgetting the things that are behind, you have to reach forth to the things that are before, pressing towards the object you had in view when starting—the utter extermination of slavery *wheresoever* it may exist." *Nov. 23, 1860; Lib. 30:198.*

The fears of this sagacious observer were quickly justified. While the abolitionists, without pause, renewed in the fall their campaign of petitions for the perfecting (in a disunion sense) of the Massachusetts Personal Liberty *Lib. 30:186.*

CHAP. I. 1861. Law, leading Republican papers, like the Boston *Journal* and *Transcript*, and the Springfield *Republican*,— alarmed at once by the very success of the party in the national *Lib.* 30:186, 189, 190. election, and by the rapid movement of the South towards secession,— earnestly advocated the repeal of the law. *Lib.* 30:205. They were reënforced by an address to the people of the State signed by the weightiest members of the legal profession, as Judge Lemuel Shaw, ex-Judge Benjamin R. Curtis, Joel Parker, Sidney Bartlett, Theophilus Parsons, and by equally shining lights in the world of scholarship and letters, as George Ticknor, Jared Sparks, and the Rev. James Walker, President of Harvard College, by George Peabody, the Rev. George Putnam, ex-Governors Henry J. Gardner and Emory Washburn, and some thirty others, representing all parties. These citizens were moved (in the immoral jargon of that day) by a "sense of responsibility to God for the preservation and transmission of the priceless blessings of civil liberty and public order which his providence has bestowed upon us." They would repeal the Personal Liberty Law from their "love of right," "their sense of the sacredness of compacts." To their aid *Lib.* 31:5. came George Ashmun, who had presided over the Chicago Convention that nominated Lincoln, and, in the last act of his truckling official life, Gov. N. P. Banks. But his suc- *Lib.* 30:178 cessor, John A. Andrew, triumphantly elected in spite of *Nov.* 19, 1859; *Lib.* 30:141. his having presided over a meeting in aid of John Brown's family, gave immediate notice in his message to the Legis- *Lib.* 31:6. lature that reaction in deference to the Slave Power would find no supporter in him.

Foiled in this direction, the "respectable" classes fell to mobbing again, being made desperate by the quick adhesion of the Gulf States, during January, to South Carolina in rebellion. Their fury was directed afresh against Wendell Phillips, whose lineage made him a sort of renegade in their eyes, and whose invectives were unendurable when directed against themselves. Scenes similar *Ante*, 3:505. to those witnessed on December 16 attended his Music- *Lib* 31:14 Hall discourse in Mr. Parker's pulpit, on "The Lesson of the Hour," on January 20; and for weeks it was deemed necessary to guard his home with volunteer defenders from among the young men of the congregation. CHAP. I. 1861.

W. L. Garrison to Oliver Johnson.

BOSTON, Jan. 19, 1861. *MS.*

It will be a fortnight, to-morrow, since I have been out-of-doors. I have had a very severe cold, or succession of colds (for I am growing more and more susceptible to such attacks), and a slow fever hanging about me; and, though the latter seems to be broken up, I am still weak, so as to make any effort burdensome.

It is on this account I have not replied to your letter, giving me an extract from Mary Ann's,[1] relative to her vision of a plot in embryo for a murderous assault upon our dear and noble friend, Wendell Phillips. I thought it best, on the whole, to say nothing to him about it; but that his precious life is in very great danger, in consequence of the malignity felt and expressed against him in this city since the John Brown meeting, there is no doubt among us. Hence, we are quite sure of a mobocratic outbreak at our annual meeting on Thursday and Friday next; and, though some of us may be exposed to personal violence, Phillips will doubtless be the object of special vengeance. The new mayor, Wightman, is bitterly opposed to us, refuses to give us any protection, and says if there is any disturbance, he will arrest our speakers, together with the Trustees of Tremont Temple! What a villain! I should not wonder if blood should be shed on the occasion, for there will be a resolute body of men present, determined to maintain liberty of speech. Whether an attempt will be made to break up the A. S. Festival at Music Hall, on Wednesday evening, remains to be seen. But all will work well in the end.

Jan. 24, 25. *Joseph M. Wightman.* *Jan. 23.*

Phillips is to speak at the Music Hall to-morrow forenoon, before Mr. Parker's congregation, and another violent demonstration is anticipated. Mayor Wightman refuses to order the police to be present to preserve order. This makes the personal peril of Phillips greater than it was before. . . . *Jan. 20.*

Dark as the times are, beyond them all is light. I would have nothing changed; for this is God's judgment-day with our guilty nation, which really deserves to be visited with civil and

[1] Mrs. Oliver Johnson. She had clairvoyant powers.

CHAP. I. — 1861. servile war, and to be turned inside out and upside down, for its unparalleled iniquity. I fervently trust this pro-slavery Union is broken beyond the possibility of restoration by Northern com-

Lib. 31 : 6, 11, 12. promises; yet, when I see our meetings everywhere mobbed down, and the cities swarming with ruffians in full sympathy with the Southern traitors, and the Northern pulpits more satanic than ever, as far as they speak out against Abolitionism, and the Republican Party constantly "shivering in the wind," I am not sure but *the whole country* is to come under the bloody sway of the Slave Power—for a time—as it has not yet done.

Mr. Garrison's illness confined him to the house through the entire month of January, so that he was unable to attend the annual meeting of the Massachusetts Anti-Slavery Society, which began its sessions at Tremont Temple on the morning of January 24, and missed being an active participant in that memorable occasion. At his request the 94th Psalm was read at the opening of the meeting by the Rev. Samuel May, Jr. The following letter was also read by Mr. Quincy:

W. L. Garrison to Edmund Quincy.

MS. and Lib. 31 : 17. BOSTON, Jan. 24, 1861.

MY DEAR COADJUTOR: . . . I am still not sufficiently strong to justify me, as a matter of common prudence, in being present at our annual State gathering to-day. "The spirit is willing," and restless for liberation, "but the flesh is weak." I believe this will be the first of the long series of anniversaries held by the Massachusetts Anti-Slavery Society, which I have failed to attend—held "through evil report" and "much tribulation"—in storm and sunshine—in the midst of impending violence, or with undisturbed composure—but always held hopefully, serenely, triumphantly. It is a great cross to me to break the connection at this crisis; especially as, judging from "the fury of the adversary," the meeting, to-day, will be the most encouraging and the most potential ever held by the Society, whether broken up by lawless violence, or permitted to proceed without molestation. The cause we advocate being not ours, but God's—not ours, but human nature's—appealing to all that is just, humane, noble, and true, and upheld by an omnipotent arm — it is beyond all defeat, unconquerable and immortal; "therefore will not we fear, though the earth be removed, and though the mountains be carried into the midst of the sea." CHAP. I. 1861.

May a Divine patience, firmness, and spirit of peace be vouchsafed to all the friends of impartial freedom who may be present at the meeting to-day, not returning railing for railing, but looking calmly and joyfully to the end of this tremendous conflict with the powers of darkness — namely, the liberation of every bondman on the American soil, and thenceforward the commencement of an era of universal reconciliation, happiness, and prosperity, such as the world has never yet witnessed.

Yours, to break every yoke,

WM. LLOYD GARRISON.

The resolutions, which were presented to the meeting by Wendell Phillips, were drawn by Mr. Garrison with his usual tact, and enunciated the fundamental principles of the abolitionists in a series of quotations from the speeches and writings of Webster, Channing, and Clay, and from the first article of the Constitution of Massachusetts. It was not easy for a Union-saving mob of Webster idolators to take exception to, or howl down, a resolution beginning: "Resolved, That (to quote the language of Daniel Webster)," and they were compelled to listen in silence, if not with composure.

The first speaker of the morning was the Rev. James Freeman Clarke, who made a forcible speech, interrupted only by occasional hisses from the rear gallery, where a crowd of turbulent fellows were gathered. The appearance of Wendell Phillips, who followed Mr. Clarke, was the signal for a pandemonium of cat-calls, yells, cheers, hisses, songs, and derisive remarks, which the orator parried and punctuated with ready wit. At last, forbearing to strain his voice in the vain attempt to make himself heard, he quietly addressed the reporters at his feet, saying: "While I speak to these pencils, I speak to a million of men. What, then, are those boys? We have got the press of the country in our hands. Whether they like us or not, they know that our speeches sell their papers. With five newspapers we may defy five hundred boys. . . . My voice Lib. 31:17.

Chap. I. 1861.

is beaten by theirs, but they cannot beat types. All hail and glory to Faust, who invented printing, for he made mobs impossible!" Those who were present on this occasion will long remember the orator's triumph in compelling, by these tactics, the very miscreants who had drowned his voice to weary of their useless clamor, and, lapsing into comparative quiet, to beg him to "speak louder," that they might hear him. He finished his speech without further difficulty, and was followed by Ralph Waldo Emerson, who had seldom appeared on an anti-slavery platform, but who came now to bear his testimony in behalf of free speech, and to face a mob for the first time. He, too, was assailed by insult and interruption, but he nevertheless held his ground and made his speech, protesting against further compromise or concession to the South. The last speaker of the morning was T. W. Higginson.[1]

Cf. Letters of L. M. Child, pp. 147–49.

The afternoon session was even more exciting, for the mob, finding the police passive, and counting on the sym-

[1] The Rev. Jacob M. Manning, the associate pastor of the Old South Church, and as liberal and progressive as his colleague (Dr. George Blagden) was the reverse, had courageously spoken at the meeting in behalf of John Brown's family, held in Tremont Temple, in November, 1859, and was among the speakers invited to participate in this meeting of the Massachusetts A. S. Society. Heartily sympathizing, he at first agreed to do so, but subsequently wrote to Mr. Garrison that he felt he ought to withdraw his promise, as the safety of his brother-in-law, then resident in South Carolina, might be endangered if he should take part at this time. "Great God, what a country!" he exclaimed —"that I cannot speak for liberty without perilling the life of my brother!" (MS. Jan. 8, 1861.) Mr. Garrison, from his sick-bed, dictated a reply, freely absolving him, and said: "If it were a question relating to a compromise of principle, then, I am sure, you would be as unwilling to allow father or mother, brother or sister, wife or child, to deter you from uttering your sentiments on the occasion alluded to, as I should be to exonerate you from the discharge of a duty which would then imperatively devolve upon you. But, as there is no moral obligation for you to speak at any particular meeting of the Anti-Slavery Society, it simply becomes a question of expediency and sound discretion, and therefore I think you have acted considerately . . . in wishing to recall your promise. . . . You have, on various occasions, shown rare moral courage and independence in bearing a frank, bold, and unequivocal testimony against the colossal sin of our country; and your last effort, on Fast Day, in your own pulpit, must satisfy all of your determination to be true to your conscientious convictions, come what may" (MS. copy, Jan. 8, 1861).

pathy of the new Democratic Mayor, became more virulent, made speaking fruitless, and began hurling the cushions from the gallery seats to the floor below. The behavior of the audience on the floor, and especially of the women, was admirable. They quietly kept their seats, and refused to be intimidated or stampeded. The avenues to the platform were guarded by trusty friends, to prevent the mobocrats from capturing the meeting as they did on December 3d. Presently the Mayor appeared with a posse of police, and, stating that the Trustees of the building had asked him to disperse the meeting, he requested the audience to leave. Unhappily for him, the Trustees were present and promptly denied his statement, demanding that he should read their letter, and, on his reluctant compliance, it appeared that they had requested him to quell the riot and protect the meeting! Convicted of falsehood in this humiliating manner, before his "fellow-citizens," the "Chief Magistrate" turned to Edmund Quincy, who was in the chair, and abjectly asked his commands. "Clear the galleries," said Mr. Quincy, and it was done. "Give us fifty policemen this evening to protect the meeting," he continued. "You shall have them," responded the Mayor, who, returning to the City Hall, straightway wrote an order to close the hall and "prevent any meeting being held there" that evening.[1] This was the last triumph of pro-slavery violence in Boston.

J. M. Wightman.

Ante, 3:505.

Lib. 31:18.

With the exception of a brief session in the Anti-Slavery Office, the next morning, the abolitionists made

[1] Doubtless there would have been a stormy time, had the evening meeting been held, for the mob, knowing the Mayor was in sympathy with them, and inflamed by liquor, were prepared for a murderous onslaught under the cover of darkness; but a fearless magistrate, resolved to execute the laws, could have protected the meeting and preserved the peace, for the police force was ample. Mr. Phillips appealed in person to Gov. Andrew, hoping that he would use the militia, and do, in the name of the State, what the recreant Mayor refused to do in the name of the city; but the Governor, with every desire to protect free speech, felt that he lacked the statutory power to interfere, unless the Mayor should call upon him to do so. This led to an agitation for a Metropolitan Police, under State control, such as New York enjoyed — or, rather, possessed; but the Legislature refused to grant it.

CHAP. I. — 1861. no further attempt to hold their meetings, but adjourned *sine die*, well knowing that the indignation excited by this outrage would be worth many conventions to the cause; and so, of course, it proved. But the spirit of compromise was still rampant, and the most abject propositions were urged for the conciliation of the seceding States and the maintenance of the Union with fresh guarantees for the protection of the Slave Power. In this the Republican leaders were conspicuous. In Congress, Charles Francis Adams, representing the Third Massachusetts District, *Lib.* 31:9. proposed the admission of New Mexico as a State, with or without slavery, and favored an amendment to the Constitution requiring that all subsequent amendments affecting slavery should be proposed by a slave State and ratified by all the States (instead of the customary three-fourths).[1] *Jan.* 12, 1861; *Lib.* 31:10. Mr. Seward, speaking in the U. S. Senate, favored the repeal of the Personal Liberty laws, and the amendment of the Constitution so as to prohibit Congress from ever abolishing or interfering with slavery in any State. Thomas Corwin of Ohio, a Republican Representative and the chairman of the Congressional Committee of Thirty-three to devise compromise measures, not only *Lib.* 31:26. urged the enforcement of the Fugitive Slave Law, but declared it to be "the duty of every free State in the Union to suppress" any incendiary publications, especially of the "newspaper press," against slavery, and "to punish their authors."[2] *MSS. E. W. Capron and E. H. Irish to J. M. McKim, Jan.* 29, 30, 1861. Andrew G. Curtin, the Republican Governor of Pennsylvania, urged the Republican legislators of that State to defeat a resolution reaffirming their party's cardinal doctrine of the non-extension of

[1] He subsequently withdrew his propositions, on the ground that it was "of no use to propose as an adjustment that which has no prospect of being received as such by the other party"; and, as a member of the Committee of Thirty-three to consider the state of the country, he finally voted against making any proposition whatever (*Lib.* 31 : 13; Wilson's 'Rise and Fall of the Slave Power,' 3 : 106).

[2] Speech of Thomas Corwin in the U. S. House of Representatives, Jan. 21, 1861; Appendix to 'Congressional Globe,' 36th Congress, 2d session, pp. 73, 74. See, also, the comments of Owen Lovejoy in his fearless speech two days later (*ibid.*, p. 85).

CHAP. I. 1861.

slavery, and appointed delegates to the so-called "Peace Congress" (convened in Washington in February) who were utterly subservient to the demands there made by the border slave States.

Had the Senators and Representatives from the seceded States only retained their seats in Congress, they could easily have insured the adoption of the measures recommended by this "Peace Congress," and substantially embodied in the Compromise bill which bore the name of its author, Mr. Crittenden of Kentucky; and the guarantees thus secured to it would have given slavery a fresh lease of life and power. They included the admission of slavery to the Territories south of latitude 36° 30′; forbade Congress to abolish the institution in places under its exclusive jurisdiction, and made it virtually perpetual in the District of Columbia; prohibited interference with the inter-State slave trade; required the United States to compensate the owner of any fugitive slave rescued from his clutches "by violence or intimidation" in the free States; empowered them to sue the county in which the rescue occurred, and the county in turn to sue the individual rescuers; and forbade that any future amendment of the Constitution should modify these stipulations or affect the fugitive-slave and three-fifths representation clauses of the original instrument.

Greeley's American Conflict, 1:376, 377, 399-402.

Even without the votes of the seceding Senators, the Crittenden Compromise commanded 19 votes in the Senate to 20 in opposition;[1] and the parallel propositions submitted by the "Peace Congress" having been also dismissed, the following amendment to the Constitution, proposed by Thomas Corwin, was adopted by the requisite two-thirds majority in both houses of Congress, a large number of Republicans voting in its favor:[2]

[1] In the House the vote was more decisive, 113 Nays to 80 Yeas.

[2] Senators Sumner, Wilson, Wade, and others in both houses of Congress were firm in resisting every step towards compromise; but even Senator Wilson spoke so apologetically concerning the Massachusetts Personal Liberty Law, in his speech of Feb. 21, in the U. S. Senate, that Mr. Garrison was compelled to criticise him sharply (*Lib.* 31 : 46).

Wilson's Rise and Fall of Slave Power, 3: 104.

"No amendment shall be made to the Constitution which will authorize or give to Congress the power to abolish or interfere, within any State, with the domestic institutions thereof, including that of persons held to labor or service by the laws of said State."

The answer of the South to this last act of cowardice was the bombardment of Sumter, and Northern legislators were thus saved the humiliation of giving the amendment the ratification which would probably otherwise have been wrung from the larger number of them. "The South," wrote George Thompson to Mr. Garrison, "has reversed your motto, and has hoisted the banner of 'No Union with *Non*-Slaveholders!' Thank God for it!"

MS. March 29, 1861.

Mr. Garrison's pen was never more active than during this critical period, and never more searching, faithful, and discriminating. Even from his sick room he sent forth, in January, a vigorous editorial in criticism of Mr. Seward's compromise speech in the Senate. After referring to the significance attached to it, on account of Mr. Seward's position in the Republican party and the admitted fact that he was to be Mr. Lincoln's Secretary of State, Mr. Garrison wrote:

Jan. 12.

Lib. 31: 10.

"Formerly, we entertained a high opinion of the statesmanlike qualities of Mr. Seward, and were ready to believe, in consequence of several acts performed by him in the service of an oppressed and despised race, that he was inspired by noble sentiments, lifting him above all personal considerations; but we have been forced, within the past year, to correct that opinion, and to change that belief. His intellectual ability is unquestionably of the first order; he writes and speaks with remarkable perspicuity, and often with great rhetorical beauty; nothing with him is hastily done; his caution is immense; he aims to be axiomatic and oracular. But it is evident that his moral nature is quite subordinate to his intellect, so as to taint his philosophy of action, and prevent him from rising to a higher level than that of an expedientist and compromiser. The key to his public life is contained in this very speech. Here it is:

"'If, in the expression of these views, I have not proposed what is desired or expected by many others, they will do me the justice to believe that I am as far from having suggested what, in many respects, would have been in harmony with cherished convictions of my own. I learned early from Jefferson that, in political affairs, we cannot always do what seems to be absolutely best. Those with whom we must necessarily act, entertaining different views, have the power and right of carrying them into practice. We must be content to lead when we can, and to follow when we cannot lead; and if we cannot at any time do for our country all the good that we would wish, we must be satisfied with doing for her all the good that we can.'

"Now, a declaration like this, expressed in such carefully considered language, carries upon its face nothing startling or objectionable; because it is the merest truism to say, that where there are many minds of conflicting views to be reconciled, mutual concessions must be made to secure the desired unity of action. And where no moral principle, no sacrifice of justice, is involved, a course like this is the dictate of common sense; otherwise, the state of society would be chaotic, and an efficient administration of public concerns impossible. But in the sentence, 'In political affairs we cannot always do what seems to be absolutely best,' there is to be found the germ of all political profligacy, and the nest-egg of all those sinful compromises which have cursed this nation since the adoption of the Federal Constitution. There is no position in which men may place themselves, or be placed by others, where they can be justified, whether to reach 'a consummation devoutly to be wished,' or to avoid formidable danger or great suffering, in violating their consciences, or conniving at what their moral sense condemns. Personal integrity and straightforward regard for the right can allow no temptation to make them swerve a hair's-breadth from the line of duty; for they are of more consequence than all the compacts and constitutions ever made. Disregardful of this, the doctrine that 'the end sanctifies the means,' or that 'we cannot always do what seems to be absolutely best,' becomes the doctrine of devils. Mr. Seward means just this: a compromise of principle to propitiate the perverse wrongdoers of the South — or his language is a mockery in this emergency. He is dealing, not with a material question of dollars and cents, but with the most momentous moral question ever presented to the world — not with well-meaning but deluded men, but with sagacious desperadoes and remorseless men-stealers. All his talk of adhering to old compromises, and making additional ones to appease the ferocious and despotic South, relates to slavery, 'the sum of all villany'— *and to nothing else.* Hence, he is for continuing to slaveholders the inhuman privilege of hunting

CHAP. I. — 1861.

their fugitive slaves in any part of the North. Hence, he is willing to vote for an amendment of the Constitution, declaring that under no circumstances shall Congress have the power to abolish or interfere with slavery in any State. Hence, his readiness to enact laws subjecting future John Browns to the punishment of death for seeking to deliver the slaves Bunker-Hill fashion, and after the example of Lafayette, Kosciusko, Pulaski, and DeKalb, as pertaining to our own Revolutionary struggle. Yet, in another speech delivered at Madison, Wisconsin, not long since, Mr. Seward solemnly declares:

"'By no word, no act, *no combination into which I might enter*, shall any one human being of all the generations to which I belong, much less of any class of human beings of *any race* or kindred *be oppressed*, or kept down in the least degree in their efforts to rise to a higher state of liberty and happiness. . . . Whenever the Constitution of the United States requires of me that this hand shall keep down the humblest of the human race, then I will lay down power, place, position, fame, everything, rather than adopt such a construction or such a rule.'

"What shall we think of the consistency or veracity of Mr. Seward in this matter of freedom? He knows, he concedes, in the speech we are criticising, that, under the United States Constitution, the fugitive slave is not entitled to safety or protection in any Northern State; and those who rush to the rescue of the enslaved millions at the South, as John Brown and his associates did, he is for hanging as felons under that same Constitution. It is time for him to lay down power, place, and position!

"Look at the present state of the country! The old Union breaking up daily, its columns falling in every direction — four Southern States already out of it, and all the others busily and openly preparing to follow — the national Government paralyzed through indecision, cowardice, or perfidy — the national flag trampled upon and discarded by the traitors, and a murderous endeavor on their part, by firing heavy shot, to sink a Government vessel entering the harbor of Charleston upon a lawful errand, compelling her to flee in disgrace and to avoid certain destruction — treason and traitors everywhere, in every slave State, in every free State, at the seat of Government, in both houses of Congress, in the army and navy, in the Executive department, at the head of the press, audacious, defiant, diabolical — the United States arsenals and fortifications already seized, or rapidly falling into the hands of the Southern conspirators, through the blackest perfidy — every movement con-

S. C., Miss., Fla., Ala.

Star of the West. Jan. 9, 1861.

templating the enforcement of the laws, and the protection of its property, on the part of the national Government, impudently denounced by the traitors and their accomplices as 'coercion,' 'tyranny,' and 'a declaration of war'—with the murderous avowal that Abraham Lincoln shall never be inaugurated President of the United States, and the unquestionable purpose of these Catilines and Arnolds to seize the Capital, and take possession of the Government by a *coup d'état*, which we have long prophesied would be their last desperate effort to keep the reins of power in their own grasp, and which we have no doubt will be successful, in spite of all the precautions of Gen. Scott.

CHAP. I. — 1861.

Winfield Scott.

"In this state of things,—when the elements are melting with fervent heat, and thunders are uttering their voices, and a great earthquake is shaking the land from centre to circumference, threatening to engulf whatever free institutions are yet visible,—Mr. Seward, with the eyes of expectant millions fastened upon him as 'the pilot to weather the storm,' rises in the Senate to utter well-turned periods in glorification of a Union no longer in existence, and to talk of 'meeting prejudice with conciliation, exaction with concession which surrenders no principle (!), and violence with the right hand of peace'! The tiger is to be propitiated by crying 'pussy-cat!' and leviathan drawn out with a hook! The word 'treason' or 'traitors' is never once mentioned—no recital is made of any of the numberless outrages committed—no call is made upon the President to be true to his oath, and to meet the public exigency with all the forces at his command—no patriotic indignation flushes his cheek—but all is calm as a summer's morning, cool, compliant, unimpassioned! His boldest word is, 'We already have disorder, and violence is begun.' How very discreet! It is a penny-whistle used to hush down a thunderstorm of the first magnitude—capping Vesuvius with a sheet of straw paper! And this is all the statesmanship of William H. Seward, in a crisis unparalleled in our national history! Stand aside! 'The hour' has come, but where is 'the man'?"[1]

[1] This article extorted a frank confession and tribute from the Boston *Courier*, then under the editorship of George Lunt, and the most virulent and disloyal journal in New England at that time: "We ask our readers to ponder carefully these telling and effective sentences, and to ask themselves whether there is not a good deal of truth as well as of force in them. They serve to show the degree of power which a man like Mr. Garrison wields, who plants himself upon an immutable principle, and firmly stands

CHAP. I. 1861. Even while commenting severely on the cowardice and recreancy of the Republican leaders whom we have named, Mr. Garrison vindicated them and their party against the false accusations hurled at them and the abolitionists alike by the Southern conspirators. Not only, he main- *Lib.* 31:26. tained, had the abolitionists uniformly recognized and conceded the Constitutional limitations of the powers of Congress respecting slavery, but the Republican platform contained not a sentiment, having a direct relation to slavery, contrary to the views entertained by all political parties twenty years ago. It was not that the Republican party was guilty of any aggression or intermeddling, any waywardness or injustice; but the South had wholly changed its former position, and insisted upon undreamed-of subserviency to its tyrannical dictation. The seceding States were therefore without excuse, guilty of "treachery, perjury, treason of the blackest character, for the worst of purposes." "Their subjugation," he declared, "and the punishment of the leading traitors, are fully authorized by the Federal Government; and when that Government ceases to maintain its rightful sovereignty, the American Union ceases to exist."

Lib. 31:27. "Under these circumstances, what is the true course to be pursued by the people of the North? Is it to vindicate this sovereignty by the sword till the treason is quelled and alle-

there, regardless of consequences. . . . His path of duty lies as clear before him as the travelled highway. He has no temptation to turn to the right hand or the left. He has no doubts, no misgivings, no questionings. Onward, straight onward, like the flight of an arrow through the air, does he move to his aim. It is not necessary for us to disclaim all sympathy with the ends and objects for which Mr. Garrison lives. To us, he and his party are all wrong; but they are consistently, manfully, and resolutely wrong. We never read a speech or an article of Mr. Garrison's without a consciousness of the power which his deep and fervid convictions give him. . . . The incurable weakness of Mr. Seward's position is, that he is ever halting between two opinions. . . . He is obliged to say one thing at Washington, and another at Rochester; one thing in the spring, and another in the autumn. . . . He blows hot and cold; he speaks with two voices; he backs and fills; he utters a brave threat, and then seems to shrink back from the echo of his own voice" (Boston *Courier*, Jan. 21, 1861; *Lib.* 31 : 20).

giance restored? Constitutionally, the sword may be wielded to this extent, and must be, whether by President Buchanan or President Lincoln, if the Union is to be preserved. The Federal Government must not pretend to be in actual operation, embracing thirty-four States, and then allow the seceding States to trample upon its flag, steal its property, and defy its authority with impunity; for it would then be (as it is at this moment) a mockery and a laughing-stock. Nevertheless, to think of whipping the South (for she will be a unit on the question of slavery) into subjection, and extorting allegiance from millions of people at the cannon's mouth, is utterly chimerical. True, it is in the power of the North to deluge her soil with blood, and inflict upon her the most terrible sufferings; but not to conquer her spirit, or change her determination.

CHAP. I.

1861.

"What, then, ought to be done? The people of the North should recognize the fact that THE UNION IS DISSOLVED, and act accordingly. They should see, in the madness of the South, the hand of God, liberating them from 'a covenant with death and an agreement with hell,' made in a time of terrible peril, and without a conception of its inevitable consequences, and which has corrupted their morals, poisoned their religion, petrified their humanity as towards the millions in bondage, tarnished their character, harassed their peace, burdened them with taxation, shackled their prosperity, and brought them into abject vassalage. . . .

"Now, then, let there be a CONVENTION OF THE FREE STATES called to organize an independent government on free and just principles; and let them say to the slave States—'Though you are without excuse for your treasonable conduct, depart in peace! Though you have laid piratical hands upon property not your own, we surrender it all in the spirit of magnanimity! And if nothing but the possession of the Capital will appease you, take even that, without a struggle! Let the line be drawn between us where free institutions end and slave institutions begin! Organize your own confederacy, if you will, based upon violence, tyranny, and blood, and relieve us from all responsibility for your evil course!'"

A somewhat similar attitude was assumed by other leaders of public opinion, who shrank from the horrors of a civil war, and the apparently hopeless task of conquering a united South with a divided North, and who

Greeley's American Conflict, 1: 358–9.

CHAP. I. 1861. believed a peaceful separation the surer and swifter way in which to shake the foundations of slavery. Few guessed the depth and fervor of the Union sentiment which the cannon-shot in Charleston harbor was to rouse.

Disappointed by Mr. Seward's "penny-whistle," Mr. Garrison anxiously watched the bearing of the President-elect, on whose patriotism, courage, and firmness the destinies of the republic rested, and waited for his utterance. *Lib.* 31:26. "It is much to the credit of Mr. Lincoln," he wrote in February, "that he has maintained his dignity and self-respect intact, and gives no countenance to any of the compromises that have yet been proposed."[1] That his inauguration would be permitted in peace seemed hardly possible, and when the telegraph announced to the country on the afternoon of the 4th of March that the Buchanan Administration had ended, and the first Republican President had actually assumed office and delivered his inaugural address without interruption or disturbance, a day of feverish anxiety was succeeded, as Mr. *Lib.* 31:38. Garrison wrote, "by a night of profoundest satisfaction and repose, . . . as though not a cloud rested upon the future."[2]

[1] This was evidently penned just after Mr. Garrison had seen a private letter from W. H. Herndon of Springfield, Ill., Mr. Lincoln's law partner, to S. E. Sewall, which concluded: "Mr. Lincoln yet remains firm as a rock. He is true game, and is strong in the faith of Justice, Right, Liberty, Man, and God. He has told me, not only once, but often and often, that rather than back down — rather than concede to traitors, his soul might go back to God from the wings of the Capitol. I believe it. He and I have been partners in law for thirteen years, and I know him" (MS. copy, Feb. 1).

[2] It was not without a little surprise, after the election of Mr. Lincoln and Gov. Andrew, that Mr. Garrison found himself frequently appealed to by aspirants for office under the new Administration to endorse their applications. Standing wholly aloof, as he did, from the Republican party organization, and being a frequent and severe critic of the acts of its leaders, he had not imagined that he had any influence to lend in that direction, but he consented with some reluctance to recommend two or three persons whom he believed worthy and competent to Governor Andrew, at the same time apologizing for doing so. The Governor promptly sent this cordial and characteristic reply (MS.):

"BOSTON, March 5, 1861.

"MY DEAR SIR: I am much obliged to you for introducing Mr. T—— of Dorchester. I shall do my best to favor the strong, real, and true-hearted

Two columns of the *Liberator* were devoted to the editor's review of the inaugural address. Containing, as the latter did, a frank and unflinching acknowledgment that all who took their oaths of office to support the Constitution and the laws were under obligation to maintain and enforce the Fugitive Slave Law, and surrender the hunted fugitive; a declaration that the President himself took his official oath "with no mental reservations"; and an expression of his willingness to see the Constitutional amendment just passed by Congress ratified by the States,—it was hardly a document to inspire the hope or the enthusiasm of the abolitionists. But, while dealing faithfully with it in these respects, Mr. Garrison treated it with his customary discrimination and fairness. Admitting the "manly courage" of Mr. Lincoln, and the "rare self-possession and equanimity" with which he had passed through the fearful ordeal of threatened violence and assassination, he commended the President's clear and simple style, and the brevity and directness of his address. His argument against Southern secession he regarded as "compact and conclusive," and certainly the Republican Party had given the South no justification for revolt.

CHAP. I. 1861.

Ante, pp. 9, 10.

"The position of the Republican party, on this subject, is very truthfully and most explicitly defined by Mr. Lincoln in his inaugural address. Wherein does it differ from that of the old Whig or the old Democratic party, so far as non-intervention with slavery at the South, or the recapture of fugitive slaves, or the suppression of slave insurrections, or the three-fifths representation, is concerned? As if this were not enough, the party, in its Chicago platform,—after recognizing 'the right of each State to order and control its own domestic institutions, according to its own judgment exclusively,'—goes out of its way to 'denounce the lawless invasion by an armed force of any State or

Lib. 31 : 38.

men who are sincerely with us in the Republican cause. And I am glad to try to help him. I will do so.

"You need never apologize for any such introduction — nor for any hint or advice you may feel disposed to give me. I hope and trust the best good of our people, of every condition, will be served by the new Administration. I shall support it faithfully in that hope and confidence, and shall do my little to give it the best direction. Faithfully yours, J. A. ANDREW."

CHAP. I. 1861.

Territory, *no matter under what pretext*, as THE GREATEST OF CRIMES'! This is a cruel stigma cast upon the memory of John Brown and his martyr-associates at Harper's Ferry. What has the South to fear from such a party as this? And how can its triumph furnish a shadow of justification for the rebellious movement of the seven Confederated States, now in open hostility to the Union?

"See what Mr. Lincoln says in his address — an address, remember! to be read by all the civilized world — respecting that thoroughly inhuman and most revolting business, the surrendering of fugitive slaves by the people of the North! After quoting the Constitutional clause, he says:

"'It is scarcely questioned that this provision was intended by those who made it for the reclaiming of what we call fugitive slaves, and *the intention of the law-giver is the law*. All members of Congress swear their support to the whole Constitution, *to this provision as much as any other*. To the proposition, then, that slaves whose cases come within the terms of this clause shall be delivered up, their oaths are unanimous.'

"Very true, but such oaths are impious, and of no validity. Whoever returns, or consents to return, a fugitive slave to the clutches of his master, is, in the sight of God, an accomplice in man-stealing. To this extent Mr. Lincoln and the Republican party are guilty. We are equally shocked and surprised that he should *gratuitously* parade this infamous pledge in his inaugural address. Nor is it any atonement when he says:

"'In any law upon this subject, ought not all the safeguards of liberty known in civilized and humane jurisprudence to be introduced, so that a free man be not in any case surrendered as a slave? And might it not be well, at the same time, to provide by law for the enforcement of that clause in the Constitution which guarantees that the citizens of each State shall be entitled to all the privileges and immunities of citizens in the several States?'

"These safeguards of liberty ought indeed to be provided — not merely 'that a free man be not in any case surrendered as a slave,' but that no fugitive should ever be carried back to bondage. The right of one man to freedom is by creation and destiny the right of every other; and President Lincoln has no better claim to be protected than any of the hunted refugees in the Dismal Swamp. He seems to have no bowels of mercy, *under the Constitution*, for those who are seeking their liberty by flight, and who deserve to be specially commiserated and aided on their way. He would modify the Fugitive Slave Law (so he said before his nomination), but only to make its operation the more effectual! And yet he is the man — *mirabile dictu!* — whose election causes seven of the slaveholding States to revolt, and in hot haste withdraw from the Union! Surely they must be desperately hard to 'conciliate'!" CHAP. I. 1861.

No transformation was ever more sudden, overwhelming, and amazing than that effected by the bombardment and capture of Fort Sumter, and President Lincoln's call for troops to suppress the rebellion. That which the South had expected would complete the demoralization of the North, and be the signal for riots and outbreaks in its great cities, evoked a whirlwind of patriotism that swept all before it, and caused "such an uprising in every city, town, and hamlet of the North, without distinction of sect or party, as to seem," wrote Mr. Garrison, "like a general resurrection from the dead." To those who were puzzled to know how he, as a disunionist, could rejoice in the determination of the Government to crush the rebellion which sought to dissolve the Union, he speedily made clear, in two lucid editorials, the difference between Northern Disunionists and Southern Secessionists, and the utter absence of any justification for the latter. Neither he nor the American Anti-Slavery Society had ever advocated the right of a State to secede from the Union *ad libitum*, without reason; and only a revolutionary right, for the causes set forth in the Declaration of Independence, could justify the South in its course. *Apr.* 12-14. *Apr.* 15. *Lib.* 31:66. *Lib.* 31:58, 62.

"On the issue raised by the secessionists," he reiterated, in rejoinder to a letter from Beriah Green, "they are wholly and fearfully in the wrong, while President Lincoln is indisputably in the right. On his side all the elements of freedom will coalesce, sympathetically and approvingly, as against their thoroughly infernal spirit and purposes, and a thousand times over wish him success in the struggle. At the same time, as pertaining to a continued union with the South, God grant that the North may speedily see the folly, danger, and iniquity of trying it any longer! Let . . . the North take the right, with not a Border Slave State left to mar her free policy, and let the South take the left, and the consequences!" *Lib.* 31:63.

CHAP. I. 1861.

On the Sunday morning following the President's call for troops, Wendell Phillips addressed an immense congregation at Music Hall on the War for the Union, the platform being decorated with the stars and stripes, "for the first time seeming to symbolize the cause of impartial freedom." Some of the very men who had hissed and hooted at him in January, were now ready to applaud him to the echo, and the scene was in every way thrilling and inspiring. The text of his discourse was suggested by Mr. Garrison:

Lib. 31:66.

Jer. 34:17.

"Therefore thus saith the Lord: Ye have not hearkened unto me in proclaiming liberty every one to his brother, and every man to his neighbor: behold, I proclaim a liberty for you, saith the Lord, to the sword, to the pestilence, and to the famine."

The selections from Scripture were likewise chosen by him, and the 50th and 51st chapters of Jeremiah seemed so remarkably applicable to the times that, when Mr. Phillips had finished his reading of them, the audience broke forth in loud applause! The peroration of the discourse, eloquent in its prophecy, fitly expressed the instinct of the abolitionists as to the certain result of the war now inaugurated.[1]

The same number of the *Liberator* in which Mr. Phillips's discourse appeared contained the following announcement, written and signed by Mr. Garrison as President of the American Anti-Slavery Society:

Lib. 31:66.

"In view of the unparalleled excitement now existing throughout the country, arising from the treasonable attempt of the Southern slave oligarchy to overturn the General Government, and to erect an exclusively slaveholding despotism upon its ruins, to the overthrow of all free institutions, it is deemed by the Executive Committee of the American Anti-Slavery Society

[1] As a manifestation of their antipathy to Mr. Phillips, and with a lack of enterprise amazing in these days of competition in journalism, the Boston dailies, with the exception of the *Advertiser*, refrained by common consent from reporting or making any allusion to this discourse. Even the Republican *Atlas and Daily Bee*, which usually gave full reports of Mr. Phillips's speeches, *and had secured one of this*, was induced to suppress it. The result was a sale of sixteen thousand copies of the *Liberator Extra* containing it.

a measure of sound expediency to postpone the usual anniversary of the Society, in the city of New York, in May next, until further notice — a decision which they are confident will be most cordially ratified by the members and friends of the Society; especially in view of the cheering fact that there is at last a North as well as a South, and that the present tremendous conflict is in its tendencies strongly and irresistibly toward the goal of universal emancipation, or else a separation between the free and slaveholding States in accordance with the principle of 'NO UNION WITH SLAVEHOLDERS!' Let nothing be done, at this solemn crisis, needlessly to check or divert the mighty current of popular feeling which is now sweeping southward with the strength and impetuosity of a thousand Niagaras, in direct conflict with that haughty and perfidious Slave Power which has so long ruled the republic with a rod of iron for its own base and satanic purposes.

"The annual meeting of the Society stands postponed until further notice."[1]

MSS. W. L. G. to O. Johnson; E. M. Davis, J. M. McKim, J. S. Gibbons, O. Johnson, to W. L. G., April 19–25.

This conclusion was the result of a correspondence between the leading members of the Society in Boston, New York, and Philadelphia, who were united in the opinion that it would be folly to attempt to arrest the public ear at such a moment. As Mr. Garrison wrote to Oliver Johnson:

MS. April 19, 1861.

"Now that civil war has begun, and a whirlwind of violence and excitement is to sweep through the country, every day increasing in intensity until its bloodiest culmination, it is for the abolitionists to 'stand still, and see the salvation of God,' rather than to attempt to add anything to the general commotion. It is no time for minute criticism of Lincoln, Republicanism, or even the other parties, now that they are fusing for a death-grapple with the Southern slave oligarchy; for they are instruments in the hands of God to carry forward and help achieve the great object of emancipation for which we have so long been striving. The war is fearfully to scourge the nation, but mercy will be mingled with judgment, and grand results are to follow, should no dividing root of bitterness rise up at the North. All our sympathies and wishes must be with the Government, as against the Southern desperadoes and buccaneers;

[1] For "the same weighty considerations" the usual May meetings in Boston were also omitted (*Lib.* 31 : 70).

CHAP. I. — 1861.

yet, of course, without any compromise of principle on our part. We need great circumspection and consummate wisdom in regard to what we say and do, under these unparalleled circumstances. We are rather, for the time being, to note the events transpiring, than seek to control them. There must be no needless turning of popular violence upon ourselves, by any false step of our own."[1]

The omission of the annual meeting called forth private protests and expressions of regret from a few anti-slavery friends, who deemed it a sacrifice of principle and dereliction from duty, and thought the outlook for the slave never more depressing than then. It was with these in mind, no less than the New Haven correspondent to whom he was more directly replying, that Mr. Garrison wrote:

Lib. 31:74.

"There seems to be some diversity of feeling and sentiment among abolitionists, in regard to the bearing of the present civil war in our land upon the anti-slavery cause. This arises from no wish or purpose, in any direction, to retreat a hair's-breadth from the line of duty originally marked out by them, and adhered to, through countless temptations and trials, with unsurpassed fidelity; but solely, we think, from a difference in the standpoint of judgment and observation occupied by the parties. By some, this tremendous conflict of hostile forces is regarded as without any cheering significance, or sign of promise, to those who have so long struggled for the utter abolition of slavery; by others, it is deemed to have a mighty bearing towards hastening the day of universal emancipation, if not intentionally on the part of the Government (and they attribute no such design to it primarily), at least by the necessities of the case,—being essentially the South against the North,—and is therefore to be viewed hopefully. It would be absurd to deny that the war presents some very paradoxical and complex features, so as to render it extremely difficult to speak of it without being misunderstood, either on one side or on the other. Nevertheless, we shall venture to express our opinions of it in a spirit of

[1] The Superintendent of Police in New York (John A. Kennedy), who had promised ample protection to the meetings of the Society in case they should be held and any violence attempted, on the pretext of suppressing "disunionism," had formerly been secretary of an anti-slavery society in Baltimore, and a partner of Benjamin Lundy in publishing the *Genius* prior to 1827, when he removed to New York (MS. April 13, 1861, Oliver Johnson to W. L. G.).

just discrimination, as far as in our power, leaving those who cannot adopt them entire liberty to criticise or refute them in our columns. . . .

"For thirty years, the abolitionists have been faithfully warning the nation that, unless the enslaved were set free, a just God would visit it with tribulation and woe proportional to its great iniquity. Now that their predictions have come to pass, are they to indulge in morbid exclamations against the natural operation of the law of immutable justice, and to see in it no evidence of the growth of conscience, the power of truth, or the approach of the long-wished-for jubilee? Surely, this would be to arraign Infinite Wisdom, to be blind to the progress of events. Surely, emancipation is nearer than when we believed, and the present struggle cannot fail to hasten it mightily, in a providential sense.

"It is alleged that the Administration is endeavoring to uphold the Union, the Constitution, and the laws, even as from the formation of the Government; but this is a verbal and technical view of the case. Facts are more potential than words, and events greater than parchment arrangements. The truth is, the old Union is *non est inventus*, and its restoration, with its pro-slavery compromises, well-nigh impossible. The conflict is really between the civilization of freedom and the barbarism of slavery — between the principles of democracy and the doctrines of absolutism — between the free North and the man-imbruting South; therefore, to this extent hopeful for the cause of impartial liberty. So that we cannot endorse the assertion, that this is 'the darkest hour for the slave in the history of American servitude.' No, it is the brightest!"

The readers of the *Liberator* had often had cause for complaint that the editorials from Mr. Garrison's pen were infrequent and irregular, but they were now treated to a stirring blast each week, and there followed successively articles on the cause and cure of the war, the relation of the anti-slavery cause to the war, the offer of General Benjamin F. Butler to suppress slave insurrections (if any should occur) in Maryland, the bewilderment of mind of the English people in relation to the struggle, and the taunts at non-resistance on the part of those who imagined that the doctrine had been "scattered to the wind" by recent events. The President and Congress were invoked

Lib. 31:70, 74.
Lib. 31:78, 82.
Lib. 31:86.
Lib. 31:94.

CHAP. I. 1861. to use their war-power to proclaim emancipation, in accordance with the doctrine laid down by John Quincy Adams twenty-five years before, and the North was warned that peace without freedom would be no peace.

Ante, 2:75; Lib. 31:74, 90.

Gen. Butler's gratuitous offer to use his Massachusetts troops in putting down any slave insurrection was still eliciting the indignant comments of the Northern press when, presto, change! the astute General opened the gates of Fortress Monroe to the fleeing slaves, and pronounced them "contraband of war"; and the anti-slavery education of the soldiers in the field and the people at home who were "no abolitionists," while anxious to save the Union, began. The "Refuge of Oppression" still gathered columns of outpourings from the Southern press, and many of these were reprinted in a tract for the further enlightenment of soldiers as to the spirit of diabolism prevalent at the South.[1] The object-lessons of Libby Prison, Belle Isle, Andersonville, and other Southern torture pens were yet to come, but already they were foreseen by the editor of the *Liberator*. Alluding to the sudden change of attitude and language towards the South on the part of many who were lately its apologists and defenders, he wrote:

Lib. 31:77, 81, 85, 89, 93.

Lib. 31:86.

"There is nothing so promotive of clearness of vision and correct judgment as to be subjected to wrongs and insults in our own persons. So long as those traitors confined their outrages and atrocities to their helpless, friendless slaves, it was all well enough, and not at all derogatory to their character as gentlemen, patriots, and Christians. They might deprive their victims of every human right, work them under the lash without wages, buy and sell them 'in lots to suit purchasers,' and subject them to every species of brutal violence as passion or cupidity prompted, and still not forfeit their claim to be honest, upright, high-minded men! Nay, for abolitionists to brand them as robbers of God's poor and needy, and the basest of oppressors, was to deal in abusive language, and to manifest a most unchristian spirit! For were they not exemplary and

[1] 'The spirit of the South towards Northern Freemen and Soldiers defending the American Flag against Traitors of the Deepest Dye.' Boston: R. F. Wallcut, 1861.

beloved Episcopalian, Presbyterian, Baptist, and Methodist brethren, whose piety was unquestionable, whose zeal for the Lord was worthy of all praise, whose revivals of religion were preëminently owned and blessed of Heaven? Were they not the very pinks of Democracy, and the most courtly and chivalrous of gentlemen? But as soon as they began to seize forts, arsenals, custom-houses, and mints belonging to the general Government, to lay their piratical hands upon Northern property, to repudiate their entire Northern indebtedness, and to trample upon the 'stars and stripes'—then, indeed, another view of their character is taken, and they are suddenly transformed from the most estimable Christian brethren and the staunchest Democratic allies into the meanest of scoundrels and the vilest of robbers!

"Truly, 'wisdom is justified of her children.' It will yet be seen and acknowledged throughout the North, in view of the shocking developments of the slaveholding spirit in this terrible conflict, that the abolitionists have correctly delineated the nature of slavery — its disregard of all the rules of morality, all the claims of a common humanity, all the principles of justice — its wolfish greed, its savage ferocity, its fiendish malignity — its utter contempt and murderous hatred of whoever or whatever interferes with the extension of its domains, or attempts to limit its power — its embodiment of the blackest perfidy, the most revolting licentiousness, the most unscrupulous villany, and the most barbarous cruelty; and as there is no sin without a sinner, no oppression without an oppressor, so the abolitionists have exaggerated nothing, but have used language guardedly, justly, and with all possible truthfulness in their exposition of the Southern character, spirit, and purposes, whether in relation to their miserable victims, or to free institutions and the cause of freedom generally. Our Northern soldiers will find that they are not in conflict with men who are governed by the laws of civilized warfare, or by any rules of honor, but with thoroughly demonized spirits, capable of perpetrating deeds of horror such as have never been surpassed in the annals of savage barbarity."

To those who asked him, "What of your peace principles now?" he replied:

"This question is exultingly put to the friends of peace and non-resistance by those whose military ardor is now at a white heat, as though it could not be satisfactorily answered, and de- *Lib.* 31 : 94.

CHAP. I. 1861.

served nothing but ridicule. Our reply to it is, that the peace principles are as beneficent and glorious as ever, and are neither disproved nor modified by anything now transpiring in the country, of a warlike character. If they had been long since embraced and carried out by the people, neither slavery nor war would now be filling the land with violence and blood. Where they prevail, no man is in peril of life or liberty; where they are rejected, and precisely to the extent they are rejected, neither life nor liberty is secure. How their violation, under any circumstances, is better than a faithful adherence to them, we have not the moral vision to perceive. They are to be held responsible for nothing which they do not legitimately produce or sanction. As they neither produce nor sanction any oppression or wrong-doing, but elevate the character, control the passions, and lead to the performance of all good offices, they are not to be discarded for those of a hostile character. . . .

"But are we not giving our sympathies to the Government as against the secession movement? Certainly — because, as between the combatants, there is no wrong or injustice on the side of the Government, while there is nothing but violence, robbery, confiscation, perfidy, lynch law, usurpation, and a most diabolical purpose, on the side of the secessionists. The weapons resorted to, on both sides, are the same; yet it is impossible not to wish success to the innocent, and defeat to the guilty party. But, in so doing, we do not compromise either our anti-slavery or our peace principles. On the contrary, we wish all the North were able to adopt those principles, understandingly, heartily, and without delay; but, according to the structure of the human mind, in the whirlwind of the present deadly conflict, this is impracticable. As, therefore, Paul said to the Jews who would not accept of the new dispensation, 'Ye that are under the law, do ye not hear the law? Cursed is every one that continueth not in all things written in the book of the law to do them' — so we measure those who, rejecting the doctrine of non-resistance, profess to believe in the right and duty of maintaining their freedom by the sword. The worst thing they can do is to be recreant to their own convictions in such a crisis as this.

"But this is, obviously, not the time to expect a dispassionate hearing on this subject. After the wind, the earthquake, and the fire, comes the still small voice. The war must go on to its consummation; and among the salutary lessons it will teach will be the impossibility of oppressing the poor and the needy, or consenting thereto by entering into 'a covenant with death,' without desolating judgments following in its train." CHAP. I. — 1861.

In this connection, also, Mr. Garrison endeavored to make clear the issues and the certain tendencies of the war to the many persons in England who, even among the abolitionists there, were confused and bewildered by the kaleidoscopic aspect of affairs from that distance. His replies to Dr. Guthrie of Edinburgh and the London *Herald of Peace* were especially effective. But there was one man who needed no instruction on the points at issue. George Thompson was already preparing himself for the task of enlightening his fellow-countrymen, and enlisting their sympathies in behalf of the American Government in its struggle with slavery in arms. *Lib.* 31:86, 98, 102.

George Thompson to W. L. Garrison.

TYNEMOUTH, Northumberland, June 7, 1861. *Lib.* 31:102.

MY DEAR GARRISON: Yours of the 21st ultimo has within the present hour reached me at this place, where I am staying for a few days, going almost daily into Newcastle to consult with my anti-slavery friends there on the progress of the cause in America, and the means we may legitimately employ to promote it. . . .

I have been a deeply interested observer of late events on your side of the ocean, and have studied them with all the powers of reflection I can command. My talk is incessantly in reference to them, and I miss no opportunity of publicly addressing my countrymen upon them. I enclose you copies of reports made of my late speeches in London and Leeds, the tenor of which I trust you will approve. I have endeavored to make myself master of the constitutional argument, in relation to the doctrine of State rights and secession, which I am often called upon to debate.

I am extremely glad to find the views expressed in your letter before me so coincident with my own. I have pondered much and deeply upon the probable issues of the present war. I was occupied in writing all day yesterday upon the subject, and could not resist the conclusion, that the present struggle *must* end in the downfall of slavery. I dare say, if I had time to

CHAP. I. — 1861.

develop my process of reasoning, it would be found that our ratiocinations are alike. May God grant that our hopes may be realized!

To me it appears that, by the conduct of the South, the North is released forever from the obligations imposed by the Constitution of '87. The despots of the South are *traitors in arms.* They have trampled the Constitution in the dust; they have disgraced the national flag; they are seeking the destruction of the North; they have reversed the Declaration of Independence; they have proclaimed the rightfulness of human slavery; they have inscribed upon the corner-stone of the atheistical edifice they seek to rear, "The black man is always, and forever, the property of the white man." If these things be so, will the North spare the accursed domestic institution? Will the armies of New England and the free West return before they have planted the flag of personal freedom side by side with that of the Union, and decreed that slavery is forever abolished in every part of the national domain? God forbid!

I am not discouraged because the abolition of slavery is not one of the *declared* objects of the President in the struggle he has commenced. I am not discouraged because the thousands who are flocking to the Federal standard, while they shout, "The Union," "The Constitution," and "Our star-spangled banner," do not also shout, "Down with Slavery!" I am not discouraged because kidnapping has been permitted in Chicago, and General Butler has played so infamous a part in Maryland, and slaves have been driven from Fort Pickens, and even Greeley has talked with "bated breath" on the subject of slavery, in recent articles in the *Tribune.* No! I have confidence in the inevitable tendency of events, and their resistless influence. The doom of slavery is sealed! Witness, the judicial blindness of the slaveholders! Witness, the madness that ever precedes destruction! Witness, the universal expectancy of a nation of slaves, waiting to be "born in a day"! Witness, the feverish excitement of the free colored population, who, when the hour strikes, and the conflagration rages, will have their part to play, and will enact it! The spirit of John Brown walks abroad! Being dead, he yet speaketh, and points with shadowy finger to Harper's Ferry and Charlestown! Witness, in every company of every regiment forming the vast army of volunteers, some few at least who have vowed to fight, not for the restoration of the Union alone, but for *a Union without slavery* — a Union of free men, of *all colors,* from Passamaquoddy Bay to the northern bank of the Rio Grande! Witness, the recent pregnant utterances of politicians, statesmen, and editors, who deal with slavery as a gangrene that must be cut out! Witness, the altered tone of that recreant and guilty church which, till the roar of Charleston cannon was heard, and the stars and stripes succumbed to the black flag of secession, hugged the men-stealers of the South to its bosom, and, while it could not fellowship the Church of the Puritans on account of its Abolitionism, could break sacramental bread with the traffickers in slaves and the souls of men!

Rev. Geo. B. Cheever's church, N. Y. City.

Need I say, my faithful friend and brother, how fervently my heart returns thanks to God that we are permitted to see this day? Need I tell you that my spirit is always with you? If my own heart condemned me for infidelity to our early vows, I should be most miserable; but I can appeal to him who knoweth all things, and say, Thou knowest how truly I have cherished, warm as when the flame was first kindled, my friendship and love for those with whom I labored —

> "When first we saw the cloud arise,
> Little as a human hand!"

Continue to trust me, and let me look forward with joyful anticipations to the day when I shall once more stand upon the soil from which I was banished by the demon of slavery, and gaze upon that vision beheld by the eye of your prophet and unequalled orator — the great and (better still) the good and gracious Phillips — "The Genius of Liberty on the banks of the Potomac, robed in light; four-and-thirty stars for her diadem, *broken fetters at her feet*, and an olive branch in her right hand."[1]

GEORGE THOMPSON.

The whirlwind of war, which was so rapidly hastening the end of slavery, was also threatening, by its absorption of public attention and drain on private resources,

[1] In 1856 Mr. Thompson had made a second visit to India, where he was prostrated, in the midst of his labors, by the climate, and he returned to England apparently a helpless paralytic. The timely pecuniary aid sent him by his American friends in 1859 saved him from sore distress, and doubtless hastened his recovery, and towards the close of 1860 he became the active (but untitled) and salaried agent in England of the American Anti-Slavery Society. The arrangement proved unexpectedly fortunate and important; for the Society, by thus sustaining Mr. Thompson in his extremity, saved and prepared him for the yeoman service which he was to perform in behalf of the American Government during the most critical period of the war.

the existence of the anti-slavery journals. The *Anti-Slavery Bugle* succumbed within a month after the fall of Sumter, and the possibility of continuing the *Standard* soon became a matter of anxious consideration. There was a proposition to merge the *Liberator* with it, in the hope that the combined list of the two papers might suffice to support one, and that Mr. Garrison, while still remaining the chief editorial writer, might be relieved of the drudgery, both editorial and mechanical, which consumed so much of his time. But he would not listen to the project, and the necessary funds to support the *Standard* were raised by private subscriptions. It was a matter of doubt how long the *Liberator* could be kept alive, but the editor was resolved to float or sink in his own craft. He was in the best of spirits when he spoke at the anti-slavery picnic at Framingham on the 4th of July, and confident that the abolition of slavery would ere long be decreed. Objecting to a resolution [1] offered by Stephen S. Foster, he said:

Lib. 31:75.

Lib. 31:111.

"I cannot say that I do not sympathize with the Government, as against Jefferson Davis and his piratical associates. There is not a drop of blood in my veins, both as an abolitionist and a peace man, that does not flow with the Northern tide of sentiment; for I see, in this grand uprising of the manhood of the North, which has been so long grovelling in the dust, a growing appreciation of the value of liberty and of free institutions, and a willingness to make any sacrifice in their defence against the barbaric and tyrannical power which avows its purpose, if it can, to crush them entirely out of existence. When the Government shall succeed (if it shall succeed) in 'conquering a peace,' in subjugating the South, and shall undertake to carry out the Constitution as of old, with all its pro-slavery compromises, then will be my time to criticise, reprove, and condemn; then will be the time for me to open all the guns that I can

[1] "That, until the Government shall take this step [of emancipation] and place itself openly and unequivocally on the side of freedom, we can give it no support or countenance in its effort to maintain its authority over the seceded States, but must continue to labor, as we have hitherto done, to heap upon it that obloquy which naturally attaches to all who are guilty of the crime of enslaving their fellow-men" (*Lib.* 31:111).

S. S. Foster

bring to bear upon it. But, blessed be God, that 'covenant with death' has been annulled, and that 'agreement with hell' no longer stands. I joyfully accept the fact, and leave all verbal criticism until a more suitable opportunity. . . .

"Under these circumstances, I take great courage, and am full of hope. I should cry, 'Shame to the people of the North!' if they did not, with their principles, and their ideas of government, come up to the support of the Administration, offering all they have of blood and treasure, until this band of conspirators shall be put down and slavery utterly obliterated. What we ought to do is to take the resolution we have just adopted,[1] put it into our hearts, plead for it everywhere, and create a great Northern sentiment which shall irresistibly demand of the Administration, under the war power, the emancipation of every slave in the land; and then God will give us peace and prosperity, and we shall have, for the first time, a 'great and glorious Union.'

"Oh, Mr. President, how it delights my heart when I think that the worst thing we propose to do for the South is the very best thing that God or men can do! That while they are confiscating our property, refusing to pay their honest Northern debts, covering the ocean with their piratical privateers, tarring and feathering, hanging, and driving out innocent Northern citizens from their borders, all we threaten to do, in the excess of our wrath, as a retaliatory measure, is to abolish their iniquitous and destructive slave system, and thus give them light for darkness, good for evil, heaven for perdition! Yes, we will make it possible for them to be a happy and prosperous people, as they never have been, and never can be, with slavery. We will make it possible for them to have free schools, and free presses, and free institutions, as we do at the North. We will make it possible for the South to be 'as the garden of God,' under the plastic touch of liberty; and for the nation to attain unparalleled glory, greatness, and renown. Assuredly, we have no enmity to the South; the enmity is on the other side. Liberty knows how to be magnanimous, forbearing, long-

[1] Also introduced by Mr. Foster: "That, as citizens deeply interested in the honor and welfare of our common country, we earnestly ask and demand of our national Government that it at once proclaim an act of emancipation to all our enslaved countrymen, wherever held, as the only honorable, just, and efficient means of settling our present national troubles, and establishing our Union upon a solid and enduring basis" (*Lib.* 31 : 111).

CHAP. I. 1861.

suffering, patient, hopeful; and therefore it is that, in the very whirlwind which is now sweeping over the land, Southern men as safely reside among us as they ever did. They are not threatened with tar and feathers, nor compelled to flee from our presence because of their Southern origin, but enjoy unimpaired all their constitutional rights. The brutality, the barbarity, the demonism, are all at the South. Yet, I pray you to remember that the slaveholders are just as merciful and forbearing as they can be in their situation — not a whit more brutal, bloody, satanic than they are obliged to be in the terrible exigencies in which, as slaveholders, they are placed. They are men of like passions with ourselves; they are of our common country; and if we had been brought up in the midst of slavery, as they have been,— if we had our property in slaves, as they have,—if we had had the same training and education that they have received,— of course, we should have been just as much disposed to do all in our power to support slavery, and to put down freedom, by the same atrocious acts, as themselves. The tree bears its natural fruit — like causes will produce like effects. But let us return them good for evil, by seizing this opportunity to deliver them from their deadliest curse — that is Christian."

Lib. 31:131. *Wilson's Anti-Slavery Measures in Congress, pp.* 14–16.

In August, the Secretary of War, Simon Cameron, in a letter to General Butler, cited the Act of Congress approved on the 6th of that month, by which slaves employed in the military and naval service of the rebellion were declared free, and authorized him further to receive and employ slaves escaping from loyal masters as well, keeping a careful record of such, that Congress might remunerate the masters after the return of peace. Mr. Garrison read this with delight, and wrote: "It goes quite as far as we could expect, and is almost tantamount to a proclamation of general emancipation"; and when, on the 31st of the same month, General Frémont issued his proclamation emancipating the slaves of actively disloyal masters in his military district (Missouri), the *Liberator* hailed it with a Laus Deo, and as the "beginning of the end." The popular response was quick and enthusiastic, even journals like the New York *Herald* and Boston *Post* admitting, for the moment, the propriety of Frémont's act; but the letter of President Lincoln revoking that

MS. Aug. 13, 1861, *to W. P. G.*

John C. Frémont.

Lib. 31:143.

Sept. 11.

portion of the proclamation chilled the hearts and hopes of all who felt that the time was ripe for radical measures. To the abolitionists the disappointment was especially keen, and faith in Lincoln's purpose or desire to use his war-powers for the destruction of slavery rapidly waned. The *Liberator* printed the letter between heavy black rules, and declared the President "guilty of a serious dereliction of duty" in not making Frémont's proclamation applicable to all the other slave States in revolt. The loyal press generally expressed disappointment and regret at the President's course, while the pro-slavery and semi-disloyal papers were jubilant, and altered their tone to one of fulsome praise of Mr. Lincoln, whom they now hoped to commit to a settled policy of non-interference with slavery; and there seemed much in the events of the next three months to justify their expectations. A period of reaction set in, during which the President permitted without protest the Order No. 3 of General Halleck (who succeeded Frémont as Commander of the Missouri department), forbidding his officers to receive fugitive slaves within the lines, and modified that portion of Secretary Cameron's annual report which advocated the confiscation and arming of the slaves of rebel masters. In his message to Congress, on its assembling in December, Mr. Lincoln proposed colonization as a scheme for disposing of the freed people who, under the name of contrabands, flocked to the camps of the Union armies, and he gave no word to awaken the hopes of the emancipationists that he would ere long initiate an active anti-slavery policy. The message seemed to Mr. Garrison "feeble and rambling," and he could find nothing to praise in it except the recommendation that Congress should recognize the independence and sovereignty of Hayti and Liberia. To Oliver Johnson he wrote:

CHAP. I. — 1861.

Lib. 31:151.

Lib. 31:150.

Lib. 31:194.

"What a wishy-washy message from the President! . . . He has evidently not a drop of anti-slavery blood in his veins; and he seems incapable of uttering a humane or generous sentiment respecting the enslaved millions in our land. No wonder

MS. Dec. 6, 1861.

New York. that such villanous papers as the *Journal of Commerce*, the *Express*, Bennett's *Herald*, and the Boston *Courier* and *Post*, are his special admirers and champions! If there be not soon an 'irrepressible conflict' in the Republican ranks, in regard to his course of policy, I shall almost despair of the country.

"In fact, I shudder at the possibility of the war terminating without the utter extinction of slavery, by a new and more atrocious compromise on the part of the North than any that has yet been made. We must continue to brand as accessories of the Southern traitors all those who, now that the Government can rightfully do it under the war power, denounce and oppose the emancipation of those in bondage. A curse on that Southern 'loyalty'[1] which is retained only by allowing it to control the policy of the Administration!"

Yet Mr. Lincoln, in his hesitancy to commit the Administration to that policy of emancipation which each day made more inevitable, could have pointed not only to the bitter opposition of the Border States, but to the timidity of the Republicans of Massachusetts, who declined, at Oct. 1. their State Convention in October, to respond to Mr. Sumner's eloquent address to them and to pass resolutions approving his utterances in favor of emancipation. The Advertiser. Journal. Republican press of Boston, too, poured contempt on the great Senator for these utterances. "The enemy in Boston," MS. Dec. 22, 1861. wrote Sumner to Garrison, in December, from Washington, "seem more malignant than ever," and he added: "You know that for some time I have been very sanguine that emancipation was at hand. Of course I am pained by the impediments which I find in the small ideas and little faith of men in public life. A courageous, earnest purpose would settle the question at once, for all time."

"Garrison's course in the *Liberator*, and in 'masterly inactivity,' has been statesmanlike. . . . He is wise MS. as a serpent," wrote Mrs. Chapman to J. M. McKim, in September. With the revocation of Frémont's proclamation, and the approaching session of Congress, the time for more aggressive measures seemed to Garrison to have come, and he drew up the following Memorial to Con-

[1] *I. e.*, the Border slaveholding States.

gress, which was extensively circulated and signed, and forwarded to Washington: CHAP. I. 1861.

"*To the Congress of the United States:* Lib. 31:154.

"The undersigned, citizens of . . . , respectfully submit —

"That, as the present formidable rebellion against the General Government manifestly finds its root and nourishment in the system of chattel slavery at the South; as the leading conspirators are slaveholders, who constitute an oligarchy avowedly hostile to all free institutions; and as, in the nature of things, no solid peace can be maintained while the cause of this treasonable revolt is permitted to exist; your honorable body is urgently implored to lose no time in enacting, under the war-power, the total abolition of slavery throughout the country — liberating unconditionally the slaves of all who are rebels, and, while not recognizing the right of property in man, allowing for the emancipated slaves of such as are loyal to the Government a fair pecuniary award, as a conciliatory measure, and to facilitate an amicable adjustment of difficulties; and thus to bring the war to a speedy and beneficent termination, and indissolubly to unite all sections and all interests of the country upon the enduring basis of universal freedom."

In an editorial on "The Time for National Deliverance," Lib. 31:162. he said, with all the emphasis of italics, to President Lincoln and his Cabinet advisers: "*To refuse to deliver those captive millions who are now legally in your power, is tantamount to the crime of their original enslavement;* and their blood shall a righteous God require at your hands. Put the trump of jubilee to your lips!"

In October Mr. Garrison visited Pennsylvania to attend the annual meeting of the State Anti-Slavery Society at Oct. 24, 25. West Chester, and wrote the "Statement of Principles" Lib. 34:175. there adopted — a succinct exposition of the position held by the Society and by the abolitionists at large, with a final word for Mr. Lincoln again. On his way to West Chester, he tarried for a day or two in New York, where a brilliant evening reception was given him at a friend's Oct. 21. house, and he "appeared in greatly improved health, full A. S. Standard, Oct. 26. of a fine animation, exhibiting (as everywhere) his characteristic mirthfulness and seriousness," Lib. 31:174. and made "a happy

CHAP. I. 1861.

speech — full of good feeling, full of high hopes, full of trust in God." Dr. George B. Cheever and Horace Greeley also participated in the occasion.

W. L. Garrison to his Wife.

MS.

New York, Oct. 21, 1861.

Oliver Johnson, W. P. Garrison.

Yesterday, Mrs. Savin, Oliver, Wendell, and myself, went to Brooklyn in the morning, to hear Ward Beecher preach. It was the first time I had been in his spacious chapel. We were provided with the best seats, near to the pulpit, and directly in front of the speaker. Old Dr. Beecher sat directly in front of me, and at the close of the services I gave him my hand, which he grasped cordially, and when I gave him my name, he seemed desirous to have me go to his house in the evening; but I was engaged elsewhere. Besides, age and time have done their work upon him: he is in a state of second childhood, with broken memory, and his speech badly affected, so that continuous conversation is beyond his ability.

Lyman Beecher.

The house, which is admirably constructed for an auditorium, holds about as many as the Tremont Temple, and was crowded in every part, aisles and all. So it is always. The immense assembly united with the choir in singing, which gave much life to that part of the service. The sermon was upon the nature and functions of conscience, and was a wide-awake and racy discourse. In the audience was Mr. Forbes of Milton Hill, with his daughter. Also, Mrs. Shaw of Staten Island, who, at the close of the proceedings, pressed eagerly forward to take me by the hand, and to express the hope that I would visit Staten Island before my return home. . . .

Boston.

John M. Forbes, Sarah B. Shaw.

Wendell and I then spent a few moments with Ward Beecher, who seemed well pleased to see us, and who playfully said he thought he could do such a heretic as I some good, if he could only see me often enough! . . .

W. P. G.

Last evening, we took tea and spent a very agreeable hour with the two female poets, Alice and Phœbe Cary, whose house is much visited. Horace Greeley was one of the company. We had some little discussion together on the peace question. He thinks there is no other way of dealing with tyranny than by knocking the tyrants in the head.

After tea, I went with Oliver and Wendell, and Phœbe Cary, to Dr. Cheever's church, to hear one of the series of anti-slavery

O. Johnson, W. P. G.

lectures he is delivering Sunday evening. The assembly was very large, and the Dr. earnest as usual, but his discourse was a hair-splitting defence of the anti-slavery character of the Constitution, and to me excessively tedious and wonderfully absurd, in view of the history of this nation. William Goodell was present, and, of course, enjoyed it to the brim, as it was but the echo of his own chop-logic. He grasped my hand warmly, and urged me to call and see him.

In Philadelphia there were more social gatherings and delightful days and evenings with the Motts, McKims, and others of that choice circle.[1] Mr. Garrison found many of his Quaker friends deeply troubled by the fact that their sons, whom they had supposed firmly grounded in the peace principles of their Society, had been among the earliest to catch the infection of patriotic fervor and enlist in the army, and there was scarcely a household from which one or more of the young men had not gone forth to the conflict. "I told them," he said, with his usual cheerful philosophy, "that however much they might regret that their sons could not meet the test when it was applied, they should at least rejoice that the boys were true to their real convictions when the shot at Sumter revealed to them that they were simply birthright Quakers, and had not fully comprehended and absorbed the principles of their fathers. They had imagined they were on the plane of the Sermon on the Mount, and they found they were only up to the level of Lexington and Bunker Hill; but they should be honored none the less for their loyalty to truth and freedom."

On his return to Boston, Mr. Garrison delivered a Sun-

[1] "Garrison is a real Bishop of souls," wrote Mrs. Chapman to Miller McKim, at this time. And again: "I enjoyed the account of your meeting in the *Standard*. Garrison is bringing up the rear like a good captain. 'Our dear chief' (as Florence Nightingale calls Sidney Herbert) is one to be proud of. He is so great as a social reformer that, as H. M. [Harriet Martineau] says, in her sketch of him in the *Once a Week*, 'he is too great, as such, to be a representative man at present; however, his example may raise up a class hereafter.' I wonder why we have never republished that sketch? I dare say Johnson did not see it, and Garrison would not give it out for the *Liberator*" (MS. Nov. 2, 1861).

Nov. 10, 1861; *Lib.* 31:182. day morning discourse on the state of the country to an audience that filled Music Hall and applauded his strongest utterances. *Nov.* 18. A week later, he and Mr. Phillips conducted the funeral services of Francis Jackson, who passed away, after a long illness, on the 14th of November, in his 73d year.[1] Like Charles F. Hovey, he left a noble bequest to the cause so dear to them both, and provided a fund which lasted beyond the abolition of slavery and helped to swell the contributions for the education of the freedmen.[2] More fortunate than Hovey, he survived to see the beginning of the end, and to know that the sum of all villanies was fast tottering to its fall.

By the capture of Port Royal and Beaufort in November, and the immediate emancipation thus effected of the thousands of slaves in the Sea Islands of South Carolina, the problem of the education and civilization of the degraded blacks of the rice and cotton belt of that section was presented to the consideration of the philanthropic people of the North, and a few weeks later it was seriously accepted and grappled with; but the last weeks of the year were absorbed in exultation over the victory on the Carolina coast and the seizure of the rebel emissaries Mason and Slidell on the steamer *Trent*. That the chief *James M. Mason.* promoter of the Fugitive Slave Law should himself be incarcerated in a Boston fort seemed a rare bit of poetic justice, and it was natural that Mr. Phillips's allusion to *Dec.* 19. it in his lecture (on "The War") at New York, in December, should be rapturously applauded. The lecture itself

[1] They were held in the same parlors of the old Hollis Street house in which the ladies of the Boston Female Anti-Slavery Society met after the mob of 1835, and received a new ally in Harriet Martineau (*ante*, 2 : 52, 57, 60).

[2] The amount was $10,000, subsequently increased by residuary rights. Mr. Garrison, who for twenty-five years was constantly indebted to Mr. Jackson's generous help in meeting the deficit of the *Liberator*, was also the recipient of a liberal bequest, and the sum of $5,000 was given in aid of the Woman's Rights movement. Through a contest of the will and an unjust decision of the Supreme Court, this last provision was subsequently annulled, in consequence of which a daughter of Mr. Jackson (Mrs. Eliza F. Eddy) twenty years later bequeathed over $50,000 for the same object, as her protest against the violation of her father's will.

occupied seven columns of the *Liberator*, and is referred to in the following letter from Mr. Garrison to Oliver Johnson: *Lib.* 31:206.

"You will see in the *Liberator*, this week, the speech of Mr. Phillips, delivered at New York, as revised and corrected by himself. And such revision, correction, alteration, and addition you never saw, in the way of emendation! More than two columns of the *Tribune's* report were in type before P. came into our office; and the manipulation these required was a caution to all reporters and type-setters! I proposed to P. to send his altered 'slips' to Barnum as a remarkable curiosity, and Winchell suggested having them photographed! But P. desired to make his speech as complete and full as he could, and I am glad you are to receive it without being put to any trouble about it. Doubtless, you will be requested to make some new alterations; for he is constantly criticising what he has spoken, and pays no regard to literal accuracy. This speech will be eagerly read, as it touches ably upon many interesting points.

MS. Dec. 26, 1861.

P. T. Barnum, the showman.

J. M. W. Yerrinton.

"Gerrit Smith at Peterboro', and Charles Sumner at Washington, both write to me in discouraging tones as to the prospects before us. The Administration has neither pluck nor definite purpose. What tremendous events will hinge upon an actual war with England!"

MSS. G. S., Dec. 23, 1861; *C. S., Dec.* 22.

In the *Liberator* for December 13, the passage from John Quincy Adams on the iniquity of the three-fifths representation clause in the Constitution, which had so long stood at the head of the first page (replaced for a time by a corresponding extract from Dr. Channing) was supplanted by Adams's declaration of the war-powers of the Government with respect to slavery; and the shibboleth, "The United States Constitution is a covenant with death and an agreement with hell," gave way to the command, "Proclaim Liberty throughout all the land, to all the inhabitants thereof."

CHAPTER II.

The Hour and the Man.—1862.

Chap. II. — 1862. Jan. 14. EARLY in the new year Mr. Garrison yielded to the urgent solicitation of friends in New York, and delivered a lecture, at Cooper Institute in that city, on "The Abolitionists and their Relations to the War," which subsequently received a wide circulation in pamphlet form.[1] (Lib. 32 : 14.) In this he vindicated the motives and methods of the Garrisonian abolitionists; replied effectively to the assertions that they were wholly responsible for the war, or had been equally guilty with the secessionists in precipitating it; answered the cry that slavery had nothing to do with the war, and the Government no right or power to touch the institution; and declared emancipation essential for the suppression of the rebellion and for ultimate peace and union. The address, which occupied two hours in delivery, abounded in cogent and forcible passages, but we have room only for two brief quotations. To the charge that the disappearance of the "Covenant with Death" motto from the head of the *Liberator* indicated a great and sudden change in his views, he replied:

Lib. 32 : 14. "Well, ladies and gentlemen, you remember what *Benedick* in the play says: 'When I said I would die a bachelor, I did not think I should live till I were married.' And when I said I would not sustain the Constitution because it was 'a covenant

[1] 'The Pulpit and Rostrum,' Nos. 26 and 27 (double number), containing the above-named lecture, a pro-slavery speech in the U. S. Senate (Jan. 23, 1862) by Garrett Davis of Kentucky, and Alexander H. Stephens's speech (March 21, 1861) declaring African slavery the corner-stone of the Southern Confederacy. New York, 1862 (*Lib.* 32 : 39).

with death and an agreement with hell,' *I had no idea that I should live to see death and hell secede.*[1] Hence it is that I am now with the Government, to enable it to constitutionally stop the further ravages of death, and to extinguish the flames of hell forever." CHAP. II. — 1862.

The other passage, forecasting the blessing which emancipation would bring to the South, and rejoicing in the certain future prosperity of that section, anticipated the verdict which the "New South," amazed by her marvellous growth and development under freedom, has already pronounced.[2]

"Slavery is a thunderbolt in the hands of the traitors to smite the Government to the dust. That thunderbolt might be seized and turned against the rebellion with fatal effect, and at the same time without injury to the South. My heart glows when I think of the good thus to be done to the oppressors as well as to the oppressed; for I could not stand here, I could not stand anywhere, and advocate vindictive and destructive measures to bring the rebels to terms. I do not believe in killing or doing injury even to enemies—God forbid! That is not my Christian philosophy. But I do say, that never before in the history of the world has God vouchsafed to a Government the power to do such a work of philanthropy and justice, in the *Lib.* 32:15.

[1] The humor of this retort was keenly relished by the audience, and by the wider public to whom the newspapers all over the North quoted it.

[2] "The 'New South' rejoices in the Union and its wide domain, and, most of all, it is proud that the blot of slavery has been removed from its escutcheon. It says, in all heartiness and sincerity, 'God be praised for this crowning glory of a wonderful century'" (James Phelan of Tennessee, in a speech prior to his election as member of Congress from the Memphis district, November, 1886).

"Bitter to my taste as were the results of the civil war, day after day has reconciled me to them, and convinced me of the wisdom of cheerful submission to the will of Him who brought them about. The union of these States has been preserved and declared indissoluble. A great and disturbing constitutional question has been finally and forever settled, and slavery has been forever abolished; it no longer tarnishes the fair fame of a great and free republic. Because it was involved in the question of constitutional right, I fought four years in its defence. I tell you now, upon the honor of my manhood, that I would fight eight years, though my hairs are white, against any attempt to reinstate it in any portion of this continent" (Z. B. Vance, Governor of North Carolina during the war, and U. S. Senator from that State since 1879, in a lecture delivered in Boston, Dec. 8, 1886; in Boston *Daily Advertiser*, Dec. 9).

CHAP. II. 1862.

extremity of its danger and for self-preservation, as He now grants to this Government. Emancipation is to destroy nothing but evil; it is to establish good; it is to transform human beings from things into men; it is to make freedom, and education, and invention, and enterprise, and prosperity, and peace, and a true Union possible and sure. Redeemed from the curse of slavery, the South shall in due time be as the garden of God. Though driven to the wall and reduced to great extremity by this rebellion, still we hold off, hold off, hold off, and reluctantly say, at last, if it must be so, but only to save ourselves from destruction, we will do this rebellious South the most beneficent act that any people ever yet did — one that will secure historic renown for the Administration, make this struggle memorable in all ages, and bring down upon the land the benediction of God! But we will not do this if we can possibly avoid it! Now, for myself, both as an act of justice to the oppressed and to serve the cause of freedom universally, I want the Government to be in haste to blow the trump of jubilee. I desire to bless and not curse the South — to make her prosperous and happy by substituting free institutions for her leprous system of slavery. I am as much interested in the safety and welfare of the slaveholders, as brother men, as I am in the liberation of their poor slaves; for we are all the children of God, and should strive to promote the happiness of all. I desire that the mission of Jesus, 'Peace on earth, good will to men,' may be fulfilled in this and in every land."

This lecture attracted much attention, and brought Mr. Garrison urgent invitations to speak in other places. Especially was it the wish of some of the most trusted and sagacious of the anti-slavery leaders that he and Mr. Phillips should declare the sentiments and demands of the abolitionists in relation to the war, both in public addresses and in personal intercourse with the President and members of his Cabinet, and the Republican leaders in Congress. They felt that if this were done, and the *Liberator* and *Standard* kept afloat, other agencies and methods useful in the past might safely be discontinued, and a greater concentration of effort secured.[1]

[1] Holding these views, Mrs. Chapman had already withdrawn from the management of the annual Subscription Festival, and J. M. McKim now resigned his position as corresponding secretary of the Pennsylvania Anti-

The annual meeting of the Massachusetts Society first claimed attention, however, and to Mr. Garrison fell, as usual, the preparation of the resolutions, which were certainly full and exhaustive. His speech, at the close of the first day's meeting, was in his happiest vein, and purposely rose-colored, as he frankly confessed, in order to offset the rather depressing effect of some of the previous speeches, Mr. Phillips's among them, which had dwelt on the shortcomings of the President and Administration touching slavery. "What have we to rejoice over?" he repeated to doubting inquirers —

CHAP. II. 1862. *Lib.* 32 : 19.

"Why, I say, the war! 'What! this fratricidal war? What! this civil war? What! this treasonable dismemberment of the Union?' Yes, thank God for it all! — for it indicates the waning power of slavery and the irresistible growth of freedom, and that the day of Northern submission is past. It is better that we should be so virtuous that the vicious cannot live with us, than to be so vile that they can endure and relish our company. No matter what may be said of the Government — how it timidly holds back — how it lacks courage, energy, and faith — how it refuses to strike the blow which alone will settle the rebellion. No matter what may be said of President Lincoln or General McClellan, by way of criticism — and a great deal can be justly said to their condemnation — one cheering fact overrides all these considerations, making them as dust in the

Lib. 32:21.

Cf. ante, 3:451.

Slavery Society. "I retire," the latter wrote, "because I believe that my peculiar work, in the position I have occupied, is done. The ultimate object of the Society, it is true, has not yet been attained, neither is its particular mission entirely accomplished. Slavery still exists; and public sentiment respecting it is not yet wholly rectified. But the signs of the times in regard to the former warrant the belief that its overthrow is near, and the progress of change in the character of the latter justifies the conviction that its regeneration will soon be sufficiently complete for all our intended purposes. The Society is now at liberty to discontinue the use of some of the instrumentalities heretofore deemed indispensable. The travelling lecturer is no longer a necessity, and the agent in the office need not feel bound to his place by a sense of obligation. This latter fact, applied to my own case, I accept as an indication of duty" (*Lib.* 32 : 75). Mr. McKim gave practical effect to his belief by speedily identifying himself with the movement to relieve and educate the freedmen; and early in the summer of 1862 he made a visit of inspection to the freed people in the Sea Islands of South Carolina, accompanied by his daughter Lucy, whose musical notation of some of the weird and pathetic slave songs was the first ever published (*Lib.* 32 : 120, 128, 191).

CHAP. II. 1862.

balance, and that is, that our free North is utterly unendurable to the slaveholding South; that we have at last so far advanced in our love of liberty and sympathy for the oppressed, as a people, that it is not possible any longer for the 'traffickers in slaves and souls of men' to walk in union with us. I call that a very cheering fact. Yes, the Union is divided; but better division than that we should be under the lash of Southern overseers! Better civil war, if it must come, than for us to crouch in the dust, and allow ourselves to be driven to the wall by a miserable and merciless slave oligarchy! This war has come because of the increasing love of liberty here at the North; and although, as a people, we do not yet come up to the high standard of duty in striking directly at the slave system for its extirpation as the root and source of all our woe — nevertheless, the sentiment of the North is deepening daily in the right direction.

"I hold that it is not wise for us to be too microscopic in endeavoring to find disagreeable and annoying things, still less to assume that everything is waxing worse and worse, and that there is little or no hope. No! broaden your views; take a more philosophical grasp of the great question; and see that, criticise and condemn as you may and should in certain directions, the fountains of the great deep are broken up — see that this is fundamentally a struggle between all the elements of freedom on the one hand, and all the elements of despotism on the other, with whatever of alloy in the mixture.

"I repeat, the war furnishes ground for high encouragement. 'Why,' some may exclaim, 'we thought you were a peace man!' Yes, verily, I am, and none the less so because of these declarations. Would the cause of peace be the gainer by the substitution of the power of the rebel traitors over the nation for the supremacy of the democratic idea? Would the cause of peace be promoted by the North basely yielding up all her rights and allowing her free institutions to be overthrown? Certainly not. Then, as a peace man, I rejoice that the issue is at last made up, and that the struggle is going on, because I see in it the sign of ultimate redemption. . . .

"I do not know that some margin of allowance may not be made even for the Administration. I would rather be overmagnanimous than wanting in justice. Supposing Mr. Lincoln could answer to-night, and we should say to him: 'Sir, with the power in your hands, slavery being the cause of the rebellion beyond all controversy, why don't you put the trump of jubilee to your lips, and proclaim universal freedom?' — possibly he might answer: 'Gentlemen, I understand this matter quite as well as you do. I do not know that I differ in opinion from you; but will you insure me the support of a united North if I do as you bid me? Are all parties and all sects at the North so convinced and so united on this point that they will stand by the Government? If so, give me the evidence of it, and I will strike the blow. But, gentlemen, looking over the entire North, and seeing in all your towns and cities papers representing a considerable, if not a formidable portion of the people, menacing and bullying the Government in case it dare to liberate the slaves, even as a matter of self-preservation, I do not feel that the hour has yet come that will render it safe for the Government to take that step.'[1] I am willing to believe that something of this feeling weighs in the mind of the President and the Cabinet, and that there is some ground for hesitancy, as a mere matter of political expediency. My reply, however, to the President would be: 'Sir, the power is in your hands as President of the United States, and Commander-in-Chief of the army and navy. Do *your* duty; give to the slaves their liberty by proclamation, as far as that can give it; and if the North shall betray you, and prefer the success of the rebellion to the preservation of the Union, let the dread responsibility be hers, but stand with God and Freedom on your side, come what may!' But men high in office are not apt to be led by such lofty moral considerations; and, therefore, we should not judge the present incumbents too harshly. Doubtless, they want to be assured of the Northern heart, feeling, coöperation, approval. Can these be safely relied upon when the decisive blow shall be struck? That is the question, and it is a very serious question. . . .

Chap. II. 1862.

"Nevertheless, I think the Administration is unnecessarily timid and not undeserving of rebuke. I think that this bellowing, bullying, treasonable party at the North has, after all, but very little left, either in point of numbers or power; the fangs of the viper are drawn, though the venomous feeling remains. Still, it has its effect, and produces a damaging, if not paralyzing, impression at Washington."

In February Mr. Garrison lectured in Greenfield, Mass., after attending the New York State Anti-Slavery Convention at Albany, and brought home a desperate cold which

Feb. 10. *Feb.* 7, 8.

[1] In June of this year, the popular vote of Illinois, Mr. Lincoln's own State, adopted three amendments to the State Constitution, cruelly discriminating against colored citizens (*Lib.* 32 : 107).

CHAP. II. 1862. Mar. 14, 18.

clung to him for several months. It was during this period that Mr. Phillips made his first visit to Washington, where he delivered two lectures before brilliant audiences. He received marked attentions in both houses of Congress, and had an interview with Mr. Lincoln which increased his belief that the President was on the road to emancipation. He at once wrote back to Boston, urging that Mr. Garrison should follow him:

MS. to Ann Phillips, Mar., 1862.

"Assure Garrison that Washington is as safe to him as New York; that I think he OUGHT to go on and lecture. He knows not the enthusiasm with which he will be received, nor the good he will do. One regret I have in going West is, that I lose the chance to come home and urge him on to it, and perhaps go with him. . . . He will be surprised, as I was, to find so many Music Hall faces there. On several occasions I came unexpectedly on two or three at a time."

Boston.

J. M. McKim.

This urgency being enforced by Mr. McKim and Oliver Johnson, Mr. Garrison wrote to the latter:

MS. Mar. 30.

"I have not yet been invited to visit Washington, and, therefore, have had no opportunity to accept or decline. But I am in no condition for public speaking, in consequence of the state of my throat and voice, and thus would be compelled to decline any invitation that might be proffered. I have paid dearly for my visit to Albany, as I did three years ago, though not to so great an extent. My cold has been severe and long protracted, but I am gradually throwing it off.

"Phillips's reception at Washington has roused up pro-slavery spite and malice in every direction. No doubt Kentuckians had very much to do in inciting the mobocratic assault upon him at Cincinnati. It is fortunate that he escaped without injury.[1] The result of it, of course, will work well for our cause."

Imprisoned by his cold and unable to speak or lecture, Mr. Garrison plied his pen industriously, and wrote three open letters, which, though addressed to George Thomp-

Lib. 32:30, 34, 38.

[1] A murderous mob assailed and broke up the meeting which Mr. Phillips attempted to address at the Cincinnati Opera House (March 24), and hurled rotten eggs and other missiles at the lecturer all exposed on the great stage. Though struck once, Mr. Phillips stood as calm and unmoved as was his wont in facing mobs, and extorted the admiration of his opponents by his fearless bearing (*Lib.* 32 : 53, 54).

son, were intended for those English abolitionists whose minds were still so befogged on the issues of the American war that they withheld their sympathies from the Federal Government. "Though," he wrote, "in view of all that has been written and published on the subject, I almost despair of removing that misapprehension in the slightest degree, yet, by the love I bear them, I feel impelled to address this letter to you — hoping it may not be wholly in vain." CHAP. II. 1862. *Lib.* 32:30.

"As for yourself," he continued, "you need nothing from me, either by way of information or guidance, at this particular juncture. . . . Your mastery of American affairs is absolute: the key to unlock them is SLAVERY, and of that key you took possession when you first came to this country in 1834, and have ever since used it with all possible skill, diligence, and success. . . . There are few Americans who are so well posted in the history of this country as yourself, while there is scarcely any one in England who seems to have any intelligent knowledge of it. Almost all your writers and public speakers are ever blundering in regard to the constitutional powers of the American Government, as such, and those pertaining to the States, in their separate capacity. Mr. Bright, in his masterly speech at Rochdale, evinced a power of analysis and correct generalization worthy of the highest praise, and has secured for himself the thanks and admiration of every true friend of free institutions. His case is as exceptional, however, as it is creditable." *Lib.* 32:30. *John Bright.*

These letters no doubt helped to illumine the clouded minds of some of the anti-slavery friends in England, but the same steamer which bore the last of them across the Atlantic, carried also a message of President Lincoln's to Congress, which proved of potent service to Thompson and the few brave men who were sustaining the cause of the North against the overwhelming tide of adverse sentiment in Great Britain. In this message — one of the clumsiest documents the author of the Gettysburg Address ever penned — Mr. Lincoln recommended the adoption of a resolution by Congress to this effect: "That the United States, in order to coöperate with any State which may *Mar.* 6. *Greeley's American Conflict,* 2:259.

CHAP. II. 1862. adopt gradual abolition of slavery, give to such State pecuniary aid, to be used by such State in its discretion, to compensate it for the inconvenience, public and private, produced by such change of system"; and this was promptly passed by both houses, though opposed by the members from the Border States for which it was intended.

The message arrested general attention as the first attempt of the President to formulate a plan looking to the abolition of slavery; and the evidence of a desire on his part to initiate measures to this end, gradual and indefinite as they were, sufficed to turn the current of popular feeling abroad, and to win sympathy hitherto withheld from the Government by those who were indifferent to the constitutional questions involved in the struggle.[1] Mr. Phillips, in a lecture before the Emancipation League of Boston,[2] four days later, welcomed the message, with his "whole heart," as "one more sign of promise." "If the President has not entered Canaan," he declared, "he has turned his face Zionward"; and he justly interpreted the message as saying, in effect: "Gentlemen of the Border States, now is your time. If you want your money, take it, and if hereafter I should take your slaves without paying, don't say I did not offer to do it."

Mar. 10. *Lib.* 32:42.

To Mr. Garrison the message caused less elation, for it proposed no limitation as to the period in which the offer might be accepted, held out no inducement for any State to emancipate its slaves immediately, and made no dis-

[1] "Shall I tell you when it was that the reaction in your favor took place? It commenced with the message of your President of the 7th [6th] of March, 1862, when he recommended the passage by Congress of a resolution promising indemnity to the planters of the slave States if, in their State legislatures, they would take means to abolish slavery" (George Thompson, speech at New York, May 10, 1864. *Lib.* 34 : 82).

[2] An organization formed in December, 1861, by Dr. Samuel G. Howe, Francis W. Bird, George L. Stearns, Frank B. Sanborn, and others, who established a weekly newspaper, the *Commonwealth*, which was for a time the organ of the League, and was edited by Moncure D. Conway and Frank B. Sanborn (*Lib.* 31 : 202; 32 : 146).

tinction between the rebel and "so-called loyal slave States." "Why wait," he asked in the *Liberator*, "for the dealers in human flesh to determine when they will deem it advisable to cease from their villany as a matter of pecuniary advantage and cunning speculation with the Government, when the Government is clothed with constitutional power to dispose of the whole matter at once, without any huckstering or delay? 'Let JUSTICE be done, though the heavens fall.' President Lincoln, delay not at your peril! 'Execute judgment in the morning — break every yoke — let the oppressed go free.'" To Oliver Johnson he wrote: "I am afraid the President's message will prove 'a decoy duck' or 'a red herring,' so as to postpone that decisive action by Congress which we are so desirous of seeing. Let us advocate no postponement of duty."

Lib. 32:42.

MS. Mar. 18, 1862.

Though not yet prepared for "decisive action," Congress was by no means inactive during the long spring session of 1862, and the record of its anti-slavery legislation was enough to show the irresistible sweep of the current towards freedom. In February it passed an act forbidding army officers to return fugitive slaves to their masters; in April it decreed immediate emancipation in the District of Columbia, and thus finally purged the nation's capital of the stain of slavery;[1] in June it forever prohibited slavery in all the Territories, and authorized the President to appoint diplomatic representatives to Hayti and Liberia; in July it declared free all slaves of rebel masters coming within the lines of the Union army or found in any place vacated by the rebels, and authorized the President to "employ persons of African descent for the suppression of the rebellion, and organize and use them in such manner as he may judge best for the public welfare." It also provided for the education of colored children, and the equal administration of the laws to the colored people, in the District of Columbia; passed a

Wilson's Anti-Slavery Measures in Congress, pp. 17–223.

[1] Loyal slave-owners were compensated at the average rate of three hundred dollars for each slave. The bill was passed by a strict party vote, the Democrats solidly opposing it.

CHAP. II. 1862. bill for the more effectual suppression of the African slave trade; and provided for the enrolment of colored soldiers. All these measures received the prompt approval of the President, but in May he again disappointed the high hopes he had thus raised, by revoking the proclamation issued ten days earlier by Major-General David Hunter, commanding the Department of the South, at Hilton Head, S. C. With delightful pithiness, this old West-Pointer announced that, as the States of Georgia, Florida, and South Carolina had taken up arms against the United States, it had become necessary to declare them under martial law. "Slavery and martial law in a free country are altogether incompatible," he continued. "The persons in these three States . . . heretofore held as slaves are therefore declared forever free."

May 19.

Greeley's American Conflict, 2:246; *Lib.* 32:83.

Mr. Lincoln did not wait to receive official notification of this from General Hunter, but based his revoking proclamation on the information contained in the public prints; and, after declaring the act unauthorized and void, and announcing that he must reserve to himself to decide "whether at any time, or in any case, it shall have become a necessity indispensable to the maintenance of the Government to exercise such supposed power," he besought the slave States to consider, ere it was too late, the offer of Congress to coöperate with them in any scheme of gradual, compensated emancipation. "You cannot," he added significantly, "be blind to the signs of the times."

Lib. 32:83.

Ante, pp. 47, 48.

"President Lincoln!" exclaimed Mr. Garrison, at the close of his sharp criticisms on the proclamation, "'canst thou draw out leviathan with a hook? Will he make many supplications unto thee?'" Nevertheless, while renewing his criticisms at the May meetings in Boston, and pressing home to the President the responsibility which the latter had now assumed of speaking or withholding the word which would give freedom to millions of his fellow-creatures, he was again careful to balance the scales justly and make all possible allowances for him

Lib. 32:82.

in his trying and difficult position, when other speakers seemed too sweeping in their denunciations.[1] "Those who hold office by the will of the people," he reminded them, "cannot be judged wholly like private men." And he further declared: "The gains of freedom have been so rapid and magnificent that we fail to appreciate them." The nineteen resolutions which he drafted for the Convention, and which were adopted by a rising vote, fully recognized these, however, while emphasizing what remained to be done. At the New York meetings, earlier in the month, he presented a carefully prepared "Statement of the Executive Committee of the American Anti-Slavery Society," referring to the omission of the annual meeting the previous year, and defining the position of the Society in view of the altered state of things.[2]

CHAP. II. 1862 *Lib.* 32:90. *Lib.* 32:90. *May* 6. *Lib.* 32:74.

Joshua R. Giddings to W. L. Garrison.

JEFFERSON, Ohio, June 12, 1862.

MS. *In Boston.*

DEAR GARRISON: Thanks for that speech before the Anti-Slavery Convention. You gave such utterance to my own feelings that I felt truly grateful on reading it this morning. I thank God that you are yet able to attend such meetings. My friends will not permit me to be present on such occasions. Indeed, it is all I dare do to read their proceedings. Even they give rise to feelings that apparently endanger my existence.

1 Stephen S. Foster, for instance, held Mr. Lincoln responsible for the enforcement of the Fugitive Slave Law in the District of Columbia, whither scores of Maryland slaves flocked after the passage of the Emancipation Act, only to be seized, imprisoned, and returned to their masters. The resolutions introduced by Mr. Garrison very properly called upon Congress to end this "frightful paradox" (*Lib.* 32 : 92).

2 In a letter urging the preparation of this Statement, Gerrit Smith wrote (April 16) to Mr. Garrison: "There is one point at which the meeting should, in my judgment, put forth a clear defence of the 'Garrisonian abolitionist.' His influence, especially in the case of such a man as yourself or Wendell Phillips, is too important to the cause of freedom that injustice should be allowed to impair it. The 'Garrisonian abolitionist' was formerly a Disunionist, and is now a Unionist; and hence he is charged with being inconsistent, or at least with being a convert. . . . There is a conversion. It is, however, *to* him, and not *of* him. There is a change; but it is *around* him, and not *in* him" (MS. and *Lib.* 32 : 74).

CHAP. II. 1862. But I rejoice to have lived so long and to have seen so much. Nor can I complain that my constitution has not done me fair service. In short, I am pretty well satisfied with the past, and am full of hope for the future. Although Lincoln has failed to come up to what you and I think he might and should have done, yet he is honest in his positions and will require time to reach our positions.

I start for Montreal[1] on Monday, and think it possible I may visit Boston before I return. Should I do so, shall hope to see [you].

God bless you! GIDDINGS.

From the May meetings in Boston Mr. Garrison went to the Yearly Meeting of Progressive Friends at Longwood, in Chester County, Pennsylvania, where he spoke repeatedly during the four days' sessions, and prepared the Testimony of the meeting on Slavery and the Rebellion, as well as on Peace. At his suggestion, a Memorial to the President was also prepared, and naturally the task of drafting it fell to him. Two weeks later a delegation appointed by the meeting waited upon President Lincoln at the White House, and Oliver Johnson as their spokesman read the Appeal:

Lib. 32 : 102. To ABRAHAM LINCOLN, *President of the United States:*

The Religious Society of Progressive Friends, in Yearly Meeting assembled at Longwood, Chester Co., Pa., from the 5th to the 7th of Sixth month, 1862, under a solemn sense of the perils besetting the country, and of the duty devolving upon them to exert whatever influence they possess to rescue it from impending destruction, beg leave respectfully but earnestly to set forth, for the consideration of President Lincoln:

That they fully share in the general grief and reprobation felt at the seditious course pursued in opposition to the General Government by the so-called "Confederate States"; regarding it as marked by all the revolting features of high-handed robbery, cruel treachery, and murderous violence, and therefore utterly to be abhorred and condemned by every lover of his country, and every friend of the human race.

That, nevertheless, this sanguinary rebellion finds its cause,

[1] Mr. Giddings had been appointed Consul-General for British North America the previous year by Mr. Lincoln.

purpose, and combustible materials in that most unchristian and barbarous system of slavery which prevails in that section of the country, and in the guilt of which the whole land has long been deeply involved by general complicity; so that it is to be contritely recognized as the penalty due to such persistent and flagrant transgression, and as the inevitable operation of the law of eternal justice. CHAP. II. 1862.

That thus heavily visited for its grinding oppression of an unfortunate race, "peeled, meted out, and trodden under foot," whose wrongs have so long cried unto Heaven for redress — and thus solemnly warned of the infatuation as well as exceeding wickedness of endeavoring to secure peace, prosperity, and unity, while leaving millions to clank their chains in the house of bondage — the nation, in its official organization, should lose no time in proclaiming immediate and universal emancipation, so that the present frightful effusion of blood may cease, liberty be established, and a permanent reconciliation effected by the removal of the sole cause of these divisions.

That in his speech delivered at Springfield, before his election to the office of Chief Magistrate, the President expressly declared: "A house divided against itself cannot stand. I believe this government cannot endure permanently half slave and half free. I do not expect the Union to be dissolved — I do not expect the house to fall — but I do expect it will cease to be divided. It will become all one thing or all the other." *Ante*, 3:420, 470.

That this Society, therefore, urgently unites with a wide-spread and constantly increasing sentiment, in beseeching the President, as the head of the nation, clothed with the constitutional power in such a fearful emergency to suppress the rebellion effectually by the removal of its cause, not to allow the present golden opportunity to pass without decreeing the entire abolition of slavery throughout the land, as a measure imperatively demanded by a due regard for the unity of the country, the safety and happiness of the people, the preservation of free institutions, and by every consideration of justice, mercy, and peace. Otherwise, we have fearful reason to apprehend that blood will continue to flow, and fierce dissensions to abound, and calamities to increase, and fiery judgments to be poured out, until the work of national destruction is consummated beyond hope of recovery.

The President received the delegation with courtesy and respect, and listened attentively to the reading of the

Lib. 32 : 102. Memorial. He questioned whether a decree of emancipation would be more binding on the South than the Constitution itself, which could not now be enforced there, but was reminded by Mr. Johnson that he did not on that account relax his efforts to enforce it, and that the memorialists believed emancipation to be indispensable to his success. He then said that he felt the magnitude of the task before him, and hoped to be rightly directed in the very trying circumstances by which he was surrounded. Finally, in response to a few words of sympathy and earnest appeal from William Barnard, who quoted the words of Mordecai to Queen Esther ("For if thou altogether holdest thy peace at this time, then shall there enlargement and deliverance arise to the Jews from another place; but thou and thy father's house shall be destroyed; and who knowest whether thou art come to the kingdom for such a time as this?"), Mr. Lincoln spoke feelingly and impressively, observing that he was deeply sensible of his need of Divine assistance. He had sometimes thought that he might be an instrument in God's hands of accomplishing a great work, and he certainly was not unwilling to be. Perhaps, however, God's way of accomplishing the end which the memorialists had in view might be different from theirs. It would be his earnest endeavor, with a firm reliance on the Divine arm, and seeking light from above, to do his duty in the place to which he had been called.[1]

All through the summer the pressure upon the President increased. Individuals and delegations waited upon him and urged him to proclaim emancipation, but two ideas still possessed his mind — to induce the Border *Ante, pp.* 47, 48. States to agree to his scheme of gradual or immediate emancipation, as they might elect; and to institute a movement for the removal and colonization of the freed people. The first scheme he again presented to Congress

1 Mr. W. D. Kelley, M. C., who was present at the above interview, has given a singularly blundering account of it in the chapter contributed by him to A. T. Rice's 'Reminiscences of Abraham Lincoln' (pp. 281–283). The proper correction was applied by Oliver Johnson in the N. Y. *Tribune* of Sept. 6, 1885.

in a message accompanying the draft of a bill curious alike for its fatuity and its financiering, for no temporal limit was suggested within which emancipation must be accomplished, and provision was actually made for the re-establishment of slavery, if any State should so elect, by gravely stipulating that in such case the State in question should refund to the United States the interest paid by the latter on the indemnity bonds they were to furnish to the States adopting gradual emancipation, and the bonds themselves should become void.[1] Nothing in the bill implied that it was to apply only to the loyal (Border) States, and under its terms the rebellious States could have claimed, had they yielded and consented to it, payment for their tens of thousands of slaves already liberated by the Union armies; the indemnity provided by the General Government being based on the census of 1860, at the outbreak of the rebellion. To assume that States which had already repudiated their debts and their Constitutional obligations, and robbed the Government of millions of dollars' worth of property, could be trusted to refund anything they had once obtained, was certainly an extraordinary manifestation of confidence; but any uneasiness lest the amazing proposition should be seriously considered by those to whom it was made, was speedily set at rest by the promptness with which most of the members of Congress from the Border States pronounced against it, and declared it useless to expect their States to respond to it. This opinion they expressed in writing, after a personal interview with the President in which he warned them that slavery in their States would perish "by mere friction and abrasion," if the war continued, and they had better sell their slaves now while the Government was willing to pay for them. "In repudiating [General Hunter's proclamation]," he added, "I gave dissatisfaction, if not offence, to many whose support the country cannot afford to lose. And this is not the end of it.

July 14, 1862. *Lib.* 32 : 115.

Lib. 32 : 119. *July* 12. *Lib.* 32 : 119.

[1] Any States granting immediate emancipation were to have cash down from the United States.

CHAP. II. 1862. The pressure in this direction is still upon me, and is increasing."

In the same interview he held out the bait of colonization of the freed people as an additional palliative, saying: "I do not speak of emancipation at once, but of a decision at once to emancipate gradually. Room in South America for colonization can be obtained cheaply and in abundance; and when numbers shall be large enough to be company and encouragement for one another, the freed people will not be so reluctant to go."[1] Five weeks later, having procured an appropriation from Congress with which to make a colonizing experiment, Mr. Lincoln invited a number of representative colored men to hold audience with him at the White House, and appealed to them to second his efforts to establish a colony in Central America, where some American speculators had recently acquired coal mines for which they wished to procure laborers. It seems scarcely credible that a man of such rare shrewdness and common-sense as Mr. Lincoln usually manifested, could have talked such amazing nonsense as he discoursed in this hour's interview. Mr. Garrison, to whom the suggestions of gradualism and colonization brought up old memories, promptly pilloried these remarks of the President in the "Refuge of Oppression," pronouncing them "puerile, absurd, illogical, impertinent, untimely." At this distance of time it is impossible to read the President's remarks with either gravity or indignation, but it is quite otherwise with the pathetic story of the dismal collapse of the experiment in colonization actually made in Hayti.[2]

Lib. 32 : 133.

Lib. 32 : 134.

Early in August Mr. Garrison visited Williamstown,

[1] The Border-State Congressmen quietly answered this by adding the cost of deportation to that of emancipation, and saying: "Stated in this form, the proposition is nothing less than the deportation from the country of sixteen hundred million dollars' worth of producing labor, and the substitution in its place of an interest-bearing debt of the same amount" (*Lib.* 32 : 119).

[2] See Mr. Charles K. Tuckerman's account in the *Magazine of American History* for October, 1886; also, *Lib.* 34 : 55. For a clever travesty by "Orpheus C. Kerr" (R. H. Newell) of the President's talk to the colored delegation, see *Lib.* 32 : 140.

Mass., and delivered an address before the Adelphic Union Society of Williams College, which had extended the first invitation of the kind ever received by him. "My 'college oration' is almost completed," he wrote to Oliver Johnson, on July 31, "and will be entirely so to-day. I have written it out in full, as you and McKim advised, and so I feel great relief in knowing certainly what I am going to say. But, oh! the bondage and drawback of reading it, as though I had never seen it before!—for I cannot remember two sentences consecutively. Such confinement in delivery will be extremely irksome to me, and, I fear, tedious to the audience; but I am 'in for it,' and must do the best I can." To his son Wendell he wrote, on Aug. 1:

Aug. 4, 1862. *MS.* *J. M. McKim.*

"My address is not quite completed, but nearly so. It is simply a serious, straightforward anti-slavery arraignment of the guilt of the nation, and showing why the present national visitation has come upon us. I have written it without a metaphor, or a single flight of the imagination, or anything to relieve its sombre aspect. To old abolitionists it would be trite, but to the mass of my audience it will, perhaps, be 'as good as new.' . . . One gets weary, however, in the constant affirmation of these moral truisms, which would seem to be as plain to every mind as the midday sun is to the vision."

MS.

W. L. Garrison to W. P. Garrison.

BOSTON, August 10, 1862.

MS.

A week ago to-day (Sunday), I was at Pittsfield, and found it to be as beautiful and attractive as eye and heart could wish. I there met Professor Fowler of Poughkeepsie, who, like myself, was on the way to Williamstown, to deliver one of the orations. . . .

John W. Fowler.

"Monday evening, the young student, Mr. G. C. Brown, whose home is in Pittsfield, and who engaged me to give the address before the Adelphic Union Society, drove us to Williamstown, a distance of twenty-two miles, in a sort of barouche, with a fine span of horses. The scenery throughout was a continual blending of the sublime and the beautiful, and some of the views of a very enchanting kind. We enjoyed our ride to the full.

Aug. 4, 1862. The day was one of the most sultry of the season. I gave my address in the afternoon, at 4 o'clock, occupying an hour and a half. It was listened to with unbroken interest, and occasionally applauded (it was too grave and serious for much applause), and was evidently well received.[1] At the close of it, Professor Bascom (who introduced me) expressed his gratification, and said he endorsed every word of it. The audience was not very large, as twenty-five cents were asked for a ticket admitting the holder to both lectures. Hardly any of the Faculty were present except Prof. Bascom. In the evening, Prof. Fowler gave his lecture, and spoke without manuscript or notes for nearly two hours and a half! His theme was "The Crisis," which he discussed with marked ability, and delivered with great energy and eloquence. . . .

John Bascom.

There is nothing new to communicate. As usual, up to this time, "all is quiet along the Potomac." Volunteering is going on rapidly in every part of the State, so that drafting will probably be required to a much less extent than was apprehended.

The draft became necessary, however, and as the time for it approached, Mr. Garrison discussed in two full and elaborate editorials the problems presented by its application to the non-resistants and abolitionists, and their duty in the premises. In these he maintained that the former (only a handful, really), who had consistently refrained from voting or taking any part in politics and government on conscientious grounds, ought to be exempt from its operation, but that all professed peace men (including the Quakers) who voted, and by their votes elected as their agents a President and members of Congress, bound by their oaths to defend the Government by military and naval force if necessary, had no just claim

Lib. 32:150, 154.

[1] The address, under the title of "Our National Visitation," was printed in full in the *Liberator* (34 : 138), and filled over six columns. "The timid people who expected all sorts of infidel propositions, were pleasantly disappointed to hear a thoroughly Christian address, and one which contained a greater amount of direct quotations from the sacred Scriptures, we venture to say, than any sermon or oration that will find utterance in this town this week. . . . The address was wonderfully vitalized and wonderfully clear — without denunciation and without bitterness," wrote the correspondent of the Springfield *Republican* (*Lib.* 34 : 136); and Mrs. Child wrote: "Garrison's address is admirable; one of the best things he ever did, which is saying a good deal" (MS., Sept. 7, 1862, to R. F. Wallcut).

to exemption. In some States the Quakers were by law free from all military liabilities, on account of their peace principles, but this, he protested, was "conceding to a sect what belongs to conscience, irrespective of sect," and so was manifestly unjust. "For he who believes in total abstinence from war as a Christian duty, though a member of no religious body, ought to have the same toleration as though he wore a Quaker dress and belonged to a Quaker society."

CHAP. II. 1862. *Lib.* 32:150.

"Now, as an apostle pertinently inquired in his own day, 'Know ye not, that to whom ye yield yourselves servants to obey, his servants ye are to whom ye obey; whether of sin unto death, or of obedience unto righteousness?'—so, we say that he who votes to empower Congress to declare war, and to provide the necessary instruments of war, and to constitute the President commander-in-chief of the army and navy, has no right, when war actually comes, to plead conscientious scruples as a peace man; but is bound to stand by his vote, or else to make confession of wrong-doing and take his position outside of the Government. He cannot be allowed to strain at a gnat, and swallow a camel; to play fast and loose with his conscience; to make the amplest provisions for war, and then beg to be excused from its dangers and hardships in deference to his peace sentiments. The Government has a right to apply this test, and the voter has no right to complain when it is rigidly enforced in his own case.

Lib. 32:150.

"But we submit to all the people, that such as wholly abstain from voting to uphold the Constitution because of its war provisions, and thus religiously exclude themselves from all share in what are deemed official honors and emoluments, ought not to be drafted in time of war, or compelled to pay an equivalent, or go to prison for disobedience. If conscience is to be respected and provided for in any case, it is in theirs.

"We know of no law, however, for their exemption; and, therefore, some of them may be drafted, and put to a trial of their faith. In that case, let them possess their souls in patience and serenity, and meet without any outcry, 'as though some strange thing had happened unto them,' whatever penalty may follow their non-compliance with the draft. There is no loss, but great gain, in suffering for righteousness' sake. They surely knew the liabilities to which they subjected themselves,

CHAP. II. 1862. when they gave in their adhesion to the principles of Non-Resistance; and they will not try to shirk the cross when it is presented, but rejoice that they are counted worthy to bear it. One thing they can and should do, in order to prevent any misconceptions as to their feelings and views in relation to the conduct of those who have risen up in rebellion; and that is, denounce it as horribly perfidious, and as having for its object the overthrow of every safeguard of popular liberty, and register their testimony that the Government has exercised no injustice towards the South, nor given any occasion for such a treasonable outbreak. Thus defining their position, it will be seen by the nation that they are acting in a manner as just and discriminating toward the Government as it is upright and conscientious on their part.

"It can hardly be asked by any Non-Resistant, 'How, if drafted, about hiring a substitute?' because what we do by another as our agent or representative, we do ourselves. To hire a substitute is, as a matter of principle, precisely the same as to go to the battle-field in person.

"'But if the alternative be, to pay a stipulated sum to the Government, or else be imprisoned or shot, may we pay the fine?' That is a matter for the individual conscience to decide. Speaking personally, we see no violation of Non-Resistance principles in paying the money; because it is a choice presented between different forms of suffering, and, 'other things being equal,' it will be natural to wish to avoid as much of it as the case will admit. Thus, a highwayman, placing his pistol to our head, demands in our helplessness, 'Your money, or your life!' To part with the money is certainly more reasonable than to part with life; nor, in yielding it, do we give any sanction to the demand. But if the highwayman should say, 'Your money, *and an acknowledgment of my right to extort it*, or your life,' then there would be no alternative but to die, or else prove recreant to truth and honesty.

"'But,' it may be said, 'though I should refuse to hire a substitute, yet, if I pay the price demanded, will not the Government take the money and apply it for that purpose? And is there any essential moral difference here?' We think there is. In hiring a substitute yourself, you actively sustain the war, and become an armed participant in it, and so violate the principles which you profess to revere. In paying a tax, you passively submit to the exaction, which, in itself, commits no violence upon others, but is only a transfer of so much property to other hands. If, then, the Government shall proceed to apply it to war purposes, the responsibility will rest with the Government, not with you. This is the light in which we regard it: still, we offer no other suggestion than this —'Let every one be fully persuaded in his own mind.' We shall honor none the less him who may feel it his duty to take the most afflicting alternative, as the most effectual method to meet the issue before the community. Of that he must be the judge; and especially must he be sure to count the cost and act intelligently."[1] CHAP. II. — 1862.

With regard to abolitionists who were not non-resistants, and who had hitherto abstained from voting on account of the pro-slavery character of the Constitution, the argument showed that as the Union was dissolved and the Government had the war-power to abolish slavery (even in the Border States, Mr. Garrison maintained), "every obstacle to CONSTITUTIONAL EMANCIPATION is taken out of the way, and the Government is, and must be, if true to itself, wholly on the side of liberty. *Such a government can receive the sanction and support of every abolitionist, whether in a moral or military point of view.*" *Lib.* 32:154.

It was a happy coincidence that the same number of the *Liberator* in which this article appeared should also contain President Lincoln's first Emancipation Proclamation, promising a final edict of freedom to the slaves in all States or parts of States which should be in rebellion against the Government on the first of January following,[2] *Sept.* 22.

[1] "A beautiful specimen of clear and unanswerable reasoning," was Gerrit Smith's comment on this editorial *(Lib.* 32 : 155).

[2] Just a month before this (Aug. 22) Mr. Lincoln had addressed his famous letter to Horace Greeley, stating that his paramount object was to save the Union, without reference to slavery. "*If I could save the Union without freeing any slave, I would do it — if I could save it by freeing all the slaves, I would do it — and if I could do it by freeing some and leaving others alone, I would also do that.* What I do about slavery and the colored race, I do because I believe it helps to save this Union; and what I forbear, I forbear because I do not believe it would help to save the Union." The encouragement of the letter lay not only in the growing popular conviction that the second alternative was the one he would be compelled to choose, but in his frank promise, "I shall try to correct errors when shown to be errors, and I shall adopt new views so fast as they appear to be true views"; and in his closing assurance that while he had thus stated his purpose according to his views of official duty, he intended no modification of his "oft-expressed

CHAP. II. 1862.

and that the editor could thus cite it as evidence of the anti-slavery purpose of the Administration. His first feeling, however, on carefully reading the document, was not one of exultation, and a friend who called to congratulate him, the morning it appeared, was surprised to find how quietly he took it, and wondered at his lack of enthusiasm; but having indulged the hope that the proclamation, if issued, would be unreserved and sweeping, he was disappointed and disturbed that the President should confine it to the rebellious States, giving them one hundred days of grace, and should couple with it his scheme for gradual and compensated emancipation in the Border States, and for colonization.[1] Still, he welcomed it as "an important step in the right direction,[2] and an act of immense historic consequence," and commended especially the clauses in which the President enjoined the army and navy to obey and enforce the anti-slavery acts already passed by Congress. He congratulated Mr. Lincoln, too, on the abuse now heaped upon him by the semi-disloyal Democratic press which had so lately praised him without stint. Only a fortnight before, he was fearing that its influence and that of the Border States had become all-powerful with the President.

Samuel May, Jr.

Lib. 32:154.

Lib. 32:158.

MS. Sept. 9, *to Oliver Johnson.*

W. L. Garrison to Oliver Johnson.

MS., in possession of Young Men's Library, Buffalo, N. Y.

BOSTON, Sept. 9, 1862.

I commend your anxiety in regard to the course to be pursued both by the *Standard* and the *Liberator*, respecting the present

personal wish that all men everywhere could be free" (Greeley's 'American Conflict,' 2 : 250). Not until two years later did it become publicly known that Mr. Lincoln had submitted the first draft of the Emancipation Proclamation to the Cabinet a month before he wrote this letter to Greeley (July 22), and was holding it in his desk until a decisive victory of the Union armies should afford him a favorable moment for issuing it. For a full account of Lincoln's steps towards emancipation, see J. G. Nicolay's and John Hay's chapter in the *Century Magazine* for December, 1888.

1 "The President can do nothing for *freedom* in a direct manner, but only by circumlocution and delay. How prompt was his action against Frémont and Hunter!" (MS. Sept. 25, 1862, W. L. G. to his daughter.)

2 "Step!" exclaimed Mr. Phillips, when this was repeated to him, "it 's a stride!"

critical state of affairs; and fully agree with you, that there has never been a time when abolitionists should weigh their words (whether written or spoken) more carefully than now, in order to avoid needless persecution and baffle pro-slavery malignity. Our work, as abolitionists, is still to impeach, censure, and condemn where we must, and approve when we can; but, in such an inflammable state of the country, the injunction: "Be ye wise as serpents, and harmless as doves," deserves to be carefully heeded. I have always believed that the anti-slavery cause has had aroused against it a great deal of uncalled-for hostility, in consequence of extravagance of speech, and want of tact and good judgment, on the part of some most desirous to promote its advancement; but this is a drawback which has ever affected the success of reformatory movements, and grows out of the incompleteness of human development.

CHAP. II.

1862.

It is very desirable, as you intimate, that the *Standard* and the *Liberator* should harmonize, as far as practicable, in the mode of dealing with such correspondents as wish to make use of their columns to express their honest but often badly expressed sentiments on men and things. In common, on the ground of free discussion, we are both often called to publish what, on the score of good taste and fair criticism, we cannot endorse; but I grant a larger indulgence than it would be proper for you to do, seeing that no one else is responsible for the *Liberator* but myself; whereas, the *Standard* is the official organ of the American Anti-Slavery Society, and on that account should be conducted with more habitual circumspection. Still, I would have the *Standard* err on the side of liberality, rather than of exclusiveness, so as to always indicate its fearlessness of the most thorough investigation and the strongest dissent; while, at the same time, I would have you exercise your own good judgment, just as you have hitherto done, in determining what shall appear in the *Standard*. I do not feel that I can give you any advice, or that you need any.

Lincoln's annual message to Congress in December made a last plea for the scheme of compensated emancipation broached in his July message, and proposed a constitutional amendment by which any State abolishing slavery by or before the year 1900 should be entitled to compensation from the Federal Government. A single point illustrates how far Mr. Lincoln yet was from put-

Chap. II. 1862. ting himself in the slave's place, and "remembering those in bonds *as bound with them*," for he frankly stated his
Lib. 32:194. wish to postpone the day of emancipation so far that the present oppressors would not live to see it, and so need not be concerned about it; whilst the slaves, consigned to life-long bondage, were to console themselves with the "inspiriting assurance" that their posterity would be free forever! But the proposed amendment made no provision whatever for the abolition of slavery in 1900 in such slave States as might not then have enacted it; and, as in the July message, the right to reëstablish it was admitted by the stipulation that in that case the Federal Government should be reimbursed.[1]

In view of this menace to the promised emancipation edict of January 1, the abolitionists had no option but to go on, and Mr. Garrison, in writing the call for the annual Subscription Festival on which the maintenance of the American Society depended, rehearsed the reasons for continued effort. The disagreeable alternative was also forced upon him, in common with all other newspaper publishers, of raising the subscription price of the *Liberator*, or suspending its publication, the price of paper having doubled in consequence of the scarcity of cotton; and, choosing the former, he advanced the price from $2.50 to $3.00 with the new year. In a frank statement of the exigencies of the *Liberator*, and a retrospective glance at its history and career, he announced that the recent marvellous change in public sentiment had wrought no advantage to its sub-
Lib. 32:202. scription-list. "Other journals," he continued, "have carefully consulted this change, and given the milk needed for new-born babes, so that more is published every day on the subject of slavery, pro and con, by the newspaper press than used to be in the course of years. That others have entered into our labors, and reaped the advantage thereof, we do not regret; it has followed in the nature

[1] These discreditable qualifications and suggestions are not mentioned by Messrs. Nicolay and Hay in their account of this message (*Century Magazine* for March, 1889).

of things, and is what we gladly looked for from the beginning. But it explains why our circulation remains unaided by the cheering revolution which has taken place."[1] A quick and generous response from long-tried friends and subscribers insured the *Liberator* another year's continuance.

Lib. 33:2, 10.

The last number of the year contained a letter from George Thompson, who, after laboring indefatigably to inform the English public on the issues involved in the American conflict, and delivering many addresses in various parts of Great Britain,[2] was now able to announce the formation of a large and influential Emancipation Society in London, for the vigorous and systematic prosecution of the same work. The nucleus of this organization was the London Emancipation Committee, a little band of Mr. Garrison's friends who had for several years

1 "How does the war affect your subscription-list? The *Liberator's* is minus at least two hundred" (MS. Sept. 9, 1862, W. L. G. to Oliver Johnson). "If slavery were really abolished, I should care very little about the continuance of the *Liberator* or *Standard*, or the American Anti-Slavery Society; but, until emancipation come, I do hope these instrumentalities will remain in the field, as hitherto. At all events, we will (if need be) 'go down with our colors nailed to the mast-head'" (MS. Dec. 14, 1862, W. L. G. to O. Johnson).

2 "Towards the close of last year, and at the beginning of the present, I delivered a large number of lectures in Lancashire and Yorkshire, including eight in the city of Manchester (six of which were in Free Trade Hall). I also gave lectures in Edinburgh, Glasgow, and elsewhere in Scotland. I formally proposed to the Union Americans in London to give the whole of my time, *gratuitously*, to the work of agitation in this country, if they would raise a fund for the payment of the necessary expenses; but there was no response. But, alas! the only agency they employed was the London *American*, which has done far more harm than good to their cause, by being the vehicle for the envenomed outpourings of G. F. Train, and the slanderous attacks upon the abolitionists of their New York correspondent. Again — the Committee of the British and Foreign Anti-Slavery Society has done nothing, and is only now thinking of saying a good word in behalf of the Proclamation. Thus, I have stood alone. The *Star* and *Daily News* have done good service among the daily London papers; and the *Spectator* and *Dial* (the latter entirely conducted by my son-in-law, Mr. Chesson), among the weekly journals, have promulgated sound views; but what are these among the multitude of papers that have gone wrong?" (MS. Nov. 7, 1862, George Thompson to W. L. G., *Lib.* 32 : 190. See, for letters and speeches of Mr. Thompson, *Lib.* 32 : 6, 27, 64, 65, 191, 204, 206; 33 : 3, 5, 7, 11, 13, 33, 34, 42, 46, 54, 63, 66, 160, 174, 207; 34 : 3, 7, 14, 29.)

CHAP. II. 1862. labored to excite public interest in the American anti-slavery movement, and to maintain the active alliance and coöperation established and fostered by him in his three visits to England. Thompson himself was the chairman, and his son-in-law, Frederick W. Chesson, the secretary, of this Committee. The enlarged Society included such men as John Stuart Mill, John Bright, Richard Cobden, Lord Houghton, Samuel Lucas, William E. Forster, Peter A. Taylor, Goldwin Smith, Justin McCarthy, Thomas Hughes, James Stansfeld, Jr., Prof. J. E. Cairnes, Herbert Spencer, Prof. Francis W. Newman, Rev. Baptist Noel, and Rev. Newman Hall, most of whom rendered direct and important service; but the organizer and tireless spirit of the movement was Mr. Chesson, to whose wide acquaintance with public men, unfailing tact and address, thorough information, and extraordinary industry and executive ability, a very large measure of credit for its success was due.

The most cordial and sympathetic relations existed between the Society and Minister Adams and Secretary Moran of the American Legation. Its first task was to evoke such expressions of popular sympathy with the American Government in all parts of the kingdom as would effectually deter the English Government from listening to Napoleon's schemes of intervention in favor of the South, and permitting the escape from English ports of other piratical cruisers like the *Alabama*, and to counteract the plottings of Mason and other rebel emissaries in London. *J. M. Mason.* To the organizations which were the legitimate and direct outgrowth of Mr. Garrison's anti-slavery missions to England[1] were largely due the suc-

[1] The Union and Emancipation Society, formed in Manchester in 1863, with Thomas Bayley Potter, M. P., as its President, and Thomas H. Barker as its indefatigable Secretary, had also many of Mr. Garrison's friends and co-workers among its members, and did an immense work in encouraging and supporting the strong Union sympathies of the suffering Lancashire operatives. Mr. Potter's labors were as disinterested as they were ardent, and his munificent pecuniary support—his personal contributions aggregating £5000—enabled the Society, during the two years of its existence, to hold three hundred meetings and distribute nearly 600,000

cessful accomplishment of that work, and the enormous advantage which thereby accrued to the American cause.[1] But without the Proclamation of Emancipation to conjure with, the task would have been infinitely greater, if not impossible. On the eve of its issue, George Thompson wrote to Mr. Garrison as follows:

George Thompson to W. L. Garrison.

Evening of Christmas Day, 1862.

MS., and Lib. 33 : 11.

In the endeavor to arrive at a sound and unprejudiced judgment on the true state of public feeling in this country, certain facts should be kept in mind.

The sentiments of our leading journals, of a portion of our public men, and of the aristocratic circles, at the present time, on the subject of slavery, are precisely similar to those which prevailed in the same quarters during the struggle for the emancipation of our own slaves. In this respect, England is neither better nor worse. *Blackwood's Magazine* and the *Times* of to-day are the same as they were in 1832 — the one the essence of Toryism, the other of Mammon. . . . On the vital question of slavery, *the heart of the people is sound.* It would be impossible to carry a pro-slavery resolution in any unpacked assembly in the kingdom. I could obtain a vote of censure from the constituents of every man who has vindicated the

pamphlets (*Lib.* 35 : 46). He clearly recognized, and continually impressed upon the workingmen of Lancashire, the fact that the struggle raging in America was their own battle, and that on the maintenance of the great republic the progress of popular institutions all over the world largely depended (*Lib.* 33 : 174). In Glasgow, the vigilance and energetic measures of Mr. Garrison's steadfast friends, Andrew Paton, William Smeal, and a few others, prevented the sailing from the Clyde of a Confederate war vessel that would have been more formidable than the *Alabama.*

1 "All the anti-slavery people, with here and there an exception, support the North; while the representatives of the old West India interests and the Conservative party generally remain true to their dishonorable traditions. . . . It has been the fashion of the *Times* to taunt the Emancipation Society with being deserted by all the old, well-remembered names. This is true of Lord Brougham, but not of Dr. Lushington. Several of the Buxtons, the Gurneys, the Croppers, and the Hughes have avowed their sympathy with the Northern cause; and . . . Mr. Henry Wilberforce, the younger son of the great philanthropist, is most earnest in his advocacy of sound views on the American question, and feels deeply the dishonor which some of his countrymen have put upon themselves by their pro-Southern sentiments" (F. W. Chesson to W. L. G., Feb. 18, 1865, *Lib.* 35 : 46).

CHAP. II. — 1862.

cause of the slaveholding rebels. The *Times* could not obtain an endorsement of its sentiments in any open meeting in the city of London or elsewhere, where an opportunity was afforded of speaking the truth. The mention of its name invariably calls forth "a groan." It should always be remembered, too, that our people are very imperfectly acquainted with the powers of your Federal Government. They know little or nothing of your Constitution — its compromises, guarantees, limitations, obligations, etc. They are consequently unable to appreciate the difficulties of your President, or to comprehend the caution, forbearance, and tenderness which he displays when speaking of slavery, slaveholders, slave States, etc. Then, again, our anti-American journals have been careful to conceal the truth. They have exposed every blunder; blazoned every pro-slavery act of general or officer in the army; have republished the harsh criticisms of Abolition speakers, and, above all, the repeated declarations of members of the Republican party, that the war was *not* for the abolition of slavery. . . .

None know better than you and I how much the Northern people themselves have done to furnish occasion to the adversary, and to justify the taunts and reproaches he has hurled against them. *You* can understand the difficulty of my position during the first year of the war, when so many ugly facts came out illustrating the pro-slavery tendencies of your public men. You know how many plagues it has needed to bring the North to hear the command,— which is not even yet obeyed,—"Let my people go!" You know how impossible it is at this moment to vindicate, as one would wish, the course of Mr. Lincoln. In no one of his utterances is there an assertion of a great principle — no appeal to right or justice. In everything he does and says, affecting the slave, there is the alloy of expediency. The slave may be free — if it should be "*necessary*," or "*convenient*," or "*agreeable to his master*." What we want to see him do is, to take his stand upon the doctrine of human equality, and man's inalienable right to life, liberty, and the pursuit of happiness. All else is paltering with conscience and with truth. . . . I firmly believe that Mr. Lincoln might, if he would, extirpate, root and branch, the accursed system; and that both God and man would support him in the deed. Oh, that he would do it — and thereby secure the peace of his soul, the blessing of the slave, the applause of mankind, the verdict of posterity, and the approbation of Heaven!

CHAPTER III.

THE PROCLAMATION.—1863.

SPECIAL preparations had been made in Boston to celebrate the promised edict of freedom on the first of January. The impressive watch-meetings held in the colored churches on New Year's eve were followed by meetings in Tremont Temple extending through the day and evening, and a grand jubilee concert in Music Hall was announced for the afternoon. It was confidently expected that the President's Proclamation would reach the city by noon, but as the day wore on without tidings of its issue, fears arose lest it might not, after all, be forthcoming, and the celebrations proceeded under a shadow of doubt and unrest. The Music Hall concert had been hastily but admirably arranged, and audience and musicians seemed alike animated by the occasion. Nothing could have been more uplifting than the fine orchestral and choral rendering of Mendelssohn's Hymn of Praise, Beethoven's Fifth Symphony, and Händel's Hallelujah Chorus, alternated with the reading, by Ralph Waldo Emerson, of his "Boston Hymn," written for the occasion, and the singing of Dr. O. W. Holmes's "Army Hymn"; [1] but the painful uncertainty about the President's action marred the otherwise perfect enjoyment of the great audience until a gentleman announced from the floor that the Proclama-

CHAP. III.

1863.

[1] The verse in Mr. Emerson's poem which won loudest applause was that on compensation:

"Pay ransom to the owner,
And fill the bag to the brim.
Who is the owner? The slave is owner,
And ever was. *Pay him!*"

CHAP. III. 1863. tion had been issued and was coming over the wires. The storm of applause which followed, and relieved the pent-up feelings of the listeners, culminated in nine rousing cheers for Abraham Lincoln, followed by three more for Mr. Garrison, who occupied a seat in the gallery, and the concert then proceeded to its triumphant finish.

Surpassing even this scene was that at the evening meeting at Tremont Temple, to which a copy of the Proclamation was unexpectedly brought, just prior to adjournment, and read with thrilling effect by Charles W. Slack. As he concluded amid a wild outburst of cheering, Frederick Douglass stepped forward and led the multitude in singing, "Blow ye the trumpet, blow!" with the chorus, never more fitting than then, "The year of jubilee has come!" Mr. Garrison unhappily missed this, as he had gone to Medford with Mr. Phillips, Mr. Emerson, and other friends to witness the unveiling of a marble bust of John Brown, at the residence of George L. Stearns; but in the *Liberator* of the following day (which was held back from the press that it might contain the Proclamation), he uttered his "Glory, Hallelujah!" and hailed the "great historic event, sublime in its magnitude, momentous and beneficent in its far-reaching consequences, and eminently just and right alike to the oppressor and the oppressed."[1] From that hour a dishonorable compromise became impossible. The Government was irrevocably committed to the emancipation policy,

Lib. 33 : 3.

[1] "Freedom's first champion in our fettered land!
Nor politician nor base citizen
Could gibbet thee, nor silence, nor withstand.
Thy trenchant and emancipating pen
The patriot Lincoln snatched with steady hand,
Writing his name and thine on parchment white,
Midst war's resistless and ensanguined flood;
Then held that proclamation high in sight
Before his fratricidal countrymen,—
'Freedom henceforth throughout the land for all,'—
And sealed the instrument with his own blood,
Bowing his mighty strength for slavery's fall;
Whilst thou, staunch friend of largest liberty,
Survived,—its ruin and our peace to see."—*A. B. Alcott to W. L. G.*

and pledged to make it effectual over all the territory covered by the Proclamation. The abolitionists had now to urge Congress and the President to complete the work and extirpate slavery by abolishing it in the Border States. This duty was set forth in the resolutions relative to the Proclamation which were adopted by the Executive Committee of the American Anti-Slavery Society, and in those passed by the Massachusetts Society at its January meeting, all of which were drafted by Garrison.[1] His speech at the same meeting was full of joy and hope. "Thirty years ago," he said, "it was midnight with the anti-slavery cause; now it is the bright noon of day, with the sun shining in his meridian splendor. Thirty years ago we were in the arctic regions, surrounded by icebergs; to-day we are in the tropics, with the flowers blooming and the birds singing around us. I say this simply as a matter of contrast and comparison."[2]

Jan. 13. Lib. 33:10.
Jan. 29. Lib. 33:22.
Lib. 33:22.
Cf. ante, 1:188.

From England came cheering reports of the revolution in public sentiment caused there by the Proclamation.

F. W. Chesson to W. L. Garrison.

LONDON, January 9, 1863.

MS. and Lib. 33:19.

I send you a copy of the *Saturday Review*, which contains an article on the Emancipation Society's address to the clergy. Do not, however, mistake this, or any similar, ebullition for an expression of the real opinion of the English people on the

1 Congress was also urged, in one of the resolutions, to establish a Freedmen's Bureau, "for the special purpose of guarding the rights and interests of the liberated bondmen, providing them with land and labor, and giving them a fair chance to develop their faculties and powers through the necessary educational instrumentalities" *(Lib.* 33:22). See, also, Report of the Freedmen's Inquiry Commission (Robert Dale Owen, James McKay, and Dr. Samuel G. Howe), appointed by Secretary Stanton, on "Negroes as Refugees, as Military Laborers, and as Soldiers" *(Lib.* 33:130).

2 Mr. Phillips, who followed Mr. Garrison, was less jubilant in tone, though not less positive as to Mr. Lincoln's purpose to stand by the Proclamation, and of the ultimate destruction of slavery; but he had just returned from Washington, where he and other Bostonians had vainly urged the President to dismiss Seward from the Cabinet as an obstructive, and his view of the immediate future was somewhat despondent *(Lib.* 33: 19, 26).

CHAP. III. slavery question, or on the issues between the North and the South. The great meetings which have been held in London and various parts of the country, during the last six weeks, to express sympathy with the anti-slavery policy of the American Government, indicate what is the true state of public feeling on this side of the Atlantic. We have endured the misrepresentations of certain organs of our press too long, and we have now determined to endure them no longer. But always remember that, from the beginning, the best of our journals have remained true to the anti-slavery cause; that the *Star*, *Daily News*,[1] *Westminster Review*, *Spectator*, *Nonconformist*, *British Standard*, *Dial*, Birmingham *Post*,[2] Manchester *Examiner*, Newcastle *Chronicle*, *Caledonian Mercury*, Belfast *Whig*,[3] and a host of other representatives of the fourth estate, have never departed from the pure faith. The working classes also have proved to be sound to the core, whenever their opinion has been tested. Witness the noble demonstration of Manchester operatives the other day, when three thousand of these noble sons of labor (many of whom were actual sufferers from the cotton famine) adopted by acclamation an address to President Lincoln, sympathizing with his Proclamation. A friend of mine who was present on the occasion tells me that the heartiness and enthusiasm of the workingmen were something glorious; that he heard them say to one another that they would rather remain unemployed for twenty years than get cotton from the South at the expense of the slave. Mr. Thompson has been in other parts of Lancashire lately, and the meetings he has addressed have been attended with the same results. Our experience in London has been equally satisfactory. It would have done you good if you had heard Baptist Noel's speech, or attended the great meeting of the working classes which we held on the 31st of December — the eve of freedom. Newman Hall's speech on this occasion was one of the best I ever listened to. He stated, in the fairest

1863.

George Thompson.

1 The chief proprietor of the *Morning Star* was Samuel Lucas, a brother-in-law of John Bright; its editors, Justin McCarthy and F. W. Chesson. The *Daily News* was edited by Thomas Walker, with the powerful aid of Harriet Martineau, who wrote scores of editorials on the American question.

2 The Birmingham *Post* published an instructive series of letters on the American question from the pen of Mr. Samuel A. Goddard, an American gentleman long resident in that city, and a brother of Mrs. Mary May. They were subsequently collected in a volume (London, 1870).

3 The Belfast *Whig* was the most influential journal in the north of Ireland. Its editor, Mr. Frank Harrison Hill, afterwards succeeded Thomas Walker as editor of the *Daily News*.

manner, every conceivable argument which had been urged in favor of the Slave Confederacy, or against the policy of the Federal Government, and then replied to them *seriatim*, demolishing every sophistry and gibbeting every falsehood, until the slavocracy had really not a rag left wherewith to conceal the revolting defects of their odious cause.

The Emancipation Society includes, as you will have seen, some of the best men in the country, without distinction of sect or party. The name of John Stuart Mill — one of the greatest in England — stands at the head of the list. We are now arranging for a demonstration in Exeter Hall, to take place on the 29th inst. Our friends in Manchester and Birmingham are organizing branch societies in those important towns; and applications for meetings and deputations are pouring in from all quarters.

Richard D. Webb.

Our friend Mr. Webb, who is doing such good service in the *Advocate*, and in other ways more private but not less useful, tells me that Professor Cairnes's admirable work [1] is about to pass into another edition. As a proof of how extensively it is read, I may say that I have made two unsuccessful attempts to obtain it from Mudie's circulating library (the greatest in the world), where there is a large number of copies. The answer on both occasions was, that every copy was in the hands of subscribers.

Jan. 7, 1863.

Mrs. Stowe's eloquent and beautiful address to the women of England is exciting great interest, and cannot fail to do much good. It was published by Sampson Low & Co. on Wednesday, in the form of a small volume; and it has since been reprinted *entire* in the columns of the *Morning Star* and the *Daily News* — a remarkable tribute to the popularity of Mrs. Stowe in this country, as well as a proof of the earnest interest which these journals take in the good work. It could not have appeared at a more favorable moment, for on Tuesday last the *Times*, with a maniacal folly, which is often linked with malignity, published an article pleading Biblical sanction for

Jan. 6, 1863.

1 'The Slave Power: Its Character, Career, and Probable Designs: Being an Attempt to Explain the Real Issues Involved in the American Contest. By J. E. Cairnes, M. A., Professor of Jurisprudence and Political Economy in Queen's College, Galway, and late Whately Professor of Political Economy in the University of Dublin.' This work was printed at Dublin by Richard D. Webb, whose full and accurate knowledge of American slavery and anti-slavery enabled him greatly to aid Prof. Cairnes in the preparation of his work.

CHAP. III. 1863. slavery, and actually suggesting that it was perhaps a religious duty on the part of the slave to refuse his freedom, even if it were offered to him! Nothing could be more calculated to stir up the religious sentiment of the country against the cause of which the *Times* has made itself the principal champion. This is another example of the manner in which the devil sometimes overreaches himself.

George Thompson to W. L. Garrison.

MS. and Lib. 33:34.

LONDON, Feb. 5, 1863.

Since I last addressed you, I have attended meetings in the following places, viz.: Sheffield, Heywood, Dumfries, Kilmarnock, Greenock, Dumbarton, Paisley, Glasgow, Stirling, Perth, Aberdeen, Dundee, Edinburgh, Galashiels, Gloucester, Cheltenham, Bristol, Bath, Stroud, Kingswood, and London. The mention of some of these towns will bring old scenes to your remembrance, when we were companions and fellow-laborers — as, thank God, we still are. . . .

Ante, 2:396, 397, 399; 3:172, 176.

Since I left Scotland, on the 22d ultimo, my meetings have been all on the American question — and such meetings! They have reminded me of those I was wont to hold in 1831, '32, and '33 — densely crowded, sublimely enthusiastic, and all but unanimous. The opposition has been of the most insignificant and contemptible kind. Before this reaches you, you will have seen the report of the meetings above and below, and in the open air around, Exeter Hall. I was the same evening engaged in holding a meeting at Stroud, which did not conclude till midnight. Three nights ago, I held a meeting near my own residence. Thousands were excluded for want of room. These outsiders were addressed by competent persons, and the cheers raised by the multitude found their way into the meeting I was addressing, and increased the excitement of my audience. I shall rest till the 10th, and then recommence my labors, which are in great demand.

Lib. 33:33, 34.

This Anti-Slavery movement is assuming gigantic proportions, and, if wisely and energetically conducted, as I trust it will be, will have a powerful, and at the same time beneficial, influence upon the counsels of your public men. It will be of vital importance in this country. It will read a salutary lesson to our public men. It will mould the decisions of our Government. It will neutralize the poison diffused by our journals. It will enlighten and stir up our ministers of religion. It will create the anti-slavery sentiment of the new generation. It will impregnate with the true fire the masses of our people. In a word, it will put England in her old and proper position. CHAP. III. 1863.

The arrival of the President's Proclamation, of the 1st of January, gave me a degree of satisfaction and joy which words cannot express. It confirmed the hopes and fulfilled the predictions in which I had indulged. In spite of all prognostications and appearances to the contrary, I had cherished a confident belief that Mr. Lincoln would execute the decree of Sept. 22. Nevertheless, the suspense was painful. My anxiety is now at an end as respects the *fiat* of emancipation, and I am waiting to see its fruits, which I trust will be abundant and peaceful.

On New Year's day, I addressed a crowded assembly of unemployed operatives in the town of Heywood, near Manchester, and spoke to them for two hours about the Slaveholders' Rebellion. They were united and vociferous in the expression of their willingness to suffer all the hardships consequent upon a want of cotton, if thereby the liberty of the victims of Southern despotism might be promoted. All honor to the half million of our working population in Lancashire, Cheshire, and elsewhere, who are bearing with heroic fortitude the grievous privations which your war has entailed upon them! The four millions of slaves in America have no sincerer friends than these lean, pale-faced, idle people, who are reconciled to their meagre fare and desolate homes by the thought that their trials are working out the deliverance of the oppressed children of your country. Their sublime resignation, their self-forgetfulness, their observance of law, their whole-souled love of the cause of human freedom, their quick and clear perception of the merits of the question between the North and the South, their superiority to the sophisms of those who would delude them, and their appreciation of the labor question involved in the "irrepressible conflict," are extorting the admiration of all classes of the community, and are reading the nation a valuable lesson.

Friday, 6th. *Feb.* 6, 1863.

I have found constant occupation for William Andrew Jackson [Jefferson Davis's late coachman]. He has been very usefully employed in Manchester, Sheffield, and other places. Last week, he accompanied me in my tour in the west of England, and this week he is engaged in South Wales. Next week he will be in Derbyshire, and will then proceed to Lancashire. I am happy to say, the impression everywhere produced by his

CHAP. III. 1863. addresses has been a favorable one. I shall be able to obtain for him as much work as he can do for some time to come.

The London Emancipation Society is growing in numbers and in power. On the 18th, I shall speak as its representative in St. James's Hall, Piccadilly, one of our finest West-End buildings. To-night I am going to hear Mr. Spurgeon lecture on the subject of slavery amongst Jews, Pagans, and Christians.

George Thompson to W. L. Garrison.

MS. and Lib. 33 : 46. LONDON, February 27 [26], 1863.

I can only send you a very imperfect acknowledgment of your letter of the 10th instant, which reached me at the house of a friend, near Manchester, on the 24th. A portion of that letter was read at the great meeting held in the Free Trade Hall, on the evening of the same day, to present an address of welcome to the captain of the *Griswold*.[1] I was at the same hour attending another immense gathering in the town of Huddersfield. I read parts of the same letter at a meeting last evening in London, at which an Address was presented to me by some kind and partial friends. The papers I send with this will give you some account of these proceedings.

Feb. 25. *Lib.* 33 : 46, 160.

It would be impossible to give you a list of all the meetings which have recently been held, for the purpose of expressing sympathy with the anti-slavery movement in the United States, and commendation of the abolition policy of the Government and Congress. My own strength has been taxed to the utmost, and has been seriously impaired by the effort I have made to meet the demands made upon me for my presence in all parts of the country. Calls to the same effect continue to pour in upon me; but, though the spirit is willing, the flesh is weak, and were I never so strong, I should be unable to accept half the invitations which are sent me.

The men who a few months ago were so bold and blatant in the advocacy of the cause of the Southern rebels, are now silent. Though some of them are in Parliament, they have thus far been mute, and we hear nothing of motions in favor of recognition, or proposals for mediation. We have now an organization which will enable us to furnish an antidote to

[1] The *George Griswold*, a vessel sent from New York to Liverpool laden with food for the suffering Lancashire operatives — the contribution of New York merchants.

any pro-slavery poison that may be diffused through the press or the legislature; and there are men in the House of Commons who are now so thoroughly conversant with the merits of the question, that any misrepresentation of facts would be met at once with an ample and overwhelming refutation. . . .

CHAP. III. 1863.

I read with deep interest your speech at the Annual Meeting of the Massachusetts Anti-Slavery Society, and have made good use of it. It came to hand very seasonably, and might have been made for the purpose of disabusing the minds of the people here.

MS. Feb. 16.

Mr. Garrison was strongly urged by Gerrit Smith and other friends to visit England during the spring and add his efforts to those of George Thompson and the London and Manchester Societies, but he was unable to do so, and tried in turn to persuade Mr. Smith and Mr. Phillips to go together. The latter was at first disposed to consider it, but finally gave up the project, in spite of many entreaties. Subsequently, Henry Ward Beecher converted an ordinary tour in Great Britain into one in behalf of the Union cause, and held that brilliant series of meetings in which he did such effective service, and found how much the labors of the Garrisonian abolitionists had done towards familiarizing the minds of the English people with the anti-slavery question in America, and enlisting and strengthening that sympathy with the North which was so essential to the success of the Government.[1]

But to return to this side of the water, and to the American Anti-Slavery Society:

[1] "During my visit to England, it was my privilege to address, in various places, very large audiences, and I never made mention of the names of any of those whom you most revere and love, without calling down the wildest demonstrations of popular enthusiasm. I never mentioned the name of Mr. Phillips, or Mr. Garrison, that it did not call forth a storm of approbation. It pleased me to know that those who were least favored in our own country were so well known in England. . . . It is true that a man is not without honor save in his own country; and I felt that I had never had before me, in an audience here, such an appreciation of the names of our early and faithful laborers in this cause as there was in that remote country, among comparative strangers" (Speech of H. W. Beecher at Third Decade Meeting, Philadelphia, Dec. 4, 1863; *Lib.* 34 : 5).

W. L. Garrison to his Wife.

MS. NEW YORK, May 14, 1863.

May 11. Our anti-slavery company was never so small before, with reference to Anniversary week. It consisted of Edmund Quincy, John T. Sargent, and myself — Phillips having preceded us in the night train, in order to be fresh for his Cooper Institute speech Monday evening. At Worcester, Mr. May and his mother joined us, and these were all the recognized abolitionists in that long and crowded train. What then?

S. May, Jr.
Mary May.

> 'It must be now that the kingdom 's coming,
> And the year of jubilo" —

and our distinctive movement is nearly swallowed up in the great revolution in Northern sentiment which has been going on against slavery and slavedom since the bombardment of Sumter. Usually, the number of clergymen has been large and conspicuous, going on to attend their several anniversary meetings; but, this time, I did not see a single one in all the crowd! . . .

May 11. Phillips's meeting at the Institute, Monday evening, was a splendid one, and he acquitted himself in a way to gather fresh laurels for his brow. His speech was reported in full in the *Tribune* of Tuesday morning. At the conclusion of it, I was loudly called for, but held back. Then calls were made for Horace Greeley, who came forward and made a few remarks in his queer-toned voice and a very awkward manner. The cries were renewed for me, and I said a few words, the applause being general and very marked. When I first entered the hall, and was conducted to a seat on the platform by the side of Mayor Opdyke, the audience broke out in repeated bursts of applause. What a change in popular sentiment and feeling from the old mobocratic, pro-slavery times! And, remember, this was a meeting called by the Sixteenth Republican Ward Association! . . .

"The State of the Country."

George Opdyke.

May 12. Our opening session at Dr. Cheever's Church was attended by a thronged house, and in all respects a great success. As the *Tribune* of yesterday contained a very full report of the proceedings, you can judge of the spirit of the occasion by a perusal of it. Our evening meeting at the Cooper Institute was also an excellent one — Theodore Tilton making the opening speech (a very good one), and Phillips following in one of his finest efforts — Henry B. Stanton concluding the meeting in an impromptu, racy, and eloquent speech, after the olden time. CHAP. III. — 1863.

Our business meetings were interesting, though small. There was a general expression of sentiment, that the Society must not be dissolved until slavery is extinct.

As usual, Mr. Garrison presented a full budget of resolutions at the New York meeting, again urging the war-powers of the President over slavery in the border States, rejoicing in the vast progress already attained, and hoping that the Society might, at its approaching thirtieth anniversary in Philadelphia, be able to "celebrate the utter extinction of the rebellion, the liberation of every bondman, the prevalence of universal peace." *Lib.* 33:78.

Two weeks later, the opening session of the New England Convention was adjourned to witness the triumphant march through Boston of the Fifty-fourth Massachusetts Regiment, the first regiment of colored troops sent from any Northern State. During the spring months, while it was being recruited and drilled at Readville, near Boston, Mr. Garrison and Mr. Phillips had repeatedly visited the camp, and witnessed the transformation which a United States uniform and military discipline wrought, within a few short weeks, in the humble, timid, poorly-clad colored men arriving from all parts of the North in response to the call of Governor Andrew, who enlisted the aid, as recruiting officers, of Frederick Douglass, William Wells Brown, and Charles Lenox Remond. *May* 28.

Robert G. Shaw, the youthful colonel of the regiment, was the son of Mr. Garrison's warm friends, Mr. and Mrs. Francis G. Shaw, of Staten Island, and among the subordinate officers were several young men of anti-slavery birth and training, who frequently visited his house and were intimate with his children.[1] His heart

[1] The "original abolitionists" did not lack representatives in the army and navy forces for the suppression of slavery and the rebellion. Among those whose sons, grandsons, or sons-in-law were thus enrolled could be named Arthur and Lewis Tappan, Mr. Garrison, James G. Birney, William Jay, Gerrit Smith, Joshua Leavitt, Abraham L. Cox, John Rankin of Ohio,

CHAP. III. — 1863.

was deeply stirred as he contemplated the perils to which these high-souled youths were soon to expose themselves in encountering an enemy who had threatened enslavement to the black soldiers, and death to their white officers, if captured in battle,[1] and whose bitterness would be intensified by the sight of their Massachusetts flag. He had not, however, anticipated the test that was soon to be brought home to himself. When it became evident that enough recruits would be obtained to form a second colored regiment, to be known as the Fifty-fifth Massachusetts, a commission as second lieutenant in it was offered to his eldest son, and the latter, who had not imbibed his father's non-resistance views, and had longed to enter the army after the adoption of the emancipation policy, eagerly embraced this opportunity of serving the cause of liberty in the way of all others that he would have chosen. The father did not shrink from the test.

W. L. Garrison to George T. Garrison.

MS. BOSTON, June 11, 1863.

Though I could have wished that you had been able understandingly and truly to adopt those principles of peace which are so sacred and divine to my own soul, yet you will bear me witness that I have not laid a straw in your way to prevent your acting up to your own highest convictions of duty; for nothing would be gained, but much lost, to have you violate these. Still, I tenderly hope that you will once more seriously review the whole matter before making the irrevocable decision. . . .

In making up a final judgment, I wish you to look all the peculiar trials and perils in the face that you, in common with all others connected with the colored regiment, will have to encounter. Personally, as my son, you will incur some risks at

Samuel Fessenden, Francis G. Shaw, Samuel May, Jr., Henry I. Bowditch, James Forten, Robert Purvis, Frederick Douglass, S. S. Jocelyn, Charles Follen, William H. Burleigh, Amasa Walker, and others. Henry Wilson, Joshua R. Giddings, William Slade, and Henry Ward Beecher contributed in like manner to the struggle (*Lib.* 35 : 139).

[1] See Jeff. Davis's message and the bill passed by the Confederate Congress on the subject (Greeley's 'American Conflict,' 2 : 523, 524).

the hands of the rebels that others will not, if it is known that you are my son. My impression is, that upon the colored regiments the Government means to rely to do the most desperate fighting and occupy the post of imminent danger. Your chance of being broken down by sickness, wounded, maimed, or killed, in the course of such a prolonged campaign, is indeed very great. True, this is not a consideration to weigh heavily against the love of liberty and the promptings of duty; but it makes me tremble in regard to the effect that may be produced upon the health and happiness of your mother, should any serious, especially a fatal, accident befall you. Her affection for you is intense, her anxiety beyond expression. . . .

CHAP. III. — 1863.

It was a proud day for the great War Governor of Massachusetts when, in the presence of Garrison and Phillips, he delivered the State and national colors for the regiment into the hands of Colonel Shaw, at the Readville camp, and nobly declared that his personal honor was identified with theirs, and that he should "stand or fall, as a man and a magistrate, with the rise or fall in history of the Fifty-fourth Massachusetts Regiment." Prouder yet was it when he reviewed, on Boston Common, the dusky troops whom he had mustered and equipped in the face of bitter prejudice and contempt, on the one hand, and timid doubtings on the other, and saw them march through Boston streets, receiving enthusiastic greetings along the entire route, and displaying as soldierly discipline and bearing as any regiment that Massachusetts had sent to the war. As they marched down State Street, singing the John Brown song, Mr. Garrison stood, by chance, on the corner of Wilson's Lane, the spot over which he had been dragged by the mob of 1835, and there, with emotion too deep for words, he watched the solid ranks go by, the fair-haired officer at their head who was never to return.

John A. Andrew.

May 18.

Lib. 33:83.

Editorially, two weeks subsequently, Mr. Garrison commented on the gratifying manner in which the emancipated slaves were vindicating the hopes of their friends and refuting the calumnious predictions so often made concerning them:

Lib. 33 : 94. "Of the multitudinous disparaging allegations that have been brought against the slave population by the enemies of impartial freedom, not one has been verified by the events of the war. Instead of not desiring their freedom, they have invariably shown the greatest eagerness to obtain it wherever our army has gone; and great has been their lamentation when, for any cause, they could not be admitted within the lines. Instead of using their freedom injuriously to themselves or others, they have behaved with marked propriety, and evinced no disposition to commit any outrage, however slight. Instead of wishing to indulge in idleness or vagrancy, they have exhibited the utmost readiness to work even for a very inadequate remuneration, and they are fast learning the lessons of thrift.[1] Instead of being a burden upon society or the Government, they more than pay their way when there is anything like a fair chance. Instead of indicating no wish to be taught, they manifest the strongest desire for rudimental instruction, and a remarkable aptitude to learn. Instead of being wild or intractable, none are so docile and obedient. Instead of showing a cowardly spirit when the heroic element is appealed to, they display as soldiers a courage for attack, and a disregard of danger and death, unsurpassed in the annals of warfare."

The steady progress of emancipation, and rapid enlistment of colored soldiers, increased the bitterness and virulence of the "Copperhead" (*i. e.*, pro-Southern) press and party. In March, there were barbarous anti-negro riots at Detroit, resulting in loss of life and the burning of forty or fifty houses. In July, the exultations over Gettysburg and Vicksburg were not yet spent when the country was shocked by the anti-draft riots in New York, during which negroes and soldiers alike were shot down, hung to lamp-posts, beaten, and thrown into the river, and hunted like wild beasts, and the Colored Orphan Asylum was burned to the ground. The Irish mob likewise sacked the Colored Sailors' Home, and the residence of those staunch abolitionists, Mr. and Mrs. James S. Gibbons. There was an

Mar. 6. *Lib.* 33 : 43.

July 13–16, 1863.

[1] For an interesting statement, by Edward S. Philbrick, of the rapid development of tastes and wants for household comforts and more abundant and varied articles of food, among the freed people of the Sea Islands of South Carolina, see *Lib.* 33 : 130.

attempt at a similar outbreak in Boston, and Mr. Garrison and his family deemed it prudent to leave their house in Dix Place for a day or two.[1] Happily the riot was crushed in its incipiency by the prompt action of the authorities; but when the Fifty-fifth Regiment departed for the South, the following week, a dress parade on the Common was abandoned, and the troops marched across the city with loaded muskets, ready for a possible attack in the Irish quarter of the "North End," where they embarked on a steamer for North Carolina.

CHAP. III. — 1863.

W. L. Garrison to George T. Garrison.

BOSTON, August 6, 1863. *MS.*

We have all been made very glad, to-day, by the receipt of your pencilled note, dated Hatteras Inlet, July 31st, announcing your safe arrival at Newbern, though a little surprised at your sudden removal with Wild's Brigade, probably to Morris Island. . . .

N. C. *Gen. E. A. Wild.*

You may readily suppose that I was very much disappointed in not being able to see you, and give you my parting blessing and a farewell grasp of the hand, when your regiment marched through Boston. Multitudes, with myself, were greatly disappointed that the regiment did not parade on the Common, where we all expected to take our farewell leave. I followed you, however, all the way down to the vessel, hoping to speak to you; but I found myself on the wrong side, and the throng was so great and the marching so continuous that I could not press my way through. After you were all on board, I went with a number of friends to the next wharf below, where we waited more than an hour, hoping to see you off and give you the parting salute. But the rain poured heavily down, and we were all compelled to beat a retreat — keenly regretting that we could not, even from a distance, shout farewell.

Not a day has passed that we have not had you in our live-

[1] "To-day, there are symptoms that a riot is brewing in this city, and, should it break out with violence, it would naturally seek to vent its fury upon such as Phillips and myself, and upon our dwellings. The whole North is volcanic. . . . My heart bleeds to think of the poor, unoffending colored people of New York, outraged, plundered, murdered by the demons in human shape who now hold mastery over New York. 'How long, O Lord, how long?'" (MS. July 14, 1863, W. L. G. to Oliver Johnson.)

CHAP. III. — 1863. liest remembrance. I miss you by my side at the table, and at the printing-office, and cannot get reconciled to the separation. Yet I have nothing but praise to give you that you have been faithful to your highest convictions, and, taking your life in your hands, are willing to lay it down, even like the brave Col. *Robert G. Shaw.* Shaw and his associates, if need be, in the cause of freedom, and for the suppression of slavery and the rebellion. True, I could have wished you could ascend to what I believe a higher plane of moral heroism and a nobler method of self-sacrifice; but as you are true to yourself, I am glad of your fidelity, and proud of your willingness to run any risk in a cause that is undeniably just and good. I have no fear that you will be found wanting at any time in the trial-hour, or in the discharge of your official duties. . . .

We shall wait for intelligence, from day to day, with the keenest interest — trusting it may be your good fortune to enter that hot-bed of nullification and treason, Charleston, with your colored associates, victorious over all opposition. The fall of that city will give more satisfaction to the entire North than that of any other place, not excepting Richmond itself. I have my doubts whether it will be accomplished for some time. Doubtless the conflict will be long and sanguinary, but in the sequel the city must surrender. . . .

Your mother's thoughts are all about you. God bless you, my boy!

Matters assumed a brighter aspect as the fall advanced. The American Anti-Slavery Society multiplied its agents *Lib.* 33:170. and meetings, and a petition to Congress for emancipation, circulated by the Women's Loyal National League, received one hundred thousand signatures.[1] Mr. Garrison, who had spent the month of August at Plymouth, Mass., lectured frequently during the autumn, chiefly in cities and towns within easy reach of Boston. The fall elections resulted triumphantly for the Republicans, thus strengthening the Administration in its emancipation policy; and now two of the Border States were moving to abolish slavery within their own limits, and to bring themselves into the ranks of the free States. Both in Missouri and in Maryland a strong party had sprung up

[1] Elizabeth Cady Stanton and Susan B. Anthony were the organizers and untiring workers in this movement ('Hist. Woman Suffrage,' 2:50–89).

advocating immediate and unconditional emancipation, and in the preliminary movements to that end which were among the issues of the November election, it found itself in the ascendancy in both States. In Tennessee and Arkansas, also, prominent slaveholders, perceiving that slavery was crumbling from mere attrition between the opposing armies on their soil, advocated immediate emancipation as the most sensible method of disposing of the vexed question and bringing matters to a settled basis, and they deemed it folly to talk of compensation. The Missouri emancipationists complained bitterly, however, that they received no encouragement or support from Mr. Lincoln, who deprecated haste and still argued in favor of gradualism, and they felt the weight of the Administration against their radical measures. The reluctance of the President to press upon the Border States the immediate abolition of slavery which he had decreed for the rebellious States, and his readiness to allow a small fraction of the (white) voting population in the latter to form new State governments and legislate for the freedmen, will be, and have been already in large measure, forgotten, while the brief address which he gave at Gettysburg, between his interview with the Missourians and his transmission to Congress of the Amnesty Message,[1] will live as long as his name and fame.

Lib. 33:197, 198.

Lib. 33:181, 198.

Raymond's History of Lincoln's Administration, p. 401.

Lib. 33:202.

Nov. 19.

[1] In his anxiety to disintegrate the rebel Confederacy politically, and to re-establish loyal State governments, Mr. Lincoln proposed, in this message, to allow one-tenth of the voters of 1860 (excepting the prominent leaders of the rebellion, and certain other classes) to organize such new governments, provided they took the oath of allegiance to the Constitution, and to the proclamations and Congressional acts relating to slavery, "so long and so far as not repealed, modified, or held void by Congress, or by decision of the Supreme Court." Legislation by such States for the freedmen must recognize and declare their permanent freedom, and provide for their education, but yet might make "temporary arrangement" for their tutelage. "While it allows those who have been in bloody rebellion to vote, it disfranchises the whole body of loyal freedmen!" wrote Mr. Garrison of it. "It opens the way for duplicity and perfidy to any extent, and virtually nullifies the confiscation act of Congress, a measure next in importance to the abolition of slavery. Mr. Lincoln's magnanimity is weakness, and his method of disposing of those who have been emancipated by his proclamation that of giving the sheep over to the guardianship of wolves. This must not be tolerated" (*Lib.* 33 : 202).

Raymond's History of Lincoln's Administration, p. 427. "Of those who were slaves at the beginning of the rebellion," recorded Mr. Lincoln in his December message, "full one hundred thousand are now in the United States military service, about half of which number actually bear arms in the ranks — thus giving the double advantage of taking so much labor from the insurgent cause, and supplying the places which otherwise must be filled with so many white men. So far as tested, it is difficult to say they are not as good soldiers as any. No servile insurrection or tendency to violence or cruelty has marked the measures of emancipation and arming the blacks."

The editor of the *Liberator* had never expected to have war correspondence a feature of his paper, but he *Lib.* 33:24, 38, 83, 114, 115, 135, 146, 175, 187, 190, 200. printed the letters which now came to him from the officers and soldiers of colored regiments, with infinitely more pleasure than he inserted the communications of *Lib.* 33:112, 116, 124. two or three non-resistant friends who deemed it more than ever the time for them to bear their testimony. To the latter he yielded space now and then, with his usual fairness and generosity, but he steadily declined to be dragged into any extended discussion of the peace *Ante, p.* 26. and non-resistance doctrine, for reasons which he had already fully set forth.

Pursuant to adjournment from its annual meeting in May, the American Anti-Slavery Society met in Philadelphia on the 3d and 4th of December, to commemorate the thirtieth anniversary of its formation, to rejoice over the emancipation, by the fiat of the American Government, of three million three hundred thousand slaves, and, in the words of the official invitation which Mr. Garrison, as President of the Society, extended to various friends of the cause, "not only to revive the remembrance of the long thirty years' warfare with the terrible forces of Slavery, and to acknowledge the hand of a wonder-working Providence in guiding the way of the little Anti-Slavery army through great moral darkness and many perils, . . . but also to renew, in the name of humanity, of conscience, and of pure and undefiled religion, the demand for the entire and speedy extinction of slavery in every part of our country." Concert Hall, the largest assembly-room in the city, was scarcely adequate for the throng of members and friends who gathered in joyful confidence that the end of their anti-slavery labors was near at hand; and in dramatic contrast to the conditions under which the Convention of 1833 had met, a slave-auction block now served as the speakers' stand, the national colors were festooned upon the walls, and a squad of colored soldiers from a neighboring camp (which bore the peaceful name of William Penn) occupied seats on the platform at the opening session. Of the forty-five survivors of the original founders of the Society, eleven [1] were present; and the racy and delightful reminiscences of the first Convention which were given by Samuel J. May, J. M. McKim, and Lucretia Mott, with an account of the women's anti-slavery societies by Mary Grew, filled what was left of the first day's sessions after the great audience had listened to Mr. Garrison's welcoming address, to letters from absent friends, and to the reading, by Dr. William H. Furness, of the Declaration of Sentiments.

The absence of Wendell Phillips and Edmund Quincy was greatly regretted. Others unable to attend, who sent letters which were read or printed, were John G. Whittier, David Thurston, Simeon S. Jocelyn, and Joshua Coffin, of the Signers of the Declaration; Arthur Tappan, Samuel Fessenden, John Rankin, Theodore and Angelina Weld, and Sarah Grimké, of the early supporters of the movement; and Joshua R. Giddings, Charles Sumner, Owen Lovejoy, B. Gratz Brown (then leading the emancipation movement in Missouri), and John Jay (subsequently Minister to Austria),[2] of the political allies of the cause.

[1] Namely, Isaac Winslow, Orson S. Murray, W. L. Garrison, Samuel J. May, Robert Purvis, Bartholomew Fussell, Enoch Mack, J. Miller McKim, Thomas Whitson, James Mott, and James McCrummell.

[2] Mr. Jay wrote: "Whatever errors of opinion or of action there may have been on the part of individuals or societies at a recent date, the political principles declared at Philadelphia have stood the test of time

CHAP. III. — 1863.

Although more than twenty years had elapsed since the cessation of personal relations between them, consequent on the division of 1840, Mr. Garrison could not refrain from sending a cordial letter of invitation to Arthur Tappan, in which he renewed his expressions of gratitude for the latter's early support and kindness, and his admiration for all he had done in the slave's cause. Mr. Tappan responded in the same spirit:

Arthur Tappan to W. L. Garrison.

MS. and Lib. 33:202.

NEW HAVEN, Nov. 17, 1863.

DEAR SIR: Few events could give me so much pleasure as the receipt of your note of the 12th inst. During the years that have intervened since we last met, I have often recalled the time when we were united in working for the slave, and regretted that any occurrence should have estranged us from each other.

I shall be glad to attend the meeting at Philadelphia, but my advanced age (78th year) and growing infirmities may prevent.

I am truly your friend,

ARTHUR TAPPAN.

John G. Whittier to W. L. Garrison.

MS. and Lib. 33:202.

AMESBURY, 24th 11 mo., 1863.

MY DEAR FRIEND: I have received thy kind letter with the accompanying circular, inviting me to attend the commemoration of the Thirtieth Anniversary of the formation of the American Anti-Slavery Society, at Philadelphia. It is with the deepest regret that I am compelled, by the feeble state of my health, to give up all hope of meeting thee and my other old and dear friends on an occasion of so much interest. How much it costs me to acquiesce in the hard necessity, thy own feelings will tell thee better than any words of mine.

and trial, and have received the emphatic endorsement of the American people; and the Anti-Slavery movement in the United States, with few exceptions that more plainly show the rule, has been marked by statesmanlike characteristics, now crowned with success, and by a love of country that no delay, injustice, or disappointment could impair or disturb" *(Lib.* 34:9).

I look back over thirty years, and call to mind all the circumstances of my journey to Philadelphia, in company with thyself and the excellent Dr. Thurston of Maine, even then, as we thought, an old man, but still living, and true as ever to the good cause. I recall the early gray morning when, with Samuel J. May, our colleague on the Committee to prepare a Declaration of Sentiments for the Convention, I climbed to the small "upper chamber" of a colored friend to hear thee read the first draft of a paper which will live as long as our national history. I see the members of the Convention, solemnized by the responsibility, rise one by one, and solemnly affix their names to that stern pledge of fidelity to freedom. Of the signers, many have passed away from earth, a few have faltered and turned back, but I believe the majority still live to rejoice over the great triumph of truth and justice, and to devote what remains of time and strength to the cause to which they consecrated their youth and manhood thirty years ago.

For, while we may well thank God and congratulate one another on the prospect of the speedy emancipation of the slaves of the United States, we must not for a moment forget that, from this hour, new and mighty responsibilities devolve upon us to aid, direct, and educate these millions, left free, indeed, but bewildered, ignorant, naked, and foodless in the wild chaos of civil war. We have to undo the accumulated wrongs of two centuries; to remake the manhood that slavery has well-nigh unmade; to see to it that the long-oppressed colored man has a fair field for development and improvement; and to tread under our feet the last vestige of that hateful prejudice which has been the strongest external support of Southern slavery. We must lift ourselves at once to the true Christian altitude where all distinctions of black and white are overlooked in the heartfelt recognition of the brotherhood of man.

I must not close this letter without confessing that I cannot be sufficiently thankful to the Divine Providence which, in a great measure through thy instrumentality, turned me so early away from what Roger Williams calls "the world's great trinity, pleasure, profit, and honor," to take side with the poor and oppressed. I am not insensible to literary reputation. I love, perhaps too well, the praise and good-will of my fellow-men; but I set a higher value on my name as appended to the Anti-Slavery Declaration of 1833 than on the title-page of any book. Looking over a life marked by many errors and shortcomings,

CHAP. III. — 1863. I rejoice that I have been able to maintain the pledge of that signature; and that, in the long intervening years,

> 'My voice, though not the loudest, has been heard
> Wherever Freedom raised her cry of pain.'

Let me, through thee, extend a warm greeting to the friends, whether of our own or the new generation, who may assemble on the occasion of commemoration. There is work yet to be done which will task the best efforts of us all. For thyself, I need not say that the love and esteem of early boyhood have lost nothing by the test of time; and

I am, very cordially, thy friend,

JOHN G. WHITTIER.

The notable speeches of the second day's sessions were *Ante, p. 77.* by Henry Ward Beecher, just returned from his English *Henry Wilson.* triumphs, Senator Wilson of Massachusetts, whom the Convention greeted with especial warmth for his part in abolishing slavery in the District of Columbia, and Frederick Douglass, who gave a graphic account of his recent interview with Mr. Lincoln, and paid an eloquent tribute to the President, who had won his entire respect and confidence. Mr. Beecher, who had not been wont to speak at the meetings of the Garrisonian abolitionists, said, in his brief remarks:

Lib. 34:5. "I am thankful for the privilege of looking on so many noble and revered faces, and so many young and enthusiastic persons, united together by so sacred a bond as that which unites you. I feel, not that I agree with you in everything, but that I am heart and soul with you in the main end. Toward that end we may take different paths, very likely, but when we come together at the end, we shall all be there. It is the end that crowns the beginning, rather than the beginning the end. I therefore feel that I am honored in being permitted to stand before you this morning, to utter these few words of sympathy and of greeting. Your cause is dear to you — just as dear to me. Your names, honored among yourselves, will never lack some wreaths, if I may be permitted to pluck any to place upon them. I thank God that he called you into existence. An uncanonical Church you are, a Church without ordination, but, in my judgment, a Church of the very best and most apostolic kind, held together by the cohesion of a rule of faith, and an interior principle.

Your ordinances are few and simple, but mighty through God. Your officers are not exactly elected. Whoever has the gifts, and the inspiration behind those gifts, he is your teacher and your leader. That is the truest form of the Church. I stand here in the midst of a part of God's great spiritual, earthly Church, happy to be in your midst; asking the privilege to call myself a brother only, asking the privilege of calling you that are advanced in years fathers and mothers, and asking the privilege also to work according to the light that is given me, and, where I differ from you, of having still your confidence that I mean right. I will never work against you, as I never have. I will work with you as far as you will let me; and we shall all be supervised by a higher Love and a diviner Wisdom, and, where mistakes are made, they will, after all, work together for the good cause. We shall meet, if not again on earth, in that land where no struggles are needed, where we shall rejoice and give thanks to Him who called, and guided, and crowned us with victory."

CHAP. III.

1863.

A Memorial to Congress asking for a Constitutional amendment to prohibit slavery forever within the limits of the United States was adopted.[1] Mr. Garrison having announced that George Thompson was soon to revisit the United States, a resolution of "fraternal welcome and warm congratulation" in advance, and of recognition of his patriotic services in support of the American Government, was also adopted; and then Mr. Garrison, with characteristic thoughtfulness, recalled the name and labors of Benjamin Lundy, "that honor may be given to whom honor is due, to one whose memory ought to be preserved to the latest generation as the distinguished pioneer in this great struggle." "If," he said, "I have in any way, however humble, done anything toward calling attention to the question of slavery, or bringing about the glorious prospect of a complete jubilee in our country at no distant day, I feel that I owe everything in this matter, instrumentally, and under God, to Benjamin

Lib. 34:17.

[1] The resolution introducing this Memorial was suggested and written by Charles Sumner, as he was on his way to Washington, the evening before the Convention (Dec. 2), and given to Henry C. Wright, whom he met on the Sound steamer to New York (MS. H. C. Wright).

CHAP. III. 1863.

Lundy." His concluding words were full of cheer, and hope, and rejoicing over the blessings to accrue to the South through emancipation.

So ended the last decade meeting of the American Anti-Slavery Society. Happy would it have been if the Society had felt warranted in making that its final gathering, and in disbanding then and there; for fate decreed that it should never again meet in such oneness of spirit.[1]

[1] A full report of the proceedings of the Third Decade Meeting was published in the *Liberator* and *Standard*, and subsequently issued in a handsome pamphlet by the Society, with an Appendix, and a Catalogue (prepared by Rev. Samuel May, Jr.) of Anti-Slavery Publications in America, from 1750 to 1863. The fiftieth anniversary of the Society was celebrated by a meeting in Philadelphia, Dec. 4, 1883. Only three of the original signers then survived — Robert Purvis, who presided; Elizur Wright, who spoke; and John G. Whittier, who sent a letter for the occasion.

CHAPTER IV.

THE REËLECTION OF LINCOLN.—1864.

THE new year opened with the shadow of a great sorrow resting upon the household in Dix Place. On the night of December 29, 1863, Mrs. Garrison was prostrated by a severe stroke of paralysis, which entirely crippled her left side, and for several days made her recovery doubtful. The blow was utterly unexpected, for she had ever enjoyed the best of health, and her energetic exertions, not only in the management of her domestic affairs, but in outside works of kindness and benevolence, were unceasing. Early in the month she had accompanied her husband and two of their sons to the Decade Meeting at Philadelphia, to her great enjoyment and the gratification of her friends in that city, for her devotion to home and children had seldom allowed her to indulge in such excursions. She returned happy in the memory of her delightful experience, and in the thought that she might attempt such visits oftener in future, now that her children no longer needed her constant maternal care, and that the approaching downfall of slavery promised more opportunities of relaxation for her husband. She had seldom looked more fresh and blooming than on the day which proved to be her last of active, vigorous health, and the friends on whom she called, on an errand in behalf of the freedmen, were impressed by her fine appearance. In the evening she attended a lecture with her husband and children, and an hour or two after she had retired for the

CHAP. IV. 1864. night, the blow fell which crippled her for the remainder of her life.[1]

The physical strain put on Mr. Garrison in the first moments of his wife's helplessness temporarily disabled him also; but he was able, in the latter part of January, to attend the Anti-Slavery Subscription Festival, and Jan. 27, 28, 1864. the annual meeting of the Massachusetts Anti-Slavery Society. At this meeting Mr. Phillips made an elaborate speech on the danger of a premature reconstruction of the seceded States, and the importance of demanding the political enfranchisement of the freedmen in any scheme that might be devised, as the only means of preventing the enactment of apprenticeship or other oppressive laws by their late masters. His text was a resolution, introduced by himself, in these terms:

Lib. 34:22. "That, in our opinion, the Government, in its haste, is ready to sacrifice the interest and honor of the North to secure a sham peace, thereby risking the introduction into Congress of a strong Confederate minority to embarrass legislation, and leaving the freedmen and the Southern States under the control of the late slaveholders, embittered by their defeat in war, and entailing on the country intestine feuds for another dozen years; and we listen in vain, either from the leaders of the Republican party or from its journals, for any such protest as would arrest national attention, or create a public opinion definite enough to avert the sacrifice."

There was good reason for exclaiming against the crude and hasty methods by which the President seemed anxious to reëstablish the machinery of local self-government (by the whites) in the conquered territory held by the Northern armies, and for demanding that no State should be readmitted to the Union until equal rights, fair-play, and protection to the freedmen had been fully secured; but

1 "How good and true she has always been!" wrote Samuel J. May, on hearing of Mrs. Garrison's paralysis. "Unselfish, she has always found her own happiness in promoting the happiness of others. She was born and brought up in a family that seemed to me full of lovingkindness; and I considered her the most equable and affectionate of them all. . . . How cheerful and bright she was at our meetings in Philadelphia, and how much she enjoyed them" (MS. Jan. 5, 1864, to W. L. G.).

to the opening sentence of the resolution Mr. Garrison, with his usual scrupulousness of phraseology, felt compelled to take exception, and he did so as follows: CHAP. IV. 1864.

"Mr. President, in consequence of a severe domestic affliction and of bodily debility, I am not mentally or physically in a condition to make a speech; and, therefore, I shall not attempt to make one. But I wish to propose an amendment to the resolution which was submitted to the meeting by my friend Mr. Phillips this forenoon, and which he advocated with his usual ability and eloquence. As it now stands, it reads thus: *Lib.* 34:23.

"'Resolved, That, in our opinion, the Government, in its haste, *is ready to sacrifice the interest and honor of the North to secure a sham peace*,' etc.

"I am not prepared to bring this charge, nor to cast this imputation. I believe that there is only one party at the North that is ready to make such a sacrifice for such an object, and that is the party of Copperheads. I would therefore propose that the resolution be amended as follows:

"'Resolved, That, in our opinion, the Government, in its haste, is *in danger of sacrificing*,' etc.

"This, Mr. President, is what I am willing to admit, and what I believe; but I would always rather err on the side of charitable judgment than of excessive condemnation. The resolution, as offered, is an impeachment of motives, not of ability or vigilance. It commits us to the assertion, that we believe the Government — meaning Mr. Lincoln in particular — is ready to do a most infamous act, namely, 'to sacrifice the interest and honor of the North to secure a sham peace,' whereby the President's Emancipation Proclamation shall be rendered null and void, and the slave oligarchy restored to their original supremacy. Now, sir, I do not believe a word of it, and therefore I cannot vote for it. To be ready to do a base thing for a base end implies both will and purpose; it means something more than liability: it amounts to perfidy. There was a time when I had little confidence in Abraham Lincoln, and very little respect for him: it was when, for almost eighteen months after secession had taken place, he was evidently averse to seeing that slavery had any vital connection with the rebellion, and so refused to strike a blow at its existence. . . . But the time

CHAP. IV. 1864. came at last when the President, unless he was determined to be wilfully and wickedly blind, was compelled to see that slavery and the rebellion were indissolubly bound up together. Then came the proclamation of unconditional and everlasting emancipation to three million three hundred thousand slaves, leaving not one to clank his fetters in any rebel State; and then, all that is vile and seditious in the Copperhead, pro-slavery, rebel-sympathizing element in the North burst forth against him, and to this hour continues to pour every vial of its wrath upon his head. Since that event, and in view of what has followed in the enrolment of tens of thousands of colored soldiers, I have changed my opinion of Abraham Lincoln. In proportion as he has fallen in the estimation of the disloyal portion of the North, he has risen in my own. True, he is open to criticism for his slowness, and needs spurring on to yet more decisive action; but I am not willing to believe that he is 'ready to sacrifice the interest and honor of the North to secure a sham peace' with the rebels. That is a very grave charge."

The amendment was earnestly opposed by Mr. Phillips, who instanced the President's attitude towards the Missouri radicals, his pains to humor Kentucky ("the Gibraltar of the Border-States obstacle"), and his recent Amnesty proclamation, in confirmation. Mr. Garrison had no apology to make for the Amnesty, which he had "elsewhere condemned in unequivocal terms," nor for the Government's course in paying the negro troops as laborers instead of as soldiers.[1] But he maintained his objection to the resolution. The vote of the Society was so close as to be doubtful for a moment, but the amendment

Ante, p. 85.

Ante, p. 85.

[1] "Laborers" received only ten dollars a month, while the pay of white soldiers was thirteen dollars. Congress at last voted equal pay to colored soldiers from Jan. 1, 1864, and the Massachusetts 54th and 55th regiments were finally awarded (by a decision of the Attorney-General) full pay from the time of their enlistment. With wonderful spirit and fortitude, they refused to receive any pay from the Government until their claim to the full amount was recognized, though in the year and a half during which the matter was unsettled their families were in want. The Legislature of Massachusetts offered them the pay withheld by the Government, but they refused it, with proper acknowledgments, and held the Government to the pledge under which they were enlisted. Gov. Andrew was unceasing in urging their claim, and addressed the President warmly on the subject, May 18, 1864 (*Lib.* 34 : 87).

was finally declared defeated, and the resolution adopted by a narrow majority. CHAP. IV. 1864.

So unusual a divergence between the two foremost leaders of the anti-slavery movement naturally attracted general attention and comment, and caused no little disturbance of mind in some of their immediate followers; but both protested that the difference was simply one of opinion and judgment, and not of fundamental principles, and Garrison defended Phillips against some of the sharp criticisms of the press, and warmly eulogized him. "The honesty of his conviction is not to be impeached," he declared, "while its soundness may be questioned without any personal feeling." "I was glad to see that you were able to be at the anti-slavery meetings," wrote Samuel J. May to Mr. Garrison, "and to attempt to qualify the only expression that marred the excellence of what Mr. Phillips said. It does seem to me that Mr. Lincoln has shown himself anxious to be and to do right, though liable to err through the influences of his education, of his evil advisers, and the complicated difficulties which beset his course of action." And J. M. McKim wrote: "Wendell's speech and resolution not only laid him open to criticism, but demanded and made necessary criticism. It was due to us all that there should be some objection, some disclaimer, and you were the person to make it. We can admire genius, love virtue, and honor fidelity, without surrendering to either, or to all combined (as in this case), our judgment."

Lib. 34:33.

Lib. 34:34.

MS. Feb. 10, 1864.

MS. Feb. 9, *to W. L. G.*

Owen Lovejoy to W. L. Garrison.

WASHINGTON (D. C.), Feb. 22, 1864. *Lib.* 34:54.

DEAR FRIEND GARRISON: I write you, although ill-health compels me to do it by the hand of another, to express to you my gratification at the position you have taken in reference to Mr. Lincoln. I am satisfied, as the old theologians used to say in regard to the world, that if he is not the best conceivable President, he is the best possible. I have known something of the facts inside during his administration, and I

CHAP. IV. — 1864. know that he has been just as radical as any of his Cabinet. And although he does not do everything that you or I would like, the question recurs, whether it is likely we can elect a man who would. It is evident that the great mass of Unionists prefer him for reëlection; and it seems to me certain that the providence of God, during another term, will grind slavery to powder. I believe now that the President is up with the average of the House.

You will notice that the House paid the hundred dollars to the master instead of the slave. And you will have noticed, perhaps, also, that Henry Winter Davis has made a report in reference to Arkansas, where he has put in the word "white" as a qualification for voting. It is my purpose (by the way), if I am ever able to be in my seat again, to move to amend by striking out the word "white." And, if possible, I mean to bring the House to a vote on it, and let them confront the question face to face.

Recurring to the President, there are a great many reports concerning him which seem to be reliable and authentic, which, after all, are not so. It was currently reported among the anti-slavery men of Illinois, that the Emancipation Proclamation was extorted from him by the outward pressure, and particularly by the delegation from the Christian Convention that met at Chicago. Now, the fact is this, as I had it from his own

Ante, p. 62. lips: He had written the Proclamation in the summer (as early as June, I think, but will not be certain as to the precise time), and called his Cabinet together, and informed them that he had written it and he meant to make it, but wanted to read it to them for any criticism or remarks as to its features or details. After having done so, Mr. Seward suggested whether it would not be well for him to withhold its publication until after we had gained some substantial advantage in the field, as at that time we had met with many reverses, and it might be considered a cry of despair. He told me he thought the suggestion a wise one, and so held on to the Proclamation until after the

Sept. 16, 1862. battle of Antietam.

I mention this as a sample of a great many others. But I am wandering from my purpose, which was simply to tell you how much pleasure your position gives me.

George Thompson. I am also very glad to see that Mr. Thompson of England speaks in friendly terms of the President. If I were acquainted with him, I would write and thank him also; and I hope you will say so to him. I congratulate him and the country on the change which has taken place in relation to slavery since he visited us before, and hope I may have the pleasure of seeing him in Washington during the session of Congress; and will be glad to introduce him to the President.

CHAP. IV. 1864.

I have also to thank you for sending me the *Liberator*. During the past sessions, when pro-slaveryism was in the ascendant, I used to read your articles to renew and strengthen my faith.

Very truly yours,

OWEN LOVEJOY.[1]

Early in February, George Thompson landed in Boston on his third and final visit to America. Both in the *Liberator* and in speeches and resolutions at the various anti-slavery conventions of the preceding months, Mr. Garrison had done his utmost to insure a fitting welcome for his bosom friend;[2] and the farewell soirées with which Thompson's admirers in London, Manchester, and Liverpool had honored him, were but a prelude to the series of ovations awaiting him in the land which he had so long loved and served, and which was ready now to recognize his heroism, his sacrifices, and his magnanimity. For whereas, in 1835, he had been secretly hurried out of Boston harbor, he was now received with special courtesies by the Customs officers of the United States, and treated as a distinguished visitor. The Collector of the port solicited his presence at a levee, a few days after he landed, and in a company comprising the representative men of the city and State he was greeted with the heartiest cheers. His first public appearance was at Music Hall, on February 16, when he addressed an immense audience on "The Popular Sentiment of England in regard to America and the Rebellion," and described the agitation which had

Feb. 6.

Lib. 34 : 25, 26, 29.

Ante, 2 : 50.

J. Z. Goodrich. Feb. 10.

Lib. 34 : 31.

[1] This worthy brother of the martyr of Alton died within five weeks after the above letter was written. Mr. Garrison then printed it, with a proper tribute to his memory (*Lib.* 34 : 54).

[2] An interesting and valuable sketch of Mr. Thompson's life and philanthropic labors, by William Farmer, ran through seven numbers of the *Liberator*, filling eighteen columns — probably the fullest and best outline of his remarkable career that has been written (*Lib.* 34 : 25, 29, 34, 37, 41, 45, 49).

kept the British Government from interfering in the American struggle. A week later, the same hall was packed to its utmost capacity on the occasion of a formal reception tendered to Mr. Thompson by leading citizens of Massachusetts, the name of John A. Andrew heading the list. Governor Andrew presided with rare felicity, declaring it to be an agreeable service, and in the direct line of his public duty, to attempt the chairmanship of the meeting, and "to accord an honorable welcome to George Thompson," both for his earlier achievements and for his recent services in behalf of the North. Mr. Thompson's response was worthy of himself and of the magnificent occasion. Mr. Garrison would fain have kept in the background, preferring that the welcome to his friend should be seen to be a spontaneous and popular one; but the audience insisted on hearing him, and gave him three cheers as he came forward to express his delight at the atonement which Boston and Massachusetts were now offering. Addressing the Governor, he said:

Feb. 23, 1864. *Lib.* 34:37. *Cf. Lib.* 27:7. *Lib.* 34:37.

"Sir, it has been the custom of those who have occupied the Executive chair in this State, to close their Fast Day and Thanksgiving proclamations with the exclamation: 'God save the Commonwealth of Massachusetts!' Now, sir, in view of the altered state of things among us, in view of this glorious meeting, justly and fairly representing the people of Massachusetts, and in view of the fact that your Excellency is here to preside on this occasion, I have to say that at last I believe Massachusetts *is* saved — saved from her old pro-slavery subserviency and degradation — saved from her blind, selfish, calculating slaveholding complicity with the South — saved to honor, justice, humanity, and impartial freedom."

Lib. 34:38.

The Boston reception was speedily followed by one at Cooper Institute, New York, with General John C. Frémont in the chair; by another at Plymouth Church, Brooklyn, with Henry Ward Beecher presiding; by others still in Springfield,[1] Lawrence, Lowell, New Bedford, and

Feb. 29. *Lib.* 34:39. *Mar.* 11. *Lib.* 34:46.

[1] The Springfield *Republican* aggravated its disgraceful course at the time of Mr. Thompson's visit in 1851 (*ante*, 3 : 322) by now repeating its calum-

Worcester, and especially at the Academy of Music in Philadelphia, on the invitation of the most prominent citizens, and with Horace Binney, Jr., presiding. But the climax of dramatic contrasts to the incidents of the Englishman's first visit to America was reached at Washington, where the House of Representatives voted him the use of its Hall for the lecture which John Pierpont and others had invited him to deliver at the Capital.[1] Vice-President Hamlin presided, and the hall was thronged by a brilliant audience, which included President Lincoln, members of the Cabinet, and a majority of both Houses of Congress. At the close of the lecture, the President, Speaker Colfax, and many Senators and Representatives congratulated Mr. Thompson. Among them was Senator Reverdy Johnson of Maryland, only a few years before counsel on the pro-slavery side in the Dred Scott case, but now an earnest advocate of the Constitutional Amendment abolishing slavery, which passed the Senate (38 to 6) two days after Mr. Thompson's lecture. Marked attentions were also shown the latter in the House and Senate, the following day; by Mr. Lincoln at the White House; and by Secretaries Stanton, Seward, and Chase.

April 4, 1864. *Lib.* 34:61.

April 6. *Lib.* 34:62.

Lib. 34:72.

April 8.

Mr. Garrison had at first intended to accompany Mr. Thompson to Washington, but decided not to do so, because, as he wrote to Oliver Johnson, who enjoyed that privilege in his stead—

"I wish him to be the one sole object of attention, and to have concentrated upon him all the honors that might be divided between us, provided we were together. I want him thus to be individually and conspicuously noticed for various reasons—especially for international ones: it will tell well in England,

MS. Mar. 14, 1864.

nies, and coolly asserting that Mr. Thompson's recent services to the Union cause were "but an act of justice and due reparation for past injuries" done by him to this country! Mr. Thompson made a scathing reply (*Lib.* 30 : 50).

[1] The invitation was signed by twenty-four Senators and twenty-two Representatives, and assured Mr. Thompson of their appreciation of his labors "as a statesman and teacher—labors which we feel persuaded have wrought an important influence for public good in both hemispheres" (*Lib.* 34 : 42).

CHAP. IV. — 1864. and help to strengthen the ties of friendship and amity between both countries. Possibly, but not probably, I may conclude to visit Washington before the final adjournment of Congress."

Oliver Johnson to W. L. Garrison.

MS. PHILADELPHIA, April 11th, 1864.

You see we are thus far on our way home. We halt here to-night to allow Mr. Thompson to be presented to the Union League, at their Club House, and to make them a brief colloquial address. It is intended to clinch the nail which he drove a week ago in the Academy of Music — or, changing the figure, to cap the climax of the former meeting. *J. M. McKim.* McKim assures us that the speech here a week ago made a grand impression, not merely upon the intelligent mass, but upon leading men, heretofore conservative. Horace Binney, Jr., the Chairman, is a man of the very highest social standing, the representative of the wealth and culture of the city. Many eminent clergymen were on the platform — among them Bishop Potter! *Alonzo Potter.* Verily the day of miracles is not past.

I wrote you, I think, of every important incident connected with our visit to Washington. *April 8.* We left there Friday morning, and were in the house of dear old Thomas Garrett by 4½ P. M. *Wilmington, Del.* In the evening there was a good audience to hear Mr. Thompson. *Lib. 34:70.* As he was rather feeble, I opened the meeting (at his earnest request) by giving the people some account of his life. He followed in a most admirable extemporaneous address, which charmed his auditors, and of which the most radical portions were loudly cheered. The influence on the city was most happy, and dear old Thomas Garrett was more than delighted. . . .

To-morrow we are off to Newark, where Mr. Thompson will speak in the evening. Then he will go to New York for a couple of days, and after that to Elmira, Syracuse, Auburn, and Rochester.

I need not tell you, my dear Garrison, that I have enjoyed every moment spent in Mr. Thompson's company. The more I see of him, the more I love and reverence him, and the more I hear him, the more I admire his eloquence. How fine are his instincts, how clear his intellect, how true his heart! How admirably poised is his mind, how rare his moral discernment, how nice his discrimination in all things! He is so generous, so catholic in spirit, so comprehensive in his aims, that he wins at once the respect and love of all whom he meets. It makes me sad at moments to think how feeble he is in body, and that age and sickness are making inroads upon his constitution. CHAP. IV. 1864.

Mr. Thompson's lecture engagements throughout the year were numerous, and took him as far west as St. Louis, in December. On the fifth of that month he wrote from Cincinnati to Mr. Garrison: "Within the last forty-eight hours I have been in two slave States, yet here I am, safe from harm, with not so much as the smell of *tar* upon me." Stranger, almost, was what befell him in Connecticut in July. *MS.*

George Thompson to W. L. Garrison.

WESLEYAN UNIVERSITY, *MS.*
MIDDLETOWN, July 20, 1864. *Wednesday.*

Times change, and men with them. Once, as you know, I was vilified and denounced by the President and professors of this institution. Now, I am respectfully invited, hospitably entertained; and students, and Faculty, and the Trustees, and the editor of the *Christian Advocate* encourage, caress, and applaud me. I had a truly splendid meeting here yesterday. These commencement meetings are rare opportunities for sowing the good seed. I had a good deal to say about *you*, and was rejoiced to find that the mention of your name drew forth loud and repeated cheers. The town is very full. I am surprised to find how many have heard me in days gone by, who I was not aware had ever come within the sound of my voice. I suppose they were the Nicodemuses of the day. . . . *Ante*, 2:139. *Daniel Curry, D.D.*

July 22.

My meeting here was a very beautiful sight, my reception most cordial. Yesterday, I went to listen to the college exercises; judge of my consternation and confusion when, without a dream of such an event, I found myself made an LL. D., amidst the acclamations of all present! This compliment was paid me as a proof of the sympathy entertained in the objects to which I have devoted myself, and as an atonement for the conduct of certain parties connected with the University, long ago. Dr. Whedon was present, concurring in the proceedings; and also Dr. Curry, the successor of Dr. Bangs in the editorship of the *Christian Advocate and Journal*. *Lib.* 34:122. *Daniel D. Whedon. Nathan Bangs.*

July 23, 1864. I shall be in Northampton on Saturday, speak again in Florence on Sunday, and be ready to welcome you next week, should you signify your intention to come. Should you say no, I shall shorten my stay, and get back to Boston, and try to spend the 1st of August with you somewhere else.

As early as January the movement in favor of Mr. Lincoln's nomination for a second term had begun to take shape in the resolutions passed by several State legislatures in favor of that course, and found constant expres-
Ante, p. 95. sion in many other ways. In his speech at the January meeting of the Massachusetts Anti-Slavery Society, Mr. Garrison had alluded to these manifestations of the popular will as proving that the loyal people did not believe the President ready "to sacrifice the interest and honor of the North to procure a sham peace," and he added, for himself:

Lib. 34:23. "Taking all things into consideration,— especially in view of the fact that he has not only decreed the liberation of every slave in Rebeldom forever, but stands repeatedly committed, as no other man does, before heaven and earth, to maintain it so long as he is in office,— in my judgment the reëlection of Abraham Lincoln to the Presidency of the United States would be the safest and wisest course, in the present state of our national affairs, on the part of those who are friendly to his Administration. No other candidate would probably carry so strong a vote in opposition to Copperhead Democracy. Such, at least, is my conviction."

Lib. 34:46. In March he repeated and emphasized this opinion in an editorial, on "The Presidency," which attracted wide attention. Declaring the approaching election to be "a matter of the gravest consideration in its relation to the stability of the Government, the suppression of the rebellion, and the abolition of slavery," he deemed it none too early to discuss who should be the Republican candidate, in view of the various schemes that were already on
S. P. Chase. B. F. Butler. J. C. Frémont. foot to prevent Mr. Lincoln's re-nomination, and to push Chase, Butler, or Frémont for the position.

"Standing, as we have stood for more than thirty years, outside of every party organization,— yet taking the deepest interest in every political struggle of national concernment as indicative of progress or retrogression,—we occupy a position not only absolutely independent of all party ties and obligations, but sufficiently elevated and disinterested to make our judgment impartial, if not conclusive to others. The crisis is too solemn to justify heat or dogmatism, or even that personal preference or rivalry which, under other circumstances, would be allowable and attended with no danger. Never was the apostolic injunction more impressive than now: 'Let every one be FULLY PERSUADED in his own mind'—and act in accordance with his clearest instincts and his highest convictions. There are, and there will be, honest differences of opinion among those who are thoroughly loyal to the Government, as to the best course to be pursued; yet it is none the less certain that the fewer these differences can be made, the less danger will there be of the success of that party at the North which is essentially, brutally, persistently pro-slavery, and eager to strike hands with the rebels of the South in an arrangement that shall be mutually satisfactory, by allowing the latter to dictate terms and have their own way. CHAP. IV. — 1864.

"In stating our convictions, we ask no approval of them on the part of our readers beyond what may seem reasonable and just."

The policy of the Copperhead party, continued Mr. Garrison, was clearly to sow dissensions in the Republican ranks, and profit by their division, but Secretary Chase had already bowed to the adverse decision of his own State *Ohio.* to his candidature, and had withdrawn his name. Frémont could have no hope of success as opposed to Lincoln, than whom no man living had so strong a hold on the mass of the people.

"Not that Mr. Lincoln is not open to criticism and censure; *Lib.* 34:46. we have both criticised and censured him again and again. Not that there is not much to grieve over, and to be surprised at, in his administration, on account of its inconsistent and paradoxical treatment of the rebellion and slavery; of this we have spoken freely. Nevertheless, there is also much to rejoice over and to be thankful for; and a thousand incidental errors and blunders are easily to be borne with on the part of him who, at one blow, severed the chains of three million three hundred thousand slaves—thus virtually abolishing the whole slave

CHAP. IV. — 1864. system (the greater necessarily including the less) in quick progression, as an act dictated alike by patriotism, justice, and humanity."

This declaration gave great satisfaction to the loyal press and public, and was a welcome evidence to Mr. Lincoln that he was not to have the influence of the abolitionists against him in the pending struggle, but could rely on their forbearance and faith in his purpose to carry the nation through to peace and freedom. Hitherto his own utterances respecting the emancipation policy had had, as George Thompson said, "the alloy of expediency." *Ante, p.* 68. Now, for the first time, he seemed to recognize the divine hand in chastisement for national oppression, and to regard the war as something more than a struggle for the Union and the Constitution, in which the question of slavery had only a subordinate part. In his honest and thoroughly characteristic letter of April 4 to A. G. Hodges of Kentucky, after frankly stating the rule which had guided his course with regard to the suppression of the rebellion, and under which, while himself "naturally anti-slavery," and believing "if slavery is not wrong, nothing is wrong," he had done no official act in deference to his mere abstract judgment and feeling on slavery, he concluded with a passage which was the forerunner of the solemn utterances in his final message to Congress and his second inaugural:

Raymond's History of Lincoln's Administration, pp. 482–3.

"In telling this tale, I attempt no compliment to my own sagacity. I claim not to have controlled events, but confess plainly that events have controlled me. Now, at the end of three years' struggle, the nation's condition is not what either party, or any man, devised or expected. God alone can claim it. Whither it is tending seems plain. If God now wills the removal of a great wrong, and wills also that we of the North, as well as you of the South, shall pay fairly for our complicity in that wrong, impartial history will find therein new causes to attest and revere the justice and goodness of God."[1]

1 "Mr. [Samuel J.] May and I have read together, this morning, the President's letter of the 4th inst. to A. G. Hodges, Esq., of Kentucky. We think it a remarkably clear and satisfactory exposition of his acts and

The Presidential theme occupied the attention of the May meetings of the American and Massachusetts Societies, to the exclusion of almost everything else, and the debates at times were earnest and exciting. Mr. Phillips, at the opening session in New York, introduced his speech with a resolution that, "while we do not criticise the wishes of the Administration, still, as abolitionists, we feel bound to declare that we see no evidence of its purpose to put the freedom of the negro on such a basis as will secure it against every peril"; and he proceeded to criticise the delays and shortcomings of Mr. Lincoln and his advisers, and the attempts to patch up a reconstructed State in Louisiana without giving suffrage to the negroes. "My charge," he said, "against the Administration, as an abolitionist, is, that it seeks to adjourn the battle from cannon shot to the forum; from Grant to the Senate-house; and to leave the poisoned remnants of the slave system for a quarter of a century to come"; and he manifested his decided opposition to Mr. Lincoln's renomination, accusing him of having, by his dilatory course respecting slavery, solidified Southern sentiment against the Union, and made a Confederacy where Jefferson Davis had only made a rebellion. "To-day," he continued, "the man who takes the helm of the vessel of State in his hand has a tenfold harder work to do than Abraham Lincoln had in March, 1861, for he has got the South, as near as such a thing can be, unanimous against him."

CHAP. IV. 1864. *May* 10. *Lib.* 34 : 81. *Lib.* 34 : 81.

In the business meetings of the Society, Mr. Phillips was even more sweeping and extravagant in his language, for he declared that he would sooner have severed his right hand than taken the responsibility which his dear and

Lib. 34 : 83.

policy on the question of slavery. It is, essentially, what he said to me when he gave me an interview at Washington, on the 7th. I am glad to see from his pen what he verbally communicated to me. My remark, since I saw him, has been, that he kindly and frankly furnished me with a key to the right understanding of the course he had pursued, and that I was glad to find that I had, in England, explained his acts correctly, and had not misunderstood either his private views or the motive of his public conduct" (MS. April 30, 1864, George Thompson at Syracuse, N. Y., to W. L. G., *Lib.* 34 : 74).

CHAP. IV. faithful friend Garrison had assumed in favoring Mr. 1864. Lincoln's reëlection. "There are no hundred men in the country," he continued, "whose united voices would be of equal importance in determining the future of the Government and country. A million dollars would have been a cheap purchase for the Administration of the *Liberator's* *May* 11. article on the Presidency." And at the final session he closed his despondent speech with a renewed avowal of his hostility to Lincoln, the day of whose reëlection, he *Lib.* 34:86. said, "I shall consider the end of the Union in my day, or its reconstruction on terms worse than Disunion."

Mr. Garrison's rejoinders to these speeches were in harmony with his previous charitable consideration for Mr. Lincoln, in view of the perils which had surrounded *Lib.* 34:82. him,—"perils and trials unknown to any man, in any *Lib.* 34:86. age of the world, in official station"; and he quoted Mr. Phillips's own words the year before, which contemplated Mr. Lincoln's being President four or eight years longer, in these terms:

Lib. 33:110. "I told him myself, and I believed it then, and I believe it now,—I meant it then, and I mean it now,—that the man who would honestly put his right hand to the plow of that proclamation, and execute it, this people would not allow to quit while the experiment was trying. Whoever starts the great experiment of emancipation, and honestly devotes his energies to making it a fact, deserves to hold the helm of the Government until that experiment is finished."

Mr. Garrison's hopeful view was shared by Miller *J. M. McKim.* McKim and George Thompson, in their speeches, and at all the public sessions the sympathy of the audiences was clearly with them and in favor of Lincoln. At the *Lib.* 34:83. business meetings of the Society, Mr. Phillips was supported by Stephen S. Foster and Parker Pillsbury, and the resolution offered by him at the outset was adopted by the close vote of 21 to 18. The regular series of resolutions introduced by Mr. Garrison, and unanimously adopted, made no allusion whatever to the Presidential question, but urged the enactment of the Thirteenth

Amendment to the Constitution, and cited the massacre of colored soldiers at Fort Pillow and elsewhere as justifying the severest accusations of the abolitionists against slavery, of which it was the natural outgrowth. CHAP. IV. 1864.

W. L. Garrison to his Wife.

NEW YORK, May 13, 1864. *MS.*

Our two public meetings, at the Cooper Institute and at Dr. Cheever's church, were attended with large and truly respectable and intelligent numbers, and went off with high interest and hearty approval. Thompson acquitted himself admirably on each occasion. Phillips was brilliant and eloquent as usual, but somewhat contradictory in statement, and decidedly opposed to the reëlection of Abraham Lincoln. Of course, I briefly expressed my dissent, and gave the reasons why I thought the people would stand by him for another term. The audiences were overwhelming in their approval of my views, though disposed generously to applaud Phillips as far as they could. I trust nothing fell from my lips which was deemed personal or unkind by dear Phillips. He is frank and outspoken in his own sentiments, and will not desire me to be less so. But I did not wish to seem to be in antagonism to himself,—for I know that our enemies would like to see us or put us at personal variance,—and so I said but very little in reply to two long speeches.

Our business meetings would have been very harmonious, had it not been for Stephen and Parker. We had some plain things said on both sides; but, on the whole, we got along better than I expected, and the Presidential election received no partisan countenance. *S. S. Foster. Parker Pillsbury.*

Before the Boston meetings occurred, Mr. Phillips had carried his hostility to Lincoln so far as to seek and accept, for the first time in his life, the votes of a political caucus, and he appeared as a delegate from his Ward in Boston at the State Convention to elect delegates to the approaching National Republican Convention at Baltimore. In this new rôle he made a speech in opposition to the resolution endorsing Mr. Lincoln, but without the slightest effect, for it was carried by acclamation. His utter fail- *May 23.* *Lib. 34:87, 94.*

CHAP. IV. 1864. Lib. 34:86. ure to influence the Convention[1] served to intensify the bitterness with which, in a speech before the Emancipation League, four days later, he spoke of Mr. Lincoln, declaring that, as the President had delayed so long before touching slavery, while he had suspended *habeas corpus* ("the barriers of liberty set up two hundred years ago") in sixty days, no negro in America owed anything to him. Mr. Lincoln, he asserted, did not desire to crush the rebellion, and he pledged himself to leave no stone unturned, from that time until November, to defeat his reëlection.

May 27. At the New England Convention, the same week, he went still farther, and accused the President of "carrying Lib. 34:93. on the war now to reëlect himself, to conciliate the disloyal white man." As at New York, he was sustained in S. S. and A. K. Foster. these extreme views by the Fosters and Parker Pillsbury, while the defence and vindication of the President fell to Mr. Garrison, Henry C. Wright,[2] and George Thompson. The final evening meeting of the two days' sessions was intensely interesting and exciting. Mr. Phillips renewed his arraignment of Lincoln, and sought to depreciate George Thompson's eulogy of the latter by impeaching his competency as a foreigner to judge as to the state of affairs in this country. This reflection elicited a rare Lib. 34:94, 95. outburst of eloquence from Thompson, who showed all his pristine fire and power, and roused the audience to

1 Mr. Phillips made special and unsuccessful efforts, also, to have an anti-Lincoln delegation sent to the Baltimore Convention from Vermont (MS. June 13, 1865, S. May, Jr., to Mary A. Estlin).

2 Radical as he always was, none of the anti-slavery workers more clearly perceived the irresistible tendency of events, the difficulties surrounding the President's Administration, and the duty of sustaining the Government, than Henry C. Wright. Travelling over a larger portion of the country than any of his associates, and thoroughly acquainted with the great West, he had peculiar opportunities for noting the drift of public sentiment and learning the opinions of all classes of people. His letters to the *Liberator* during 1864, when he was constantly on his lecture missions, East and West, and watching the dangerous plots in Indiana and Illinois of the "Knights of the Golden Circle," testify to his sound sense and judgment. On Lincoln's reëlection, he declared, the preservation of the republic, the destruction of slavery, and the rights of the laboring classes everywhere depended (*Lib.* 34 : 103, 106, 110, 147, 158, 163).

Parker Pillsbury.

the highest pitch of feeling. Mr. Garrison quoted, as the most effective reply possible to Mr. Phillips's present attacks on the President, from speeches which his colaborer had made in 1861 and 1862, before either proclamation of emancipation had been issued, and in which he had repeatedly praised Lincoln as in advance of public sentiment, and declared himself satisfied with the rapid progress of events. Passing from these, he replied specifically to Phillips's current criticisms and complaints, expressing his conviction that the people could not do better, politically speaking, than to reëlect Lincoln, and that they ought, as a matter of justice and to vindicate the democratic principle, to keep him in office until he should be the acknowledged President of the whole United States. He also animadverted upon the Convention which was to meet in Cleveland the following week, to nominate Frémont for the Presidency:

Lib. 34:94.

May 31, 1864.

"Gen. Frémont, as yet, has not shown a single State, a single county, a single town or hamlet in his support. Who represents him from Massachusetts, on the call for the Cleveland Convention? Two men, both non-voters, I believe, and neither of them has a particle of political influence. Now I call that the step from the sublime to the ridiculous. Is that the best Massachusetts can do for Frémont? For, remember, I am speaking now of the 'coming man' in the next election, who is to run Abraham Lincoln off the track. If I were speaking on a moral issue, I should speak in a very different manner of those whose names appear on that call; for the man who stands alone in a moral cause, though all the world be against him, if God be for him, stands in a majority, and is conqueror. But when you come to politics, that is another sphere. Then you must have men and money; then you must have votes; then you must have something of political influence and respectability. But, with one exception, the signers to the call for the Cleveland Convention have not one ounce of political weight in this country.

Lib. 34:94.

S. S. Foster, Karl Heinzen.

Cf. ante, 2:436.

B. Gratz Brown.

Mr. President, we are getting on well. We are to have all our friends contend for, in the end. There is no difference among us in this respect. We all go for equal rights, without regard to race or color. We have not relaxed our vigilance or

CHAP. IV. 1864. our testimony; and I am sorry to hear any intimation thrown out that we do not call for the amplest justice."

Mr. Phillips was dissatisfied because the *National A. S. Standard* would not commend the Cleveland movement and oppose Lincoln, but the course of the paper was sustained by the Executive Committee. "If I am required either to set the *Standard* in opposition to Lincoln's re-election," wrote Oliver Johnson to Mr. Garrison, "or to suppress my honest convictions in regard to the Frémont movement, its candidates and platform, I shall resign the editorial chair." *MS. June 20, 1864.*

The Republican National Convention met in Baltimore on the 7th of June, and unanimously nominated Mr. Lincoln for a second term. Among those who witnessed its proceedings, from the gallery, was Mr. Garrison. He was revisiting Baltimore for the first time since 1830, having just come from the Progressive Friends' Meeting at Longwood, with Theodore Tilton, editor of the New York *Independent*. Of the Convention Mr. Garrison wrote, on his return:

Lib. 34:102. "It was well worth going from one end of the country to the other to witness its proceedings; yet it came in my way incidentally, and I was glad to have the opportunity to be 'a looker-on in Venice.' As a delegated body representing all the loyal States and Territories in the Union, it presented an imposing appearance, and indicated, both in the choice of its candidates and platform it adopted, the overwhelming sentiment of THE PEOPLE. Prior to its coming together, all the loyal States had, with a unanimity unexampled since the days of George Washington, officially declared in favor of the reëlection of ABRAHAM LINCOLN; so that its duty was simply to record its votes for the man thus unmistakably designated. From Maine to Oregon, the response was the same, with the single exception of the Radical delegates from Missouri, who, on the first ballot, voted for General Grant, in accordance with their instructions; and then transferred their votes to Abraham Lincoln, making the grand total of 519 for his reëlection. Though this unanimity was strongly to be desired for the weightiest considerations, it was hardly to be expected; for what had the enemies of the Administration left undone to create division in the ranks?

When the result was announced, the enthusiasm was indescribable; and yet it was not comparable to the electric outbreak which followed the adoption of the following resolution:

CHAP. IV. 1864.

"'3. Resolved, That as slavery was the cause and now constitutes the strength of this rebellion, and as it must be always and everywhere hostile to the principles of republican government, justice and the national safety demand its utter and complete extirpation from the soil of the republic; and that we uphold and maintain the acts and proclamations by which the Government, in its own defence, has aimed a death-blow at this gigantic evil. We are in favor, furthermore, of such an amendment to the Constitution, to be made by the people in conformity with its provisions, as shall terminate and forever prohibit the existence of slavery within the limits or the jurisdiction of the United States.'

"The whole body of delegates sprang to their feet as by one impulse, giving vent to their feelings in prolonged cheering and warm congratulations,— again and again renewing their joyful demonstrations in the most enthusiastic manner. Was not a spectacle like that rich compensation for more than thirty years of universal personal opprobrium, bitter persecution, and murderous outlawry? It is impossible for me to describe my emotions on that occasion—for what had God wrought! It was the first NATIONAL VERDICT ever recorded, in form and fact, in letter and spirit, against slavery, as a system 'incompatible with the principles of republican government,' and therefore no longer to be tolerated in the land. It was the sublime decree—'Let the covenant with death be annulled, and the agreement with hell no longer stand!' It was a full endorsement of all the abolition 'fanaticism' and 'incendiarism' with which I had stood branded for so many years. The time for my complete vindication had come, from the Atlantic to the Pacific—the vindication of all who had labored for the extinction of 'the sum of all villanies,' whether through evil report or good report—yea, the vindication of Eternal Truth and Justice!"

W. L. Garrison to his Wife.

BALTIMORE, June 8, 1864. *MS.*

June 6.

I arrived here in the evening train on Monday, and met with a very kind welcome from the Needleses, who were expecting my coming, with George Thompson as my companion. Since then, I have been constantly occupied in seeing the city, which

CHAP. IV. 1864. has almost wholly grown out of my recollections. It is ahead of Boston in population and extent, but has not as many good residences or handsome stores. The old jail that I once had the honor and happiness to occupy for a time has been torn down, and a new and handsome prison erected upon its site; so the charm was broken, and it was useless to think of visiting my old cell.[1]

"High walls and huge the body may confine," etc.

The city is very quiet and very clean; and the general appearance of the people, including the colored people, is creditable.

Yesterday and to-day, I have attended the National Convention for the nomination of President and Vice-President of the U. S. It has been a full one, and its proceedings have been such as to gladden my heart, and almost make me fear that I am at home dreaming, and not in the State of Maryland. Even my friend Phillips would have been highly gratified

[1] "Our travelling companion was no other than that fanatical, heretical, and incendiary gentleman, Mr. William Lloyd Garrison of Bunker Hill — whose company in the cars, a few years ago, would not have rendered a journey southward eminently enviable; to whom, however, on his late journey, as far south of Mason and Dixon as we could get, all hats went off, all hands were thrust in welcome, and all hospitable honors shown — in the midst of which the bewildered man stood a modest and meek-minded conservative before those more fiery radicals on whom the new pentecost has fallen with its tongues of flame. Not having been in Baltimore since he was there imprisoned, thirty-four years ago, and never in his life having been in Washington (honest man!), his journey was full of strange emotions at every turn. Condemned as a criminal for speaking in a slave city against slavery, he returned to that city to find it so far regenerated that to-day Baltimore is ready to give a larger proportional vote than Boston for universal liberty. The court in which Mr. Garrison was tried and sentenced is now presided over by a radical Abolitionist — Judge Hugh L. Bond, one of the most indefatigable and influential Unionists in the State, who, to gratify our curiosity, hunted up from the old records of the court the time-yellowed papers of indictment against Mr. Garrison, which that gentleman, putting on his spectacles, perused with eyes as full of merriment as we noticed in Horace Greeley's, on being dismissed from his contempt of Judge Barnard's court. As we had threatened to put Mr. Garrison into his old cell, and shut him up for a night, we were disappointed to learn that the city authorities, not foreseeing how they were spoiling a good historical incident, had torn down the old jail and built a new one in its place — where, however, not the opposers but abettors of slavery and treason are now confined! Thus the gallows which was built for Mordecai, is used for hanging Haman! Eight or nine of the original jurymen who gave the verdict against Mr. Garrison are still living, and Judge Bond jocosely threatened to summon them all into court, that Mr. Garrison might forgive them in public! We bargained in advance for a photograph of the scene" (Theodore Tilton, in the *Independent*; *Lib.* 34 : 104).

with the tone and spirit of the Convention. In the speeches made, every allusion made to slavery as a curse to be extirpated, and a crime no longer to be tolerated, has been most enthusiastically responded to; in several instances the assembly rising to their feet, and giving vent to their feelings in rousing cheers. . . . Each evening there has been a mass meeting held in Monument Square, addresses made, and the most radical sentiments rapturously applauded, without a single Copperhead daring to peep or mutter. This evening there will be an immense ratification meeting held in the same Square, with speech-making, etc., etc.

CHAP. IV.

1864.

I have been introduced to various members of the Convention[1] — among them the redoubtable Parson Brownlow, who looks very sick, and is probably not long for this world. I have made up my mind not to speak in public, either here or in Washington, though there is a desire to hear me in both places. . . .

Wm. G. Brownlow.

I am very well indeed, and find the jaunt, with all its fatigues, good for me.

WASHINGTON, June 9, 1864.

MS.

If I am not dreaming, I am at last in the Capital of the United States. Right from the cars, this forenoon, Judge Bond of Baltimore and Tilton took me up to the White House, and forthwith introduced me to the President, who was receiving a group of persons fresh from the Baltimore Convention, congratulating him on his renomination. He received me very heartily, and expressed a desire to see me again, and I expect to do so to-morrow. He referred to my imprisonment in Baltimore thirty-four years ago, and said: "Then you could not get out of prison; now you cannot get in" — referring playfully to the demolition of the old prison. I was . . . introduced to a large number [of persons] from various parts of the country, many of them of more or less prominence. Leaving the East

Hugh L. Bond. Theodore Tilton.

[1] The temporary president of the Convention was the Rev. Robert J. Breckinridge, D. D., of Kentucky, Mr. Garrison's old-time Colonization antagonist *(ante,* 1 : 448–450), now a warm advocate of the Constitutional Amendment. Another indication of the revolution in public sentiment was the action of the General Conference of the M. E. Church, at Philadelphia in May, excluding from membership all persons guilty of holding, buying or selling slaves, and receiving a deputation from the colored Conference, in session at the same time; and of the Old School and New School Presbyterian General Assemblies, at Newark, N. J., and Dayton, O., in favor of emancipation *(Lib.* 34 : 99).

Edwin M. Stanton.

Room, we went to see Secretary Stanton, and had a long private interview with him of a most interesting character. I was very much pleased with him, and have no doubt of his thorough-going anti-slavery spirit and purpose.[1] But I cannot give particulars.

Secretary Chase is out of the city. Neither Seward nor Blair will get a call.

From the White House, we then went to the Capitol, and there found Congress in session. We sent in our cards to Sumner and Wilson, who instantly came out and insisted on our going upon the floor of the Senate, where we really had no right to be. Sumner conducted me to John P. Hale's chair, which I occupied for some time — Hale not being present. A great number of the Senators were introduced to me; among them were Fessenden, Wade, Wilkinson, Morgan, etc. Quite a sensation was produced by my presence. Sumner and Wilson were exceedingly marked in their attentions.

W. P. Fessenden, B. F. Wade, M. S. Wilkinson, E. D. Morgan.

Tilton and I went afterwards to see where we could find a room at the principal hotel to occupy, but our application was in vain. Every hotel is more than full. Fortunately for us, Senator Wilson insisted on our coming to his hotel (the Washington), and by his influence got a room for us. We have dined and taken tea with Wilson, who is unremitting in his attentions. To-morrow we shall go to the House of Representatives — to Arlington Heights — etc., etc. . . .

MS.

WASHINGTON, June 10, 1864.
At the White House.

I am now at the White House, with Tilton, waiting to have a second interview with the President. He has been receiving, for the last hour, the delegates from the several States that voted for his nomination at the Baltimore Convention. I have no special desire to see him again, except that yesterday he expressed the hope that I would call again; for I know he must be bored with callers.

[1] As a boy, Stanton had often sat on the knees of Benjamin Lundy, who used to visit his father's house when on his anti-slavery missions. In a letter urging Mr. Garrison to visit Washington, Senator Wilson wrote (MS. Feby. 11, 1864) that, in a recent interview with Secretary Stanton, the latter stated that his father gave Lundy the money to start his paper, and "then remarked that there was *one person whom he wished to see* before he died, and *that person was yourself.* I therefore write to request you to pay your numerous friends here a visit, and at the same time gratify the wish of the Hon. Secretary."

PHILADELPHIA, June 11, 1864. *MS.*

It is now 3 o'clock P. M. I left Washington this morning, and have just arrived here — very dusty and tired, but in good health and spirits.

Yesterday noon, Tilton and I had an hour's private interview with the President at the White House, and it was a very satisfactory one indeed. There is no mistake about it in regard to Mr. Lincoln's desire to do all that he can see it right and possible for him to do to uproot slavery, and give fair-play to the emancipated. I was much pleased with his spirit, and the familiar and candid way in which he unbosomed himself.

William Whiting.

Last evening I spent with Solicitor Whiting (the brother of Anna), and had a good time.[1]

In his interview with the President, Mr. Garrison said to him: "Mr. Lincoln, I want to tell you frankly that for every word I have ever spoken in your favor, I have spoken ten in favor of General Frémont"; and he went on to explain how difficult he had found it to commend the President when the latter was revoking the proclamations of Frémont and Hunter, and reiterating his purpose to save the Union, if he could, without destroying slavery; "but, Mr. President," he continued, "from the hour that you issued the Emancipation Proclamation, and showed your purpose to stand by it, I have given you my hearty support and confidence." Mr. Lincoln received this good-naturedly, set forth the difficulties under which he had labored, and expressed his anxiety to secure the adoption of the Constitutional Amendment, that the question might be forever settled and not hazarded by his possible death or failure of reëlection. The resolution in favor of it adopted at Baltimore had been prepared and introduced at his own suggestion.

The Amendment failed to pass the House of Representatives before Congress adjourned for the summer,[2] but

[1] Solicitor William Whiting, whom Secretary Stanton appointed to expound the war powers of the Government under the Constitution, especially as relating to slavery, was a son of Mr. Garrison's early and steadfast supporter, Col. William Whiting of Concord, Mass.

[2] The vote was 93 in favor to 65 against, less than the necessary two-thirds.

CHAP. IV. 1864. was saved from final defeat by a motion to reconsider, which carried it over to the winter session. Thanks to the untiring exertions of Senator Sumner, the long spring session did not end until the Fugitive Slave Laws of 1793 and 1850 had both been swept from the statute-books. One of the obstacles he encountered was reported in the following private note:

Lib. 34:99, 118.

Charles Sumner to W. L. Garrison.

MS.

SENATE CHAMBER,
23d April, '64.

DEAR MR. GARRISON:

You will see what has occurred in the Senate. We were on the point of passing a little bill repealing "all acts or parts of acts" for the surrender of fugitive slaves, when John Sherman of Ohio interfered to keep alive the old act of 1793; and Foster of Connecticut has followed with an elaborate speech vindicating the atrocity.

L. S. Foster; ante, 1:392.

The vote in favor of slave-hunting stood 24 to 17, including *ten* Republicans in the majority.[1] If the anti-slavery sentiment had not become so sluggish, this could not have taken place. Cannot you help to revive it? The *practical measures* are to clean the statute-book of all support of slavery.

Ever yours,
CHARLES SUMNER.

Not only was the repeal of both laws secured by Mr. Sumner, but through his efforts the coastwise slave-trade, which Mr. Garrison had earned his prison-cell by denouncing in 1830, was abolished, and the exclusion of colored witnesses from United States Courts prohibited. No less cheering than these gains was the action of the newly-reconstructed States of Arkansas and Louisiana, in adopting free Constitutions, the former by popular vote, and the latter by a Constitutional Convention; but in both cases

[1] The position taken by these Republican opponents was, that, having sworn to support the Constitution with its slave-hunting proviso, they could not vote to repeal all acts for the rendition of fugitive slaves, though they had already voted for the Constitutional Amendment abolishing slavery! Such of these conscientious gentlemen as he could not convert, Mr. Sumner persuaded to absent themselves when the final vote was taken, and Messrs. Sherman and Foster were among these (*Lib.* 34 : 118).

only a fraction of the voters of 1860 participated, and the influence of the Administration at Washington was controlling. Much more significant, therefore, was the regeneration of Maryland, which worked out its own salvation, and adopted, in June, a Constitutional amendment by which, on its ratification by the people in October, slavery was at once and unconditionally abolished, without any pecuniary compensation to the masters.[1]

CHAP. IV. 1864. *Lib.* 34:107.

In November came the triumphant reëlection of Lincoln, an event whose importance was justly estimated by the friends of Union and Emancipation abroad, anxious watchers of the progress of the campaign. To these Mr. Garrison's support of the President had given the liveliest satisfaction, which was increased by his rejoinders to two letters written by Prof. Francis W. Newman of London University, a solitary sympathizer with the utter distrust of Mr. Lincoln shown by Mr. Phillips and his followers. In the first of these Mr. Garrison wrote:

Lib. 34:6, 54, 157, 177, 185. *Lib.* 34:106, 114, 118, 158.

"I am neither the partisan nor eulogist of President Lincoln, in a political sense. Since his inauguration, I have seen occasion sharply to animadvert upon his course, as well as occasion to praise him. At all times I have endeavored to judge him fairly, according to the possibilities of his situation and the necessities of the country. In no instance, however, have I censured him for not acting upon the highest abstract principles of justice and humanity, and disregarding his Constitutional obligations. His freedom to follow his convictions of duty as an individual is one thing—as the President of the United States, it is limited by the functions of his office; for the people do not elect a President to play the part of reformer or philanthropist, nor to enforce upon the nation his own peculiar ethical or humanitary ideas, without regard to his oath or

Lib. 34:114.

1 Potential in causing this remarkable conversion was the perception of the poor whites of Maryland that the free enlistment of colored troops in the State would wonderfully aid in filling the State's quota, and relieve themselves from entering the army. See the speech of Henry Winter Davis in Congress, Feb. 25, 1864, *Lib.* 34 : 65. The amendment, though adopted by 53 to 27 votes in the Convention, would have failed of ratification but for the soldier vote, which gave it a bare majority (*Lib.* 34 : 107, 171). For Mr. Garrison's jubilant letter on its ratification by the people, see *Lib.* 34 : 198.

CHAP. IV. — 1864.

their will. His primary and all-comprehensive duty is to maintain the Union and execute the Constitution, in good faith, according to the best of his ability, without reference to the views of any clique or party in the land, and for the general welfare. And herein lies the injustice of your criticism upon him. You seem to regard him as occupying a position and wielding powers virtually autocratic, so that he may do just as he pleases — yea, just as though there were no people to consult, no popular sentiment to ascertain, no legal restrictions to bind."[1]

Harriet Martineau to W. L. Garrison.

MS.

AMBLESIDE, August 10, 1864.

I have been thinking of you with strong sympathy for a long time past. Indeed, as you know, I always did; but I mean particularly since your precious wife's illness, and since the peculiar trial . . . of your being misunderstood and unkindly treated by old comrades and disciples who should have distrusted their own judgment rather than doubt *you*. . . . If there was any way in which I could publicly express my own views in the matter, I should be very glad to bear my testimony to what seems to me our entire agreement on the question of Mr. Lincoln's character, deserts, and claims to reëlection; and to express my hearty admiration of the magnanimity of your conduct, as well as of the justness and clearness of your views in the most critical hour of the history of your Republic. All who know me here know what I think; and if it could be of any use (which I hardly suppose), its being understood on your side of the water, I should be glad that it *was* known.

J. E. Cairnes.

Professor Cairnes called here ten days ago. I seldom or never see any visitor now (being too ill), except near neighbors and friends; but I could not send away *that* stranger-friend (for we had never met) without a word, and I rejoice that he came. He had been travelling, and had not seen the *Liberator* containing Mr. Newman's letter. He took it away with him; and when he brought it back next day, he expressed strong surprise,— well as he knows Mr. Newman,— at the absurdity, and regret

F. W. Newman.

[1] "I regarded your father as a man of noble nature, but with concentrated views — I do not say 'narrow,' because they were as wide as a race and included their emancipation. But in his reply to Prof. Newman there was that largeness of view and recognition of outside difficulties which we call the statesmanlike quality of mind" (MS. May 14, 1887, Geo. Jacob Holyoake to W. P. G.).

at the tone of that letter. . . . Professor Cairnes and I were anxious each to know what the other thought of Mr. Lincoln, and of your course; and it was pleasant to find how entirely we agreed. . . . CHAP. IV. — 1864.

We judge it best to avow on all reasonable occasions our wish for Mr. Lincoln's reëlection, and our respect for the patriotism and wisdom of abolitionists who are forbearing with his human frailties, for the sake of the national welfare. . . . I say as much as circumstances permit in honor of Mr. Lincoln in the *Daily News*, and I shall try my best to work in that, the best possible direction.

Yours, dear friend, affectionately,

H. MARTINEAU.

Thomas Hughes to W. L. Garrison.

3 OLD SQUARE, LINCOLN'S INN,
LONDON, Sept. 9, 1864. *MS.* *Lib.* 34:158.

MY DEAR SIR: I cannot resist writing you a line, though you have probably scarcely ever heard my name, to say how right and wise I and many other Englishmen think the course you have taken upon the question of supporting Mr. Lincoln for re-election. I was much pained by Professor Newman's letter to you; still more by the line which many of the leading American abolitionists have taken upon the question, and by the tone they have thought fit to adopt as to yourself. I think I may safely say that the great majority of Englishmen who have really taken the trouble to study the question, agree with me in thinking that Mr. Lincoln has proved himself thoroughly honest and trustworthy in the fearfully difficult and trying position in which your nation have placed him, and that these qualities far more than outweigh his faults, which have been only such as arise from caution and distrust of himself.

It would be impertinent in me to add any opinions of my own as to your great revolution. My only excuse for writing at all is, that I have taken the deepest interest for many years in American politics, and especially in the noble stand which you and others have made against slavery in the United States; and I could not remain silent when some of the ablest and best of your own friends are turning against you for conduct which seems to me most wise, and consistent with all you have said and written for the last thirty years.

Whatever other issue your tremendous struggle may have, it seems clear that God will, through it, make an end of slavery on

Chap. IV. — 1864.

your continent; and that end will have been cheaply purchased even if the Union should perish.

Believe me, with all good wishes for your own and your country's future,

Most truly yours,

Thos. Hughes.

As we have already stated, one of Mr. Lincoln's chief offences, in the eyes of Mr. Phillips and his supporters, was his apparent willingness to have Louisiana readmitted to the Union without enfranchising the freedmen. They pointed to the fact that when the free colored men of New Orleans, who had raised a regiment for the defence of the city within forty-eight hours, pending a threatened rebel attack, had asked to be enrolled as voters at the election which soon after ensued for the reorganization of the State, the Military Governor who had invoked their aid, and was now ordering the election, and the General commanding the Department, refused their application. Military power could abrogate the provisions of the old State Constitution so far as to allow white soldiers and sailors to vote, but declined to recognize those who were black. The assumption that Mr. Lincoln was either hostile or indifferent to the matter was erroneous, however. On the contrary, he favored the extension of the suffrage to such colored men as were qualified by intelligence or by having borne arms in defense of the Union, and he suggested that a provision to that effect be made in the new Constitution.[1] In May, Miller McKim wrote from Washington to Mr. Garrison: "I have had an interview with the President since I have been here—not of my seeking. I . . . have seen some of the correspondence between Mr. Lincoln and New Orleans. It is greatly to Mr. Lincoln's credit as a friend to the black man. Mr. Lincoln is in advance of his party on the question of negro suffrage. Not in advance of all, but of the majority."

Brig.-Gen. Geo. F. Shepley. Gen. N. P. Banks. Lib. 34:55, 63.

Letter to Gov. Michael Hahn.

MS. May 5, 1864.

[1] Under pressure from General Banks, a clause authorizing the Legislature to extend the suffrage to such citizens was finally inserted (*Lib.* 34:182).

In his reply to Professor Newman, who had especially dwelt upon the Louisiana question, and condemned the President for not enfranchising the colored men of that State, Mr. Garrison asked:

"By what political precedent or administrative policy, in any country, could he have been justified if he had attempted to do this? When was it ever known that liberation from bondage was accompanied by a recognition of political equality? Chattels personal may be instantly translated from the auction-block into freemen; but when were they ever taken at the same time to the ballot-box, and invested with all political rights and immunities? According to the laws of development and progress, it is not practicable. To denounce or complain of President Lincoln for not disregarding public sentiment, and not flying in the face of these laws, is hardly just. Besides, I doubt whether he has the constitutional right to decide this matter. Ever since this government was organized, the right of suffrage has been determined by each State in the Union for itself, so that there is no uniformity in regard to it. In some free States, colored citizens are allowed to vote; in others, they are not. It is always a State, never a national, matter. In honestly seeking to preserve the Union, it is not for President Lincoln to seek, by a special edict applied to a particular State or locality, to do violence to a universal rule, accepted and acted upon from the beginning till now by the States in their individual sovereignty. Under the war power, he had the constitutional right to emancipate the slaves in every rebel State, and also to insist that, in any plan of reconstruction that might be agreed upon, slavery should be admitted to be dead, beyond power of resurrection. That being accomplished, I question whether he could safely or advantageously—to say the least—enforce a rule, *ab initio,* touching the ballot, which abolishes complexional distinctions; any more than he could safely or advantageously decree that all women (whose title is equally good) should enjoy the electoral right, and help form the State. Nor, if the freed blacks were admitted to the polls by Presidential fiat, do I see any permanent advantage likely to be secured by it; for, submitted to as a necessity at the outset, as soon as the State was organized and left to manage its own affairs, the white population, with their superior intelligence, wealth, and power, would unquestionably alter the franchise in accordance with their prejudices, and exclude those thus summarily brought to the polls. Coercion would gain

Lib. 34:118.

CHAP. IV. 1864. nothing. In other words,—as in your own country,—universal suffrage will be hard to win and to hold without a general preparation of feeling and sentiment. But it will come, both at the South and with you; yet only by a struggle *on the part of the disfranchised*, and a growing conviction of its justice, 'in the good time coming.' With the abolition of slavery in the South, prejudice or 'colorphobia,' the natural product of the system, will gradually disappear — as in the case of your West India colonies — and black men will win their way to wealth, distinction, eminence, and official station. I ask only a charitable judgment for President Lincoln respecting this matter, whether in Louisiana or any other State."[1]

In the closing numbers of the *Liberator* volume, Mr. Garrison laid stress on the grave problems involved in
Lib. 34:194. the reconstruction of the rebellious States, at the hands of Congress, and on the duty of securing the enactment of
Lib. 34:190. the Thirteenth Amendment, abolishing slavery. For this Amendment the President, in his Message to Congress, made an earnest plea, and solemnly renewed his vow never to retract or modify his Proclamation, or to return to slavery any person emancipated by its terms, or by any
Lib. 34:199. of the acts of Congress. "If the people should," he added, "by whatever mode or means, make it an Executive duty to reënslave such persons, another, not I, must be their instrument to perform it."

Once more the expediency of consolidating the *Liberator* and *Standard* was privately considered, the ever-increasing cost of paper making it difficult to sustain

[1] Another indictment, constantly reiterated, against Mr. Lincoln was his assent to the Labor System established in Louisiana by General Banks, who was accused of having forced the freedmen back under their old masters and reduced them to a state of serfdom scarcely better than slavery. Mr. Garrison refused to accept these assertions until he could investigate the matter, and it subsequently appeared that they were altogether unjust and exaggerated. The Labor System, which insured employment at fair wages to the men, and provisions and shelter for their families, saved hundreds from the demoralization and death which decimated them when they swarmed about the Union camps; and the Educational System, which went hand in hand with it, gave instruction to more than 11,000 children. Both departments were under the charge of radical abolitionists and friends of Mr. Garrison, Major B. Rush Plumly of Philadelphia, and Rev. Edwin M. Wheelock of New Hampshire (*Lib.* 34 : 155, 160, 181, 182; 35 : 30, 34).

both,[1] but it was finally decided to increase the price of each, and try to prolong their individual existence until the passage and ratification of the Amendment should warrant their discontinuance. To Oliver Johnson, who had strongly urged their union, on the ground that Mr. Garrison would thus be relieved of the toil of the printing-office, and could, by editorial correspondence with the *Standard*, easily satisfy the *Liberator* subscribers, whose interest in the paper was largely personal to him, the latter wrote:

MS. Nov. 26, 1864.

"I am not insensible to the compliment intended to be conveyed in the assurance, that it is what *I* write that alone interests the readers of the *Liberator;* but I am not willing to believe, after an editorial experience of thirty-eight years, that, aside from my own lucubrations, I have neither the tact nor the talent to make an interesting journal. This touches me too closely. If the *Liberator* has been at all effective in the past, it has been owing to its completeness, as a whole, from week to week, and not to what I have written. This is the true value of every journal. My selections have cost me much labor, and they have been made with all possible discrimination as to their interest, ability, and appositeness. The amount of communicated original matter has always been much larger than that of the *Standard;* and though not always of special interest or value,

[1] An additional embarrassment arose, in the case of the *Liberator*, from the action of the Hovey Committee, who had hitherto paid for one hundred copies of the paper, for gratuitous circulation. They now stopped the appropriation, "on the alleged ground . . . that the *Liberator*, for the countenance it has given to President Lincoln and his administration, 'has no more claim to be circulated by the Committee than any other *Republican* paper'" (*Lib.* 34 : 210). The Draper Brothers of Hopedale, Mass., Edward Harris of Woonsocket, R. I., Samuel E. Sewall, and others voluntarily assumed the burden thus dropped by the Committee. From Henry Ward Beecher there came the following gay and characteristic note (MS.):

BROOKLYN, Feb. 4, 1865.

MY DEAR MR. GARRISON: I have had the *Liberator* sent to me, free, for several years; on the principle, I presume, that I *needed* it. So long as I was in a state of nature, I consented to have a free gospel preached to me. But, as I have made up my mind, at length, that slavery is an evil, and ought to be abolished, I suppose that I can find no good reason for taking the *Liberator* without paying for it. I am truly yours, H. W. BEECHER.

Please find a check for $25.00.

CHAP. IV. — 1864.

it has made the *Liberator* less a transcript, and more readable on that account.

"The *Liberator* has an historic position and a moral prestige which would be lost should it be merged in the *Standard*. True, the loss would be the same should the paper be discontinued; but I shall try to prevent this by increasing the subscription price for the next volume. I confess to a strong desire to keep it along till the Amendment of the Constitution is secured, and slavery abolished. It will then have accomplished its anti-slavery mission. . . .

"Though you may still feel that the plan you have urged, as to the union of the two papers, is wisest and best, I know you will readily acquiesce in the decision to which I have come; especially as that decision seems to accord with the judgment of the Executive Committee at the present time.

"Accept, dear Johnson, a renewal of my grateful acknowledgments for your many kindnesses, and the lively interest you have ever evinced in my welfare and happiness. I have not a more attached or a more disinterested friend in the world than yourself. And the anti-slavery cause has never found a truer advocate or a more faithful laborer than you have been from the hour you espoused it."

CHAPTER V.

THE JUBILEE.—1865.

SWIFTLY following the example of Maryland, Missouri joined the ranks of the free States at the beginning of the new year, and abolished slavery within her borders without a day of grace or a cent of compensation to the slave-masters.[1] As if shamed to decency by this signal repentance of her neighbor, Illinois tardily repealed her infamous "Black Laws"; and on the last day of January the Thirteenth Amendment to the Constitution, forever abolishing slavery in the United States, triumphantly passed the House of Representatives at Washington by the requisite two-thirds majority. "With devout thanksgiving to God, and emotions of joy which no language can express," Mr. Garrison announced the event to his readers, and when the salute of one hundred guns in its honor was fired by Gov. Andrew's order, he went up to the Common to enjoy the sight and listen to the reverberations. At the Governor's suggestion and request, the church bells were rung throughout the State; and it was while sitting in the quiet Friends' Meeting at Amesbury that Mr. Whittier heard these, and, divining the caŭse, framed in thought his inspired lines of praise and thanksgiving ("Laus Deo!"), which Mr. Garrison never wearied of repeating. A Jubilee Meeting was speedily convened in Music Hall, which was crowded with an enthusiastic audience, and when the chairman (Josiah

CHAP. V. — 1865. Jan. 11. — Lib. 35:28. — Lib. 35:18. — Feb. 4.

[1] The new Constitution was adopted in State Convention without submission to popular vote. The clause abolishing slavery passed by a vote of 60 to 4 (*Lib.* 35 : 11).

Chap. V. 1865.

Quincy, Jr.) introduced Mr. Garrison as the first speaker of the evening, the latter received such an ovation that he was unable to proceed for several minutes. His speech was naturally exultant, anticipating the future greatness and prosperity of the country, and its influence upon other nations, and (by way of impressing upon his hearers the full significance of this latest triumph) rehearsing the pro-slavery clauses of the Constitution which were now abrogated by the Amendment. We quote his words of rejoicing, at the beginning:

Lib. 35:22.

"*Mr. Chairman, Ladies and Gentlemen:* In the long course of history, there are events of such transcendant sublimity and importance as to make all human speech utterly inadequate to portray the emotions they excite. The event we are here to celebrate is one of these — grand, inspiring, glorious, beyond all power of utterance, and far-reaching beyond all finite computation. (Applause.) . . .

"Sir, no such transition of feeling and sentiment as has taken place within the last four years, stands recorded on the historic page; a change that seems as absolute as it is stupendous. Allow me to confess that, in view of it, and of the mighty consequences that must result from it to unborn generations, I feel to-night in a thoroughly methodistical state of mind — disposed at the top of my voice, and to the utmost stretch of my lungs, to shout 'Glory!' 'Alleluia!' 'Amen and amen!' (Rapturous applause —'Glory!' 'Alleluia!' 'Amen and amen!' being repeated with great unction by various persons in the audience.) Gladly and gratefully would I exclaim with one of old, 'The Lord hath done great things for us, whereof we are glad.' (Applause.) With the rejoicing Psalmist I would say to the old and the young, 'O give thanks unto the Lord, for he is good; for his mercy endureth forever. To him alone that doeth great wonders; for his mercy endureth forever. To him that overthrew Pharaoh and his host in the Red sea; for his mercy endureth forever. And brought out Israel from among them, with a strong hand, and with a stretched-out arm; for his mercy endureth forever.' (Loud applause.) 'Let everything that hath breath praise the Lord!'

"Mr. Chairman, friends and strangers stop me in the streets, daily, to congratulate me on having been permitted to live to witness the almost miraculous change which has taken place in the feelings and sentiments of the people on the subject of slavery, and in favor of the long rejected but ever just and humane doctrine of immediate and universal emancipation. Ah, sir, no man living better understands or more joyfully recognizes the vastness of that change than I do. But most truly can I say that it causes within me no feeling of personal pride or exultation — God forbid! But I am unspeakably happy to believe, not only that this vast assembly, but that the great mass of my countrymen, are now heartily disposed to admit that, in disinterestedly seeking, by all righteous instrumentalities, for more than thirty years, the utter abolition of slavery, I have not acted the part of a madman, fanatic, incendiary, or traitor (immense applause), but have at all times been of sound mind (laughter and cheers), a true friend of liberty and humanity, animated by the highest patriotism, and devoted to the welfare, peace, unity, and ever increasing prosperity and glory of my native land! (Cheers.) And the same verdict you will render in vindication of the clear-sighted, untiring, intrepid, unselfish, uncompromising anti-slavery phalanx, who, through years of conflict and persecution — misrepresented, misunderstood, ridiculed, and anathematized from one end of the country to the other — have labored 'in season and out of season' to bring about this glorious result. (Renewed applause.) You will, I venture to think and say, agree with me, that only RADICAL ABOLITIONISM is, at this trial-hour, LOYALTY, JUSTICE, IMPARTIAL FREEDOM, NATIONAL SALVATION — the Golden Rule blended with the Declaration of Independence! (Great applause.) . . .

"Do we realize the grandeur of the event we are assembled to celebrate? It is not merely negro emancipation, but universal emancipation. (Cheers.) It is not merely disenthralling four millions, but thirty-four millions. (Renewed cheers.) It is not merely liberating bodies, but souls — outwardly and inwardly alike. It is an act, not in hostility to the South, but for the general welfare — the good of the whole country. It is not to depress or injure any class, but to promote all human interests. In fine, it is the Declaration of Independence, no longer an abstract manifesto, containing certain 'glittering generalities,' simply to vindicate our Revolutionary fathers for seceding from the mother country; but it is that Declaration CONSTITUTIONALIZED — made THE SUPREME LAW OF THE LAND —

Lib. 35 : 23.

for the protection of the rights and liberties of all who dwell on the American soil. (Cheers.)"[1]

And now came an invitation from the citizens of Newburyport, begging their former townsman, to whom, during the entire anti-slavery struggle, they had as a community turned the cold shoulder, to return to his old home and receive their congratulations on the triumphant culmination of his life-work. "The town of your nativity sends you greeting on the successful passage of the act of Congress," concluded the letter, which bore the signatures of twenty-eight of the leading citizens. In compliance with this request, which was as gratifying as it was unexpected, Mr. Garrison visited his birthplace on the 22d of February, and delivered an address to an audience which packed the City Hall to overflowing and received him with the greatest enthusiasm. The editor of the *Herald* presided and made the welcoming address, and Whittier, too modest, as usual, to appear in person, wrote for the occasion the beautiful hymn included in his collected works — not less felicitous than his "Laus Deo," nor less in consonance with Mr. Garrison's spirit and devout thought. This, too, the latter constantly read and quoted as expressing better than any words of his own the song of praise in his heart:

MS. Feb. 8.

Lib. 35:34, 35.

Geo. J. L. Colby.

Household Ed., p. 357.

"Not unto us who did but seek
The word that burned within to speak,
Not unto us this day belong
The triumph and exulting song.

. . . .

"Nor skill, nor strength, nor zeal of ours
Has mined and heaved the hostile towers;
Not by our hands is turned the key
That sets the sighing captives free.

"A redder sea than Egypt's wave
Is piled and parted for the slave;

[1] Another meeting to celebrate the Amendment was held in Tremont Temple, February 13, under the auspices of the colored people; Phillips, Garrison, and Thompson being among the speakers (*Lib.* 35 : 27).

A darker cloud moves on in light,
A fiercer fire is guide by night!

"The praise, O Lord! is Thine alone,
In Thy own way Thy work is done!
Our poor gifts at Thy feet we cast,
To whom be glory, first and last!"

"The remembrance of my recent visit to Newburyport," wrote Mr. Garrison to Jacob Horton, "and the generous and handsome reception which was accorded to me by the citizens, for dear Liberty's sake, will carry with it a delightful aroma while memory lasts." The demonstration, tardy atonement as it was on the part of the old town, was typical of the utter revolution in public sentiment towards the editor of the *Liberator*, and of the general respect and confidence which he now enjoyed. His opinions were sought and his influence solicited by men prominent in public or political life, and in a way at times quite amusing to him, as when one of the Republican leaders of Massachusetts begged him to urge Mr. Lincoln to summon Governor Andrew to his Cabinet. "The President recognizes you as one of '*the Powers*'—a Radical with a substratum of common sense and practical wisdom. He will heed your suggestions," wrote this gentleman. But Mr. Garrison disclaimed any such influence, and did not now attempt to dabble in political wire-pulling or Cabinet-making. His only intercourse with the President was the social hour he spent with him in June, 1864, and the only favors he ever asked of him were the careful consideration of charges against an officer under arrest, whom he believed to be innocent, but who must nevertheless stand or fall by the evidence that might be adduced; and the acknowledgment of a painting[1] presented to Mr. Lincoln by citizens of Boston several months before, no word from its recipient having

MS. Mar. 17, 1865.

MS. Jan. 18, 1865, J. M. Forbes to W. L. G.

Ante, p. 117.

[1] "Waiting for the Hour," an oil painting by W. T. Carleton of Boston, representing a Watch Meeting of Slaves on the night before the Emancipation Proclamation, Dec. 31, 1862.

CHAP. V. 1865. ever reached the donors. The officer in question was released, and the following "ingenuous and appreciative letter" of thanks sent for the picture:

President Lincoln to W. L. Garrison.

MS. and Lib. 35:27.

EXECUTIVE MANSION,
WASHINGTON, 7th February, 1865.

MY DEAR MR. GARRISON:

I have your kind letter of the 21st of January, and can only beg that you will pardon the seeming neglect occasioned by my constant engagements. When I received the spirited and admirable painting, "Waiting for the Hour," I directed my Secretary not to acknowledge its arrival at once, preferring to make my personal acknowledgment of the thoughtful kindness of the donors; and, waiting for some leisure hour, I have committed the discourtesy of not replying at all.

I hope you will believe that my thanks, though late, are most cordial, and I request that you will convey them to those associated with you in this flattering and generous gift.

I am, very truly, your friend and servant,
A. LINCOLN.[1]

W. T. Sherman. Jan. 16, 1865. *Lib.* 35:24. An order of General Sherman, assigning the abandoned lands in the Sea Islands for settlement by the freedmen, having occasioned some misapprehension and adverse comment, the Secretary of War deemed it advisable to write to Mr. Garrison personally concerning it:

Edwin M. Stanton to W. L. Garrison.

MS. Private.

WAR DEPARTMENT,
WASHINGTON CITY, Feb. 12, 1865.

DEAR SIR: I take the liberty of enclosing to you a copy of the "Minutes" of an interview between General Sherman and *(Sic.)* myself with the Colored Ministers and Church Members of

[1] "It was my privilege once, and once only, to talk with Abraham Lincoln, at Petersburg, Va., April 6, 1865. His face, his figure, his attitudes, his words, form the most remarkable picture in my memory, and will while memory lasts. I spoke to him of the country's gratitude for his great deliverance of the slaves. His sad face beamed for a moment with happiness as he answered in exact substance, and very nearly in words: 'I have been only an instrument. The logic and moral power of Garrison, and the anti-slavery people of the country and the army, have done all'" (Daniel H. Chamberlain, ex-Governor of South Carolina, in N. Y. *Tribune*, Nov. 4, 1883).

Savannah, during my late visit to that city. The occasion was one of deep interest to me, and will no doubt be interesting to you, besides serving to correct misapprehensions and misgivings in the minds of many persons. The order of General Sherman assigning lands to the colored people was made the day after that interview. His order has been criticised as evincing hostility to the blacks by setting them apart by themselves, as if they were an inferior race. But you will not fail to observe that this point was distinctly presented to the Ministers and others present, all of whom, with one exception, expressed a decided sentiment in favor of their separation, and assigned their reasons. The question was one upon which the General and myself felt much embarrassment, but we thought the intelligent persons whom we consulted were best able to form an enlightened judgment by which we could safely be guided.

CHAP. V. — 1865.

With great regard, I am truly yours,

EDWIN M. STANTON.

The dramatic incidents of the war had been many and striking, and each month brought its fresh example of retributive justice, of strange contrast and coincidence. There was the occupation of General Lee's estate at Arlington as a Freedmen's village (with its Garrison and Lovejoy Streets) and national cemetery; of John Tyler's and Henry A. Wise's residences by schools for colored children — the daughter of John Brown teaching in the latter, with her father's portrait hanging on the wall; and of Jefferson Davis's plantation on the Mississippi as a "contraband" camp, and its final purchase and cultivation by his former slaves; the teaching of a freedman's school in Maryland by the son of Frederick Douglass, near the place whence his father had escaped; the burning of Harper's Ferry by General Hector Tyndale of Philadelphia, who three years before had visited the town with his fellow-citizen, J. M. McKim, to claim the body of John Brown and take it to the North;[1] the appointment of

Lib. 34: 1, 128.

Lib. 32: 155; 34: 19; 35: 45.

Lib. 34: 15, 121.

Lib. 33: 136.

Lib. 33: 27.

1 "That right hand which lifted the coffin of John Brown to its place at the station, by the orders of his Government put the first torch to the hotel in which he [Tyndale] was insulted! And the conflagration was not stopped until, with poetic justice, he commanded his brigade to spare the engine-house, the Gibraltar from which the brave old man fired his first gun at Virginia slavery" (Speech of Wendell Phillips, Jan. 29, 1863. *Lib.* 33 : 27).

CHAP. V. 1865. John Brown's trusted friend, George L. Stearns, as Assistant Adjutant-General of the United States for the enrolment of colored troops, with headquarters at Nashville—"appointed to do, under the stars and stripes, in broad daylight, by wholesale, what Virginia murdered Brown for trying to do in detail." (*Speech of Wendell Phillips, Jan. 28, 1864. Lib. 34:22.*) There was the case of an indignant Union General (*Brig.-Gen. Edward A. Wild.*) who directed a brutal slave-owner to be tied up and flogged by the slave women whom he had himself been scourging. (*Lib. 34:91.*) Colored schools in South Carolina and Louisiana and a camp of colored soldiers in Kansas bore the name of William Lloyd Garrison; (*Lib. 35:179; 33:144.*) and one of the gunners who aimed the first great Parrott gun at Charleston was a *Liberator* subscriber. (*Lib. 34:114.*) But scenes and events still more dramatic and impressive were to come, and it is not probable that the United States will ever see the parallel in this respect of the ninety days ending with the month of April, 1865.

Threatened by the triumphant Northern march of Sherman's army, the rebel forces defending Fort Sumter and Charleston abandoned both, and they fell into the hands of the Union forces on the 18th of February. Three days later the 55th Massachusetts Regiment entered the city, singing exultantly the John Brown song; (*Lib. 35:39.*) and when Lieut. George Thompson Garrison halted his company in the streets, he was greeted by James Redpath, the biographer of John Brown, and the then correspondent of the New York *Tribune*. (*Lib. 35:56.*) Redpath it was who now went promptly to work to establish free schools in the deserted "cradle of secession," ignoring all complexional distinctions among the pupils. The slave-pens were broken open, and mottoes from Isaiah, Garrison, and John Brown inscribed therein; (*Lib. 35:39.*) and the steps of the auction-block in the Mart, up which so many thousands of unhappy victims had walked to meet their fate, were sent to Boston, there to be exhibited in meetings in behalf of the freedmen, and to incite contributions for the educational societies. Their first appearance was at Music Hall, (*March 9.*) together with the sign ("MART") which had hung in front of the auction-house, and the lock of the room in which women had been subjected to examination before sale; and all three relics of barbarism were then presented to the local Freedmen's Aid Society by Charles Carleton Coffin, war correspondent of the Boston *Journal*, who had brought them from Charleston. Mr. Garrison's ascent of the steps, from which he made his speech, was the event of the evening; and when he had put the "accursed thing under his feet," the scene was "one of unusual interest and excitement, the audience raising thunders of applause and waving hundreds of white handkerchiefs." "I attended," he wrote to a friend, "a similar meeting, for a similar purpose, at Lowell on Wednesday evening last, and, on taking the block, was greeted with the strongest demonstrations of applause, prolonged and repeated, as though there were to be no end to them. What a revolution!"

CHAP. V. — 1865.

Lib 35:42.

MS. Mar. 17, *to Jacob Horton.*

Mar. 15.

With the rebellion rapidly approaching its "last ditch," the Confederacy in such straits that even General Lee advocated arming the blacks for its defence, the doom of slavery assured, and the President of the United States, in his inaugural address, reverently recognizing the justice of the Divine judgments meted out to North and South alike for their guilty complicity in enslaving their fellow-creatures, Mr. Garrison felt that the time had come for him to prepare the "Nunc dimittis" of the *Liberator*. The issue of March 24th contained this formal announcement of his purpose:

Century Magazine, Aug., 1888.

Mar. 4.

"We have concluded to discontinue the *Liberator* at the close of the present year, which will complete its THIRTY-FIFTH volume. As we commenced its publication for the express purpose of effecting the extinction of slavery, and as that sublime event has been consummated by a constitutional decree of the nation, so that henceforth no slave is to be held within the domains of the American Union, it seems to us historically fitting that the *Liberator* should simply cover the whole period of the struggle, and terminate with it. Unless, therefore, something should occur beyond our present belief or anticipation to make it necessary to change our decision, we shall not prolong the existence of the paper beyond this YEAR OF JUBILEE; and have

Lib. 34:46.

CHAP. V. — 1865. instructed our General Agent to take no subscription for a longer period."

The first days of April brought the downfall of Richmond and that memorable Monday morning when "Massa Linkum," entering the city with only a corporal's guard of attendants, was received with the wildest demonstrations by the emancipated blacks, and almost overwhelmed by their tokens of joy and gratitude. Mr. Garrison was one of the multitude assembled in Faneuil Hall on the afternoon of the following day to exult over the event, and to enjoy the unwonted spectacle of Robert C. Winthrop and Frederick Douglass speaking from the same platform. There were loud calls for himself after Douglass had finished his brilliant speech, but he had already left the hall in order to speak at a Freedmen's Aid meeting in Chelsea, where the steps of the auction-block were again a feature of the occasion. Just before he was invited to mount them (over a rebel flag captured by his son's regiment), a telegram was put into his hands, and the applause with which his ascent of the steps was greeted was redoubled when he read aloud to the audience a dispatch from the Secretary of War, inviting him to be present, as a guest of the Government, at the ceremony of raising the stars and stripes on Fort Sumter, on April 14, the fourth anniversary of the surrender of the fort and inauguration of the war.[1] A similar invitation was extended to George Thompson, and a state-room was assigned for their joint use on the steamer *Arago*, which conveyed the invited guests from New York to Charleston. On reaching New York, Mr. Garrison received the following telegram:

April 3. *April 4.*

"WASHINGTON, April 7, 1865.

"The Adjutant-General has been directed to give Captain Garrison a furlough while you are at Charleston. I hope Mr. Thompson accompanies you. A formal invitation was for-

Lieut. G. T. Garrison.

[1] Major-General Robert Anderson had been appointed to perform the act, and Henry Ward Beecher engaged to deliver an oration on the occasion.

warded to him[1] to your care, by mail, and a duplicate will be sent to Fortress Monroe, where I expect to join your party. CHAP. V. 1865.

"EDWIN M. STANTON."

The announcement that Mr. Garrison was to go to Fort Sumter caused general delight and approbation. "Nothing more satisfies me that slavery is annihilated beyond any hope of resurrection than the deference, kindness, and congratulation extended to me by those who are the unerring representatives of public opinion," he wrote to his wife, on the eve of his embarking. *MS. Apr. 7.* "The American Anti-Slavery Society may reasonably conclude that its specific mission is ended."

W. L. Garrison to his Wife.

SUNDAY MORNING, April 9, 1865. *MS.*

Yesterday, at 12 o'clock, M., the *Arago* slowly and majestically left the pier on her way down the harbor for Charleston; *New York harbor.* with a fair wind, a bright sky, and a slight undulation of the waves. There was nothing to be desired in the matter of favorable omens. Up to this hour, everything has gone with us as though we had the elements under our own control — a splendid sunset last evening — a night so brilliant and entrancing that I did not turn into my berth till a late hour. This day the air is warmer, and as beautiful as it can be, and we have come with so little motion that scarcely any have been sea-sick, and, for a wonder, I have experienced no trouble whatever on that score. . . . Everything has been provided on a liberal scale, and we are

1 "I could write much of my own feelings," said George Thompson, in a letter to R. F. Wallcut (April 8), "as I look back upon the thirty years and six months which have elapsed since I landed on the shores from which I am now departing. Then I was denounced by a slaveholding President for preaching the doctrine of Universal Liberty. To-day, I am the guest of an anti-slavery President, on board a United States Government vessel, on an expedition to the city of Charleston, S. C., to see a flag raised which is not only the symbol of Union, but of Freedom. . . . In former years, the question was often put to me, Why don't you go to the South? To-day I answer, I am going; going to celebrate the triumph of Garrisonian abolitionism in Charleston; going in company with Garrison himself; going to tread a once slave-cursed soil soon to be 'redeemed, regenerated, and disenthralled by the irresistible Genius of Universal Emancipation'" (*Lib.* 35 : 58).

Chap. V. — 1865.

living as though we were at a first-class hotel. When we go round Cape Hatteras, we shall probably be put to a much severer test.

Noah H. Swayne. William D. Kelley. Charles Anderson. Robert Anderson. Richard S. Storrs, Jr. Capt. Francis A. Davies. Samuel Scoville. Henry Wilson. John A. Dix. Abner Doubleday.

We have about eighty invited guests on board, bound to see the flag raised at Sumter. Among these are Judge Swayne of the U. S. Supreme Court; Judge Kelley of Philadelphia; Lieut.-Governor Anderson (brother of the General) of Ohio; General Anderson and a portion of his family; Rev. Henry Ward Beecher, with his wife and children; Rev. Dr. Storrs of Brooklyn, who is to perform the religious services this forenoon; Professor Davies of West Point, and other Professors; Rev. Mr. Scoville, son-in-law of Mr. Beecher, with his wife; Senator Wilson; General Dix and General Doubleday; several merchants; and others whom I [am] unable to identify by name or profession. All on board have been very courteous and attentive to George Thompson and myself, and they are manifestly pleased that we are on board. I have had several talks with General Anderson, and he is particularly gratified that we are of the company. He is a very amiable and modest man, and looks and reminds me more of John Brown than any one I have seen. He seems to be quite religious in his spirit, and reverently recognizes the hand of God in all the wonderful events which have taken place.

Henry M. Smith.

The New York *Times*, *Tribune*, and *Herald* have their reporters on board. Mr. Smith, editor of the Chicago *Tribune*, is his own reporter.

There is no stiffness of manners. Every one is ready for conversational interchange; and though we are heterogeneous in the professions and pursuits of life, yet there is entire harmony on the slavery question. Secretary Stanton has evidently made his selections with care.[1]

[1] "Social intercourse was universal; conversation taking a wide range, but having special reference to the state of the country, and its future peace and security. Great apprehension was very generally expressed lest a mistaken leniency should be shown to the leading actors in this horrible rebellion, and concessions made in the reconstruction of the revolted States which would breed another explosion, and again endanger the stability of our Government. Judge Holt was particularly strong and emphatic upon these points. There seemed to be but one feeling; and that was, that sound policy as well as abstract right demanded that the fullest justice should be meted out to the colored population of the South, whose terrible wrongs had brought this tempest of fire and blood upon the land, and upon whose loyalty and valor the chief reliance must be placed in holding the South hereafter to the performance of her constitutional duties" (W. L. G. in *Lib.* 35 : 66).

SUNDAY, 6 P. M. CHAP. V. 1865.

We have passed Cape Henry, and [are] going up to Fortress Monroe, where we shall arrive in the course of another hour. How long we shall remain there, we cannot tell; probably not more than an hour or two. Several additional guests are to come on board, among them Secretary Stanton, if he can leave his post.[1] . . .

Dear Thompson and I have a state-room together. He is very kind and attentive to me, bringing me my coffee before I leave my berth in the morning, as he rises earlier, and assiduous to do all in his power to make the jaunt pleasant to me.

As all has gone well with us thus far, I trust it will to the end. But my thoughts are more with you and the dear ones at home than at Fort Sumter, saving that the prospect of our seeing George brings him before me continually. Will it not be a joyful surprise to him to meet me and Mr. Thompson? *G. T. Garrison.*

W. L. Garrison to his Wife.

CHARLESTON, S. C., April 15, 1865.

We had a fine passage from Fortress Monroe to Hilton Head, where we arrived on Tuesday night. *April* 11. I experienced no seasickness of any account, and therefore enjoyed the trip exceedingly. We had a beautiful moon with us all the way each night, and at times the scene was magical. Our good friends, Mr. and Mrs. Severance, Mr. Pillsbury (brother of Parker),[2] Mr. Dodge, and a number of others were there to give me a warm welcome to the shores of Carolina. *T. C. and C. M. Severance, Gilbert Pillsbury, J. G. Dodge.* The next day we went in the steamer *Delaware* to Savannah, and passed by Fort Pulaski and many other objects of interest, and saw the remains of the formidable obstructions placed in the Savannah river to keep our war vessels at bay. We found carriages waiting for us on our arrival, and went through the principal streets of Savannah, which is a city of mingled gentility and squalor, but entirely dead in regard to all business affairs. Thursday evening we left Hilton Head *April* 13. in the *Arago* for Charleston, where we arrived at daybreak, outside of the bar. At 11 we left for Fort Sumter, and got there a *April* 14. little after 12. A large concourse present. The exercises of

[1] The pressure of official business compelled him to relinquish the trip, most fortunately, as it proved.

[2] Mr. Severance was Collector of the Port at Hilton Head. Mr. Pillsbury soon afterwards became the Republican Mayor of Charleston.

CHAP. V. — 1865.

the highest interest. Beecher's discourse a good one. The enthusiasm immense. Everything went off grandly. Have no time for particulars, as I expected to return home this evening in the *Arago*, but have concluded to remain one week longer, and go again to Savannah and Florida, along with Henry Ward Beecher and family, Tilton, George Thompson, Henry Wilson, etc., etc. Shall probably go to Richmond before getting home. So, be entirely easy about me.

Theodore Tilton.

To-day, we have had three thousand colored people turned out to greet us, and a great procession to escort us, with a band of music, through the principal streets, all the way raising shouts to make the welkin ring! Also, a long procession of girls and boys.[1] We have had a magnificent meeting in Zion's Church—thousands present—which was powerfully addressed by Judge Kelley, George Thompson, Theo. Tilton, Henry Wilson, and also by myself. My reception was beyond all description enthusiastic, and my feelings were unutterable.

Wm. D. Kelley.

G. T. Garrison.

As for our dear George, I have not yet seen him, but expect to in the course of a few hours. He returned with his company last evening, from the interior, with 1,200 slaves, now freemen. I understand he is in good health, and long to embrace him for your sake and mine. When I get back, I shall have a volume of interesting things to communicate to you and the children. God preserve and bless you all! I can add no more, for the boat leaves immediately.

With the exception of a brief editorial in the *Liberator*, on his return, the above is the only personal record left by Mr. Garrison of his experiences in South Carolina. Writing hurriedly in both instances, he failed to note several incidents which we must mention here, quoting from the narratives of others who accompanied him. First in order was a visit, on the day before the Sumter festivities, to Mitchelville, a village of three thousand inhabitants—"the first self-governing settlement of freedmen in the country."[2] Here the members of the *Arago's* party

April 13.

Lib. 35:76.

[1] Two thousand school children had been enrolled and organized by James Redpath in less than two months.

[2] Situated a mile and a half from Hilton Head, and named in honor of the lamented General O. M. Mitchel, who had shown himself an earnest friend of the emancipated race during his command of that Department, until his death in October, 1862.

were received in a church densely crowded by the colored people, who thrilled their guests by the fervor with which they sang their hymns and songs, beginning with those which they had been wont to sing in their days of bondage, and ending with "The Day of Jubilo hab Come," and "John Brown's Body." The meeting was emotional throughout, and "from the most hysterical contraband to the dispassionate judge there was no reserve or restraint in the general flow of tears." Mr. Garrison, who was "rapturously welcomed," began his address by reading Moses's triumphal song, Exodus xv., "and then, for half an hour, magnetized his colored constituents, as he detailed the early history of the anti-slavery movement in America, and sang the praises of the Proclamation which had answered all their prayers." He was followed by Judge Kelley, Theodore Tilton, Judge Kellogg, Joseph Hoxie, and George Thompson, the second of whom aroused the audience most thoroughly.

CHAP. V. — 1865.

Lib. 35:76.

Wm. D. Kelley. Stephen Wright Kellogg.

Of the Sumter celebration, Mr. Garrison wrote:

"The day proved to be very fine, and was ushered in by salvos of artillery. All the vessels in the harbor, including the naval fleet, put on their gayest attire, and the national ensign floated from all the principal fortifications, except Fort Sumter. The services at the Fort were in the highest degree impressive. . . . The speech of General Anderson, previous to hoisting the identical flag which, after an honorable and gallant defence in 1861, he was compelled to lower, was very brief, but uttered with deep feeling; and the address of Mr. Beecher was as happily conceived as it was eloquently expressed, and elicited the most rapturous applause from an immense assembly, thrilled by the sublimity of the scene.

Lib. 35:66.

Robert Anderson.

"To add to the joy and exultation of the occasion, the intelligence had most opportunely arrived that morning of the surrender of General Lee with his army to General Grant; thus giving assurance that the rebellion had gone down just as the 'stars and stripes' were about to be unfurled on Sumter — henceforth the banner of universal emancipation!

"Previous to the raising of the flag the steamer *Planter*, Capt. Robert Smalls, which, it will be remembered, ran the rebel gauntlet in 1862, came to the fort loaded down with between

CHAP. V. 1865. 2000 and 3000 of the emancipated race, of all ages and sizes. Their appearance was warmly welcomed, and their joy seemed to be unbounded. Capt. Smalls was subsequently introduced to many distinguished gentlemen, to whom he narrated his interesting adventure with lively satisfaction.

April 14. "On the evening of that day, a handsome banquet was given at the Charleston Hotel, by General Gillmore, to the invited guests who came in the *Arago;* at the conclusion of which eloquent and stirring speeches were made by Judge Holt, Judge Kelley, Hon. Joseph Hoxie, Lieut.-Governor Anderson, George Thompson, Theodore Tilton, and others. *The* speech of *Joseph Holt. Lib.* 35:69. the occasion was made by Judge Holt, which was one of the most forcible speeches to which we ever listened, and delivered with great energy."[1]

Mr. Thompson and Mr. Garrison were also among the speakers at the banquet, the latter being heartily cheered as he rose to respond to the toast in his honor. Brief as were his remarks, we can quote only the opening and concluding paragraphs:

Lib. 35:76. "My friends, I am so unused to speaking—in this place (cheers and laughter)—that I arise with feelings natural to a first appearance. You would scarce expect one of my age—and antecedents—to speak in public on this stage, or anywhere else in the city of Charleston, South Carolina. (Cheers.) And yet, why should I not speak here? Why should I not speak anywhere in my native land? Why should I not have spoken here twenty years ago, or forty, as freely as any one? What crime had I committed against the laws of my country? I have loved liberty, for myself, for all who are dear to me, for all who dwell on the American soil, for all mankind. The head and front of my offending hath this extent, no more. . . .

"I am here in Charleston, South Carolina. She is smitten to the dust. She has been brought down from her pride of place. The chalice was put to her lips, and she drunk it to the dregs. I have never been her enemy, nor the enemy of the South. Nay,

[1] Major-General Anderson, in responding to a toast in his honor, had paid a warm tribute to Secretary Stanton, General Dix, and Judge Holt for the support which, as members of Buchanan's Cabinet, they had given him during his defence of Sumter in 1861; and Judge Holt, in his reply, urged that no mercy or forbearance should be shown the guilty leaders of the rebellion, whose treasonable plottings he had seen in Washington during the stormy winter of 1860–61.

I have been the friend of the South, and, in the desire to save her from this great retribution, demanded in the name of the living God that every fetter should be broken, and the oppressed set free.[1] I have not come here with reference to any flag but that of freedom. If your Union does not symbolize universal emancipation, it brings no Union for me. If your Constitution does not guarantee freedom for all, it is not a Constitution I can subscribe to. If your flag is stained by the blood of a brother held in bondage, I repudiate it, in the name of God. I came here to witness the unfurling of a flag under which every human being is to be recognized as entitled to his freedom. Therefore, with a clean conscience, without any compromise of principles, I accepted the invitation of the Government of the United States to be present, and witness the ceremonies that have taken place to-day.

"And now let me give the sentiment which has been, and ever will be, the governing passion of my soul: 'Liberty for each, for all, and for ever.' (Cheers.)"

Before retiring for the night to his room at the Charleston Hotel, the editor of the *Liberator* paid a fraternal visit to the office of the Charleston *Courier*,[2] where, true

[1] The following tribute to Mr. Garrison by a South Carolinian will not be out of place here. In an address on the "Parallelisms of Negro Slavery and Protection in the United States," delivered in Brooklyn, N. Y., March 19, 1886, Mr. John J. Dargan, President of the South Carolina Free Trade Association, said: "The North furnished, up to the outbreak of the war, many able and zealous defenders of the right of human bondage. But in the fulness of time there arose a party in New England led by William Lloyd Garrison. Words fail me when I contemplate the moral stature of this man. Grand, noble embodiment of liberty and justice, of courage and perseverance. He was for putting aside all calculations on consequences, and doing right, giving justice, and establishing freedom. . . . For . . . his fearless fight for liberty in America, his native State of Massachusetts had then only vituperation and imprisonment and stones and the hangman's halter to bestow upon him. But now it has come to pass that a citizen of South Carolina, upon whose soil he dared not set his foot twenty-five years ago, lest he be swung to the first convenient tree, as a malefactor blacker in crime than that unrepentant one who hung by Christ on the cross — a South Carolinian now proclaims his unbounded admiration for the man's courage and foresight, and his immeasurable gratitude to him for doing more, probably, than any other one man to liberate South Carolina from the curse of negro slavery."

[2] This journal, but recently a noisy secession sheet, was now conducted by Northern men who had taken possession of the deserted office and types, and made a loyal paper of it.

to his instincts, he took the composing-stick and put in type a paragraph of Mr. Beecher's oration of that afternoon, on which the printers were at work.

Courier, April 15, 1865.

April 15. The next morning[1] a visit was paid to the grave of Calhoun, the party consisting of Messrs. Beecher, Garrison, Thompson, Tilton, and others. One of these (Rev. A. P. Putnam) shall describe the incident:

Lib. 35 : 76. "One of the most impressive scenes I have witnessed was Wm. Lloyd Garrison standing at the grave of John C. Calhoun. *April 15.* It was on the very morning when Abraham Lincoln died. The cemetery is a small one opposite St. Philip's church. The monument of the great advocate of slavery and nullification is built of brick, and covered with a large, plain slab of marble, inscribed with the simple name, Calhoun. He who slept beneath was the very soul of the hated institution when Garrison began his mighty warfare against it. The latter had now lived to see the power of his great antagonist pass away; and just as the *Abraham Lincoln.* illustrious Emancipator who gave to the system its final blow was breathing his last, the reformer laid his hand upon the monument before him, and said impressively, 'Down into a deeper grave than this slavery has gone, and for it there is no resurrection.' It was a fitting hour for such words to be spoken. Garrison was the proper man to speak them. The tomb of Calhoun was the appropriate place for their utterance. It was a scene that a painter might well attempt to reproduce upon canvas. Later in the morning, I entered the vast building which is known as 'Zion's Church,' and which is used by the colored people as their principal place of worship. It was crowded with an immense audience of three or four thousand blacks. Gen. Saxton[2] was presiding over the meeting, and around him in the pulpit were some of the most eminent public men and leading abolitionists in the country. The space in front was filled with

[1] "On Saturday morning . . . I was standing in front of St. Michael's church with William Lloyd Garrison. Just then the band of the 127th Regiment came down Meeting Street, playing 'Old John Brown' most superbly. 'Only listen to that in Charleston streets!' exclaimed Garrison, and we both broke into tears. I had many such startling and almost incredible surprises during my visit" (Rev. Theodore L. Cuyler in the *Evangelist*, *Lib.* 35 : 70).

[2] Major-General Rufus Saxton, the philanthropic Commander of the Department, and worthy successor to General Mitchel in his vigilant regard for the interests of the freedmen.

military officers, teachers, and missionaries from the North, and members of the excursion parties of the *Arago* and the *Oceanus*.[1] Garrison was standing in the pulpit, receiving an address from a liberated slave who stood below, and whose name was Samuel Dickerson. The negro spoke in behalf of the emancipated thousands who surrounded him, and in words of thrilling eloquence extended a joyful welcome to their distinguished visitor and friend. They all recognized in him the leader of the great movement which had broken their chains. Pointing to two little girls near by, who were neatly dressed, and were holding beautiful bouquets in their hands, the freedman said, in most pathetic and impassioned tones, that, but a brief time before, he had no power to claim them as his own, although they were bone of his bone and flesh of his flesh. 'Now, sir,' he continued, 'through your labors and those of your noble coadjutors, they are mine, and no man can take them from me. Accept these flowers as the token of our gratitude and love, and take them with you to your home, and keep them as a simple offering from those for whom you have done so much.' I do not pretend to give the language of this eloquent black orator, but only the main thought of his speech. Hardly one of the distinguished men who followed him spoke with greater accuracy, as none of them did with greater power.

"The little girls ascended the pulpit stairs, and presented their flowers to Mr. Garrison, who made a most fitting and touching reply. It seemed to me that it must have been the proudest moment in the reformer's life. To stand in the city of Charleston, S. C., in the presence of a vast assemblage of freed men and women, whose fetters he had done so much to break, and to receive from little emancipated children the humble memorial of the thankfulness and affection of the poor who were ready to perish, must indeed have been a sufficient reward for the laborious services he had rendered, and all the obloquy he had endured in their behalf, through more than thirty years of conflict with wrong. . . .

[1] The *Oceanus* was a steamer chartered by residents of Brooklyn, N. Y., mostly members of Mr. Beecher's church, for the excursion, and carried on this occasion 186 passengers, among whom were Joshua Leavitt, Hon. Edgar Ketchum, Aaron M. Powell, Revs. O. B. Frothingham, John W. Chadwick, A. P. Putnam, and Theo. L. Cuyler. An interesting and valuable record of this trip was subsequently published, which included a report of the speeches at the above-described meeting—'The Trip of the Steamer *Oceanus* to Fort Sumter and Charleston, S. C.,' Brooklyn, 1865.

CHAP. V. — 1865.

"The enthusiasm of that assembled multitude at the first mention by one of the speakers of the name of Abraham Lincoln was such as to defy description. It was intense, wild, and almost fearful. The vast crowd cheered, and clapped their hands and waved their handkerchiefs — some screaming for joy, and others raising their hands and clasping them in gratitude to God, and hundreds weeping the tears they could not repress as they thought of their great friend and benefactor. How little did any of us dream that, on that very morning, he lay silent in death at Washington!"

It had been intended to hold this meeting in the open air, and stands for the speakers had been erected in Citadel Square, which was thronged at an early hour. When Mr. Garrison arrived on the scene, at ten o'clock, he was greeted with deafening shouts, and the enthusiastic freedmen, defying all attempts to restrain them, lifted him aloft and bore him in triumph on their shoulders to the speakers' stand. The adjournment to the church was made on Senator Wilson's account, as he could not speak out-of-doors, and the meeting was opened by the speech of welcome already alluded to, for which, and for Mr. Garrison's rejoinder, we must here find room. Advancing to the pulpit with his children, Samuel Dickerson thus addressed Mr. Garrison:

Lib. 35:72.

"SIR: It is with pleasure that is inexpressible that I welcome you here among us, the long, the steadfast friend of the poor, down-trodden slave. Sir, I have read of you. I have read of the mighty labors you have had for the consummation of this glorious object. Here you see stand before you your handiwork. These children were robbed from me, and I stood desolate. Many a night I pressed a sleepless pillow from the time I returned to my couch until the close of the morning. I lost a dear wife, and after her death that little one, who is the counterpart of her mother's countenance, was taken from me. I appealed for her with all the love and reason of a father. The rejection came forth in these words: 'Annoy me not, or I will sell them off to another State.' I thank God that, through your instrumentality, under the folds of that glorious flag which treason tried to triumph over, you have restored them to me. And I tell you it is not this heart alone, but there are mothers, there are fathers, there are sisters, and there are brothers, the pulsations of whose hearts are unimaginable. The greeting that they would give you, sir, it is almost impossible for me to express; but simply, sir, we welcome and look upon you as our saviour. We thank you for what you have done for us. Take this wreath from these children; and when you go home, never mind how faded they may be, preserve them, encase them, and keep them as a token of affection from one who has lived and loved. (Cheers.)"

CHAP. V.
—
1865.

Mr. Garrison spoke as follows:

"MY DEAR FRIEND: I have no language to express the feelings of my heart on listening to your kind and strengthening words, on receiving these beautiful tokens of your gratitude, and on looking into the faces of this vast multitude, now happily liberated from the galling fetters of slavery. Let me say at the outset, 'Not unto us, not unto us, but unto God be all the glory' for what has been done in regard to your emancipation. I have been actively engaged in this work for almost forty years — for I began when I was quite young to plead the cause of the enslaved in this country. But I never expected to look you in the face, never supposed you would hear of anything I might do in your behalf. I knew only one thing — all that I wanted to know — that you were a grievously oppressed people; and that, on every consideration of justice, humanity, and right, you were entitled to immediate and unconditional freedom.

Lib. 35:72.

"I hate slavery as I hate nothing else in this world. It is not only a crime, but the sum of all criminality; not only a sin, but the sin of sins against Almighty God. I cannot be at peace with it at any time, to any extent, under any circumstances. That I have been permitted to witness its overthrow calls for expressions of devout thanksgiving to Heaven.

"It was not on account of your complexion or race, as a people, that I espoused your cause, but because you were the children of a common Father, created in the same divine image, having the same inalienable rights, and as much entitled to liberty as the proudest slaveholder that ever walked the earth.

"For many a year I have been an outlaw at the South for your sakes, and a large price was set upon my head, simply because I endeavored to remember those in bonds as bound with them. Yes — God is my witness! — I have faithfully tried, in the face of the fiercest opposition and under the most depressing circumstances, to make your cause my cause; my wife and

CHAP. V. — 1865. children your wives and children, subjected to the same outrage and degradation; myself on the same auction-block, to be sold to the highest bidder. Thank God, this day you are free! (Great cheering.) And be resolved that, once free, you will be free forever. No — not one of you ever will, ever can, consent again to be a bondman. Liberty or death, but never slavery! (Cheers.)

"It gives me joy to assure you, that the American Government will stand by you to establish your freedom, against whatever claims your former masters may bring. The time was when it gave you no protection, but was on the side of the oppressor, where there was power. Now all is changed! Once I could not feel any gladness at the sight of the American flag, because it was stained with your blood, and under it four millions of slaves were daily driven to unrequited labor. Now it floats purged of its gory stains; it symbolizes freedom for all, without distinction of race or color. The Government has its hold upon the throat of the monster Slavery, and is strangling the life out of it.

"In conclusion, I thank you, my friend, for your affecting and grateful address, and for these handsome tokens of our Heavenly Father's wisdom and goodness, and will try to preserve them in accordance with your wishes. O, be assured, I never doubted that I had the gratitude and affection of the entire colored population of the United States, even though personally unknown to so many of them; because I knew that upon me heavily rested the wrath and hatred of your cruel oppressors. I was sure, therefore, if I had them against me, I had you with me. (Applause.) But, as it is now time to organize this meeting, it will not be proper for me to go on with these remarks any further, except to say that, long as I have labored in your behalf, while God gives me reason and strength I shall demand for you everything I claim for the whitest of the white in this country. (Great cheering.)"

Beyond the words of panegyric with which he subsequently introduced Senator Wilson and George Thompson to the eager assemblage, Mr. Garrison made no further speech at this meeting, preferring to yield the time to others. One other experience yet awaited him when, in company with Senator Wilson and others, he *April* 15. visited towards evening the camp of the 55th Massachu-

CHAP. V. 1865.

setts Regiment, about three miles from the city, to find and embrace his soldier-son. There were gathered, in all the rags and wretchedness in which they had made their exodus, the twelve hundred plantation slaves or "contrabands" whom his son's company had just convoyed from the interior to the coast. They presented a picture of the misery and degradation of slavery and slave-life such as Mr. Garrison had never before witnessed, and had scarcely conceived; and most deeply was he affected by it, and by the manifestations of gratitude with which the poor creatures gathered about him when told by some of the officers that he had always been their friend. Even more touching was an incident which pointed the difference between their low estate and that of the blacks of Charleston. "Well, my friends," said Mr. Garrison to them before leaving the camp, "you are free at last—let us give three cheers for freedom!" and, leading off, he gave the first cheer. To his amazement, there was no response, the poor creatures looking at him in wonder, and he had to give the second and third cheers also without them. *They did not know how to cheer.*

On Monday morning the little group of the *Arago's* passengers who had remained behind, on the steamer's return to New York, left Charleston for the purpose of visiting Florida. The incidents of their departure were thus described by Mr. Beecher:

Lib. 35:84.

"The streets were full of colored people. I supposed that they had just come in from plantations—for they were being brought into Charleston by hundreds and thousands by our soldiers returning from raids through the adjacent country; but they said they were going to see Mr. Garrison and Mr. Thompson off. And we could have found our way to the steamer by following this crowd. When we reached the wharf, it was black; and yet it glowed like a garden. They had but little to bring as testimonials of their remembrance and gratitude; but what they had they brought. One had a little bunch of roses. Another had a bunch of jessamines and honeysuckles. Others had bunches of various kinds of flowers. I saw Mr. Tilton loaded down with these treasures that had been

Theodore Tilton.

CHAP. V. — 1865.

showered upon him, and struggling beneath his burden as he came on board. And they were thrown up on the steamer to Mr. Thompson and Mr. Garrison, and whatever person showed himself by the rail. And they lay about in bowlsful, and basketsful, and heaps in the corners so abundant that we knew not how to dispose of them. They were all they had to bring by which to express their gratitude towards those that they supposed had befriended them. No, not all; one poor, decrepit old woman came with a straw basket containing about two quarts of ground-nuts, which she wished to give us. A young woman came with some dainty little cakes that had been carefully prepared in some kitchen. There were various little delicacies brought for us, that we might eat them and remember the givers. I shall not forget these scenes. I shall not forget the cheers and acclamations of that dusky throng, as speeches were made to them. And when the boat moved off, I felt that we had left behind many of the Lord's elect, and that it were better for a man that a millstone were hanged about his neck, and that he were drowned in the depth of the sea, than that he should lay one finger of harm on these little ones of Christ."

A spirited meeting was held on the wharf, James Redpath presiding, and Samuel Dickerson made an eloquent farewell speech, to which Garrison, Thompson, and Tilton responded. Major Delaney, a colored member of General Saxton's staff, also spoke. The hundreds of school children present sang patriotic songs with great energy. As the steamer swung off, Dickerson was seen kneeling at the end of the wharf, with one arm about his little daughters, and holding above them with the other an American flag; and with this tableau ended the never-to-be-forgotten experiences of the three days in Charleston. Gathering a mass of the flowers which the grateful freedmen had showered upon their friends, George Thompson disappeared for a time, as the steamer made her way out of the harbor, and then, returning, led his companion to their state-room, where he had fairly covered the latter's berth with the fragrant offerings. "Garrison!" he said, "you began your warfare at the North in the face of rotten eggs and brickbats. Behold, you end it at Charleston on a bed of roses!"

The intended journey to Florida was rudely interrupted by the news of President Lincoln's assassination, which reached the party at Beaufort. To quote Mr. Beecher: *April* 14, 1865.

"We had returned to Beaufort, and were on the eve of going upon shore to enjoy a social interview, before setting out for Savannah, when a telegram came to Senator Wilson from Gen. Gillmore. As the boy that brought it passed me, I jocosely asked him some questions about it. Presently Senator Wilson came out of his cabin, much agitated, and said, 'Good God! the President is killed!' and read the dispatch. It was not grief, it was sickness that I felt. *Lib.* 35:84.

"In one half-hour we had wheeled upon our keel, and were plowing our way back to Hilton Head, whither we had telegraphed to have steam raised upon the *Suwo Nada*, that we might leave immediately for the North. We could see no more sights. We had no more heart for pleasure. The heavens seemed dark. Nothing was left, for the hour, but God, and his immutable providence, and his decrees. I leaned on them, and was strengthened. But, oh, the sadness of that company, and our nights' and our days' voyaging back! We knew nothing but this: that the President had been assassinated. All the rest was reserved for our coming into the harbor. We hoped to have returned with great cheer, and to have come up this noblest bay of the world to see it lined with tokens of joy and beauty; but, instead of that, on a dreary morning, drenched, chilled, and seasick, we came creeping up the bay under a cloudy sky, fit symbol of our nation's loss, and betook ourselves to our several homes."

No stop was made at Fortress Monroe on the return voyage, which was so hastily ordered that the steamer had only one hour's supply of coal left on reaching New York. Mr. Garrison often spoke of the immense relief it was to all, on landing, to find that the assassination of the President had not affected the stability of the Government of the country in the slightest, and that the North was as united in feeling as it was after the fall of Sumter in 1861.

Lieut. Garrison's furlough was voluntarily extended by Secretary Stanton to enable him to accompany his father to Boston. In September, 1865, the Secretary visited

CHAP. V. — 1865. Boston and renewed his acquaintance with Mr. Garrison, to whom he wrote on his arrival:

MS. Sept. 18, 1865. "One of the anticipated pleasures of my visit to Boston was to see you, and it will occasion me much regret should anything prevent our meeting. The invitation to witness the ceremonies at Fort Sumter was a just tribute to your great labors and sacrifices in the cause [of] freedom and human rights, and without your presence much of the significance of the event would have been incomplete. . . . Although conscious that the terms of commendation in which my services during the war are so kindly mentioned by you, are beyond my merit, I am happy to know that they are approved by you, who from earliest youth have been an object of my respect and admiration. With sincere regard, I shall ever be faithfully your friend."

CHAPTER VI.

END OF "THE LIBERATOR."—1865.

THE debates at the January meetings of the Massachusetts Society in Boston had turned almost wholly upon the question of reconstruction and negro suffrage; Mr. Phillips vigorously opposing the readmission of Louisiana or any other of the seceded States with the word white in their constitutions, and declaring that "no emancipation can be effectual, and no freedom real, unless the negro has the ballot and the States are prohibited from enacting laws making any distinction among their citizens on account of race or color." Mr. Garrison urged that those Northern States which denied suffrage to the blacks within their own borders could not, with any consistency, make a similar denial on the part of the Southern States a sufficient reason for refusing them readmission to the Union, and he therefore proposed the following resolutions as supplementary to the series introduced by Mr. Phillips:

Jan. 26, 27, 1865.

Lib. 35:18.

"7. Resolved, That if, as reconstructed, Louisiana ought not to be admitted to the Union because she excludes her colored population from the polls, then Connecticut, New Jersey, Pennsylvania, and all the Western States ought not to be in the Union for the same reason; and while they are guilty of this proscription, it is not for them to demand of Louisiana a broader scope of republican liberality than they are willing to take in their own case.[1]

Lib. 35:18.

[1] Mr. Garrison had already pointed out, in an editorial reviewing the whole subject of "Equal Political Rights," that the new Constitution of Louisiana was really more favorable to the colored people than that of any

CHAP. VI. — 1865.

"Whereas, ever since the organization of the National Government till now, every State in the Union has claimed and exercised the right to determine on what conditions any of its inhabitants shall wield the ballot — the General Government taking no cognizance of the special inclusion or exclusion pertaining to its electoral law; and whereas, it is not to be presumed that any State will consent to have this established prerogative wrested from it, and a wholly different rule forcibly prescribed, either on the plea of military occupancy or by act of Congress, without an amendment of the National Constitution; and whereas, by the conflicting laws or constitutions of the several States in the matter of voting, colored citizens who are electors in one State are disfranchised in another, and thus this usage is attended with invidious and oppressive features, and ought not longer to prevail among a people claiming to be one in nationality of spirit, purpose, and destiny; and whereas, with a wise regard to the future peace and welfare of the republic, and especially the allegiance of the Southern section of it, no one class should be left to ostracize another, under the plea of State sovereignty; therefore,

"8. Resolved, That Congress should lose no time in submitting to the people an amendment of the Constitution, making the electoral law uniform in all the States, without regard to complexional distinctions."

Both of these resolutions, with a third, providing for the dissolution of the Society on the final adoption and ratification of the Thirteenth Amendment, were laid on the table at the final session, while those proposed by Mr. Phillips (which also suggested a Constitutional amendment forbidding all discriminations against color) were adopted. So far as the claims made in behalf of the colored race were concerned, there was no vital difference between the speakers or the resolutions, but there was an essential difference in the spirit in which public men and measures were named and criticised; and this, on the part of some, had become so distasteful to Mr. Garrison that he preferred to absent himself from the second day's ses-

of the Northern States outside of New England, all which (with Connecticut) were more or less proscriptive. See *Lib.* 35 : 133. His own position coincided with Sumner's, that the seceded States were in a Territorial condition, and there should be no haste in readmitting them (*Lib.* 35 : 6).

sions which the Society voted to hold, in extension of the original call. "Old things have passed away," he declared, "and behold, all things have become new." Chap. VI. 1865.

"I recognize the fact, with devout gratitude to God. I will not cast imputations upon the motives of any man, or any body of men, for this sudden change, nor taunt them with being bayoneted up to it by abolitionists. I have no such impeachment to make. I thank God that they are now 'clothed, and sitting in their right minds'; and that is all I care to know. I give them my heart and my hand — and, instead of prognosticating only evil, and filling the air with doubts and apprehensions of danger in the future, I choose rather to believe that the people have passed the Rubicon, that they have burned the bridge behind them; that they have drawn the sword and thrown away the scabbard, and never mean to make any further compromise with slavery, but do mean to annihilate it. To say that this Government is disposed to put Union first and the black man afterwards, is to assert what is not true. The Government does not say so. The Government affirms, before the civilized world, that it puts liberty with Union! — the liberty of the black man alongside of the Union, or else no Union. What is gained by casting wrong imputations? What is the use of prophesying evil, only evil, and that continually? Is that the way to encourage the people to go forward? If their faces are simply turned Zionward, let us thank God that they are so turned, even if they have not taken a step toward Zion. Their faces are in the right direction; and God speed them onward until they reach Zion and sing its songs of praise! . . . Let us, then, cheer on the vast multitude whose hearts are beginning to palpitate with our own. Let us rejoice that they have entirely changed, in spirit and feeling, towards us and the cause of the oppressed; and not say or insinuate that they will betray freedom for Union the earliest moment they can. Let us be just, magnanimous, hopeful, coöperative, and thus stimulate them to complete the work so well begun. That is the philosophy upon which I act." *Lib.* 35:26.

Several of the speakers having bluntly intimated, at the same meeting, that he had fallen behind, and, being no longer the man for the crisis, should now yield the leadership to Mr. Phillips, he repudiated any claim to leadership, declaring that he had been "one only of a multitude of *Lib.* 35:25.

CHAP. VI. 1865. noble men and women in various parts of the country, whose combined efforts have all been necessary to bring about the marvellous change in public sentiment which we now see, and over which we now rejoice."

Lib. 35:25. "I cannot allow," he continued, "because it is not true, that Mr. Phillips is more firmly anchored in anti-slavery principle than I am, or more inexorable in the application of that principle. Have I not always declared, that all proscriptive complexional distinctions are cruel, unnatural, and wicked before God? I deny here, not in the spirit of rivalry but as a matter of justice, that he precedes me, or the humblest member of this Society, a hair's-breadth in demanding that equal justice be done to the black man as to the white man. I protest, therefore, against this alleged difference between Mr. Phillips and myself — as though there had been a retreat, or standing still, or getting 'behind the times,' on my part, and a bold, radical advance on his part, separating us from each other. There is no such antagonism, isolation, retraction, or precedence. Neither is he in advance, nor am I behind; neither does he lead, nor are the abolitionists led. We all stand side by side, shoulder to shoulder, and march in a solid phalanx against the common foe — God alone being our 'leader.' Wherein we may chance to differ relates not to the principles we cherish, the doctrines we disseminate, or the claims we make for the colored population, whether bond or free; but solely as to the relative amount of praise or blame, of satisfaction or complaint, to be expressed or awarded concerning certain public men and measures in their bearing upon the cause so dear to us all. And herein we shall differ in opinion, more or less, according to the standpoint we occupy, the information we possess, or the ability we have to perceive and understand the relation of events in this tremendous convulsion of the country."

Mr. Phillips also uttered his protest against the attempt to extol him at the expense of his friend:

Lib. 35:26. "Allow me," he said, "one word, which I utter with the greater pleasure and frankness because my friend, Mr. Garrison, has left the hall, that there is nothing more unpleasant to me than any allusion to him and myself as antagonists. Whatever may have been the immediate cause of my anti-slavery life and action, he is, in so true and full a sense, the creator of the anti-slavery *movement*, that I may well say I have never uttered an anti-slavery word which I did not owe to his inspiration; I have never done an anti-slavery act of which the primary merit was not his. More than that: in my experience of nigh thirty years, I have never met the anti-slavery man or woman, who had struck any effectual blow at the slave system in this country, whose action was not born out of the heart and conscience of Wm. Lloyd Garrison. I do not forget the half-dozen anti-slavery sermons which sparkle along our history,— the quiet scruples of some tender consciences,— the passive disapprobation of Friends, their protection of individual fugitives, or the devoted life of Lundy,— still, the anti-slavery *movement* is Garrison's work, and, as agitators, we all owe to him the breath of our nostrils; and I do not see to-day, that, in regard to the great principles of the cause, there is any difference between him and myself. . . . Whatever, therefore, may be the conclusion of this debate, I recognize the same leading mind at the head of the anti-slavery struggle. In times past, none but his own modest lips ever dreamed of denying him that title; in time to come, we shall need, find, and welcome the same leader."

CHAP. VI.

1865.

The question whether the American Anti-Slavery Society should dissolve or continue its operations caused an unusually large attendance at the annual meeting in May, in New York, not only of the old and long-tried members, but of others, hitherto seldom seen at these meetings, whose attitude towards the Society had suddenly changed from indifference or hostility to a professed conviction that its dissolution would now be an alarming peril to the freedom and enfranchisement of the blacks. Mr. Garrison at once introduced the subject in these resolutions:

"Whereas, . . . it is decreed by the nation that all fetters shall be broken, every bondman set free; and

Lib. 35:81.

"Whereas, it is not for Abolitionists to affect exclusiveness, or to seek isolation from the great mass of the people, when the reasons which compelled them to take such a position no longer exist; therefore,

"Resolved, That, uniting our thanksgivings to God with those of the emancipated millions at the South for the wonders he has wrought, and rejoicing with joy unspeakable that 'the year of

CHAP. VI. 1865. jubilee is come,' so that further anti-slavery agitation is uncalled for, we close the operations and the existence of this Society with the present anniversary."

To this, Mr. Phillips opposed the following motion:

Lib. 35:81. "Resolved, That since the Constitutional Amendment abolishing slavery is not yet ratified, and consequently the system of slavery stands in the eye of the law untouched; and whereas, there are still thousands of slaves legally held within the United States; therefore, this Society calls upon its members for fresh and untiring diligence in finishing the work to which they originally pledged themselves, and putting the liberty of the negro beyond peril."

May 9, 10. *Lib.* 35:81, 82, 85, 86. The debate on these propositions continued through two days, that of Mr. Phillips being supported by C. L. Remond, Frederick Douglass, Robert Purvis, S. S. Foster, and Anna E. Dickinson, while Samuel May, Jr., Oliver Johnson, and William I. Bowditch favored continuing the Society only until the Thirteenth Amendment should have been officially ratified. The point having been made that the Society was pledged to continue until negro suffrage should be secured, because the elevation of the free people of color was one of the objects set forth in its Declaration and Constitution, Mr. Garrison rejoined that, as the author of the Declaration, he felt competent to interpret it.

Lib. 35:81. "This Society," he continued, "is 'The American *Anti-Slavery* Society.' That was the object. The thought never entered my mind then, nor has it at any time since, that when slavery had received its death-wound, there would be any disposition or occasion to continue the Anti-Slavery Society a moment longer. But, of course, in looking over the country, we saw the free colored people more or less laboring under disabilities and suffering from injustice, and we declared that, incidentally, we did not mean to overlook them, but should vindicate their rights and endeavor to get justice done to them. The point is here. We organized expressly for the abolition of slavery; we called our Society an *Anti-Slavery* Society. The other work was incidental. Now, I believe slavery is abolished in this country; abolished constitutionally; abolished by a decree of this nation, never, never to be reversed; and, therefore, that it is ludicrous for us, a mere handful of people, with little means, with no agents in the field, no longer separate, and swallowed up in the great ocean of popular feeling against slavery, to assume that we are of special importance, and that we ought not to dissolve our association, under such circumstances, lest the nation should go to ruin! I will not be guilty of any such absurdity." CHAP. VI. 1865.

Mr. Phillips, with impassioned rhetoric, insisted that the Thirteenth Amendment was not yet legally ratified, belittled the Freedmen's aid and educational movements which were already accomplishing noble results, and declared that he was not going to haul down his flag. "I never shall leave the negro until, so far as God gives me the power, I achieve it [absolute equality before the law—absolute civil equality]." "Who proposes to do so?" asked Mr. Garrison, who further punctuated the speech, when printed in the *Liberator*, with a keen running commentary. To him the constant insinuation that those opposed to prolonging the Society's existence were deserters or backsliders, seemed alike offensive and amusing; and when Robert Purvis and Anna E. Dickinson pathetically entreated him to remain at his post, and "hold the standard," he replied with a dignity, power, and eloquence of which the printed report gives hardly an adequate impression. We can quote only the alpha and omega of his speech:

Lib. 35:82.

Lib. 35:82.

"If this were a struggle about fundamental principles, it would be a grave occasion to me, and I should regard this discussion as of very considerable importance. But as there is really nothing of principle at all involved in it—as it is only a question of usefulness, only a matter of opinion whether this Society has essentially consummated its mission, as originally designed—I feel perfectly indifferent as to the manner in which it shall be decided. Nothing is more clear in my own mind, nothing has ever been more clear, than that this is the fitting time to dissolve our organization, and to mingle with the millions of our fellow-countrymen in one common effort to establish justice and liberty throughout the land. (Applause.) . . .

Lib. 35:85, 86.

CHAP. VI. — 1865.

"My friends, let us not any longer affect superiority when we are not superior (hear, hear) — let us not assume to be better than other people when we are not any better. (Applause, and cries of Hear, hear.) When they are reiterating all that we say, and disposed to do all that we wish to have done, what more can we ask? And yet I know the desire to keep together, because of past memories and labors, is a very natural one. But let us challenge and command the respect of the nation, and of the friends of freedom throughout the world, by a wise and sensible conclusion. Of course, we are not to cease laboring in regard to whatever remains to be done; but let us work with the millions, and not exclusively as the American Anti-Slavery Society. As co-workers are everywhere found, as our voices are everywhere listened to with approbation and our sentiments cordially endorsed, let us not continue to be isolated. My friend, Mr. Phillips, says he has been used to isolation, and he thinks he can endure it some time longer. My answer is, that when one stands alone with God for truth, for liberty, for righteousness, he may glory in his isolation; but when the principle which kept him isolated has at last conquered, then to glory in isolation seems to me no evidence of courage or fidelity. (Applause.)

"Friends of the American Anti-Slavery Society, this is no 'death-bed scene' to me! There are some in our ranks who seem to grow discouraged and morbid in proportion as light abounds and victory crowns our efforts (applause); and it seems as if the hour of the triumph of universal justice is the hour for them to feel the saddest and most melancholy! We have had something said about a funeral here to-day. A funeral because Abolitionism sweeps the nation! A funeral? Nay, thanks be to God who giveth us the victory, it is a day of jubilee, and not a day to talk about funerals or death-beds! It is a resurrection from the dead, rather; it is an ascension and beatification! Slavery is in its grave, and there is no power in this nation that can ever bring it back. But if the heavens should disappear, and the earth be removed out of its place,— if slavery should, by a miracle, come back,— what then? We shall then have millions of supporters to rally with us for a fresh onset!

"I thank you, beloved friends, who have for so many years done me the honor to make me the President of the American Anti-Slavery Society. I never should have accepted that post if it had been a popular one. I took it because it was unpopular; because we, as a body, were everywhere denounced, proscribed, outlawed. To-day, it is popular to be President of the American Anti-Slavery Society. Hence, my connection with it terminates here and now, both as a member and as its presiding officer. I bid you an affectionate adieu."

CHAP. VI.

1865.

The final vote was taken after another appeal from Mr. Phillips, and resulted in the rejection of Mr. Garrison's resolutions by a vote of 118 to 48, and so the continuance of the Society was decided. Tumultuous applause greeted the announcement of the result, which was renewed when the Nominating Committee reported Mr. Garrison's name for reëlection as President for the ensuing year; but he of course declined to serve, and Mr. Phillips, who was then chosen as his successor, offered a resolution of fervid tribute to the retiring President, which was adopted by a rising vote, and acknowledged in a few grateful words by the recipient.[1]

Thus did Mr. Garrison dissolve his connection with the Society which, more than any other man, he had founded, and over which he had presided for twenty-two years. Doubtless he would have been willing to continue

[1] The tribute was certainly sincere and heartfelt on the part of the majority of the Society who voted it, and was accepted in that sense by Mr. Garrison; but the Nominating Committee did not deem it necessary to pay a similar compliment to the retiring members of the Executive Committee, only one of whom was renominated. Edmund Quincy, Anne Warren Weston, Sydney Howard Gay, Samuel May, Jr., and Henry C. Wright, all shared Mr. Garrison's views essentially, and with him withdrew from the Society. A resolution of thanks to the retiring editors of the *Standard* (Oliver Johnson and Edmund Quincy), with especial commendation of their conduct of the paper during the war, was introduced by S. May, Jr., but was adroitly referred to the new and hostile Executive Committee, who finally passed it in an emasculated form which the subjects of it refused to accept and returned with trenchant letters (*Lib.* 35 : 98). Mr. Quincy could not resist the opportunity to poke a little fun at the Society and its Executive Committee. "Regarding, as I do," said he, "the existence of an *Anti-Slavery* Society at this time as not merely an anachronism and an absurdity, but as an *impossibility*, I must regard the ladies and gentlemen in question, officially, as Non-existent, and the Society they profess to represent as a Nonentity. Holding these views, I cannot consent, by accepting this Resolution, at once to deny them and to stultify myself." See, also, Oliver Johnson's farewell to the readers of the *Standard* (*Lib.* 35 : 88), and pp. 387–390 of his 'Garrison and his Times,' for a full and accurate statement of the causes which led to the division in the anti-slavery ranks.

CHAP. VI. 1865.

in that position until the last State had ratified the Constitutional Amendment, if he had believed that the Society would then dissolve; but he saw that it had passed under the control of those with whose habitual attitude he could no longer sympathize, and that it was useless to try to coöperate with them. He perceived, too, that the force of habit was strong with many of the old friends of the cause, to whom the annual meetings and festivals and conventions had been meat and drink for many years, and who, reluctant to break up old and delightful associations, inclined a willing ear to the arguments that the Society was never more needed than now. When such came to him almost in tears at having been compelled to vote against his proposition, he cheerily assured them that he was not disturbed in the least by it, and begged them not to be, as it was not a matter of the slightest importance. For himself, his course was clear, and the step resolutely taken of resigning the position he had so long held, and declaring himself a co-worker with the great multitude now in favor of freedom and equality, increased the weight and influence in public estimation which his conduct during the previous year had secured him.

He absented himself (as did Edmund Quincy and Samuel May, Jr.) from the sessions of the New England Convention in Boston, and delivered in Providence, the following day, an address on the assassination of President Lincoln, before the Union League of Rhode Island. In this he candidly reviewed Mr. Lincoln's course on the slavery question, from the time of his election until his death, exposing its fluctuations and inconsistencies, yet recognizing also the vast difficulties by which he was surrounded, and paying a just and discriminating tribute to his lofty traits of character — this man of "absolute faith in the people, sound judgment, ready tact, abiding cheerfulness, inflexible perseverance, large common sense, strong powers of reasoning, incorruptible integrity, and unalloyed patriotism." He repeated the address in Lynn

May 31. June 1. Lib. 35:108.

on the following Sunday to a great audience, and then made his annual pilgrimage to the Progressive Friends' Meeting at Longwood, with George Thompson as his companion. *June* 4, 1865. *June* 8–10.

"Think of six long, consecutive sessions, with the mercury ranging towards 90, and the meeting-house packed like a bee-hive in winter," he wrote to his wife. "The laboring oar as to talking and speechifying fell, as usual, to my lot; in addition to which I had to preside as chairman. . . . I drew up nearly all the Testimonies that were adopted by the Yearly Meeting — on Peace, Temperance, the Rebellion, Slavery, etc." *MS. June* 11.

The remainder of June and the whole of July he spent quietly at Rockledge,[1] going daily to the city to attend to his editorial duties, yet contriving to obtain much needed rest, and enjoying the charm and seclusion of his suburban retreat. His letters to his wife, who was spending several weeks at Providence at this time, under treatment for her paralysis, continually allude to his delight in the "romantic and cosy home." "The foliage of the trees is complete, and the birds are as merry and vocal as though just liberated from bondage."[2] *MSS. July* 20, *June* 22, 1865.

From the day the Constitutional Amendment was

[1] At the end of August, 1864, the Garrison family left the house in Dix Place which they had occupied for eleven years, and removed to Roxbury, where a pleasant frame house, situated on high ground near the old Roxbury fort of Revolutionary days, was purchased. A picturesque ledge of rocks adjoined the estate, which consisted of nearly half an acre of ground, and the whole region was one of much natural beauty. The house, which was soon christened "Rockledge," was elevated by terraces thirty feet above Highland street, and had abundance of air and sunlight, which the surrounding foliage in no wise interrupted, while the upper windows commanded extensive views of the harbor and country. The change from city life was beneficial not on sanitary grounds alone. The distance from town (a half-hour's ride by horse-car) was sufficient to check the constant stream of callers and visitors to whom Dix Place had been of such convenient access, and to abate that liberal hospitality which Mrs. Garrison's disablement now forbade.

[2] In July he was surprised by receiving an official notice of his having been made an honorary member of the Phi Beta Kappa Society at Cambridge. This was brought about by his old friend, Dr. Henry I. Bowditch, who thought it time that Harvard should honor the founder of the anti-slavery movement (MS. July 23, 1865, W. L. G. to H. E. G.).

CHAP. VI. 1865. passed by Congress Mr. Garrison took the ground (held also by Senator Sumner) that its ratification by three-fourths of the loyal States would be sufficient for its adoption, as the seceded States, which had not yet been readmitted to a place in the national councils, were manifestly incompetent to pass upon it; and as the requisite number had acted before the 4th of July, he regarded the Amendment as legally carried then, and for the first time in many years spent the national holiday in Boston, enjoying its celebration.

The question of giving the ballot to the freedmen was constantly agitated during the summer, and the Republican press and leaders, including some of the most con-
Lib. 35:101, 105, 106, 118, 121, 125. servative, steadily gravitated towards its adoption as an article of party faith. Several of the fall State Conven-
Lib. 35:173. tions declared in favor of negro suffrage, and where there was hesitation actually to adopt the principle, the importance of securing the rights of the freedmen before readmitting any State was recognized and affirmed.
Lib. 35:159, 161, 162. Nevertheless, the Republican State of Connecticut defeated, in October, by a majority of 6500, an amendment to its own Constitution enfranchising its colored citizens,
Lib. 35:159. and the new State of Colorado inserted the word white in its Constitution. The disloyal element at the South were encouraged by this, and by symptoms that President Johnson regarded them with less disfavor than formerly, and desired their readmission to representation as soon as their legislatures should have endorsed the Thirteenth Amendment and repudiated the rebel debt. Swallowing
Wilson's Rise and Fall of Slave Power, 3: 600–602. this bitter pill, they proceeded to enact proscriptive laws against the freedmen, and tried to regain control of them by inhuman codes paralleling those which prevailed in slavery days. Outrages upon the blacks were of daily occurrence, and systematic efforts were made to terrorize and subject them. "These atrocities excite in us no surprise,"
Lib. 35:134. wrote Mr. Garrison, who regarded them as confirming all that the abolitionists had asserted as to Southern barbarity towards the negro. Still, while his heart was saddened

by these cruel demonstrations, he felt assured that they would be overruled for good, and would "help to consolidate the loyal sentiment of the country in opposition to any relaxation of the strong arm of the General Government," and "to the admission of any one of the revolted States into the Union for an indefinite period." In common with others, he tried to regard hopefully the course of the new President, and to believe that his intentions were right;[1] but hope grew fainter from month to month, as Johnson's purpose to restore the entire political control of the returning States to the whites, without any guarantees whatever for the protection of the freedmen, became evident. "The aspect of things at the South is somewhat portentous," he wrote to Henry C. Wright, in October. "If the rebel States, 'reconstructed' so as to leave the colored people at the mercy of the savage whites, are suddenly admitted into the Union, there will assuredly be a terrible state of affairs, perhaps leading to a war of extermination. I begin to feel more uneasy about the President."

CHAP. VI. 1865. *Andrew Johnson.* *MS. Oct.* 2.

Late in September he attended the Champlain Valley Agricultural Fair, at Vergennes, Vermont, in company with the Rev. Edwin H. Chapin, and had "an unspeakably pleasant" time and a cordial reception. Both, in their addresses, dwelt upon the questions of the day and the importance of negro suffrage. A fortnight later Mr. Garrison was in Philadelphia, on business connected with the American Freedman's Aid Commission, an organization comprising the principal Freedmen's Educational and Aid Associations in the East and West, which had hitherto been working independently of each other, but were now brought into harmonious operation through the efforts of J. M. McKim. Of this new organization Bishop Matthew Simpson was made President, and Mr. Garrison First Vice-President, Mr. McKim being the Corresponding

Sept. 28. *Lib.* 35:163. *Oct.* 11. *Lib.* 35:170.

[1] No one was more hopeful than Mr. Phillips. "I have never expressed a doubt with regard to President Johnson," he said in May; "I believe in him. I believe he means suffrage" (*Lib.* 35 : 86).

CHAP. VI. — 1865. Secretary of the Eastern Department.[1] Later in the month Mr. Garrison and Mr. McKim visited Maine in behalf of the Commission, holding large meetings and forming auxiliary associations in Portland and Bangor.[2]

As the autumn advanced, the treasury of the *Liberator* again ran low, and, in order to replenish it and enable him to carry the paper to the end of the year, the editor reluctantly left his post and undertook a lecture tour in the West, which occupied five weeks and absorbed the month of November and the first week of December.

Nov. 2. The trip, which began at Lockport, N. Y., was a hard and exhausting one for Mr. Garrison. He gave his lecture (a two hours' discourse on "The Past, Present, and Future of Our Country") from four to six times each week, and suffered both from hoarseness and ophthalmia; but he lost no appointment, and had the satisfaction of earning fifteen hundred dollars — more than his year's salary — in a single month. As usual, too, the social enjoyments of the journey were more than a compensation for its hardships. In almost every city he was the recipient of courtesies and attentions from old and new friends; beyond Michigan
Nov. 16–20. all was new to him, and he saw Chicago and the Missis-
Nov. 22. sippi River (at Quincy) for the first time. Unexpected glimpses of George Thompson (also on a Western lecture tour), at Detroit, and Gerrit Smith, at Chicago, were among the pleasant incidents of the journey. At Prince-
Nov. 20. ton, Illinois, he paid his respects to the widow and children of Owen Lovejoy, and at Springfield was the guest of W.
Nov. 26. H. Herndon, Lincoln's law partner, with whom he visited the tomb of the martyr-President. On his return journey he travelled with members of Congress on their way to

[1] Its object was "to promote the education and elevation of the Freedmen, and to coöperate to this end with the Bureau of Refugees, Freedmen, and Abandoned Lands," which had been established early in the year by Congress, with General O. O. Howard as Chief Commissioner.

[2] At Portland, Mr. Garrison's early antagonist, John Neal (*ante*, 1: 99, 383), entered heartily into the movement. "Mr. Garrison and I used to have some hot contests," said Mr. Neal. "Who was wrong and who was right?" asked Governor Israel Washburne. "I was wrong," said Mr. Neal, frankly, "and Mr. Garrison was right" (*Lib.* 35: 174).

Washington for the opening of the new session. "I am constantly urging the importance of not admitting any of the rebel States into the Union until a longer probation," he wrote to his wife, "and find leading men to accept my views." *MS. Nov. 29.*

After his long absence at the West,[1] Mr. Garrison had hoped to devote the last three weeks of the year wholly to the *Liberator*, but he had scarcely reached Boston before he was summoned to New York to attend a committee meeting of the American Freedman's Aid Commission; and three days later he was compelled to fulfil an engagement at Philadelphia, for a lecture at the Academy of Music. Even while he was speaking, the telegraph wires were bearing to every part of the land the official proclamation of Secretary Seward, issued that day, announcing the ratification of the Thirteenth Amendment, and its consequent incorporation as a part of the Constitution. Hurrying back to Boston, the editor of the *Liberator* took the composing-stick and himself set up the proclamation for insertion in the number just going to press,— the last issue but one of the paper,— and to it appended this pæan: *Dec. 15. Dec. 18. Dec. 22.*

"With our own hands we have put in type this unspeakably cheering and important official announcement that, at last, the old 'covenant with death' is annulled, and the 'agreement with hell' no longer stands. Not a slave is left to clank his fetters, of the millions that were lately held in seemingly hopeless bondage. Not a slaveholder may dare to present his claim of property in man, or assume the prerogative of trafficking in human flesh and blood. Henceforth, personal freedom is secured for all who dwell on the American soil, irrespective of complexion or race. It is not merely the abolition of slavery, with the old recognized right of each State to establish the system *ad libitum*, but it is the prohibition, by 'the supreme law of the land,' duly ratified, to enslave a human being in any part of our national domains, or to restore what has been overthrown. It is, *Lib. 35:202.*

1 During this and many previous absences, Charles K. Whipple kindly assumed much of the editorial care of the paper. Samuel May, Jr., and Edmund Quincy contributed editorials, the latter giving an admirable review of the *Liberator's* career, in the last number before Mr. Garrison's return (*Lib.* 35 : 190).

CHAP. VI. — 1865.

consequently, the complete triumph as well as utter termination of the Anti-Slavery struggle, as such.

"Rejoice, and give praise and glory to God, ye who have so long and so untiringly participated in all the trials and vicissitudes of that mighty conflict! Having sown in tears, now reap in joy. Hail, redeemed, regenerated America! Hail, North and South, East and West! Hail, the cause of Peace, of Liberty, of Righteousness, thus mightily strengthened and signally glorified! Hail, the Present, with its transcendent claims, its new duties, its imperative obligations, its sublime opportunities! Hail, the Future, with its pregnant hopes, its glorious promises, its illimitable powers of expansion and development! Hail, ye ransomed millions, no more to be chained, scourged, mutilated, bought and sold in the market, robbed of all rights, hunted as partridges upon the mountains in your flight to obtain deliverance from the house of bondage, branded and scorned as a connecting link between the human race and the brute creation! Hail, all nations, tribes, kindreds, and peoples, 'made of one blood,' interested in a common redemption, heirs of the same immortal destiny! Hail, angels in glory and spirits of the just made perfect, and tune your harps anew, singing, 'Great and marvellous are thy works, Lord God Almighty; just and true are thy ways, thou King of saints! Who shall not fear thee, O Lord, and glorify thy name? for thou only art holy: for all nations shall come and worship before thee: for thy judgments are made manifest.'"

For the one remaining number of the *Liberator* Mr. Garrison's children besought him to at once prepare his valedictory editorial, leaving to others the drudgery of the proof-reading and mechanical details of the paper. The proofs he insisted on reading himself, and the outside pages he also "made up" from the galleys, but the inside pages he finally allowed his friend and assistant, Winchell Yerrinton, to make up, under his direction; a considerable portion of the editorial page being given to letters of congratulation and farewell from old and tried friends. When these were inserted, less than a column's space was left in which to complete his valedictory, and, the number being already late for the press, he wrote the remainder of it with the printers standing at his elbow for "copy," which he doled out to them a few lines at a time. The final paragraph he set with his own hands, and then stepped to the imposing-table or stone[1] to insert it in the vacant place awaiting it. Evening had come, and the little group[2] in the printing-office gathered silently about to witness the closing act. As the form was locked for the last time by the senior Yerrinton, all present felt a

[1] This old stand, which had done duty in the *Liberator* office for twenty-five or thirty years, was purchased by a brother printer and abolitionist, George W. Stacy of Milford, Mass., and subsequently (1885) returned by him to Mr. Garrison's family. "How many days and nights have I wearily bent over it in getting ready the paper for prompt publication!" wrote Mr. Garrison to Mr. Stacy (MS. Oct. 23, 1878). "What a 'stone of stumbling' and a 'rock of offence' it was to all the enemies of emancipation!"

[2] Consisting, besides Mr. Garrison, of his sons George and Frank, and J. B. and J. M. W. Yerrinton, the printers of the paper. In expressing his sadness at the termination of their long business connection, Mr. Garrison wrote to the senior Yerrinton: "The little printing-office has daily brought us together, and enabled us to know each other as intimately as it is possible, in every phase of human thought and feeling. I wish to improve this opportunity to testify to the unfailing good temper and kindness of spirit and manner which you have manifested amidst all the annoyances and perplexities connected with type-setting, bad proof, illegible manuscript, etc., etc. Never has there been a sharp or hasty word between us. Your disposition has been so good that mine must have been crabbed indeed at any time to have caused a ripple upon the surface of our feelings towards each other. Blessed with good health, you have been always at your post — not even indulging, for once, in that occasional recreation which seems to be almost indispensable to the recuperation of mind and body. Such assiduity and steadiness I have never known, and call for especial recognition. But your work on the *Liberator* has not been a mere mechanical performance. You have mingled with it the liveliest interest in the welfare of the paper, in the principles it has inculcated, in the humane and godlike object it has aimed to achieve. . . . For many a year it was anything but reputable to be even the printer of the *Liberator;* but that reproach is now wiped out, and in the future will make your memory honored" (MS. Jan. 1, 1866). To the son, J. M. Winchell Yerrinton, Mr. Garrison sent this tribute: "I have known you ever since you were a little boy; and in all the wide range of my acquaintance there is no one I more highly respect and esteem. . . . The best phonographic reporter in this country, you have held an important relation to those grand reformatory changes which have taken place within the last quarter of a century. But for your marvellous skill, where would have been the eloquent speeches of Phillips and others but in the dim remembrance of those who listened to them? And your heart has been in the work. In many ways and on an extended scale, you have been a public benefactor, and a most efficient instrument in disseminating light and knowledge —'thoughts that breathe, and words that burn'" (MS. Jan. 1, 1866).

CHAP. VI. 1865. sense of loss and bereavement. Mr. Garrison alone preserved his wonted cheerfulness and serenity. From the death-bed of the *Liberator*, he went directly to a Committee meeting of the New England Freedmen's Aid Society, his face towards the resurrection and the life of Freedom.

The last number of the *Liberator* fitly reproduced the Salutatory from the first, followed by the editor's

Lib. 35 : 206.

VALEDICTORY.

THE LAST NUMBER OF THE LIBERATOR.

"The last! the last! the last!
O, by that little word
How many thoughts are stirred
That sister of THE PAST!"

The present number of the *Liberator* is the completion of its thirty-fifth volume, and the termination of its existence.

Commencing my editorial career when only twenty years of age, I have followed it continuously till I have attained my sixtieth year — first, in connection with the *Free Press*, in Newburyport, in the spring of 1826; next, with the *National Philanthropist*, in Boston, in 1827; next, with the *Journal of the Times*, in Bennington, Vt., in 1828–9; next, with the *Genius of Universal Emancipation*, in Baltimore, in 1829–30; and, finally, with the *Liberator*, in Boston, from the 1st of January, 1831, to the 1st of January, 1866; — at the start, probably the youngest member of the editorial fraternity in the land, now, perhaps, the oldest, not in years, but in continuous service,— unless Mr. Bryant, of the New York *Evening Post*, be an exception.

Whether I shall again be connected with the press, in a similar capacity, is quite problematical; but, at my period of life, I feel no prompting to start a new journal at my own risk, and with the certainty of struggling against wind and tide, as I have done in the past.

I began the publication of the *Liberator* without a subscriber, and I end it — it gives me unalloyed satisfaction to say — without a farthing as the pecuniary result of the patronage extended to it during thirty-five years of unremitted labors.

From the immense change wrought in the national feeling and sentiment on the subject of slavery, the *Liberator* derived no advantage at any time in regard to its circulation. The original "disturber of the peace," nothing was left undone at the beginning, and up to the hour of the late rebellion, by Southern slaveholding villany on the one hand, and Northern pro-slavery malice on the other, to represent it as too vile a sheet to be countenanced by any claiming to be Christian or patriotic; and it always required rare moral courage or singular personal independence to be among its patrons. Never had a journal to look such opposition in the face — never was one so constantly belied and caricatured. If it had advocated all the crimes forbidden by the moral law of God and the statutes of the State, instead of vindicating the sacred claims of oppressed and bleeding humanity, it could not have been more vehemently denounced or more indignantly repudiated. To this day — such is the force of prejudice — there are multitudes who cannot be induced to read a single number of it, even on the score of curiosity, though their views on the slavery question are now precisely those which it has uniformly advocated. Yet no journal has been conducted with such fairness and impartiality; none has granted such freedom in its columns to its opponents; none has so scrupulously and uniformly presented all sides of every question discussed in its pages; none has so readily and exhaustively published, without note or comment, what its enemies have said to its disparagement and the vilification of its editor; none has vindicated primitive Christianity, in its spirit and purpose — "the higher law," in its supremacy over nations and governments as well as individual conscience — the Golden Rule, in its binding obligation upon all classes — the Declaration of Independence, with its self-evident truths — the rights of human nature, without distinction of race, complexion, or sex — more earnestly or more uncompromisingly; none has exerted a higher moral or more broadly reformatory influence upon those who have given it a careful perusal; and none has gone beyond it in asserting the Fatherhood of God and the brotherhood of man. All this may be claimed for it without egotism or presumption. It has ever been "a terror to evil-doers, and a praise to them that do well." It has excited the fierce hostility of all that is vile and demoniacal in the land, and won the affection and regard of the purest and noblest of the age. To me it has been unspeakably cheering, and the richest compensation for whatever of peril, suffering, and defamation I have been called to encounter, that one uniform testimony has been borne, by those who have had its weekly perusal, as to the elevating and quick-

CHAP. VI. 1865.

ening influence of the *Liberator* upon their character and lives; and the deep grief they are expressing in view of its discontinuance is overwhelmingly affecting to my feelings. Many of these date their subscriptions from the commencement of the paper, and they have allowed nothing in its columns to pass without a rigid scrutiny. They speak, therefore, experimentally, and "testify of that which they have seen and do know." Let them be assured that my regret in the separation which is to take place between us, in consequence of the discontinuance of the *Liberator*, is at least as poignant as their own; and let them feel, as I do, comforted by the thought that it relates only to the weekly method of communicating with each other, and not to the principles we have espoused in the past, or the hopes and aims we cherish as to the future.

Although the *Liberator* was designed to be, and has ever been, mainly devoted to the abolition of slavery, yet it has been instrumental in aiding the cause of reform in many of its most important aspects.

I have never consulted either the subscription-list of the paper or public sentiment in printing, or omitting to print, any article touching any matter whatever. Personally, I have never asked any one to become a subscriber, nor any one to contribute to its support, nor presented its claims for a better circulation in any lecture or speech, or at any one of the multitudinous anti-slavery gatherings in the land. Had I done so, no doubt its subscription-list might have been much enlarged.

In this connection, I must be permitted to express my surprise that I am gravely informed, in various quarters, that this is no time to retire from public labor; that though the chains of the captive have been broken, he is yet to be vindicated in regard to the full possession of equal civil and political rights; that the freedmen in every part of the South are subjected to many insults and outrages; that the old slaveholding spirit is showing itself in every available form; that there is imminent danger that, in the hurry of reconstruction and readmission to the Union, the late rebel States will be left free to work any amount of mischief; that there is manifestly a severe struggle yet to come with the Southern "powers of darkness," which will require the utmost vigilance and the most determined efforts on the part of the friends of impartial liberty — etc., etc., etc. Surely, it is not meant by all this that I am therefore bound to continue the publication of the *Liberator*; for that is a matter for me to determine, and no one else. As I commenced its publication without asking leave of any one, so I claim to be competent to decide when it may fitly close its career.

Again — it cannot be meant, by this presentation of the existing state of things at the South, either to impeach my intelligence, or to impute to me a lack of interest in behalf of that race for the liberation and elevation of which I have labored so many years! If, when they had no friends, and no hope of earthly redemption, I did not hesitate to make their cause my own, is it to be supposed that, with their yokes broken, and their friends and advocates multiplied indefinitely, I can be any the less disposed to stand by them to the last — to insist on the full measure of justice and equity being meted out to them — to retain in my breast a lively and permanent interest in all that relates to their present condition and future welfare?

I shall sound no trumpet and make no parade as to what I shall do for the future. After having gone through with such a struggle as has never been paralleled in duration in the life of any reformer, and for nearly forty years been the target at which all poisonous and deadly missiles have been hurled, and having seen our great national iniquity blotted out, and freedom "proclaimed throughout all the land to all the inhabitants thereof," and a thousand presses and pulpits supporting the claims of the colored population to fair treatment where not one could be found to do this in the early days of the anti-slavery conflict, I might — it seems to me — be permitted to take a little repose in my advanced years, if I desired to do so. But, as yet, I have neither asked nor wished to be relieved of any burdens or labors connected with the good old cause. I see a mighty work of enlightenment and regeneration yet to be accomplished at the South, and many cruel wrongs done to the freedmen which are yet to be redressed; and I neither counsel others to turn away from the field of conflict, under the delusion that no more remains to be done, nor contemplate such a course in my own case.

The object for which the *Liberator* was commenced — the extermination of chattel slavery — having been gloriously consummated, it seems to me specially appropriate to let its existence cover the historic period of the great struggle; leaving what remains to be done to complete the work of emancipation to other instrumentalities (of which I hope to avail myself), under new auspices, with more abundant means, and with millions instead of hundreds for allies.

CHAP. VI. 1865.

Most happy am I to be no longer in conflict with the mass of my fellow-countrymen on the subject of slavery. For no man of any refinement or sensibility can be indifferent to the approbation of his fellow-men, if it be rightly earned. But to obtain it by going with the multitude to do evil — by pandering to despotic power or a corrupt public sentiment — is self-degradation and personal dishonor:

"For more true joy Marcellus exiled feels
Than Cæsar with a Senate at his heels."

Better to be always in a minority of one with God — branded as madman, incendiary, fanatic, heretic, infidel — frowned upon by "the powers that be," and mobbed by the populace — or consigned ignominiously to the gallows, like him whose "soul is marching on," though his "body lies mouldering in the grave," or burnt to ashes at the stake like Wickliffe, or nailed to the cross like him who "gave himself for the world," — in defence of the RIGHT, than like Herod, having the shouts of a multitude crying, "It is the voice of a god, and not of a man!"

John Brown.

Farewell, tried and faithful patrons! Farewell, generous benefactors, without whose voluntary but essential pecuniary contributions the *Liberator* must have long since been discontinued! Farewell, noble men and women who have wrought so long and so successfully, under God, to break every yoke! Hail, ye ransomed millions! Hail, year of jubilee! With a grateful heart and a fresh baptism of the soul, my last invocation shall be:

"Spirit of Freedom, on! —
Oh! pause not in thy flight
Till every clime is won
To worship in thy light:
Speed on thy glorious way,
And wake the sleeping lands!
Millions are watching for the ray,
And lift to thee their hands.
Still 'Onward!' be thy cry —
Thy banner on the blast;
And, like a tempest, as thou rushest by,
Despots shall shrink aghast.
On! till thy name is known
Throughout the peopled earth;
On! till thou reign'st alone,
Man's heritage by birth;
On! till from every vale, and where the mountains rise,
The beacon lights of Liberty shall kindle to the skies!"

WM. LLOYD GARRISON.

BOSTON, DECEMBER 29, 1865.

CHAPTER VII.

THE NATIONAL TESTIMONIAL.—1866.

NO act of Mr. Garrison's could have afforded more convincing proof of his unselfishness than his voluntary discontinuance of the *Liberator*, and his joyful recognition of the accomplishment of its immediate object.[1] Certainly it was not without a pang of regret that he gave up the paper and its office, the loss of which and of his long-established editorial routine made him feel, as he expressed it, "like a hen plucked of her feathers." Old habits he could not at once shake off. Many of his exchanges continued to come to him, and he would read and clip from them as industriously as though he were still purveying for the *Liberator*; and during the few weeks in which the office of the Massachusetts Anti-Slavery Society (which had also been the subscription-office of the *Liberator*) was continued, he went to it almost daily, as of old. The Society itself voted, at the January meeting, by a majority of three to one, not to disband, after a debate in which the argument in favor of dissolution was sustained by Mr. Quincy, Mr. May, and Mr. Garrison, who all withdrew from the organization. The importance of continuing it was urged with much intensity of feeling and language by Mr. Phillips and his supporters, whose imputation that the retiring members were deserting the cause was warmly resented by Mr.

CHAP. VII.

1866.

Jan. 24, 25.

S. May, Jr.

1 "The Euthanasia of the *Liberator*" was celebrated by Edmund Quincy in the N. Y. *Independent* of Jan. 11, 1866. Notable articles on the career of the paper and its editor also appeared in the London *Daily News* of Jan. 9 (by Harriet Martineau), N. Y. *Nation* (by O. B. Frothingham), and N. Y. *Tribune* (by H. B. Stanton) of Jan. 4, and in other leading journals.

Garrison in the debate, and subsequently in the N. Y. *Independent*. The Society whose existence was declared of such vital consequence continued the *Standard*, but did nothing more for the next four years than hold an annual meeting. Its office was closed.

Feb. 8, 1866.

In February, Mr. Garrison made his second and final visit to Washington, for the sake of spending a few days with his daughter, who had recently become Mrs. Henry Villard and gone there to reside. He lectured in Philadelphia to a large audience, on his way thither, and spent ten days at the Capital at a peculiarly exciting time, when the apostasy of Andrew Johnson to the party which had elected him first became open and pronounced, through his veto of the Freedmen's Bureau Bill, and his disgraceful harangue in denunciation of Congress to a crowd in front of the White House, on Washington's Birthday.

Jan. 3, 1866. *Feb.* 3. *Feb.* 17–26. *Feb.* 22.

W. L. Garrison to W. P. Garrison.

MS.

WASHINGTON, Feb. 22, 1866.

I have come here at a very interesting and opportune period. This is a live Congress, and every day is big with events of national importance. I have heard several very radical speeches in the Senate — one by Senator Yates, "flat-footed" in favor of universal (male) suffrage; another by Senator Wade, on his proposed amendment of the Constitution, allowing no man to be reëlected to the office of President of the United States — a very bold speech in its utterance; and a third, by Senator Trumbull, distinguished for logical power and vigor of treatment, pulverizing the President's veto [of the Freedmen's Bureau Bill], and showing him to have falsified all its provisions and purposes. I have also listened to the reading of a speech by that Kentucky factionist, Garrett Davis, in support of the veto. The Copperhead strength is very weak, in intellect and numbers, in both houses of Congress.

Richard Yates. B. F. Wade. Lyman Trumbull.

Last evening, I called with Harry at Secretary Stanton's residence, but he and his wife had gone out to spend the evening.

Henry Villard.

This forenoon, I had a brief interview with General Howard, who is, of course, full of uncertainty as to what is to be the

O. O. Howard, Supt. Freedmen's Bureau.

duration or power of the Bureau; but he told me that he had an interview with the President yesterday, who gave him to understand that he should speedily announce, by proclamation, that the war has ended and peace been restored; and that the Bureau would continue until a year from that date, according to the terms of the bill constituting the Bureau. He is not, however, to be depended on, especially as all Rebeldom and Copperdom are so warmly espousing his cause. To-morrow promises to be a very lively day in the Senate, on the subject. Senator Wilson is to introduce another bill, providing for the continuance of the Bureau two years from May next, with enlarged powers; but if it pass, the President will doubtless veto it, as in the former instance.

CHAP. VII. 1866.

Henry Wilson.

To-day (22d) Washington is all astir. The day is superb as to the weather — like an April day in Boston — and Pennsylvania Avenue is thronged by all sorts of people. An immense mass of secessionists and Copperheads are holding a meeting at the Theatre, to sustain the recreant President; and I understand he is to address them! I am sure the bottomless pit is equally jubilant.

I have just come, with Franky, from the Capitol, where a most fitting and eloquent eulogium has been bestowed upon the character and services of the late Henry Winter Davis by Senator Creswell of Maryland. The hall of the House was crowded in every part. The Judges of the Supreme Court were present — the leading military men — dignitaries of all kinds — Senators and Representatives, etc. I got in after the oration began, and was standing back near the door, when Speaker Colfax got his eye upon me, and instantly sent a messenger to conduct me to a seat near to Secretary Stanton, Judge Chase, and other notables. After the services, I spoke to Stanton, who expressed great regret that he was not at home last evening, and said he would not be absent again if I would call.[1] I was introduced to a large number of Senators, Representatives, and persons from various parts of the country, and warmly received.

F. J. G.

J. A. J. Creswell.

Schuyler Colfax.

E. M. Stanton.
S. P. Chase.

To-morrow evening I am to lecture in the Union League Hall. . . . On Sunday evening I expect to address the colored people in one of their churches.

[1] Mr. Garrison's first call on reaching Washington was on Senator Sumner (Feb. 18). "Sumner almost made a declamatory speech about universal suffrage, and intends making another in the Senate on the same subject" (MS. Feb. 19, 1866, W. L. G. to H. E. G.).

CHAP. VII. 1866. The Union League Hall was a small room holding but four hundred persons, but it was the only one that could be obtained for Mr. Garrison's lecture, all other halls and churches (including the Unitarian) being refused to the gentleman who had invited him to speak in Washington. *Wm. R. Hooper.* The Odd Fellows' Hall was first engaged, but the proprietors, on learning the name of the lecturer, demanded a bond that no colored person should be admitted, which was of course refused.

It was a larger and more enthusiastic assemblage which Mr. Garrison addressed in the Rev. Henry Highland Garnet's church, the following Sunday evening, *Feb. 25.* and he received a fervent welcome from his colored friends. On both occasions he expressed himself with emphasis concerning the President's veto and speech; and, on his way northward, he lectured to a great audience at the Academy of Music in Brooklyn, *Feb. 27.* declaring that the language in which Andrew Johnson had assailed Congress, in his speech at the White House, was in itself a sufficient ground for his impeachment and removal from office. This proposition he urged further in an article in the N. Y. *Independent,* *Mar. 29, 1866.* the last but one that he was able to write that year, and in a lecture which he delivered in Auburn, Syracuse, and elsewhere. *Mar. 7, 8.*

In the month of January he had experienced a severe fall in Boston, as he was on his way to spend the evening at the house of James T. Fields, with Mrs. Stowe, *Harriet Beecher Stowe.* Governor Andrew, and other friends, and struck the icy pavement with such violence that his right hand and shoulder were badly bruised, and his arm almost paralyzed for a time. He had hardly recovered from the effects of it when he had the misfortune to fall a second time, as he was hurrying to a train, and again struck heavily on his right arm and shoulder. *MS. June 6, 1866, W. L. G. to S. J. May.* This accident caused him many months of suffering, and effectually disabled him from any literary or other work for the rest of the year. It supplied, too, a sufficient reason for his not attempting a task to which he was strongly urged by his friends, namely, the preparation of a History of the Anti-Slavery Movement in the United States. While he was at work on the last number of the *Liberator*, he had received an earnest request to undertake such a work, from the publishing firm of Ticknor & Fields, who subsequently made a very liberal proposition to that end. Mr. Garrison provisionally accepted it, but he had many doubts and misgivings on the subject, and, after two years of alternating resolution and hesitation, he abandoned the idea. The only overt step he took towards it was the hiring of an office in the city, to which the files of the *Liberator* were taken for his examination and review; but the days and weeks he had proposed to devote to them were spent in writing letters and clipping the current newspapers, and the first line of the History was never written. "Be merciful!" he wrote to one of his children, who was impatient to have him begin the work. "It is a matter requiring the gravest deliberation before I actually commit myself one way or another. I confess, I do not feel competent to the mighty task, and fear I shall make a failure of it, if I try." Nearly two years later, in writing to Samuel J. May, in commendation of the 'Recollections of the Anti-Slavery Conflict' which the latter was then publishing serially in the Boston *Christian Register*, he thus expressed himself:

CHAP. VII. 1866. *Dec.* 27, 1865. *MS. July* 3, 1866. *MS. July* 5. 1868. *MS. Mar.* 25, 1866, *to W. P. G.*

"I am now thinking seriously of devoting the next year, if spared, to writing a History of the Anti-Slavery Struggle, and shall feel grateful for any aid you can render me. Unfortunately, my memory of persons and events grows more and more like a sieve; and a good memory is a most important auxiliary in such a connection. How to shape the work will be puzzling — the subject is so vast, the actors so many, the incidents so multitudinous. You lovingly fear I shall not do justice to myself. Certainly, how to dispose of myself, without seeming to be egotistical by personal references on the one hand, or affectedly modest by omitting them on the other, will be a difficult and delicate task. But I shall try to avoid extremes, and to write with all possible simplicity and directness. It is of very little consequence in regard to any record of ourselves. Time

MS. Dec. 9, 1867.

CHAP. VII. 1866. makes mockery of fame. Enough that the Right has triumphed, that Slavery is overthrown, and that God is glorified."

During the spring and summer months of 1866, Mr. Garrison tried various treatments and remedies for his torturing pains, but time alone brought him relief or cure. Whist became a favorite diversion to him, and he spent many an evening playing the game with his children and with George Thompson, who had now become a neighbor in Roxbury and was almost daily interchanging calls with his old comrade. More than ever Mr. Garrison devoted himself to his wife, who, though sadly crippled, found much solace in reading and in correspondence with her absent children. *June 14.* The domestic event of the year was the birth at Rockledge of their first grandchild, *Agnes Garrison.* whose advent gave them unspeakable delight, and whom Mr. Garrison never wearied of carrying in his arms, lulling to sleep, or entertaining with song or piano.

He refused to sign a petition, presented by George Shea of New York, for Jefferson Davis's release from Fortress Monroe, and had no disposition to join Gerrit Smith and Horace Greeley in that movement. Always opposed to capital punishment, he declared that if Davis, with his colossal guilt, escaped the gallows, hanging ought certainly to be forever abolished. The election, in the fall of 1866, of a former compositor on the *Liberator* *Chas. L. Mitchell.* as the first colored member of the Massachusetts Legislature afforded him great satisfaction.

Deprived of his income from the *Liberator*, prevented by his injuries from writing or lecturing, his wife permanently crippled, and his children not yet in a position to relieve him of pecuniary care, Mr. Garrison naturally contemplated his rapidly melting resources with much anxiety, unaware that a movement was already on foot to relieve him from all future concern on that score, and to make him comfortably independent for the remainder of his days. *Mar. 28.* Near the end of March, a number of gentlemen met at the house of Dr. Henry I. Bowditch, and formed themselves into a Committee for the purpose of raising a national testimonial to Mr. Garrison, in grateful and honorable recognition of his part in bringing about the great consummation of universal freedom and homogeneous institutions in the United States. Ex-Governor Andrew accepted the chairmanship with great heartiness, and wrote the Address to the Public, to which a national character was unmistakably given by the approving signatures — gladly appended in every case — of the Governor, Lieutenant-Governor, and Chief Justice of Massachusetts, the State's Senators and Representatives in Congress, Senators and Representatives from sixteen other States (including Missouri), the Chief Justice of the United States, the President of the Senate, the eminent poets and littérateurs of the country, and leading citizens of New York, Philadelphia, Baltimore, and Chicago. The press also cordially endorsed the movement, which was so quietly initiated that Mr. Garrison knew nothing of it for several weeks, and was taken utterly by surprise when it was announced to him. The following is a transcript of the circular to the Public:

John A. Andrew.

L. S. Foster.

Emerson, Whittier, Longfellow, Lowell, Bryant.

National Testimonial to William Lloyd Garrison.

The accomplishment of the Great Work of Emancipation in the United States directs our minds to the duty of some fit public recognition of the man who must in all future time be regarded as its visible leader.

WILLIAM LLOYD GARRISON, then in the twenty-sixth year of his age, established the *Liberator* newspaper in 1831, and thenceforward devoted his abilities and his career to the promotion of "immediate and unconditional emancipation." After the lapse of thirty-five years of the most exacting labor, of controversy, peril, and misconception, he has been permitted to see the object gained to which he, at first almost alone, consecrated his life. The generation which immediately preceded ours regarded him only as a wild enthusiast, a fanatic, or a public enemy. The present generation sees in him the bold and honest reformer, the man of original, self-poised, heroic will, inspired by a vision of universal justice made actual in the practice of nations; who, daring to attack without reserve the worst and

CHAP. VII. most powerful oppression of his country and his time, has outlived the Giant Wrong he assailed, and has triumphed over the sophistries by which it was maintained.

1866.

In this difficult and perilous work, his labors have been so exclusively directed to the single aim of the overthrow of American Slavery, and so absorbing and severe, that, with abilities capable of winning fortune as well as reputation, he is now, in respect to worldly honors and emoluments, as he was at the commencement of his career.

We ask simply to arrest the attention of the American people to the obligations they owe to this American.

Although he contended for the rights of human nature — and thus, in a degree, made mankind his constituency — yet *here* was the field of his enterprise, and *ours* was the land to be immediately redeemed.

He was the advocate of no private interest, he was the representative of no sect or party; with no hope of worldly profit to be reaped from the measures and the principles he urged, he was the conspicuous, the acknowledged, the prophetic leader of the movement in behalf of the American Slave — now consummated by the Edict of Universal Emancipation.

It cannot mar the dignity of his position as a man of honest intellectual and moral independence, to receive a substantial testimonial of the good-will and grateful respect of his friends and countrymen; nor can it be more than an honorable recognition on the part of the uncounted multitudes, of all parties and sections, who must confess themselves to have become his debtors, to give to him such a testimonial, and to make it substantial.

We, the undersigned, do therefore invite all people who rejoice in the destruction of Slavery, in the reëstablishment of the Union on the basis of Universal Freedom, who appreciate his past service in the cause of Liberty, and the dignity and judgment with which he has accepted and interpreted the more recent events of public history, to unite with us in presenting a national testimonial of not less than *Fifty Thousand Dollars* to our fellow-countryman — WILLIAM LLOYD GARRISON.[1]

APRIL 25, 1866.

[1] The following letters were appended to the circular:

DEAR SIR: WASHINGTON, April 11, 1866.

I am glad that you and others have taken in hand the project of a testimonial to Mr. Garrison. His earnest and disinterested labors in the great

Mr. Garrison often said that he prized this document, with its signatures, more than all the pecuniary results that might follow from it. As to these he was never sanguine, having seen many an ambitious attempt to reward public benefactors or commemorate popular heroes fail miserably, and knowing well that the career of even a successful reformer does not appeal to the popular fancy like that of a victorious general or an idolized political leader. And in truth, with all its weight of names, the Garrison Testimonial owed its success in a very large measure to the untiring devotion of the Secretary and Assistant Treasurer, Rev. Samuel May, Jr., to the practical work of securing subscriptions.[1] For two years, under many disadvantages, he gave himself unremittingly to the task, until, in the spring of 1868, the result was announced to Mr. Garrison in the following letter:

CHAP. VII. — 1866.

The Testimonial Committee to W. L. Garrison.

BOSTON, March 10, 1868.

Boston Daily Advertiser, May 16, 1868.

DEAR SIR: The undersigned, a committee appointed to obtain for you a national testimonial in acknowledgment of your preëminent services in forwarding the abolition of American slavery, having brought our labors nearly to a close, think the time has arrived to present you with a statement of the result. We have received in all, after deducting every necessary expense, thirty-one thousand dollars, which we are happy now

cause of Emancipation, of which he may almost be said to be the pioneer, may be most fitly so recognized. His best reward is the triumph of the cause, achieved already, though not yet perfected; but let there be added to that most precious sense of grand results from work nobly done, such a recognition by the people as will be equally honorable to them and to him.

Yours very truly,

S. P. CHASE.

Charles Sumner, in a letter to the Committee, said: "Mr. Garrison's sublime dedication of himself all alone to this cause, at a moment when it was disregarded, can never be forgotten in the history of this country. I trust that no effort will be spared to carry out the idea of securing an honorable token of the grateful sentiments which his name must always inspire among the friends of Human Rights."

[1] Mr. May also visited Washington and secured the signatures attached to the Address to the Public.

CHAP. VII. — 1866.

to place in your hands; and this sum we have reason to believe will be increased one or two thousand dollars more from sources where we know a subscription has been undertaken, but is not yet finished.

The testimonial is in every sense national. Contributions to it have come from every quarter of the country, from all classes, the rich and the poor, the educated and the unlearned, from persons of both sexes, of every religious and political opinion, and of every race. The sums we have received have been given always cheerfully, often joyfully, the donors declaring it a privilege and an honor to share in the offering. Distinguished philanthropists of other countries have also, unsolicited, added their offerings to this testimonial fund.

It gives us the highest gratification to present this national tribute to you as the leader and inspirer of the movement against American slavery, which has resulted in one of the greatest moral triumphs the world has ever witnessed. Having devoted yourself from early manhood wholly to the cause of human freedom, regardless of all personal dangers and sacrifices, you have now the joy of living in a country of which all the inhabitants are free. Whatever trials and sufferings may await the race for which you have labored, they can never again be reduced to slavery.

Our pleasure on this occasion is saddened only by the recollection that our chairman, the late Governor Andrew, who entered into the plan of the committee with all the energy of his sympathetic nature, using both his tongue and pen to promote it, cannot place his name with ours here. No one would have rejoiced more than he in the accomplishment of this effort.

We trust, Mr. Garrison, the offering we present will cheer you and Mrs. Garrison during the remainder of your lives, be they longer or shorter, not merely by the material resources which it brings, but by the precious recollection that it is the gift of a grateful generation of your countrymen and friends. May you long be spared, a living example, to your country and the world.

Your friends,
SAMUEL E. SEWALL,
J. INGERSOLL BOWDITCH,
WILLIAM E. COFFIN,
WILLIAM ENDICOTT, JR.,
SAMUEL MAY, JR.,
EDMUND QUINCY,
THOMAS RUSSELL,
ROBERT C. WATERSTON.

Saml May Jr.

W. L. Garrison to the Testimonial Committee.

BOSTON, March 12, 1868.

RESPECTED FRIENDS: In replying to your very kind letter of the 10th instant, transferring to my hands the truly generous sum obtained by you as a national testimonial, in recognition of my labors in the anti-slavery cause through a long and perilous struggle, I shall try in vain to find words adequately to express my feelings. I can only tender to you my heartfelt thanks for this signal proof of your personal esteem and good-will. I am so constituted as not to fear the frowns of men, when conscious of being in the right; yet no one should desire more strongly than I have always done to secure the regards of the wise, the good, and the true, next to the approval of my own conscience as unto God. All controversy, where no principle is involved, no right to be vindicated, no wrong to be redressed, is utterly distasteful to my temperament. If, therefore, for a long series of years, I was "a disturber of the peace" and "a troubler of Israel," it was not of my choice or seeking; but necessity was laid upon me so to act, by the heinous wrongfulness of chattel slavery, by the Christian obligation to remember those in bonds as bound with them, by the irresistible claims of outraged human nature, and by a more than patriotic interest in the welfare of my native land. Little indeed did I know or anticipate how prolonged or how virulent would be the struggle, when I lifted up the standard of immediate emancipation, and essayed to rouse the nation to a sense of its guilt and danger. But, having put my hand to the plow, how could I look back? For, in a cause so righteous, I could not doubt that, having turned the furrows, if I sowed in tears I should one day reap in joy. But, whether permitted to live to witness the abolition of slavery or not, I felt assured that, as I demanded nothing that was not clearly in accordance with justice and humanity, some time or other, if remembered at all, I should stand vindicated in the eyes of my countrymen. In the very first number of the *Liberator* I said:

"It is pretended, that I am retarding the cause of emancipation by the coarseness of my invective and the precipitancy of my measures. The charge is not true. On this question my influence, humble as it is, is felt at this moment to a considerable extent, and shall be felt in coming years, not perniciously but beneficially—not as a curse but as a blessing; and posterity will bear testimony that I was right." *Ante*, 1:225.

Happily, I have not had to wait for posterity for my vindication—a generous and complete vindication. But, by the

CHAP. VII. 1866.

mighty power of a wonder-working Providence, I have been permitted to see the gory system of slavery annihilated, and its four millions of captives set free. My reproach has been turned into commendation, and my shame into honor. In approval of this testimonial, I see the honored name of Chief Justice Chase, of the U. S. Supreme Court, himself an early and fearless champion in the same good cause — that of the Hon. James Speed of Kentucky, late Attorney-General of the United States — the names of Senators and Representatives in Congress from Maine to Oregon — the names of the Governor, Lieutenant-Governor, and Chief Justice of Massachusetts — the names of eminent merchants, lawyers, collegiate professors, poets, philanthropists, editors, etc., etc. In view of a list so broadly representative, and distinguished for such intellectual, moral, and political weight — added to this the list of approving contributors to the fund — I feel the profoundest humility mingled with the deepest gratitude. Some of these I have never seen, and probably shall never see in the flesh; but I wish to thank each one of them as in his immediate presence. Among the contributors abroad are the honored names of John Bright, John Stuart Mill, William E. Forster, Thomas B. Potter, Samuel Morley, John Cropper, and Arthur Albright. The moral verdict rendered by such an array is prized by me incomparably above all the gold and silver ever coined. While it has particular reference to my career, for the reasons set forth in the appeal, it also means much more than this — namely, the vindication of the anti-slavery movement as such, and of all who have faithfully labored to secure its triumph. Its design, therefore, is neither pecuniary reward nor personal exaltation; but is vitalized and made all-embracing by the sublime historical event to which it relates.

Having never sought the applause of my fellow-men, nor asked any favors at their hands, nor claimed to be more than others in labors and sacrifices in the cause of the oppressed, I trust no one will be found so unjust as to impute to me a wish to have any of my co-laborers thrown into the shade. Long before I took up the advocacy of the rights of man, without regard to race or complexion, many had done the same, in their way and according to the light given them. Liberty has never been without her witnesses on earth. The Declaration of Independence contains, in its "self-evident truths," all the abolitionism I have ever enunciated. So does the Golden Rule. Certainly I have never sought to put myself up, nor any fellow-worker down. As to where I have stood and what I have done, by the help of God, for the extinction of slavery in this land, the fury of the oppressor in the past is a more sure certificate than any that can now be given me by the friends of freedom. Yet, without co-workers from the greatest to the least, and in every position in society, my labors had been almost in vain, and peradventure the year of jubilee indefinitely postponed.

Of this testimonial I may be permitted to say, that none was ever more unsought or more unexpected; none more spontaneous or more honorable was ever proffered. Under the guise of self-abnegation, I might decline it; but I have labored in vain if I have now to prove my disinterestedness by refusing to accept this mark "of the good-will and grateful respect of friends and countrymen." He who insists upon always giving, but never receiving, may possibly discover that he is actuated by a false pride and a selfish exclusiveness. Perceiving the spirit and object which have prompted this testimonial, and the complete justification of a once hated but now gloriously triumphant cause embodied in it, I accept it in no dependent sense, nor as a pecuniary reward for any sacrifices made or labors performed, but with becoming self-respect, and with untrammelled freedom of thought, speech, and action. I accept it, moreover, not as relating to any other question than that of slavery, not as an approval of all my methods of action or modes of expression (for some of these I should be quite sure to alter on a critical revision, now that the heat and smoke of the conflict are ended), but exactly for what it is intended to sanction and commend, to wit — the cause of universal freedom, and an unswerving advocacy of that cause, at whatever cost or peril. By the abolition of slavery, notwithstanding the pangs and dangers of our present transitional state, we may ultimately hope for all crowning mercies upon our beloved country. For brass there shall be brought forth gold, and for iron silver, and for wood brass, and for stones iron. Every man shall sit under his own vine, and there shall be none to molest or make afraid.

My pleasure, gentlemen of the committee, is saddened in this connection, as well as your own, in view of the sudden demise of your lamented chairman, ex-Governor Andrew, who honored me with his friendship and confidence when friends and supporters were "few and far between," and who took a more than friendly interest in the inception and completion of this testimonial, himself writing the appeal to the people, and exerting his influence to get it responded to, to the full extent therein

CHAP. VII. — 1866.

designated. Were he now living, no one would take more pleasure in the result than himself. His loss is a national bereavement. For, since the tragical death of President Lincoln, what public man has been so widely lamented as himself? So gentle, yet so forcible! so conciliating, yet so outspoken! so modest, yet so intrepid! so yielding where no sense of duty was involved, yet so inflexible in the maintenance of his principles! so full of "the milk of human kindness," yet so like a flame of fire against injustice! so thoroughly domestic in his affections and habits, yet so ready at all times to be sacrificed in the service of his country! — among the most manly of men, the most upright of statesmen, and the best of patriots! What he did as Governor of the Commonwealth, during the late slaveholding rebellion, both for the State which he represented and the nation whose liberties he upheld, is it not a signal part of the history of the times, to be admiringly rehearsed by a grateful posterity? In him the hunted fugitive slave always found an advocate ready to interpose all his legal ability and forensic eloquence to shield him from the terrible fate of rendition; for the millions in bondage he cherished the deepest sympathy; and the entire colored population of the republic should ever cherish his memory with grateful emotions.

Again warmly thanking you as a committee, and all who have in any manner participated in procuring this testimonial, I remain, with the highest personal regard,

Yours, for a free country and a free world,

WM. LLOYD GARRISON.

The English contributions alluded to by Mr. Garrison aggregated nearly three hundred pounds, and some of these were transmitted through James Russell Lowell, who made it the occasion for writing the following note:

J. R. Lowell to W. L. Garrison.

MS.

ELMWOOD, 29th Dec., 1866.

MY DEAR SIR: In sending me some subscriptions by friends in England towards the "Garrison Testimonial," Mr. Thomas C. Ryley copies a passage from the letter of Mr. Bright, enclosing a £5 contribution. As I am sure the extract must give pleasure to you and yours, I recopy it:

John Bright.

"It is true I have ten times more applications for subscriptions than I can comply with, but I gladly send you £5 towards the Garrison fund. I know no nobler man than Wm. Lloyd Garrison, and no man more rejoices that he has lived to see the great day of freedom than I do. I hope he will believe that our small contributions to the fund but faintly express the esteem and affection which his English friends feel towards him." CHAP. VII. 1866.

Allow me, my dear sir, to add my own hearty sympathy with Mr. Bright's words, and to say that nothing could have been more in keeping with the uniform wisdom of your anti-slavery leadership than the time you chose for resigning it.

With great respect,

Very truly yours,

J. R. LOWELL.

CHAPTER VIII.

To England and the Continent.—1867.

Chap. VIII.
—
1867.

FROM the time the destruction of slavery was an assured fact, Mr. Garrison had cherished the hope that he might once more revisit his transatlantic coadjutors, and rejoice with them that Cowper's boast, "Slaves cannot breathe in England!" could now be applied to America. The fact that his daughter and her husband, and his youngest son, were then abroad and urging him to join them; the hope that travel and change of scene might accelerate his recovery; the temptation to visit the International Exposition at Paris; and an appointment by the American Freedman's Union Commission to represent it at an International Anti-Slavery Conference to be held in that city in August,—all combined to determine his going, and George Thompson, after three years' residence in America, decided to return to England with him.

On the 8th of May, they sailed together from Boston on the *Cuba*. A host of friends gathered at East Boston to see them off, and preparations had been made to escort them down the harbor with the Revenue Cutter, which Collector Russell offered for the purpose, but a heavy rain prevented this. Mr. Waterston, of the Testimonial Committee, announced to Mr. Garrison that Thirty Thousand Dollars had been collected and placed to his credit, and as the *Cuba* swung into the stream and began her voyage, the guns of the gaily dressed Revenue Cutter fired a parting salute in his honor, which was repeated by the boys of the School Ship *Massachusetts*, who manned the yards of that vessel and gave three rousing cheers.

Thomas Russell. Rev. Robert C. Waterston.

The voyage to Liverpool was quick and uneventful. Mr. Garrison proceeded directly to Paris, parting with Mr. Thompson at London, and crossing the Channel, for the first time, between Folkestone and Boulogne. The wretched accommodation for passengers on the Channel steamers amazed him, and in trying to compute the yearly aggregate of misery caused thereby to tens of thousands of travellers, he became, as he declared, "too indignant to be seasick." The next four weeks he devoted to sight-seeing in Paris, in company with his children, and was charmed by the gay and brilliant city. He made many visits to the great Exposition, and never wearied of strolling or driving through the parks and along the boulevards, or of excursions to St. Cloud and Versailles. The shop windows had an especial fascination for him. He had never before shown any interest in diamonds or precious stones, but the great jewelry shops in the Palais Royal arcades fairly dazzled him. Every day brought its novel experience, and was so fully occupied that he found scant time for recording his impressions; hence, his letters present little that is quotable. He saw the great military display of the 6th of June, when Napoleon entertained his guests the Czar Alexander and King William of Prussia (accompanied by Bismarck) with a review of sixty thousand troops in the Bois de Boulogne.

May 9–18, 1867.

May 20.

"As a spectacle," he wrote, "it was the most gorgeous and the most imposing of any I have ever witnessed, or ever expect to witness. The sun shone clearly out, adding to the brilliancy and effectiveness of the scene. . . . Of course, in a moral point of view, this mighty warlike display gave me no pleasure, but rather much pain at seeing such a perversion of human nature in support of usurpation and oppression. As the royal party rode out of the park, they were fired upon by a Pole, who doubtless intended to kill the Emperor of Russia, but he only succeeded in killing the horse of an officer riding by the side of the royal carriage, the pistol bursting in his hand. He was immediately arrested.

MS. June 7, to H. E. G.

"I have dined with Madame Coignet and Miss Dowling, who have been at the head of the Freedmen's movement in Paris.

John Lemoinne. . . . I there met the Editor of the *Journal des Débats*, but as he could not speak English, nothing passed between us. I have *Nicholas Tourgueneff; ante, 3:421.* also dined with Monsieur Tourgueneff, my Russian admirer, and a nobleman by nature as well as by station. . . . I have also had a very agreeable interview with the celebrated *Edouard Laboulaye.* Professor Laboulaye, who strongly reminded me, in his sweet, gentle manners, and in the shape of his head, of the lamented *Charles Follen.* Professor Follen. Even he is not allowed to address a class or assemblage of persons in more than two places in the whole city of Paris! Everything here is under governmental espionage and dictation, and therefore in a volcanic condition, although the volcano is capped for the present."

Augustin Cochin. Mr. Garrison met still another eminent Frenchman:

MS. June 14, 1867, to W.L.G., Jr. "Two or three days ago, I wrote a letter to M. Cochin, expressive of my admiration of his character and works in relation to Slavery and the Results of Emancipation, and my desire to have an interview with him, if agreeable, before leaving Paris for London. He immediately wrote a very cordial note in reply, and then drove in his carriage a long distance to our hotel, and sent up his card, with the letter. As I happened to be all alone, . . . I could not read his letter, which was written in French; and as the servant who brought me the letter and card could not understand a word of English, I could not make any response; and so M. Cochin had to drive home without seeing me! He left an invitation to have me take *Henry Villard.* breakfast with him the next morning, and Harry, at my request, went along with me to act as my interpreter. We were very heartily received; but though Cochin, I am assured, can speak very well in English, yet his diffidence was apparently so great about it that he chose to carry on the conversation wholly in French, talking with great fluency and animation, Harry interpreting what he said as he went along. We stopped only twenty or thirty minutes, declining to take the breakfast which we saw spread in another room, though he assured us that his wife (whom we did not see, as she probably expected to see me at breakfast) could speak English readily. Cochin is in the prime of life, has a fine countenance, and in his manners is a finished gentleman, as well as one of the most eminent men in France for his literary and scientific ability. His family descent is old and high."

This was only one of many experiences in which his ignorance of any language but his own was a sad drawback to Mr. Garrison's happiness. He was, however, constantly meeting countrymen and friends in Paris, and he was pleased to be recognized and addressed by two of the colored waiters at the American restaurant of the Exposition. He spent a very agreeable evening with William Cullen Bryant, whom he had never before met, and who had been appointed a fellow-delegate with him to the Anti-Slavery Conference.

CHAP. VIII. 1867. June 1.

On the 15th of June he returned to London, accompanied by his daughter and son. He had little time for looking about the city and noting the changes since his last visit in 1846, before he was overwhelmed by letters and notes of invitation, and proffered courtesies from friends in London and in other parts of the kingdom. After George Thompson, his first call was on John Bright, whom he happened never to have met in his previous visits. Their interview was delightful for its cordiality and informality, seeming rather like the meeting of old friends. The next day he paid his respects to the Duke and Duchess of Argyll, at Argyll Lodge, Kensington, desiring to testify his appreciation of the Duke's unfaltering support of the Northern cause during the civil war, and his grateful remembrance of the friendship and support of the Duchess of Sutherland, whose daughter, a young girl in 1840, now greeted him as the Duchess of Argyll. Five of her twelve children were brought into the room to see him whose name had ever been an honored one in her mother's house. A day or two later he received a note from the (Dowager) Duchess of Sutherland herself, who was now a great invalid and sojourning at Chiswick House, one of the seats of the Duke of Devonshire.

June 19. June 20.

The Duchess of Sutherland to W. L. Garrison.

CHISWICK, June 21. *MS.*

DEAR SIR:

I did not hear without great emotion that you are returned to England, and I look forward with great happiness to meet you in these better times. I am anxious to know how long you stay,

Chap. VIII. — 1867.

for if your time allows of a little delay, I would wait a little in hopes of being rather more free from violent pain.

Believe me, dear sir, yours sincerely,

Harriet Sutherland.

I have been very ill for the last month.

To this, Mr. Garrison replied that he hesitated to intrude on her in her invalid condition; but she quickly responded: "However unwell, I would not on any account not see you," and she requested him to come to luncheon at Chiswick House, and sent her carriage for him and his children. She was still too unwell to leave her room, and the Duke and Duchess of Argyll and Marquis of Lorne entertained her guests at luncheon, and did the honors of the house. Mr. Garrison was ushered without delay into the chamber of the Duchess, by her daughter, and welcomed with great warmth and feeling. She made him bring his children in to see her, after luncheon, and when the house, with its treasures of art, its rooms in which Fox and Canning had died, and its beautiful grounds with their superb cedars of Lebanon, had been shown them by their attentive hosts, and they were about to return to the city, Mr. Garrison was again taken to his staunch friend for the parting which was final for this life. The Duchess died in the following year.

MS. June 24. *June 26.* *Oct. 27, 1868.*

Under the escort of Mr. F. W. Chesson (Mr. Thompson's son-in-law), Mr. Garrison visited the House of Commons, and was introduced to John Stuart Mill and James Stansfeld, Jr., the latter the son-in-law of his old friend, Wm. H. Ashurst; and at Stansfeld's house, a few evenings later, he renewed with delight his acquaintance with Joseph Mazzini.

June 20, 1867. *June 23.*

"Of course," he afterwards wrote, "a quarter of a century makes perceptible changes in us all — changes which are rendered the more striking by a separation for so long a term. But Mazzini's altered appearance affected me sadly. There were, indeed, the same finely shaped head; the same dark, lustrous eyes; the same classical features; the same grand intellect; the same lofty and indomitable spirit; the same combination of

Introduction to Life and Writings of Mazzini, 1872.

true modesty and heroic assertion, of exceeding benignity and inspirational power, as in the earlier days; but, physically, he was greatly attenuated, stricken in countenance, broken in health, and evidently near the close of his earthly pilgrimage. But, no marvel! During our long absence from each other, what mighty intellectual forces he had brought into play! what exhausting vigils he had been obliged to keep, and labors to perform! what cruel betrayals, what hairbreadth escapes, what fiery trials had been his! . . . Through all these trying vicissitudes he had passed, and well might the outward man show signs of marked infirmity — to say nothing of the flight of time. But I was painfully convinced that he had greatly injured himself — his nervous temperament being finely wrought — by his one bad habit of excessive smoking; a habit which had mastered his self-control, the evil effects of which he readily admitted, which (as he told me) was fastened upon him by his long solitary imprisonment, and from the craving demands of which he was endeavoring to escape by an effort to lessen the number of cigars used by him daily. Lamenting that so great a soul should be in such self-imposed bondage, I earnestly besought him to summon all his powers, and, both for his own safety and as a noble example to others, resolve to go for 'immediate and unconditional emancipation.' Nothing could be more respectful, more sweet, more gentle than the manner in which he received my entreaty."

Other friends whom he met were Peter A. Taylor, M. P. for Leicester, and his wife, ardent friends of the North in the war days, Thomas Hughes, and Justin McCarthy, then editing the *Morning Star*. Invitations to breakfast or dinner came to him from the son and grandson of his early friend, Sir Thomas Fowell Buxton, and from Lord Houghton, at whose house he met Anthony Trollope and Hepworth Dixon. Trollope had a low opinion of the negro, and discussed him from the ethnological standpoint in a manner that stirred Mr. Garrison's indignation, and led him to handle the novelist in a vigorous and summary fashion delightful to his host, who recalled the incident ten years later. A day was spent at Richmond with the Duc d'Aumale and his nephews, the Comte de Paris and Duc de Chartres, at the house of Mr. and Mrs. Auguste

CHAP. VIII. 1867. Laugel, the latter a daughter of Mrs. Chapman. In addition to all these occupations, Mr. Garrison was besieged by callers at his lodgings, and had little time to prepare himself for the impending demonstration in his honor which he greatly dreaded.

Morning Star, June 24, 1867. Announcement was made, shortly after his arrival in London, that "a Public Breakfast in honor of William Lloyd Garrison, the leader of the Anti-Slavery Party in the United States," would be held at St. James's Hall, on Saturday, June 29, at noon, and that John Bright, Esq., M. P., would preside on the occasion. The price of tickets was placed at ten shillings each, and the presence of ladies was invited. The Committee of Arrangements consisted of more than fifty gentlemen, all of them well known, and most of them eminent for their political, social, literary, or scientific standing. The Duke of Argyll headed the list as Chairman, with the Hon. E. Lyulph Stanley as Vice-Chairman, and they were supported by Lord Houghton, Lord Alfred Spencer Churchill, and Sir George Young; by members of Parliament like John Bright, John Stuart Mill, William E. Forster, James Stansfeld, Jr., Charles and Sir Thomas Fowell Buxton, Peter A. Taylor, Thomas Hughes, Thomas Bayley Potter, and Joseph Cowen; by members of the bar like Serjeant Parry, W. Vernon Harcourt, and William Shaen; by philosophers, scientists, and littérateurs like Herbert Spencer F. D. Maurice and T. H. Huxley, Goldwin Smith, Richard H. Hutton, William Howitt, Frederic Harrison, and William Black; and by journalists like Justin McCarthy, A. H. Dymond, and F. W. Chesson.

That these names were lent in no perfunctory spirit is evident from the fact that four-fifths of the Committee were present at the Breakfast. The fine hall was thronged. Upwards of three hundred ladies and gentlemen sat down at the tables, which occupied the floor of the hall. The galleries, too, were filled with eager spectators, and a hundred persons tried in vain to buy breakfast tickets at the door. Seldom had an audience so distinguished for intellectual and moral worth been assembled in London. Mr. Bright presided, with Mr. Garrison on his right, and the Duke and Duchess of Argyll on his left. On the right of Mr. Garrison sat Earl and Countess Russell and their daughter, and at the same or other tables were John Stuart Mill, Herbert Spencer, Professors Maurice and Huxley, William E. Forster, and many other members of Parliament, Sir Charles and Lady Trevelyan (daughter of Zachary Macaulay), Miss Cobden, Lady Lyell and Miss Lyell, Professor Fawcett and wife, Professor Beesly, Victor Schoelcher,[1] W. Vernon Harcourt, Jacob Bright, Justin McCarthy, Edward Miall, Frederic Harrison, Geo. J. Holyoake, William Black, and scores of others. Of Mr. Garrison's English anti-slavery friends there were the Ashursts, Stansfelds, Shaens, Taylors, Thompsons, and Chessons; and Richard D. Webb came over from Ireland for the occasion. America was represented by the U. S. Consul at London (Mr. Morse), and by a number of anti-slavery friends who were happily in London—Mrs. Chapman's daughters and the Rev. William Henry Channing being among these, while Miss Sarah Remond, Bishop Payne of the African M. E. Church, Rev. J. Sella Martin, and William and Ellen Craft well represented the enfranchised race. The American Minister sent the following letter, which was read by Mr. Chesson:

CHAP. VIII. 1867.

Henry Fawcett. E. S. Beesly.

54 PORTLAND PLACE, June 25, 1867.

To F. W. Chesson. W. L. G. Breakfast, p. 15.

SIR: Permit me to express my great gratification in receiving the honor of an invitation to be present on the interesting occasion so complimentary to my countryman, Mr. Garrison. It cannot but be gratifying to perceive so cordial a disposition among Englishmen to recognize his long and arduous services in the cause of philanthropy. It is with much regret that I find myself unable, from the pressure of my engagements on that day, to attend; but I pray you to assure the Committee of the obligation I feel myself to be under for their courtesy.

I am, very truly yours,
C. F. ADAMS.

[1] As Colonial Minister under the French Republic of 1848, Schoelcher precipitated the abolition of slavery in the French colonies.

Mr. Chesson also read a letter from the Comte de Paris:

To F. W. Chesson. W. L. G. Breakfast, p. 16.

YORK HOUSE, Twickenham, S. W., June 26.

SIR: Engagements of long standing will prevent me from being present at the breakfast which will be given on Saturday to Mr. Garrison. I regret it extremely, and I hasten to beg you to thank the Committee in the Comtesse de Paris's name, as well as my own, for the amiable invitation which you have transmitted to us.

I wish at least to avail myself of that opportunity to tell you how much I sympathize with the mark of esteem and respect which you are about to give to the courageous and indefatigable champion of emancipation. The abolition of slavery is indeed a cause dear to every liberal heart, whatever may be its country; and as we all belong to an epoch which, besides its faults, has also its greatness, we may be proud to see it wipe off this shameful stain on our civilization.

The cause of humanity has definitively triumphed, thanks to the energy of a free people. Slavery is henceforth condemned by public opinion, even in the countries where the law allows it still an ephemeral existence. But those who have served this cause can never forget that at a time when its success appeared only as an impracticable utopia, it had enlisted already a handful of eloquent defenders, and that prominent amongst them was William Lloyd Garrison.

After consecrating his life to a task so difficult at the outset, he has had the happiness to see the accomplishment of the salutary revolution for which he labored. He has at last been conspicuous, even for his moderation, in the midst of that American people which, formed in the manly school of liberty, has shown itself as great in victory as in adversity. While we pay deserved homage to those who receive during this life the recompense of their devotion to their principles, it is impossible not to associate with them the memory of those who have been the martyrs of their cause, from the name, already historical, of Lincoln, to the last of those who are inscribed on the long and precious lists published in America, and so justly called "The Roll of Honor."

In receiving a man whose character honors America, I thank you, Sir, for having thought of me, and for having counted on my sympathy for all that is great and noble in that country, which I have seen in the midst of such a terrible crisis.

I remain, Sir, yours truly,

LOUIS PHILLIPPE D'ORLÉANS, Comte de Paris.

Letters expressing sympathy with the objects of the meeting were also received from the Earl of Shaftesbury, Lord Houghton, Sir Charles Lyell, Sir T. F. Buxton, Goldwin Smith, Charles Buxton, M. P., Professor J. E. Cairnes, Thomas Hughes, M. P., and many others unable to attend. Of these we give but one:

CHAP. VIII. 1867.

Sir Charles Lyell to F. W. Chesson.

73 HARLEY STREET, June 22, 1867.

W. L. G. Breakfast, p. 17.

DEAR SIR: I regret that my engagements are such as to prevent me from assisting in the arrangements for a public breakfast to Mr. Garrison, who has done so much for a cause in which I warmly sympathize.

I will do what I can in making the intended meeting known among those who I know will be glad to contribute to its success.

Believe me, dear Sir,
Very truly yours,
CHARLES LYELL.[1]

Those who were familiar with Mr. Bright's oratory averred that he had never spoken with more grace and simple eloquence, or with deeper tenderness and feeling, than characterized the beautiful address with which he introduced the post-prandial exercises of the occasion. Its effect upon his audience was most impressive, and a common baptism of spirit seemed to pervade the great assembly, which listened as if entranced. His opening words were as follows:

W. L. G. Breakfast, p. 17.

"The position in which I am placed this morning is one very unusual for me, and one that I find somewhat difficult; but I consider it a signal distinction to be permitted to take a prominent part in the proceedings of this day, which are intended to commemorate one of the greatest of the great triumphs of freedom, and to do honor to a most eminent instrument in the achievement

[1] Here it will not be inappropriate to cite the following private tribute from Charles Darwin (MSS. to W. P. G., October, 1879): "I thank you also for the Memorials of Garrison, a man to be forever revered." "It will ever be a deep gratification to me to know that your Father, whom I honor from the bottom of my soul, should have heard and approved of the few words which I wrote many years ago on Slavery." (See the 'Journal of a Voyage,' *passim*, and particularly the chapter on Brazil.)

CHAP. VIII. — 1867

of that freedom. (Hear, hear.) There may be, perhaps, those who ask what is this triumph of which I speak. To put it briefly, and, indeed, only to put one part of it, I may say that it is a triumph which has had the effect of raising 4,000,000 of human beings from the very lowest depth of social and political degradation to that lofty height which men have attained when they possess equality of rights in the first country on the globe. (Cheers.) More than this, it is a triumph which has pronounced the irreversible doom of slavery in all countries and for all time. (Renewed cheers.) Another question suggests itself — How has this great matter been accomplished? The answer suggests itself in another question — How is it that any great matter is accomplished? By love of justice, by constant devotion to a great cause, and by an unfaltering faith that that which is right will in the end succeed. (Hear, hear.)"

Recalling the trials and perils attending the earlier stages of Mr. Garrison's career — his imprisonment at Baltimore, the Boston mob, and the Georgia law — Mr. Bright continued:

W. L. G. Breakfast, p. 19.

"Now, these were menaces and perils such as we have not in our time been accustomed to in this country in any of our political movements — (hear, hear) — and we shall take a very poor measure indeed of the conduct of the leaders of the emancipation party in the United States if we estimate them by any of those who have been concerned in political movements amongst us. But, notwithstanding all drawbacks, the cause was gathering strength, and Mr. Garrison found himself by and by surrounded by a small but increasing band of men and women who were devoted to this cause, as he himself was. We have in this country a very noble woman who taught the English people much upon this question about thirty years ago; I allude to Harriet Martineau. (Cheers.) I recollect well the impression with which I read a most powerful and touching paper which she had written, and which was published in the number of the *Westminster Review* for December, 1838. It was entitled 'The Martyr Age of the United States.' The paper introduced to the English public the great names which were appearing on the scene in connection with this cause in America. . . . When I read that article by Harriet Martineau, and the description of those men and women there given, I was led, I know not how, to think of a very striking passage which I am sure must be

Ante, 2:97, 189.

W. L. G. Breakfast, p. 20.

familiar to most here, because it is to be found in the Epistle to the Hebrews. After the writer of that epistle has described the great men and fathers of the nation, he says: 'Time would fail me to tell of Gideon, of Barak, of Samson, of Jephtha, of David, of Samuel, and the Prophets, who through faith subdued kingdoms, wrought righteousness, obtained promises, stopped the mouths of lions, quenched the violence of fire, escaped the edge of the sword, out of weakness were made strong, waxed valiant in fight, turned to flight the armies of the aliens.' I ask if this grand passage of the inspired writer may not be applied to that heroic band who have made America the perpetual home of freedom? (Enthusiastic cheers.) . . .

CHAP. VIII. — 1867.

"Then came the outbreak which had been so often foretold, so often menaced; and the ground reeled under the nation during four years of agony, until at last, after the smoke of the battle-field had cleared away, the horrid shape which had cast its shadow over a whole continent had vanished, and was gone for ever. (Loud cheers.) An ancient and renowned poet has said:

W. L. G. Breakfast, p. 21.

> 'Unholy is the voice
> Of loud thanksgiving over slaughtered men.'

It becomes us not to rejoice, but to be humbled, that a chastisement so terrible should have fallen upon any of our race; but we may be thankful for this — that that chastisement was at least not sent in vain. (Hear.) This great triumph in the field was not all; there came after it another great triumph — a triumph over passion, and there came up before the world the spectacle, not of armies and military commanders, but of the magnanimity and mercy of a powerful and victorious nation. (Cheers.) The vanquished were treated as vanquished, in the history of the world, have never before been treated. There was an universal feeling in the North that every care should be taken of those who had so recently and marvellously been enfranchised. Immediately we found that the privileges of independent labor were open to them, schools were established, in which their sons might obtain an education that would raise them to an intellectual position never reached by their fathers; and at length full political rights were conferred upon those who, a few short years, or rather months, before, had been called chattels, and things to be bought and sold in any market. (Hear, hear.) And we may feel assured, that those persons in the Northern States who befriended the negro in his bondage will not now fail to assist his struggles for a higher position. May we

CHAP. VIII. 1867.

not say, reviewing what has taken place — and I have only glanced in the briefest possible way at the chief aspects of this great question — that probably history has no sadder, and yet, if we take a different view, I may say also probably no brighter page? (Cheers.) To Mr. Garrison more than to any other man this is due; his is the creation of that opinion which has made slavery hateful, and which has made freedom possible in America. (Hear, hear.) His name is venerated in his own country — venerated where not long ago it was a name of obloquy and reproach. His name is venerated in this country and in Europe wheresoever Christianity softens the hearts and lessens the sorrows of men; and I venture to say that in time to come, near or remote I know not, his name will become the herald and the synonym of good to millions of men who will dwell on the now almost unknown continent of Africa. (Loud cheers.)

"But we must not allow our own land to be forgotten or depreciated, even whilst we are saying what our feelings bid us say of our friend beside me and of our other friends across the water. We, too, can share in the triumph I have described, and in the honors which the world is willing to shower upon our guest, and upon those who, like him, are unwearied in doing good. We have had slaves in the colonial territories that owned the sway of this country. Our position was different from that in which the Americans stood towards theirs; the negroes were far from being so numerous, and they were not in our midst, but 4,000 miles away. We had no prejudices of color to overcome, we had a Parliament that was omnipotent in those colonies, and public opinion acting upon that Parliament was too powerful for the Englishmen who were interested in the continuance of slavery. We liberated our slaves; for the English soil did not reject the bondman, but, the moment he touched it, made him free. We have now in our memory Clarkson, and Wilberforce, and Buxton, and Sturge; and even now we have within this hall the most eloquent living English champion of the freedom of the slave in my friend and our friend, George Thompson. (Great cheering.) Well, then, I may presume to say that we are sharers in that good work which has raised our guest to eminence; and we may divide it with the country from which he comes. (Hear, hear.) Our country is still his; for did not his fathers bear allegiance to our ancient monarchy, and were they not at one time citizens of this commonwealth; and may we not add that the freedom which now overspreads his noble nation first sprang into life amongst our own ancestors? (Enthusiastic cheering.)

"To Mr. Garrison, as is stated in one of the letters which have just been read — to William Lloyd Garrison it has been given, in a manner not often permitted to those who do great things of this kind, to see the ripe fruit of his vast labors. Over a territory large enough to make many realms, he has seen hopeless toil supplanted by compensated industry; and where the bondman dragged his chain, there freedom is established forever. (Loud cheers.) We now welcome him amongst us as a friend whom some of us have known long; for I have watched his career with no common interest, even when I was too young to take much part in public affairs; and I have kept within my heart his name, and the names of those who have been associated with him in every step which he has taken; and in public debate in the halls of peace, and even on the blood-soiled fields of war, my heart has always been with those who were the friends of freedom. (Renewed cheering.) We welcome him, then, with a cordiality which knows no stint and no limit for him and for his noble associates, both men and women; and we venture to speak a verdict which, I believe, will be sanctioned by all mankind, not only those who live now, but those who shall come after, to whom their perseverance and their success shall be a lesson and a help in the future struggles which remain for men to make. One of our oldest and greatest poets has furnished me with a line that well expresses that verdict. Are not William Lloyd Garrison and his fellow-laborers in that world's work — are they not

'On Fame's eternal bead-roll worthy to be filed?'"

The enthusiastic plaudits which followed Mr. Bright's peroration were renewed when the Duke of Argyll came forward to propose the formal Address of Welcome, which had been written by Goldwin Smith. He prefaced his reading of it with a brief speech, from which we also quote:

"Mr. Chairman, Ladies and Gentlemen: It is hard to follow an address of such extraordinary beauty, simplicity, and power; but it now becomes my duty at your command, Sir, to move an address of hearty congratulation to our distinguished guest, William Lloyd Garrison. (Cheers.) Sir, this country is from time to time honored by the presence of many distinguished *W. L. G. Breakfast, pp.* 24-29.

CHAP. VIII. 1867.

and of a few illustrious men; but for the most part we are contented to receive them with that private cordiality and hospitality with which, I trust, we shall always receive strangers who visit our shores. The people of this country are not preëminently an emotional people; they are not naturally fond of public demonstrations; and it is only upon rare occasions that we give, or can give, such a reception as that we see here this day. There must be something peculiar in the Cause which a man has served, in the service which he has rendered, and in our own relations with the People whom he represents, to justify or to account for such a reception. (Hear, hear.) As regards the Cause, it is not too much to say that the Cause of negro emancipation in the United States of America has been the greatest cause which, in ancient or in modern times, has been pleaded at the bar of the moral judgment of mankind. (Cheers.) I know that to some this will sound as the language of exaggerated feeling; but I can only say that I have expressed myself in language which I believe conveys the literal truth. (Hear, hear.)

"I have, indeed, often heard it said in deprecation of the amount of interest which was bestowed in this country on the cause of negro emancipation in America, that we are apt to forget the forms of suffering which are immediately at our own doors, over which we have some control, and to express exaggerated feeling as to the forms of suffering with which we have nothing to do, and for which we are not responsible. I have never objected to that language in so far as it might tend to recall us to the duties which lie immediately around us, and in so far as it might tend to make us feel the forgetfulness of which we are sometimes guilty, of the misery and poverty in our own country; but, on the other hand, I will never admit — for I think it would be confounding great moral distinctions — that the miseries which arise by way of natural consequence out of the poverty and the vices of mankind, are to be compared with those miseries which are the direct result of positive law and of a positive institution, giving to man property in man. (Loud cheers.) . . .

"If such be the Cause, what are we to say of the Man and of the services which he has rendered to that cause? We honor Mr. Garrison, in the first place, for the immense pluck and courage which he displayed. (Cheers.) Sir, you have truly said that there is no comparison between the contests in which he has had to fight and the most bitter contests of our own public life. In looking back, no doubt, to the contest which was maintained in this country some thirty-five years ago against slavery in our colonies, we may recollect that Clarkson and Wilberforce were denounced as fanatics, and had to encounter much opprobrium; but it must not be forgotten that, so far as regards the entwining of the roots of slavery into the social system, in the opinions and interests of mankind, there was no comparison whatever between the circumstances of that contest here and those which attended it in America. (Hear, hear.) The number of persons who, in this country, were enlisted on the side of slavery by personal interest was always comparatively few; whilst, in attacking slavery at its headquarters in the United States, Mr. Garrison had to encounter the fiercest passions which could be roused. (Hear, hear.) That is, indeed, a tremendous sea which runs upon the surface of the human mind when the storms of passion and of self-interest run counter to the secret currents of conscience and the sense of right. (Cheers.)

"Such was the stormy sea on which Mr. Garrison embarked at first — if I may use the simile — almost in a one-oared boat. He stood alone. (Cheers.) And so in our reception this day of Mr. Garrison, we are entitled to think of him as representing the increased power and force which is exerted in our own times by the moral opinions of mankind. (Hear, hear.) It is true, indeed, that we have lately seen some of the most tremendous and bloody wars which history records; and I, for one, must admit that the time has not yet come — it is not even yet in sight — when we can beat our swords into ploughshares and our spears into pruning-hooks; but if we look to the great events to which I have referred, we shall see that in our own time the march of great battalions has generally been in the wake of the march of great principles — (hear, hear) — that in the freedom of Italy, in the consolidation of Germany, and still more in the recent contest in America, we are to look to the triumphs of opinion as, in the main, the triumphs which have been won. (Cheers.) I can understand the joy which must be felt by a great sovereign, or by a great general, when, standing amidst the heaps of slain, he can feel that he has won the independence of a country, or, still better, has established the independence of a race. We can all, however, understand still better the joy of him who, like our distinguished friend, after years of obloquy and oppression, and being denounced as the fanatical supporter of extreme opinions, finds himself acknowledged at last by his

CHAP. VIII. countrymen and the world as the prophet and apostle of a triumphant and accepted cause. (Cheers.)

1867.

"One word in regard to the nation which Mr. Garrison represents. Let us remember with joy and thankfulness that only a few years ago the present reception could not have been given to Mr. Garrison. He was not then the representative of a people, of a country, or of a government. He was the representative only of a party in the United States, and I have always held that public receptions or meetings in foreign countries, or at least in other countries, for I will not call America a foreign country — (immense cheering) — I mean public assemblies or conventions taking part with particular parties of another country, are sometimes almost as apt to do as much harm as good. (Hear, hear.) Now, thank God, Mr. Garrison appears before us as the representative of the United States; freedom is now the policy of the Government and the assured policy of the country, and we can to-day accept and welcome Mr. Garrison, not merely as the liberator of the slaves, but as the representative also of the American Government. (Cheers.) This country desires to maintain with the American people not merely relations of amity and peace; it desires to have their friendship and affection. (Cheers.) It is not merely that that country has sprung from us in former times. It is that it is still to a great extent springing from England. (Hear, hear.) It is hardly possible to go into any house of the farming class in that part of the country with which I am particularly connected, without being told that a brother or a sister, a daughter or a son, has gone to the United States of America, and is flourishing in the free States of Ohio or Illinois. (Cheers.) I think we ought to feel, every one of us, that in going to America we are going only to a second home. (Cheers.) Such are the relations which I trust we shall see established between the two countries. (Hear, hear.) Surely it is time to forget ancient differences — (loud cheers) — differences dating from the days of Burgoyne's retreat, or our failure before the ramparts of New Orleans. I maintain that there is hardly an Englishman in this country — I am sure there is no one in this room — who is not almost as proud of Washington as he is of Wellington — (cheers) — the memory of both belonging, indeed, to the common heritage of our race. (Hear, hear.)

"Therefore, on all these grounds — on the ground of the Cause of which he was the great champion, of the peculiar services which he has rendered to that cause, and of the People whom he represents, we desire to give Mr. Garrison a hearty welcome. (Cheers.)"

CHAP. VIII. — 1867.

The Duke then read the Address:

"*To William Lloyd Garrison, Esq.*

"Sir: We heartily welcome you to England in the name of thousands of Englishmen who have watched with admiring sympathy your labors for the redemption of the negro race from slavery, and for that which is a higher object than the redemption of any single race, the vindication of the universal principles of humanity and justice; and who, having sympathized with you in the struggle, now rejoice with you in the victory.

W. L. G. Breakfast, pp. 29, 30.

"Forty years ago, when you commenced your efforts, slavery appeared to be rapidly advancing to complete ascendency in America. Not only was it dominant in the Southern States, but even in the free States it had bowed the constituencies, society, and, in too many instances, even the churches to its will. Commerce, linked to it by interest, lent it her support. A great party, compactly organized and vigorously wielded, placed in its hands the power of the State. It bestowed political offices and honors, and was thereby enabled to command the apostate homage of political ambition. Other nations felt the prevalence in your national councils of its insolent and domineering spirit. There was a moment, most critical in the history of America and of the world, when it seemed as though that continent, with all its resources and all its hopes, was about to become the heritage of the slave power.

"But Providence interposes to prevent the permanent triumph of evil. It interposes, not visibly or by the thunderbolt, but by inspiring and sustaining high moral effort and heroic lives.

"You commenced your crusade against slavery in isolation, in weakness, and in obscurity. The emissaries of authority with difficulty found the office of the *Liberator* in a mean room, where its editor was aided only by a negro boy, and supported by a few insignificant persons (so the officers termed them) of all colors. You were denounced, persecuted, and hunted down by mobs of wealthy men alarmed for the interests of their class. You were led out by one of these mobs, and saved from their violence and the imminent peril of death almost by a miracle. You were not turned from your path of devotion to your cause,

Ante, 1: 244, 245.

CHAP. VIII. 1867. and to the highest interests of your country, by denunciation, persecution, or the fear of death. You have lived to stand victorious and honored in the very stronghold of slavery; to see
Ante, p. 141. the flag of the Republic, now truly free, replace the flag of
Ante, pp. 141–144. slavery on Fort Sumter; and to proclaim the doctrines of the *Liberator* in the city, and beside the grave, of Calhoun.

"Enemies of war, we most heartily wish, and doubt not that you wish as heartily as we do, that this deliverance could have been wrought out by peaceful means. But the fierce passions engendered by slavery in the slave-owner determined it otherwise; and we feel at liberty to rejoice, since the struggle was inevitable, that its issue has been the preservation, not the extinction, of all that we hold most dear. We are, however, not more thankful for the victories of freedom in the field than for the moderation and mercy shown by the victors, which have exalted and hallowed their cause and ours in the eyes of all nations.

"We shall now watch with anxious hope the development, amidst the difficulties which still beset the regeneration of the South, of a happier order of things in the States rescued from slavery, and the growth of free communities in which your name, with the names of your fellow-workers in the same cause, will be held in grateful and lasting remembrance.

"Once more we welcome you to a country in which you will find many sincere admirers and warm friends."

Earl Russell, at the invitation of Mr. Bright, now came forward to second the Address. Remembering his unfriendly attitude towards the American Government during the critical period of the rebellion, the Committee of Arrangements had not thought of inviting him to the Breakfast, and were surprised at receiving an intimation from him that he wished to be present. Even then they refrained from asking him until they had consulted Mr. Garrison, who unhesitatingly assented. Earl Russell's motive for wishing to take part in the proceedings was revealed in his speech, which was as honorable to him as it was surprising and gratifying to his audience. He said:

W. L. G. Breakfast, pp. 31–33. "As one of his sincere admirers and warm friends, I heartily join in this welcome to Mr. Garrison, and I hold it a distinguished honor to share in the tribute of admiration which is being offered to him this day. It is the characteristic of our race that, amidst evils unnumbered, and miseries unrelieved, though often deeply felt, and institutions which condemn millions to what seems a hopeless servitude, the Almighty has planted in some breasts a feeling of indignation against wrong, a zeal to redress the evils which press upon the most wretched of their fellow-men, that raises up deliverers for mankind, who will not rest until the evils they struggle against are done away, until the balance is redressed, and the fortunes of their race seem to brighten. Such a spirit is found in our guest of to-day. Mr. Garrison felt for the evils of his fellow-men of an oppressed race; he devoted himself to the object of removing them; he was ready to encounter death itself in the pursuit of that salutary and worthy object; and he has been happy enough to live to see the victory of freedom over slavery, and to grapple with it in the form which has prevailed both in America and our own colonies, and which my noble friend who spoke before me has well designated as one of the worst evils that have afflicted mankind. (Cheers.)

"Having said this with respect to Mr. Garrison, you will permit me to join in another sentiment which has been expressed by the Duke of Argyll,—that this may be an occasion which will tend to draw closer the ties of friendship and affection which ought to bind us to the United States of America. (Loud cheers.) So far, unfortunately, the condition of mankind has been such that men seem to seek every occasion of difference with each other, in order to found upon those differences relations of hostility and mutual hatred. Difference of class, difference of race, difference of religion, difference of situation, difference of domestic institutions, all seem to be grounds on which those who are natural enemies to love and affection seek to implant sentiments of hatred and hostility, leading often to bloody wars, and consequences the most calamitous to mankind. If this be so, and I am afraid it is little in our power to prevent those causes from having this operation, may we not consider that the ties existing between us and the United States of America, having our birth from the same ancestors, having both the blessings of Christianity, having (though with different institutions) the same love of freedom, should lead us to replace by a thorough and entire affection the old leaven of hatred and ill-will which has sometimes troubled their connection? Should not these considerations impress us with affection

CHAP. VIII. and regard for our brethren in America, and make us perpetually friends? (Loud cheers.)

1867.

"Well, I have my own faults to acknowledge in this respect, because I certainly thought, when the Slave States of America endeavored to establish their independence, and at the same time to continue and perpetuate the institution of slavery, that the Northern States ought at once to have proclaimed not only their own abhorrence, but the abolition and destruction, of slavery. Distance and want of knowledge of the circumstances of America made me fall into error in that respect. (Hear, hear.) I was afterwards convinced by the distinguished man who represents the United States in this country—I mean Mr. Adams—I was convinced by him in frequent conversations we had on the subject, that I had not rendered due justice to President Lincoln, who was the friend of freedom, and not only the friend, but ultimately the martyr of freedom. (Cheers.) I now, therefore, acknowledge that the task which the Government of the United States had to perform was a totally different task, and a much more difficult one, than we had ourselves to perform when, more than thirty years ago, we abolished slavery in our West India Islands; not having that slavery mixed with our domestic institutions; not having it involved and twined into all our relations, whether political or social; but merely looking upon it as a question for the mass of mankind, as an obligation imposed upon us by our adherence to Christianity, not as having what the United States had, the utmost difficulty in disentangling all the intricacies of the question, and prevailing upon men whose interests, and even their very existence, seemed bound up with it, to abandon their false gods. (Cheers.) Not having that difficulty before us, I did not do justice to the efforts made by the United States; but I am now persuaded that President Lincoln did all that it was possible to do, and that we are bound to give our tribute of admiration to the excellent policy which the President and his Government pursued, and which has resulted in the great consummation we see before us—the entire liberation of 4,000,000 of negro slaves from the bondage in which they were held. (Great cheering.)

"I may well say, as my noble friend has just said, that all those animosities which prevailed some eighty years ago, between the people of this country and the people of the United States of America, have entirely disappeared from our breasts, and that on the 4th of July, which is approaching, we all of us can feel as much admiration for the memory of General Washington,— a man, I believe, of the purest glory amongst all the great men who have existed in modern times,— and as much rejoicing over the triumphs of freedom and the spread of free institutions as the Americans themselves. (Loud cheers.)

CHAP. VIII.

1867.

"There is this further ground for sympathy and for rejoicing in common, that we and they have combined in treating the race of Africa as a free community, free to enter into the paths of industry, free to distinguish themselves in intellectual progress as much as any race of our own color. Having this additional source of sympathy and fellow-feeling, let us hope that the friendship of the United States and the United Kingdom of Great Britain and Ireland may endure unbroken, and that Mr. Garrison may carry with him, amongst other gratifications, this reflection, that our meeting here to-day has tended to the better union of two races who ought never to be separated. (Great cheering.)"

Any one of the above speeches would have made the occasion noteworthy and significant, but it remained for John Stuart Mill, who followed Earl Russell, to point, with philosophic thoughtfulness, the moral of Mr. Garrison's experience. Mr. Mill said:

W. L. G. Breakfast, pp. 33-35.

"The speakers who have preceded me have, with an eloquence far beyond anything which I can command, laid before our honored guest the homage of admiration and gratitude which we all feel is due to his heroic life. Instead of idly expatiating upon things which have been far better said than I could say them, I would rather endeavor to recall one or two lessons, applicable to ourselves, which may be drawn from his career. A noble work nobly done always contains in itself, not one, but many lessons; and in the case of him whose character and deeds we are here to commemorate, two may be singled out specially deserving to be laid to heart by all who would wish to leave the world better than they found it.

"The first lesson is,— Aim at something great; aim at things which are difficult; and there is no great thing which is not difficult. Do not pare down your undertaking to what you can hope to see successful in the next few years, or in the years of your own life. Fear not the reproach of Quixotism or of fanaticism; but after you have well weighed what you undertake, if you see your way clearly, and are convinced that you

CHAP. VIII. are right, go forward, even though you, like Mr. Garrison, do

1867. it at the risk of being torn to pieces by the very men through whose changed hearts your purpose will one day be accomplished. Fight on with all your strength against whatever odds, and with however small a band of supporters. If you are right, the time will come when that small band will swell into a multitude. You will at least lay the foundations of something memorable, and you may, like Mr. Garrison,— though you ought not to need or expect so great a reward,— be spared to see that work completed which, when you began it, you only hoped it might be given to you to help forward a few stages on its way.

"The other lesson which it appears to me important to enforce, amongst the many that may be drawn from our friend's life, is this: If you aim at something noble and succeed in it, you will generally find that you have succeeded not in that alone. A hundred other good and noble things which you never dreamed of will have been accomplished by the way, and the more certainly, the sharper and more agonizing has been the struggle which preceded the victory. The heart and mind of a nation are never stirred from their foundations without manifold good fruits. In the case of the great American contest, these fruits have been already great, and are daily becoming greater. The prejudices which beset every form of society — and of which there was a plentiful crop in America — are rapidly melting away. The chains of prescription have been broken; it is not only the slave who has been freed — the mind of America has been emancipated. The whole intellect of the country has been set thinking about the fundamental questions of society and government; and the new problems which have to be solved, and the new difficulties which have to be encountered, are calling forth new activity of thought, and that great nation is saved, probably for a long time to come, from the most formidable danger of a completely settled state of society and opinion — intellectual and moral stagnation.

"This, then, is an additional item of the debt which America and mankind owe to Mr. Garrison and his noble associates; and it is well calculated to deepen our sense of the truth which his whole career most strikingly illustrates — that though our best-directed efforts may often seem wasted and lost, nothing coming of them that can be pointed to and distinctly identified as a definite gain to humanity; though this may happen ninety-nine times in every hundred, the hundredth time the result may be so great and dazzling that we had never dared to hope for it, and should have regarded him who had predicted it to us as sanguine beyond the bounds of mental sanity. So has it been with Mr. Garrison. (Loud cheers.)"

CHAP. VIII. — 1867.

The Address having been unanimously adopted by the audience, Mr. Garrison rose to acknowledge it amid an enthusiastic ovation. Not anticipating that he was to encounter such a greeting from the foremost men of intellect in Great Britain, he had made small preparation for his part of the programme, and, with the exception of jotting down a few notes as heads of what he wished to say, he went trusting to the inspiration of the moment. His opening words, spoken under perceptible embarrassment, and with unaffected modesty and feeling, were listened to with the closest attention:

W. L. G. Breakfast, pp. 36, 37, and London Morning Star, July 1, 1867.

"Mr. Chairman, Ladies and Gentlemen: For this marked expression of your personal respect, and appreciation of my labors in the cause of human freedom, and of your esteem and friendship for the land of my nativity, I offer you, one and all, my grateful acknowledgments. But I am so profoundly impressed by the formidable array of rank, genius, intellect, scholarship, and moral and religious worth which I see before me, that I fear I shall not be able to address you, except with a fluttering pulse and a stammering tongue. For me this is, indeed, an anomalous position! Assuredly, this is treatment with which I have not been very familiar! For more than thirty years I had to look the fierce and unrelenting hostility of my countrymen in the face, with few to cheer me onward. In all the South I was an outlaw, and could not have gone there, though an American citizen guiltless of wrong, and though that flag [here the speaker pointed to the United States ensign] had been over my head, except at the peril of my life; nay, with the certainty of finding a bloody grave. (Hear, hear.) In all the North I was looked upon with hatred and contempt. The whole nation, subjugated to the awful power of slavery, rose up in mobocratic tumult against any and every effort to liberate the millions held in bondage on its soil. And yet I demanded nothing that was not perfectly just and reasonable — in exact accordance with the Declaration of Independence and the Golden Rule. I was not the enemy of any man living. I cherish no personal enmities, I know nothing of them in my heart. Even whilst the slaveholders were seeking my destruction, I never for a moment entertained any other feeling towards them than an earnest desire, under God, to deliver them from a deadly curse and an awful sin. (Hear, hear.) It was neither a sectional nor a personal matter at all; it had exclusive reference to the eternal law of justice between man and man, and the rights of human nature itself.

"Sir, I have always found in America that a shower of brickbats had a tonic effect, materially strengthening to the backbone. But, sir, the shower of compliments and applause which has greeted me on this occasion would assuredly cause my heart to fail me, were it not that this generous reception is only incidentally personal to myself. You, ladies and gentlemen, are here mainly to celebrate the triumph of humanity over its most brutal foes; to rejoice that universal emancipation has at last been proclaimed throughout the United States; and to express, as you have already done through the mouths of the eloquent speakers who have preceded me, sentiments of peace and of good-will towards the American Republic. Sure I am that these sentiments will be heartily reciprocated by my countrymen.

"I must here disclaim, with all sincerity of soul, any special praise for anything that I have done. I have simply tried to maintain the integrity of my soul before God, and to do my duty. I have refused to go with the multitude to do evil. I have endeavored to save my country from ruin. But then I ought to have done it all; and, having done it all, I feel it is nothing to speak of, nothing to be complimented upon. We ought to do our duty always — we ought to rejoice if even through persecution, if even through the cross, we are compelled to look duty in the face.

"And now, rejoicing here with you at the marvellous change which has taken place across the Atlantic, I am unable to express the satisfaction I feel in believing that, henceforth, my country will be a mighty power for good in the world. While she held a seventh portion of her vast population in a state of chattelism, it was in vain that she boasted of her democratic principles and her free institutions; ostentatiously holding her Declaration of Independence in one hand, and brutally wielding her slave-driving lash in the other! Marvellous inconsistency and unparalleled assurance! But now, God be praised, she is free — free to advance the cause of liberty throughout the world! (Loud cheers.)"

Recalling his first visit to England, Mr. Garrison amused his auditors with the story of Buxton's mistaking him for a black man, and then, passing to the World's Convention of 1840, and his reasons for declining to enter it, he improved the opportunity to pay a tribute to Mr. Mill for the "masterly ability" with which he had recently advocated, in Parliament, the rights of woman — "rights which pertain to all the human race, the exclusive possession of which cannot be safely entrusted to those who are for class interests, and who reject the doctrine of human equality." He also eulogized George Thompson's anti-slavery labors in the United States, and said of the American abolitionists: *Ante*, 1: 351.

"Putting myself entirely out of the question, I believe that in no land, at any time, was there ever a more devoted, self-sacrificing, and uncompromising band of men and women. Nothing can be said to their credit which they do not deserve. With apostolic zeal, they counted nothing dear to them for the sake of the slave, and him dehumanized. But whatever has been achieved through them is all of God, to whom alone is the glory due. . . . *W. L. G. Breakfast*, *pp*. 39, 40.

"Henceforth, through all coming time, advocates of justice and friends of reform, be not discouraged; for you will and you must succeed, if you have a righteous cause. No matter at the outset how few may be disposed to rally round the standard you have raised — if you battle unflinchingly and without compromise — if yours be a faith that cannot be shaken, because it is linked to the Eternal Throne — it is only a question of time when victory shall come to reward your toils. Seemingly, no system of iniquity was ever more strongly intrenched, or more sure and absolute in its sway, than that of American slavery; yet it has perished.

'In the earthquake God has spoken:
He has smitten with His thunder
The iron walls asunder,
And the gates of brass are broken.'

So it has been, so it is, so it ever will be throughout the earth, in every conflict for the right. (Great cheering.)"

After showing that "on the issue raised by the Confederate States, never was there a more causeless war in the

CHAP. VIII. 1867. world," Mr. Garrison concluded his speech with a grateful recognition of the support given the Union and Emancipation cause by enlightened Englishmen and a portion of the English press, saying:

W. L. G. Breakfast, pp. 44–46.

"Before I sit down, I desire to return my thanks to those on this side of the Atlantic who, in the midst of our terrible struggle, were able to understand its nature, and to give a clear and unequivocal testimony in behalf of the right. (Hear, hear.) I may, perhaps, be permitted to name one or two for a noble example. The Duke of Argyll, a peer of the realm, who, I think, all will now confess was, in point of clearness of vision, soundness of understanding, and accuracy of opinion relative to the real merits of the American struggle, without a peer. (Cheers.) Then there is our respected and honored chairman. (Great cheering.) We always felt greatly encouraged and strengthened when we got hold of his telling speeches. They were exactly to our mind. I cannot, of course, enumerate all who stood up firmly in behalf of President Lincoln and his administration — a Mill, a Forster, a Stansfeld, a Hughes, a Potter, a Taylor, and a Monckton Milnes, now the Right Hon. Lord Houghton — but, without meaning to be invidious, I offer my thanks to those I have named. (Hear, hear, and a voice: "And Cobden.") Yes, the lamented Cobden, of course — (cheers) — who, if he had been living now, doubtless would have been here on this occasion. (Hear, hear.) Then there are Professors Goldwin Smith, Cairnes, Newman, and Huxley. Amongst the newspapers I must name the *Daily News* — (cheers) — the *Morning Star* — (cheers) — the *Spectator*, and the *Nonconformist*. (Cheers.) If my memory be not utterly at fault, I believe the *Times* was rather inclined to bring discredit upon the American Government, but only succeeded in bringing discredit upon itself. (Cheers.) However, let us hope for better *Times* to come. (Hear, hear, and a laugh.)

"I cannot tell you with what pleasure I listened to the ingenuous speech of Earl Russell. (Hear, hear.) I know there was at one time a good deal of feeling in our country in regard to some sentiments which had fallen from his lips, and which seemed to me if not hostile to, at least equivocal about, our position. I do not wonder that there was a good deal of misconception and misapprehension on the subject, at so great a distance. It was a very mixed-up question for a long time, until President Lincoln sent forth his immortal proclamation of emancipation — (cheers) — and then the pulse of England beat to the music of that jubilee bell. Earl Russell cannot exalt himself more than he has done this day, by making a manly confession of his mistake. (Cheers.) I am sure that he who, in his place in the Cabinet, agitated the question of emancipation for the West Indies, never could have entertained a sentiment of hostility to the emancipation of the slaves in America. Russell and Reform — the words are synonymous (cheers); and having championed the old Reform through Parliament with great courage and fidelity, I expect to see him soon, with another Reform Bill, furthering still more the work on behalf of the rights of men and the glory and prosperity of England.

"Now, in parting, let me say, we must not allow ourselves to be divided — England from America, America from England. By every consideration under heaven, let us resolve to keep the peace. (Great cheering.) If we have old grudges, let them be thrown to the winds. (Hear, hear.) Let there be peace — a true and just peace — peace by forbearance — (hear, hear) — peace by generous concession — for the sake of the cause of mankind, and that together England and America may lead the nations of the world to freedom and glory. (Cheers.) There is your country's flag, there is mine. Let them be blended. (Renewed cheers.) I will conclude by quoting some lines written by my friend, Mr. Thompson, some years ago, which will express all my feelings:

George Thompson.

'Then let us haste these bonds to knit,
And in the work be handy,
That we may blend "God Save the Queen"
With "Yankee Doodle Dandy."'

(Prolonged cheers.)"

George Thompson, who also received the heartiest applause, followed Mr. Garrison with wonted eloquence; and after brief remarks by Mr. Stansfeld, Mr. Vernon Harcourt, and Mr. E. Lyulph Stanley, Mr. Bright closed the meeting with a few words in acknowledgment of the vote of thanks tendered him. "Wherever there is a friend of freedom," he said, "the proceedings of this day will give him pleasure; and wherever there is a human being suffering oppression, I trust that what we have done to-day may give him hope."

So remarkable a demonstration as that at St. James's

CHAP. VIII. Hall could not fail to command general attention, and the 1867. secular and religious press of London teemed with editorials about the Breakfast and the speeches made thereat. Even the *Times* confessed its "brilliant" character, and that "Mr. Garrison was fairly entitled to the homage paid him by peers and philosophers." The unusual, if not unprecedented, spectacle of an ex-Prime Minister honestly confessing the error of his course in a critical period of international relations also excited wide comment, and the cabled announcement of it in the American papers caused equal surprise and pleasure. So pro-Southern a paper as the London *Morning Post* had only words of praise for the speeches of Earl Russell and Mr. Bright, and for Mr. Garrison himself.[1]

The attention of the provinces was at once aroused, and invitations from other cities eager to imitate the example of London and do him honor poured in upon *July* 1. Mr. Garrison. He spent his last evening in London at the House of Commons, hearing brief speeches by Gladstone, Bright, and Disraeli; and saying good-bye in the *T. Hughes, T. B. Potter, P. A. Taylor, James Stansfeld, Jr.* lobby to Bright, Hughes, Potter, Taylor, and Stansfeld. *July 2–6.* The next day he was off for Manchester, where he and his companions were entertained at the Trevelyan (Temperance) Hotel, as the guests of the United Kingdom Alliance, the powerful organization having for its object the total suppression of the liquor traffic. A public dinner was given him on the evening of July 4th, Thomas Bazley, M. P. for Manchester, presiding, and George Thompson coming down from London to participate. The address of welcome was moved by Rev. S. Alfred Steinthal, an old friend and correspondent of the *Liberator*, and Jacob Bright was among the speakers. At a Ladies' Reception given him at the same place the following evening, Mr.

[1] The Proceedings of the Breakfast were published in a neat volume (pp. 96) by William Tweedie, 337 Strand, London, 1868, with an Introduction by F. W. Chesson, and Opinions of the Press. To Mr. Chesson, who initiated the movement for the Breakfast, and, as Honorary Secretary, practically managed it, the credit for the remarkable character and success of the occasion was largely due.

Garrison described the heroic women of the anti-slavery movement in America, and in extolling Lucretia Mott, the Grimkés, Mrs. Foster, Mrs. Child, and Mrs. Chapman, he did not forget to name also the clear-sighted Elizabeth Heyrick of England.

CHAP. VIII. 1867.

Ante, 1: 146.

Newcastle-on-Tyne was next visited, and four delightful days were spent with Mr. and Mrs. John Mawson and family in their beautiful home at Gateshead. Mr. Mawson presided at the crowded soirée given to Mr. Garrison on the evening of July 9, in the Assembly Rooms at Newcastle, and his voice faltered with emotion as he testified that their guest, after receiving a nation's thanks and obtaining a world-wide renown, was yet "the same gentle, loving, earnest, true man he was twenty years ago." Not the least interesting and touching feature of the occasion was the presentation of a second welcoming address from the workingmen of the neighboring seaport town of North Shields, to whom, in common with their fellow-toilers of the North of England, Mr. Garrison had just paid a glowing tribute for their steadfast loyalty, in the face of imminent starvation, to the Union cause—"a spectacle," he declared, "such as the world has never seen for moral sublimity. . . . Such workingmen and such operatives," he continued, "are capable of rising to any height, and . . . whatever they do not have now politically as their just claim, ought to be given to them without any delay whatever."[1] The Address was read by Joseph Cowen, Jr., proprietor of the Newcastle *Daily Chronicle*, and an unfaltering supporter of the North:

July 6–10.

To William Lloyd Garrison.

Newcastle Chronicle, July 10, 1867.

HONORED SIR: The members of the North Shields Reform League, embracing the opportunity of your visit to Newcastle

[1] "Had the Confederacy over which Jefferson Davis presided emerged triumphantly from the struggle with the North in 1865, instead of being beaten at all points, we should not have witnessed any extension of the franchise in 1867. The agitation which William Lloyd Garrison carried to so successful an issue in America, had a potent influence in securing the rights of citizenship for the artisans and the agriculturists of England" (Newcastle *Daily Chronicle*, Nov. 16, 1885).

CHAP. VIII. 1867. after a lengthened interval of time, and at the close of the labor of your life, desire, on behalf of a large body of workingmen in this seaport town, to congratulate you, and through you your fellow-countrymen, upon one of the most glorious achievements of our age — the Emancipation of the Colored Race in America.

Some of us, though living remote from you, on the margin of the North Sea, have held unfaltering faith in you and your work for fully a quarter of a century; in fact, ever since Harriet Martineau introduced your name to the English people. When our countrymen in America have sent stray copies of the *Liberator* here to our reading-rooms, we have never failed to peruse with absorbing interest the reports of the great anti-slavery agitation in your country, and we have been cheered in our work here by a knowledge of what was being done across the Atlantic.

Feeling all through the great conflict which swept over your country, that the cause of the North was the cause of the slave, our sympathies were with the Northern people in the darkest crisis of their history. Happily, the reëstablishment of the Federal authority in the South is coincident with the emancipation of the slave. And it is to the great anti-slavery party in America, who, through good report and evil report, allowed the national conscience no peace until victory was achieved, and who sternly refused all compromise with evil, that this great result is due.

There is not a thoughtful toiler amongst the industrial masses of these Northern counties who does not feel a higher sense of manhood, and a firmer faith in great principles, when he sees that in the result of your work, as in much else in this life, "They that sow in tears shall reap in joy; he that goeth forth weeping, bearing precious seed, shall doubtless come again with rejoicing, bringing his sheaves with him."

In this spirit we welcome you, our dear old friend, once more to Northumberland.

Signed on behalf of the North Shields Reform League,

ROBERT ROBSON, President.
ROBERT SUTHERLAND, Treasurer.
JOHN CHARLTON, Secretary.

July 12. Edinburgh followed Newcastle with an evening reception to Mr. Garrison, tendered by the Ladies' Emancipation Society, and for a week he and his children were the guests of his dear and faithful friend, Mrs. Elizabeth Pease Nichol, at Huntly Lodge, enjoying social intercourse with her and other friends, and driving about the city and its beautiful suburbs. Among the new acquaintances whom they met was that delightful writer and gentleman, Dr. John Brown, author of 'Rab and his Friends.' CHAP. VIII. 1867.

On the day of his departure for Glasgow, Mr. Garrison was presented with the freedom of the city of Edinburgh, at a special meeting of the Town Council; the Lord Provost presiding, and the Magistrates and members of the Council, with the City Clerk and City Chamberlain, attending in their robes of office. This signal honor was tendered to Mr. Garrison "in respect of his long and meritorious exertions to abolish slavery in the United States of America"; and the Lord Provost, in making the presentation speech, described slavery as he had himself seen it when visiting the United States before the war, and recalled the active part which Edinburgh had borne in the struggle for West India emancipation. Mr. Garrison accepted this, like all previous honors, as bestowed not on himself alone, but on all his fellow-abolitionists, and "as a symbolical olive-branch to the people of the United States, and an expression of International amity and good-will. It is in that light," he said, "that my joy is full, and my heart beats responsively." The significance of the compliment was increased by his being the first American to receive it, and his pleasure in it was enhanced by the fact that George Thompson had been similarly honored many years previous, so that they were now "fellow-citizens."[1] His speech of acceptance was the best of all he delivered in Great Britain, at least so far as *July* 18. *Ante*, 3:153.

1 "The presentation to me of the 'freedom of the city' by the Lord Provost and Magistracy of Edinburgh was a notable mark of respect, taking me utterly by surprise. It is rather curious that the person who preceded me in receiving it was Prince Alfred, Lord Palmerston preceding him. It was given to the illustrious John Hampden. You [see], therefore, that different considerations lead to its bestowment. It was most worthily given to George Thompson several years ago. Of course, it possesses no

CHAP. VIII. — 1867. pertains to the form, since he could do no less than prepare it carefully in advance of the ceremony.

In Glasgow he had to encounter two demonstrations— a public breakfast, initiated by the Smeals and Patons and their anti-slavery associates, and an evening meeting —at each of which a fervid and impressive address, handsomely engrossed, was presented to him.

July 19, 1867.

"Elsewhere, Sir," said the venerable Dr. William Anderson, in reading that at the breakfast, "you have repeatedly said, in reply to the commendations of friends, that you have only done your duty; but you cannot surely have signified, in saying so, that you protested against their laudations. Why, Sir, it is precisely because you have done your duty that we hold you in admiration, and tender you our expression of it. And you must not check the flow of our feelings by any expression which might be construed as if you gave us back the proffered cup of our praise, only partially accepted. We never felt ourselves less in danger of being seduced by courtesy into the use of expressions which savored of flattery."

North British Daily Mail, Glasgow, July 20, 1867.

"Mr. Chairman," said Mr. Garrison in reply to this broadside, "it is hardly worth while here or anywhere to inquire minutely into the various methods and instrumentalities by which slavery in the United States has been abolished. Those who labored with me were enabled to do something towards the event. Those who labored on this side of the Atlantic had a share in the same glorious work, and are entitled to thanks and to gratitude, as well as those in my own country. It took everything that has transpired since the struggle commenced to bring it about, and every one who gave anything, however small, to the treasury—every one who offered up a heartfelt prayer to God for the deliverance of the oppressed—every one who, in any manner, at any time, and to however small an extent, threw his influence into the scale of justice, had a hand in this blessed work, and it includes at last a mighty host. . . . It has been done by the promulgation of the truth; it has been done by the act

interest or value to me beyond its being a high official recognition of the rectitude and grandeur of the anti-slavery movement in the United States, and, through me, a vindication of American abolitionists generally" (MS. Paris, Aug. 20, 1867, W. L. G. to Samuel May, Jr.). Mr. Garrison did not know that Mrs. Nichol had quietly suggested the propriety of thus honoring him to the Lord Provost.

of the slaveholders themselves to a great extent. The abolitionists were very active and indefatigable during the struggle to put down slavery; but, if possible, they were outdone in activity by the slaveholders themselves. . . . For the very acts to which they resorted to uphold and perpetuate slavery, having been monstrous, cruel, and unnatural, reacted in favor of the good cause, which always succeeded a great deal better when we were assailed by them, denounced by them, and injured by them than in any other way; and so 'God makes the wrath of man to praise Him, and the remainder of wrath He restrains.' Oh, the cowardice of tyrants and the weakness of a colossal wrong!"

The evening meeting was under the auspices of the Scottish National Reform League, and was a very lively affair, for Mr. James Moir, who, with the Smeals and Patons, had been among the few Glasgow citizens friendly to the North during the war, while the shipyards on the Clyde were busy turning out privateers and blockade-runners, aroused the protests and hisses of a portion of the audience by the vigor with which he denounced the Southern rebellion and the attitude of the governing classes of Great Britain respecting it. It was interesting to see how quickly these manifestations of dissent subsided when Mr. Garrison rose and took up the theme, and there was no sign of opposition when he endorsed what Mr. Moir had said, and declared that the Southern rebellion was "the most perfidious and most wicked rebellion recorded on the pages of history," with "no extenuation whatever."

Ante, p. 67.

"Slavery," he told them, "was not the product of Republicanism. It was older than the Constitution of the United States — as old as the settlement of the colonies under the power and patronage of Great Britain. It was not because of our Republican institutions or ideas that we held slaves in bondage, but in violation of them; and therefore those principles or ideas stand untarnished before the world, notwithstanding our guilty apostasy in the past, and I hold that the Declaration of American Independence is yet to be the Declaration of the world. Whatever freedom for the people — all the people — shall be wrought out on our soil, will be an example to the peoples of all parts of

No. British Daily Mail, Glasgow, July 20, 1867.

CHAP. VIII. 1867. the world; and the truth embodied in that famous instrument, that all governments derive their just powers from the consent of the governed, is to course round the globe, and whatever cannot answer to it in time must fall. The best and the strongest government in the world must be that where the greatest number are interested in its administration. The more brains you have, the better government; and the more people who can be summoned to give judgment in regard to the laws or the form of the government, the more sure will be the verdict in regard to what ought to be done. The people may err—they often do; they may be badly deceived—they often are; but the people as such are never wilfully deceived, nor are they hostile to their own interests. They may be deceived, but they will by-and-bye understand the deceptions and deal with the deceivers; but you cannot possibly have a broader basis for any government than that which includes all the people, with all their rights in their hands, and with an equal power to maintain their rights."[1]

The Address, which was adopted with great enthusiasm, recognized, like that of the North Shields workingmen, the influence of the American conflict on the movement for extending the franchise of Great Britain.

No. British Daily Mail, Glasgow, July 20, 1867.

"We rejoice with you," it said, "that the Slaveholders' Confederacy—'that fatal and perfidious barque, built i' the eclipse, and rigged with curses dark'—has sunk to rise no more. The eager joy with which the enemies of liberty in Europe, and their allies among the aristocracy of Britain, hailed that infamous attempt to solve all questions affecting capital and labor by making the laborer capital, aroused our countrymen from that political apathy which is fatal to a free state, and so encouraged the advocates of popular liberty in this country again to raise the standard of Reform. Your success won half our battle. Though our efforts to secure to all our countrymen the rights of citizenship have not, like yours, been crowned with complete success, yet we rejoice that political monopoly in this country has just received another heavy blow, and ere long must likewise totter to its fall. We look forward with hope to the time when the British people, truly represented in a reformed Parliament, in firm and friendly union with the Ameri-

[1] "You can fool all the people some of the time, and you can fool some of the people all the time, but you cannot fool all the people all the time," was Abraham Lincoln's homely way of putting it.

can people, may jointly lead the nations towards a nobler civilization, true liberty, and lasting peace. We shall ever remember, Sir, that to your labors much of our success is due. And as the memories of the early founders of our national liberty and greatness are to-day cherished equally by Britain and America, so in the future, we believe, shall your name, and the names of your noble coadjutors, be held in honor by both branches of the Anglo-Saxon race." CHAP. VIII. 1867.

With these demonstrations Mr. Garrison's public labors ended for a season, greatly to his relief, for he was much worn by the excitement and fatigue of so much talking, both in public and in private. On his way North he had had little recreation — a glimpse of York Minster and a visit *July* 6. to Melrose Abbey and Abbotsford being his chief diver- *July* 10. sions — and he had hoped now to make a trip through the Highlands with his companions; but the weather was rainy and unpropitious, and that had to be abandoned. A visit to the English Lake District was also relinquished for the same reason, and because it would have been an aggravation to go there and not see Harriet Martineau, whose ill-health rendered it doubtful whether she could receive them. Naturally, she was one of the first persons to whom Mr. Garrison wrote on his arrival in London, and several letters were interchanged by them.

Harriet Martineau to W. L. Garrison.

THE KNOLL, AMBLESIDE, June 19, 1867. *MS.*

MY DEAR FRIEND:

Your letter has moved me deeply. I could write sheets full; but, if I write at all, it must be very briefly, and I do wish to write with my own hand. After the months and years that my mind has been full of you, and my sympathy has been all awake and alive, as you were passing through the experience of success, after such a struggle, it seems strange to send you such a note as this must be. But I am *not* better, and I must be content to do only what I can.

It seems to my companion (my dear niece Jane) and myself that I ought to tell you the case about your coming (as it regards us) precisely as it appears to us. You must then judge for yourself what to do. I need not say that no amount of

CHAP. VIII. 1867. fatigue or other suffering would deter me for a moment from attempting to see you. It is not *that* which is in question. But my disease is enlargement of the heart, and my life is precarious to the last degree; and strong emotion of any kind is dangerous accordingly. I could not see *you* without strong emotion. It is not a question of self-command, but the heart stops when I am feeble, or startled, or in any way moved, and it is always very doubtful whether it will go on again. For this reason, and because of my being soon exhausted, and also, at times, because I can hear scarcely at all, I have not, for a long time past, seen any person whatever but the family and my most intimate neighbors. Sometimes, however, I am, for the hour together, able to talk and to listen, and to enjoy seeing a friend's face.

Now, here you have the facts; and I must leave the decision to yourself. I would see you, if possible, and should be grateful and happy to do so; but I might be unable, and I dare not ask you to come so far for such a chance. If you do come, you had better not let me know the time, perhaps, that there may be no exhaustion from expectation before we meet. . . . Our valley is in full beauty at present. The Arnolds (Dr. A.'s widow and daughter) would be delighted to see you, after honoring your name and revering your life for thirty years; and my niece would be delighted to take you across the valley to Fox How, to see the good man's portrait, and the house he built, and his venerable widow. It seems unnatural not to ask you to be my guest; but I might as soon propose to go up the mountains with you! — I who cannot stand for two minutes.

Thomas Arnold.

How happy Mrs. Chapman is about her daughter's engagement to Mr. Dicey! It is such a happiness to see that old friend of ours happy! I think her, as I always did, the greatest woman I ever heard or read of. She is still the great blessing of my life.

Maria W. Chapman. Edward Dicey.

I do hope you will mend in health by your travels. I rejoice to see that you are to be greeted with honors in London.

With veneration and affection, I am your old and grateful friend,

H. Martineau.

Harriet Martineau to W. L. Garrison.

MS. Ambleside, June 25, 1867.

My Dear Friend:

I really cannot resist telling you how happy you have made me by the present of your likeness and that of your dear wife, and by the hearty affection of your letter. It would do me more harm to be silent towards you than it possibly can to write these few lines. Few strangers would recognize the face before me as the same that hangs over my study chimney-piece,— the portrait I brought with me from America in 1836; but I see the identity, and am rejoiced to know your later aspect,— the face that looked in upon me at Tynemouth being between the two. I believe your decision about our not meeting is the right one, much as we should have wished otherwise. We must take it as one of the trials of the illness, to be accepted cheerfully.

Ante, 2: 395.

If you should come this way, after all, it would be a true kindness in you to call at Fox How, where the Arnolds will be at home for some time to come. The eldest son once told me that he remembered the impression made on him in childhood, one winter evening early in 1839, by his father's voice in reading to Mrs. A. "The Martyr Age," then just out in the *Westminster Review*. The boy was too young to enter into the story, but the deep emotion of his father's voice thrilled him, and that has been the association with your name in his mind ever since. Then, again, you know W. E. Forster is the husband of Dr. Arnold's eldest daughter; and you can be in no doubt how he feels towards you. I do hope you are seeing him in London, in spite of his anxious business in Parliament. . . .

Matthew Arnold.

My dear friend, there is one word more that I must say. I value unspeakably your sympathy, and your sense of my sympathy, in the great interest which has occupied so much of our lives; but it leads you to overrate very much any sacrifices I have made or risked. I will not pretend to deny that what I have done has been of some use; but what I have suffered is so little that I am ashamed to hear of it from a confessor like you.

It was only repute and comfort for one single year in the United States that I risked, and so much evil-speaking since as angry people chose to utter,— quite harmlessly to me, as long as the sea rolled between them and me. You, of all men, least need to be told how harmless the slanders and scoldings of strangers are; and I don't know that they have done me any harm. I certainly never cared for them, at home or abroad. . . .

I do not suffer very much, as long as we can preserve perfect quiet; and we have no cares or troubles in this house. All about me is love and peace.

I am your affectionate old friend,

H. MARTINEAU.

CHAP. VIII. 1867. During their stay in Glasgow, Mr. Garrison and his children were the guests of Mr. A. F. Stoddard, an American merchant, a nephew of Arthur Tappan; and the views of the lower Highlands from his beautiful residence on the Clyde, at Port Glasgow, were the only glimpses they obtained of them. On the 24th of July they returned to London for a fortnight of comparative respite, and quiet social enjoyment.

Aug. 3. They again passed a delightful evening with Mazzini at the house of Mrs. Stansfeld's brother, William H. Ashurst, Jr., and saw him for the last time. A day or two later there came this note from him:

Joseph Mazzini to W. L. Garrison.

MS. Aug. 3, 18 Fulham Road, S. W.

MY DEAR FRIEND: We may never more see one another. Will you accept my photograph, and think of me sometimes? God bless you, and all those you love!

Ever faithfully yours, JOS. MAZZINI.

How deeply the apostle of Italian liberty and unity was loved and reverenced by his American fellow-reformer, the latter endeavored to express in his reply to the above; and five years later, after Mazzini's death, it was his privilege to do so more fully and publicly in the Introduction which he then prepared for an American edition of Mazzini's writings.[1] Few men have better understood and appreciated one another, or been more magnetically drawn, each to the other, than they.

W. L. Garrison to his Wife.

PARIS, August 12, 1867.

Aug. 8. H. Villard. Last Thursday I called to see William E. Forster, member of Parliament (Harry accompanying me), and spent a pleasant

[1] 'Joseph Mazzini: His Life, Writings, and Political Principles. With an Introduction by William Lloyd Garrison.' New York: Hurd & Houghton, 1872. The justice and discrimination of Mr. Garrison's tribute were warmly attested by Mazzini's most intimate friends, Madam Emilie Ashurst Venturi, the translator of his works, and Madam Jessie White Mario, wife of his Italian compatriot.

half-hour with him. On taking our leave, he advised us to be at the House of Commons by 4 o'clock P. M., saying the great debate on the Reform Bill, as it had been sent down from the House of Lords, would come off that night, and he would try to get us admitted to the galleries. We gladly complied with his suggestion. Between four and five hundred members were present. It was an occasion of historic interest, and the discussion on both sides was marked with great ability. Gladstone and John Bright spoke with more than their wonted eloquence and power, and I deemed myself very fortunate to have heard them in their best trim. No other person who spoke was at all comparable to either of them. As a parliamentary speaker, Gladstone takes the lead; as a popular orator, Bright has no peer. During a brief recess, Mr. Forster took me to the coffee-room of the House, and hospitably gave me a supper; introducing me there to Lord Amberley (the eldest son of Lord John Russell), who sails this month for a six months' tour in the United States; to the Archbishop of Canterbury, by whose side I afterwards sat in the House, in a privileged seat; and to several members of Parliament. John Stuart Mill sat by my side while I was eating, and we had a social conversation together. He was very strong in his expressions of personal esteem for myself, and hoped I should be able to visit him at his residence at Avignon, in France, where he spends his parliamentary vacation. He is as modest as he is gifted in intellect, though not much as a speaker. I am glad to have made his acquaintance.

From the 10th to the 29th of August Mr. Garrison and his children were in Paris, enjoying the sights of the city and the Exposition, and favored with delightful weather. That Paris had another side than the bright and joyous one usually apparent, he learned on the Emperor's fête-day, when the Boulevards swarmed with "the lame, the halt, and the blind," allowed by special dispensation to emerge from their retreats for that day and drive their trade of beggary on the great thoroughfares of the city. The sight of such misery and degradation powerfully affected him. His inability to speak or understand French was again a trial to him. "Here I am," he wrote, "in a city with nearly two millions of inhabitants, with not one of whom can I intelligibly carry on any conversation,—

CHAP. VIII. 1867. an exceptional case like that of Prof. Laboulaye being very rare. Even he, though accurate, is a good deal fettered and limited in his English speech."

His regret was augmented during the two days' sessions of the International Anti-Slavery Conference, which met in Paris on the 26th and 27th of August, in the Salle Herz, for he could neither understand nor enjoy the eloquent speeches of Laboulaye (who presided, in the absence of the venerable Duc de Broglie) and Cochin,[1] or even the brief remarks of his friend and fellow-countryman, John C. Palfrey,[2] who ventured to address the meeting in French; and the exordium of his own carefully prepared speech, on the second day, was a lament that he was obliged to listen to the French and Spanish speakers as though he had neither a head nor a heart to respond to their noble sentiments, and a declaration of his "abiding faith in the feasibility of a universal language, at some period or other."

The Conference was convened by the French Emancipation Committee, the Spanish Abolition Society, and the British and Foreign Anti-Slavery Society, and both delegate and non-delegate members (including among the latter the women, to whom Prof. Laboulaye paid a graceful compliment) were invited to vote on the resolutions presented as the conclusions of the assembly. Of discussions there were none, for, under the stringent laws of the Second Empire respecting public meetings, a special authorization for the gathering had to be obtained from the Minister of the Interior, and the limitation to two days compelled a pre-arranged and inflexible programme. The various papers read or contributed dealt with the East African slave trade, slavery in Cuba and Brazil, and the results of emancipation in the British Colonies and the United States; and addresses beseeching their

[1] M. Cochin reminded Mr. Garrison and his children of Wendell Phillips in his personal appearance.

[2] Other American members of the Conference were James A. Thome of Cleveland *(ante,* 1 : 454) and Levi Coffin of Cincinnati.

sympathy and coöperation in suppressing slavery and the slave trade in their dominions were subsequently presented in the name of the Conference to the sovereigns of Brazil, Portugal, Spain, Turkey, Egypt, and Zanzibar.

CHAP. VIII. 1867.

Mr. Garrison, who was warmly recognized and greeted by the Conference as its most eminent member, gave a brief retrospect of the anti-slavery struggle in America, and presented the cheering statistics furnished him by the American Freedman's Union Commission as to the work already accomplished in the education and elevation of the freedmen, upon whom the elective franchise had now been conferred, under the reconstruction law recently enacted by Congress. He closed with words of cheer to the abolitionists of Spain, Portugal, and Brazil, and with a warm tribute to the Duc de Broglie, whom, as the coadjutor of Wilberforce, Clarkson, Buxton, and Macaulay, he had hoped to meet; to the French Republicans of 1848, who, during their brief control of the Government, had promptly abolished slavery in the Colonies; and to Laboulaye, Cochin, Gasparin, Hugo, and Schoelcher,[1] "for their powerful testimonies against slavery universally, their clear perception and faithful exposure to the people of France of the real nature and object of the late slaveholding rebellion in the United States, and their valuable support of the American Government in the hour of its greatest extremity."

Mar. 23, 1867.

Report of Paris A. S. Conference, p. 38.

Circumstances beyond his control prevented Mr. Garrison from fulfilling a conditional promise made before leaving London, to return and attend a grand Temperance fête at the Crystal Palace on Sept. 3d. The disappointment to the thirty thousand people gathered there on that day, many of them from distant parts of the kingdom,

[1] Victor Schoelcher (*ante*, p. 197) had resided in London since the Coup d'État of 1851, and declined to attend the Conference while France was still under the Emperor's heel. It was difficult for Laboulaye and Cochin, in their addresses, to conceal the bitterness and humiliation with which they regarded the espionage and repression of public assemblies by the official censor.

CHAP. VIII. 1867. was very great; but he sent a letter of testimony which was printed and distributed to the multitude.

On the 29th of August Mr. Garrison and his children left Paris for Switzerland, where they spent the entire month of September. They were accompanied during the first fortnight by their friends, Mr. and Mrs. George A. Blanchard of Concord, New Hampshire, and by Richard D. Webb, who had come from Dublin for the purpose and to attend the Anti-Slavery Conference as well. More delightful company it would have been hard to find. The Blanchards were the best of fellow-travellers, and Mr. Webb's wit and jollity were inexhaustible, keeping the party in constant merriment. Their course followed the *Aug.* 31. usual track from Geneva to Chamonix, where Mr. Garri- *Sept.* 1. son's agility in descending the Flégère made him foot-sore for days; but the glorious views of the Mont Blanc range, surpassing anything he had ever seen, were ample recompense. His spirits rose with the increasing grandeur of the scenery and he sang exuberantly. The familiar lines from Byron and Coleridge were frequently repeated by him and Mr. Webb, who discussed many a topic of mutual interest as they drove or walked or sat together during their journeyings and restings; and their friendship of twenty-seven years ripened to the closest mutual affection.[1] The weather was perfect, the skies cloudless. They *Sept.* 4. had a day of rare delight at a little pension near Castle

[1] "I . . . spent three weeks with the Garrisons in Paris and Switzerland. It was a time of intense enjoyment, for I exceedingly liked my companions. . . . As to Mr. Garrison himself, he is the most delightful man I have ever known — magnanimous, generous, considerate, and, as far as I can see, every way morally excellent. I can perceive that he has large faith, is very credulous, is not deeply read, and has little of the curiosity or thirst for knowledge which educated people are prone to. But, take him for all in all, I know no such other man. His children are most affectionate and free with him — yet they have their own opinions and express them freely, even when they differ most widely from his" (MS. Feb. 5, 1868, R. D. Webb to E. Quincy). "People who travel together have an excellent opportunity of knowing and testing one another. . . . I have never on the whole known a man who bears to be more thoroughly known, or is so sure to be loved and reverenced" (MS. Oct. 9, 1867, R. D. Webb to E. P. Nichol).

Chillon, after their descent of the Tête Noire pass; and at Interlaken they tarried more than a week, making the usual excursions to Berne, and Lauterbrunnen, and Giessbach, and revelling in the view of the peerless Jungfrau. The last half of the month was spent quietly at Lucerne, under less propitious skies, and without the lively companionship of their friends. After an ascent of the Rigi, and a glimpse of Zurich, the Falls of the Rhine, and Constance, Mr. Garrison and his son returned to England by way of Stuttgart, Heidelberg, Frankfort, and Brussels, seeing the Rhine, also, from Mayence to Cologne.

Sept. 5–13, 1867. *Sept.* 27. *Sept.* 29, 30. *Oct.* 2–8. *Oct.* 6.

One more week was given to London, and two evenings of this were occupied by receptions and suppers tendered by the National Freedmen's Aid Union, at Devonshire House, the headquarters of the Society of Friends in London, and the National Temperance League, in the Strand. The former was presided over by the venerable and indefatigable abolitionist, Joseph Cooper, whom Mr. Garrison had met on his first visit to England; at the latter, the famous caricaturist, George Cruikshank, was present, and made a humorous and lively speech, though then just entering his 76th year. On both occasions, George Thompson shared the honors and the speaking with Mr. Garrison; and at Birmingham and Leeds, also, where large and enthusiastic meetings were held, they both spoke with much vigor. That at Birmingham was under the auspices of the National Freedmen's Aid Union and the Birmingham and Midland Freedmen's Aid Association, and was preceded by a breakfast to Mr. Garrison, at which an ex-Confederate General, R. V. Richardson of Tennessee, spoke and made voluntary confession that the freedmen "were confiding, warm-hearted, faithful, sympathetic, possessed of great physical energy and power, and only required to be educated to make excellent citizens."[1]

Oct. 9–16. *Oct.* 14. *Oct.* 15.

[1] "I am writing this with a Southern Confederate General (Richardson of Tennessee) by my side, and a Major (Saunders) of the same stripe — both very courteous, friendly, complimentary! What strange things turn up in the course of time!" (MS. Oct. 19, 1867, W. L. G. to H. E. G.)

CHAP. VIII. — 1867.

The following letter was read by Arthur Albright, Mr. Garrison's host in Birmingham, through whose untiring efforts, largely, the magnificent sum of £100,000 had already been raised and sent to America in aid of the freedmen:

W. E. Gladstone to Arthur Albright.

MS. PENMAEN-MAWR, Aug. 22, '67.

DEAR SIR: I have received your letter of the 20th, and I sincerely regret that I am unable to comply with your request. During the recess of Parliament, my limited hours for taking part in public proceedings must be reserved for direct local claims and for those of my constituents. Even these, indeed, I am far from being able to meet as I could wish. Had I been in more favorable circumstances, I should have hailed an opportunity of paying public honor to such a man as Mr. Garrison.

I remain, Sir, your faithful servant,

W. E. GLADSTONE.

The Leeds meeting occurred on the 21st of October, and celebrated, by this happy coincidence, the anniversary of the Boston Mob.[1] Between Birmingham and Leeds a night was spent at Stratford-on-Avon, by invitation of Mr. E. F. Flower, well known to Americans for his ever-ready hospitality, and for his successful efforts while Mayor to preserve and restore Shakespeare's birthplace. Hardly less than his pardonable satisfaction over this achievement was his pride in the exploits of his earlier years, when, as a youth in Illinois, he had been so efficient an agent of the Underground Railroad that he was compelled at last to flee for his life from the State.

The culminating demonstrations in Mr. Garrison's honor were those which occurred at the annual meetings of the United Kingdom Alliance at Manchester, on the 22d of October, where he spoke twice in response to resolutions of welcome — at the morning session of the Council, and at the great public meeting in Free Trade Hall in the evening; his fellow-countryman, General Neal Dow, and

[1] Edward Baines, M. P. for Leeds, presided at the reception in that city, where Mr. Garrison was the guest of his old friend, Joseph Lupton.

Cardinal Manning being among the other speakers, and Sir Wilfred Lawson occupying the chair. The vast hall was packed to overflowing with an audience of five thousand persons, whose enthusiasm was tumultuous when Mr. Garrison rose to speak. Rising *en masse*, they greeted him with prolonged cheering and waving of handkerchiefs, and when he could finally make himself heard, he declared himself almost overwhelmed by the "marvellous and sublime spectacle" of such a gathering, which far surpassed in size and earnestness any temperance meeting he had ever seen. At a Vegetarian banquet the following evening, he made a brief speech, confessing that he was not a convert to that theory, but that if the demonstration of its soundness were to rest on the vigorous octogenarian who presided, the case would certainly be made out.

John Mawson came to Manchester to take a last farewell of Mr. Garrison,[1] and James Haughton was there from Dublin to renew the old friendship. Other friends were at Liverpool to say the parting word — George Thompson, Richard D. Webb, and Miss Estlin of Bristol among them. On the morning of the 25th a complimentary breakfast was given to Mr. Garrison by Mr. James R. Jeffrey, a prominent merchant of Liverpool, and the evening of the same day was spent with a delightful company at the home of Mr. and Mrs. William Crosfield, the latter a niece of James Cropper. The next day Mr. Garrison, with his son, sailed for home on the *Java*, having as fellow-passengers Dr. Henry I. Bowditch, Miss Anne Warren Weston, and other friends, whose cheerful companionship mitigated the discomforts of the rough and uncomfortable voyage; and on the 6th of November Boston was reached and the fourth transatlantic journey ended.

Mary A. Estlin.

Oct. 26.

[1] Less than two months later (Dec. 18) Mr. Mawson was killed by an explosion of nitro-glycerine on the town moor of Newcastle. "He was one of the most affectionate, loving, magnetic persons I ever knew, and had one of the most charming homes . . . into which I ever entered. . . . His face had almost an angelic radiance about it" (MS. Jan. 11, 1868, W. L. G. to H. C. Wright).

CHAPTER IX.

JOURNALIST AT LARGE.—1868–1876.

CHAP. IX. 1868–76.

WITH renewed health, Mr. Garrison again tried to face the task of writing a History of the Anti-Slavery Movement; but an invitation to become a regular paid contributor to the New York *Independent*, with liberty to write as often as he chose, and to select his own topics, proved irresistibly attractive. His name was attached to all his articles, and he practically enjoyed all the freedom and opportunity of utterance which the *Liberator* had afforded him, with none of the responsibility and drudgery of editorial life. Moreover, he now addressed sixty thousand readers instead of twenty-five hundred. "You will speak," wrote Oliver Johnson, who had become the associate editor of the *Independent*, "to a great audience, to many of whom your real sentiments are hardly known, and some of whom, doubtless, are filled with prejudice against you." And a few weeks later he wrote: "One of the very best and ablest of our orthodox ministers expressed himself as highly delighted with your articles, and said they were not only specimens of fine English, but pervaded by an eminently noble and Christian spirit."

MS. Jan. 27, 1868.

MS. Apr. 7, 1868.

In the hundred articles which he contributed to that paper during the next seven or eight years, Mr. Garrison discussed all the reforms and topics of the day which attracted him, whether pertaining to the freedmen and the reconstruction problem, temperance, the rights of women, peace, popular religion, or the issues of the two Presidential campaigns. Nor was his active interest in these by any means confined to writing about them in the *Independent*, but by voice and pen, on the platform, and in many avenues of the press, he was constantly bearing his testimony, and giving the prestige of his name and vigorous support. For the years included in this chapter we shall, abandoning the chronological presentation hitherto observed, deal with successive topics, and shall quote briefly Mr. Garrison's utterances on questions which still await their just settlement.

THE FREEDMEN.— As an officer and member of the Executive Committee of the New England branch of the Freedman's Union Commission, Mr. Garrison attended many committee meetings during the closing years of the organization, and occasionally presided or spoke at the public meetings of the Society and its tributary organizations in other places. As one of the Trustees for the expenditure of the money left to the Anti-Slavery cause by Francis Jackson (which did not become available until two years after slavery was abolished), he urged that the entire fund should be devoted to the education of the freedmen, as the nearest possible method of carrying out Mr. Jackson's wishes; and in this he was sustained by two of his co-Trustees, Edmund Quincy and Samuel May. Mr. Phillips, on the other hand, advocated its appropriation for the support of the *Anti-Slavery Standard*, on the ground that the political enfranchisement of the freedmen, which the *Standard* (not alone, however, but in common with some of the ablest and most influential journals in the country) was especially urging, was more important than their education. Others of the Trustees sided with Mr. Phillips,[1] and, for the sake of adjusting the matter, Mr. Garrison proposed that five thousand dollars be given to the freedmen, and the balance ($4200) to the *Standard;* but when Congress, a month or two later, passed the Reconstruction Act enfranchising the freedmen, the special

1868-69.

[1] Namely, Charles K. Whipple and William I. Bowditch. Edmund Jackson, the testator's brother, favored giving one-quarter of the amount to the *Standard* and the rest to the freedmen.

CHAP. IX. 1868–76. plea for the continuance of the *Standard* seemed to him no longer weighty or plausible, and he again expressed his opinion that the entire fund should go to the freedmen. *John Codman.* The Master in Chancery to whom the matter was referred by the Supreme Court of Massachusetts, coincided in this view, and, acting upon his recommendation, the Court directed the Trustees to so appropriate the money; but, the majority refusing to obey the mandate, they were removed by the Court, who directed Messrs. Garrison, May, and Quincy to nominate four persons in their place, and the money finally reached the treasury of the New England branch of the Freedman's Union Commission. This fresh controversy with old co-laborers was inexpressibly painful to Mr. Garrison, who felt obliged, by the sharp reflections on his course which appeared in the *Standard*, to write an exhaustive review of the whole matter, and a vindication of himself, which was printed by *A. S. Standard, Mar. 14, 1868.* that paper and was both unanswered and unanswerable.

At the numerous jubilations held by the colored people over the adoption of the Fifteenth Amendment to the Constitution, which gave them the elective franchise, Mr. *Apr. 15, May 18, 1870.* Garrison was in much request. He spoke at the Faneuil Hall celebration in Boston, and at Providence, but had to decline invitations from New York, Baltimore, Richmond, and Vicksburg — the last-named being extended by the Mayor and citizens. Four years later, after Charles Sumner's death, he urged the passage of the Civil Rights Bill by Congress, and protested against its emasculation by the omission of the clause forbidding all complexional distinctions in the public schools.

Independent, Apr. 16, 1874. "The common school," he wrote, "must be open to all and for all, whether white or black, whether native or foreign. Those who, for any reason, do not choose to avail themselves of its benefits, may consult their own choice or prejudice, as the case may be; but they must not make it subservient to their exclusiveness. To gratify them in this respect would be to lay the axe at the root of our free institutions and to engender animosities that no community can afford to tolerate."

And again:

"For one, I would prefer to have the bill defeated as it stands, rather than adopted with the sanction of separate schools on account of complexional distinctions by Congress. I deny the constitutional right of that body or of any State Legislature to approve or recognize any such distinctions; and I am surprised that so plain a point has not been earnestly maintained by the advocates of the bill at Washington as originally reported.

W. L. G. to Hon. C. T. Garland, Feb. 1, 1875. Washington Chronicle, Feb. 5, 1875.

"The Constitution of the United States is the supreme law of the land; and, as amended, Congress may as lawfully set up a king to rule over us as to stamp with the badge of inferiority, by a senseless proscription on account of the color of the skin, any enfranchised American citizen. How the land would rock with excitement if the Irish, German, Scandinavian, or any other foreign population now naturalized, and with the ballot in their hands, should be invidiously excluded from our common schools and compelled to herd together. Even demagogues would then grow eloquently patriotic amid the thunderings and lightnings of popular indignation, and somebody would be very likely to see his political prospects blasted."

As a shining example of the success of co-education, irrespective of color or sex, he pointed to Berea College in Kentucky, saying: "It is the most interesting educational institution to contemplate in the United States, and deserves the highest encomiums and the most liberal patronage for the good it has wrought and the grand example it has furnished how to pacificate and bless the entire South."[1]

Independent, Apr. 16, 1874.

With perfect consistency, he deprecated the attempt, on the part of the colored people in a town near Boston, to start a church of their own, when they were free to connect themselves with any of the white churches in the place, as establishing "a precedent which logically ends in endorsing the old pro-slavery doctrine that there should be no fraternization between the two races on account of color."

MS. Dec. 8, 1874, to N. T. Allen.

TEMPERANCE.— In the political revulsion which marked the autumn of 1867, the opponents of the prohibitory law in

[1] His own deep interest in this college was emphasized by his singling it out for a bequest at his death.

CHAP. IX. 1868–76. Massachusetts succeeded in electing a Legislature pledged to its repeal, and the announcement of this unpleasant and unexpected event greeted Mr. Garrison on his arrival from England, the same week; but neither this, nor the reverses of the Republican party in other States, though of grave moment on the eve of the first Presidential election after the war, disturbed his buoyant and hopeful mind. In the lecture on his summer's experiences in Europe which he gave a few weeks later at Music Hall, (*Nov.* 29, 1867.) and repeated in other places, he predicted a speedy reaction in favor of the law in Massachusetts, and of the Republican party in the country at large; and at a great temperance rally held in Boston the following May, he (*May* 13, 1868.) was one of the principal speakers. The Legislature elected in the fall of 1868 reënacted the law, and, in the annually-renewed conflict of the next three or four years, he frequently wrote and spoke in behalf of prohibition—in the *Independent* and at various temperance meetings.

(*Independent Mar.* 3, 1870.) "Whether as a question of public safety or general prosperity, of enlightened patriotism or disinterested philanthropy, of personal freedom or popular government," he wrote in 1870, "I am an inflexible, uncompromising prohibitionist. If there is anything left to us worth contending for, in matters of legislation, or as a principle of society, or with reference to the common weal, surely it must be the right not merely to restrain but to suppress that traffic which produces more pauperism, more crime, more lunacy, more misery in every conceivable shape than all other predisposing causes put together. Where such suppression is not generally practicable, there must be a comparatively low standard of public virtue, a great lack of moral stamina, deplorable ignorance of physiological law, and criminal disregard of the duties and responsibilities of American citizenship. . . .

"The licensed sale of intoxicating liquors, no matter how guardedly, for drinking purposes, not only injures and imperils the individual consumer, but brings woe into the family circle, riot and murder into the community, and makes the State accessory to three-fourths of all the pauperism and crime within its borders. No such sale can be granted without moral culpability. It cannot be too often reiterated that there are some acts which no legislative assembly, no representative body, NOT THE PEOPLE THEMSELVES, though in entire agreement, have a right to do or sanction; and they are those acts from which necessarily and inevitably flow more of evil than good, more of damage than recompense, more of wretchedness than solace, more of peril than security, and which lead to a violation of those physical and moral laws which are binding upon the whole human race. The Legislature of Massachusetts may not find, therefore, in any amount of opposition to the prohibitory law, any warrant or justification for passing a license law as a substitute. Even if it shall feel constrained to repeal the former, on the ground of the impracticability of its enforcement, it has no moral, and therefore should exercise no legal, right to enact the latter, thus throwing around the most demoralizing of all licenses the sanction of the Commonwealth." CHAP. IX. 1868–76.

When, by the passage of a local-option law in 1871, the question of License or No License was submitted to popular vote, Mr. Garrison cast his first (and only) ballot since that he had given for Amasa Walker in 1834. *Ante*, 1:455. He did not favor the formation of a Prohibitory political party, however, and, after Mr. Phillips's defeat as the candidate of the Prohibition and Labor parties for Governor in the fall of 1870, he expressed his disbelief in third-party movements, in an article on "Moral and Political Action." *Ind. Nov.* 24, 1870. Time had only confirmed the objections to them first evoked by the Liberty Party. *Ante*, 2:244, 245, 311, 349, 436.

"I trust not to be misapprehended. I am not for divorcing moral from political action, nor do I deprecate an earnest interest in the results of our State and national elections. *Ind. Nov.* 24, 1870. Perhaps there are few who watch those results with more vigilance than I do; or who despise more heartily the hollow outcry that men are not to be made good — *i. e.*, better citizens — by legislative enactments. But I fail to see the wisdom or expediency of adding a third wheel to a mill when there is not sufficient water-power to turn the two great wheels which are already in position, which are ample to do all the work required, and which only need a greater supply of water to move with celerity and efficiency in accordance with the law of gravitation. This was the conviction I cherished throughout the anti-slavery struggle, and it remains unchanged, unless in growing more profound."

Robert C. Pitman. Boston Journal, Nov. 4, 1871.

MS. May 10, 1876, J. H. Coulter to W. L. G.

Likewise, when Judge Pitman was the Prohibition candidate in 1871, Mr. Garrison deprecated a movement which could only draw votes from the Republican nominee, who was a firm Prohibitionist, to the advantage of his Democratic and License opponent. In 1876 he declined an overture to stand as the candidate of the Prohibition party for President.

He always avoided public dinners where wine and cigars were permitted, and, in declining a pressing invitation to the annual dinner of the New England Society of New York, in 1877, he wrote, in a private note to the president: "I will frankly state, that one reason why I decline participating in such commemorations is the habitual wine-drinking and smoking so generally indulged in — a custom, I am sure, that would be far 'more honored in the breach than in the observance.'"[1]

THE RIGHTS OF WOMEN.— The question of woman suffrage was first submitted to popular vote in Kansas in the fall of 1867, when amendments to the State Constitution enfranchising women and negroes were both defeated after a long and exciting canvass, in which Lucy Stone, Henry B. Blackwell, Susan B. Anthony, and Elizabeth Cady Stanton bore an active part. A curious outcome of this contest was a temporary partnership between Mrs. Stanton and Miss Anthony and George Francis Train, a notorious charlatan, who was exciting the mirth of the country by posing as a self-constituted candidate for President. Imagining that an espousal of the women's cause would further his own success, he had delivered, just before the election, several of his disjointed harangues in favor of their amendment, while opposing contemptuously that establishing negro suffrage; and he now offered to furnish capital with which to start a woman-suffrage paper in New York, in which, also, he was to ventilate his own vagaries on trade, finance, and other topics. His offer was eagerly

[1] The president (Mr. Daniel F. Appleton) was so pleased by this that he asked permission to print it as a postscript to the formal letter of declination in the pamphlet report of the proceedings, where it appears.

accepted, and in the series of meetings which they held in the principal cities on their return journey from Kansas to New York, the ladies named shared the speaking with him, and listened without protest to his constant ridicule and vulgar abuse of the negro.

CHAP. IX.
1868–76.

The annoyance and mortification felt by many suffragists at this entangling alliance and its consequent degradation of the movement, led to the formation at Cleveland, in November, 1869, of the American Woman Suffrage Association, of which Henry Ward Beecher was made President, and to the subsequent establishment at Boston of the *Woman's Journal*. To both of these movements Mr. Garrison gave his active coöperation, and was especially helpful in launching the *Journal*, of which, for a time, he was an associate editor with Mrs. Mary A. Livermore, Mrs. Julia Ward Howe, Mrs. Lucy Stone, and T. W. Higginson. He was one of the Vice-Presidents also of the American and of the Massachusetts Woman Suffrage Associations, and President of the former for two years. In the wintry months of February and March, 1870, he made two journeys to Vermont, and addressed suffrage conventions at Rutland and Burlington in company with Mrs. Howe and Mrs. Livermore, the question of a constitutional amendment being then before the State Board of Censors. From the exposure thus incurred he narrowly escaped a severe illness, and the gradual impairment of his health may be said to date from that time. When well enough, he never failed to attend the semi-annual suffrage conventions in Boston, in January and May; and at the annual hearings at the State House before the Committees on suffrage and other bills affecting the rights of person and property of women, he was ever a faithful champion. He spoke also at many suffrage meetings in other cities and States, and wrote repeatedly on the subject for the *Independent*, and to conventions in distant places which he could not attend.[1]

Jan., 1870.

[1] See *Independent*, Dec. 31, 1868, Dec. 23, 1869, March 17, May 19, 1870, March 2, July 1, Dec. 7, 1871, April 3, 1873; *Woman's Journal*, *passim*, 1870–

W. L. Garrison to Henry Ward Beecher.

MS. BOSTON, May 10, 1870.

MY DEAR FRIEND: I regret to be obliged to substitute a brief letter for my presence at the mass convention of the American Woman Suffrage Association at Steinway Hall to-morrow; for I had anticipated great pleasure in seeing (many of them for the first time) so strong an array of eminent advocates of equal rights, drawn together by a common inspiration from various parts of the country. But, while the spirit is willing, the flesh is weak; hence the cause of my absence.

The claim of woman to the ballot is so reasonable, in such exact conformity to the theory of popular government, and so important in its bearings upon whatever concerns the interests of the people, that I marvel that any man with ordinary intelligence and sense of justice, on giving any consideration to the subject, can resist or decry it. I have carefully read and weighed all the objections that have been brought against it; but, among them all, I have neither seen nor heard a single one possessing any force whatever. Many of them are so utterly at variance with each other as to be mere jargon; and the remainder of them are marked with such shallowness of reasoning and emptiness of declamation as signally to demonstrate the impossibility of a sound argument being framed against a truly just issue.

Rev. Horace Bushnell.

No man has written, no man can write, more absurdly on the subject than the distinguished author of the work entitled 'A Reform against Nature.' Yet, while advancing all sorts of preposterous reasons against giving woman the ballot, he sums up all that need be urged in favor of the measure in the following cogent paragraph:

"Little as he means it, man is nevertheless gravitating steadily toward some practice of wrong against the sex; laying up usages that are oppressive, maxims unjust, laws of really despotic mastership — all, it would

---

79; 'History of Woman Suffrage,' Vol. 3, pp. 122, 343, 368. In other ways, too, he had opportunity to bear his testimony in behalf of equal rights for the sexes. Called upon, at a dinner of the American Institute of Homœopathy (Boston, June 10, 1869), to respond to a toast on "Reform and Reformers," he urged that women should stand on an equality with men in the medical profession, and the Institute voted by an overwhelming majority, the next day, to admit them as members, winning the honor of being the first medical body that had ever done so.

seem, because the wrong is in him, and, *having the power*, must needs be somehow issued in the deed; even though he disavows it, and protests he would not have it."

Yes! "having the power"! Therefore he contemns, subordinates, oppresses! And he is "gravitating steadily" in that direction. It is not a rightful but a usurped power that is thus degrading him and injuring woman, and a "despotic mastership" is the inevitable sequence. The simple remedy for all this injustice is to restore to woman that share of power, especially in matters of legislation, which has been wrested from her; in other words, to concede equal political rights. No class legislation was ever yet just or beneficent. Where all are entitled to a voice and vote in public affairs, there the laws will be the most equitable, and the government the most effective in its administration.

Dr. Bushnell says:

"Suffrage is a right given, never a right to be demanded because it inheres beforehand in the person; and neither men nor women have any title to it, save what is grounded in consideration of benefit."

Suffrage is a right primarily given — by whom? Where did Hancock and Adams, Washington and Jefferson, Revolutionary Federalists and Republicans, Dr. Bushnell and the opposers of woman suffrage generally, get their right to vote? Who gave them authority to choose their own rulers? Women claim no other title to it than men assert for themselves; and that claim is as valid in the one case as it is in the other. It is sure to be accorded in the end, and the sooner the better. No matter how many stubborn or stupid men may resist, no matter how many weak-minded or timorous women may say nay, it will nevertheless be triumphant, adding new lustre to the nineteenth century.

Yours, very cordially,

WM. LLOYD GARRISON.

With an optimism natural and common to many, after the marvellous events of the previous decade, Mr. Garrison was confident in 1870 that women would be enfranchised by a Sixteenth Amendment to the United States Constitution before 1876. He scouted, however, an attempt to prove that political equality had been already obtained by the 14th and 15th Amendments "as on a par with Bishop Berkeley's sublimated theory that there

CHAP. IX. 1868-76. is no such thing as matter, it being only a projection of the mind or spirit."

MS. Jan. 4, 1872, W. L. G. to E.M.Davis. "It is precisely like the attempt made, by certain individuals, to prove that there were no pro-slavery clauses or provisions to be found in the United States Constitution, sticking to the letter thereof, and disregarding all the historical facts pertaining to its adoption, the clear understanding of it by the people, and the uniform concurrence of all legislative and judicial proceedings under it pertaining to slavery and the slave trade. Such criticism is neither fair nor sensible, and totally at variance with the truth. In the name of common sense, with nineteen-twentieths of the male voters of the land hostile to woman suffrage, how has it been possible for them to consent to any amendment of the Constitution granting what they stoutly resist?"[1]

MISCELLANEOUS TOPICS.—Never before had Mr. Garrison been able to address so large a clerical audience as the *Independent* afforded him—a fact of which he did not lose sight, for he dwelt much upon the duty and the unrivalled opportunity of the pulpits to deal with living issues and condemn present wrong and injustice. He criticised the pulpit method of preaching; inquired, in a clever catechism, what really constitutes a "Christian," and maintained the rights of conscience against all assumptions of infallibility, whether Papal or Protestant. When the decision of the Cincinnati Board of Education to discontinue Bible-reading in the schools was agitating that city, and exciting much discussion throughout the country, he warmly commended the action of the Board, deeming it as reasonable to insist "that only the Protestant religion shall be tolerated in the land as that our Protestant Bible *shall* be read in the public schools."

Ind. Feb. 27, Sept. 3, 1868. Ind. Sept. 10, 1868. Ind. July 14, 1870. Ind. Nov. 11, 1869.

Ibid. "If," he continued, "this root of bitterness extracted, the Catholics, or any other sect, shall refuse to accept of the common schools for the instruction of their children, and proceed to

[1] Some spirited verses on "Human Equality," supplemental to, and in the style of, Burns's "A man 's a man for a' that," were written by Mr. Garrison for one of the gatherings of the New England Women's Club, of which he became an honorary member in 1872.

establish separate schools to represent their sectarian spirit and purpose, they can do so; but they may not therefore be gratified by the overthrow of that impartial, beneficent system which must be inflexibly adhered to as essential to the general welfare, the support of free institutions, the life of the Republic. So men who do not choose to vote may stay away from the polls; but they may not arbitrarily insist that the people shall not be allowed to carry on the government, and cast their ballots to that end." CHAP. IX. 1868-76.

No suitable occasion for bearing peace and non-resistance testimonies was neglected by Mr. Garrison, and he strenuously and successfully opposed, with others, the enactment of a bill for compulsory military drill in the public schools of Massachusetts, which had already passed 1865. its second reading in the Legislature. One day in the fall of 1875, he received a call from a young Japanese student in Boston University, who had been sent to the United States by his Government with the ultimate view of obtaining a military and naval education. A perusal of Charles Sumner's oration on the "True Grandeur of 1845. Nations" had first caused the youth to reflect on the nature of war and the military profession, and he now came to hear what Mr. Garrison had to say on the subject. To the two enthusiastic young girls — fellow-students — who accompanied and introduced him, the rapt expression of his face, as he listened to a kind and impressive statement of the underlying principles of peace and non-resistance, remains a vivid and memorable picture. "Mr. Garrison's words did more harm to my military pride and inclinations than even the 'True Grandeur of Nations,'" he said to them as they left the house. Returning to Japan, he informed his Government that his conscience forbade him to enter upon a military career, and was promptly cast into prison for his contumacy; but he unflinchingly adhered to his resolution. He was released after a time, and degraded to a position which gave him a scanty subsistence; but, when last heard from, he was still true to his principles.

CHAP. IX. 1868-76. When Mrs. Josephine E. Butler of England instituted the agitation against the laws of Parliament which, under the specious name of the Contagious Diseases Acts, provided for the licensing of prostitution in the garrison towns of Great Britain, Mr. Garrison was prompt to welcome the movement, and make it known to the American public, in an article full of burning indignation over the iniquity of the Acts. Of Mrs. Butler and her noble women associates he said:

Ind. Aug. 31, 1871.

Ibid. "To her, and to them all, I desire thus publicly to pay my homage; regretting that I can find no words adequately to express my admiration of the moral courage they have displayed, the intellectual and moral force they have brought into the field, the masterly ability with which they have conducted the argument, the noble dignity of character which they have exemplified under the vilest provocation, and the exalted purity of sentiment to which they have given utterance. They have helped to make the present age illustrious, and deserve the plaudits of mankind. Had they been represented in the British Parliament, no such infamous acts could have been passed or proposed. Such legislation is possible only where women are excluded; and it furnishes another potential argument for their political enfranchisement to the full extent enjoyed by men."

1877. A few years later, it was his privilege to coöperate personally with them in their own country, and to give them timely encouragement and aid. He also heartily seconded Dr. William G. Eliot of St. Louis in his long and arduous struggle for the repeal of the ordinances licensing prostitution in that city, which ended triumphantly in April, 1879.

Ind. Mar. 6, 1873.

On the so-called "Labor question," Mr. Garrison thus expressed himself to a correspondent who had appealed for his aid in a movement for "industrial reform":

W. L. Garrison to W. G. H. Smart.

Boston Globe, Sept., 1875.

ROXBURY, August 18, 1875.

You ask me to "consider the evils that now oppress society, especially the toiling masses, whose only dependence is the labor of their hands," and you seem to regard these evils [as] almost as intolerable and iniquitous as were those which characterized the atrocious system of chattel slavery. That society is afflicted with many evils that are to be deplored, and that ought to be removed, is undeniable; but that there is any analogy or comparison between the condition and chances of "the toiling masses" and those to which the millions recently brought out of the house of bondage were subjected, I cannot admit and do not believe. Besides the very aged and the very young, there are comparatively few who are not more or less toiling with their brains or hands, in order to procure the means of subsistence. "The toiling masses," therefore, can only be another appellation for the American people. What have they to complain of in regard to constitution and laws for which they are not directly responsible? What outside power is subjecting them to wrongs and deprivations which call in thunder-tones for another emancipation crusade? What inside power is comparable to their own collective will and unquestionable strength? What new safeguards for their freedom, safety, and happiness do they need, that they have not the means to establish? Is not the government of them, by them, and for them (ostracized womanhood excepted), to be moulded as they shall judge best? Or, if in any case it is not for them, upon whom rests the responsibility but themselves? . . .

CHAP. IX. — 1868–76.

Cf. ante, p. 204.

You express the conviction that the present relation of capital to labor is "hastening the nation to its ruin," and that, if some remedy is not applied, it is difficult to see "how a bloody struggle is to be prevented." I entertain no such fears. Our danger lies in sensual indulgence, in a licentious perversion of liberty, in the prevalence of intemperance, and in whatever tends to the demoralization of the people.

Cf. ante, 3: 224, 225.

Abhorring all injustice, class legislation, and usurpation of power,

I remain, very respectfully yours,

William Lloyd Garrison.

Retrospect.— While constantly using the salient lessons of the anti-slavery conflict by way of illustration and analogy in his treatment of current topics, Mr. Garrison had no disposition to reproach pro-slavery or personal antagonists with their past delinquencies, unless compelled to do so in order to vindicate the truth of history. There were several occasions on which he performed such neces-

Mar. 20, 1874.

sary tasks very effectively.[1] His best contribution of this nature was a letter addressed to the Boston *Journal* on the gross conduct of the Massachusetts Legislature, when, on the death of Millard Fillmore, they passed resolutions commending the signer of the Fugitive Slave Law as entitled to the "affectionate remembrance of the American people, and an honorable place in the long line of their illustrious public servants." The shame of this perfunctory and insincere act was rendered all the more glaring by the eulogies which the same body was forced to pay immediately afterwards to Charles Sumner, whose death at Washington occurred the day after the Legislature of his State had thus disgraced itself.

Mar. 11, 1874.

May's Recollections of the A. S. Conflict. Wilson's Rise and Fall of the SlavePower. MS. May 2, 1870, W. L. G. to H. Wilson.

Both Samuel J. May and Henry Wilson appealed to Mr. Garrison for facts and criticism while they were preparing their respective contributions to anti-slavery history, and he was very frank in his strictures on certain passages in the latter's chapters touching the abolitionists. These were modified in some degree before they appeared in the printed work, but were still left inaccurate and unsatisfactory,[2] and the third and last volume, finished by another

1 See articles on "The Late Bishop [John Henry] Hopkins" of Vermont (*Independent*, Jan. 30, 1868); "A Pro-Slavery Calumny Refuted" (*Ind.* Dec. 10, 1868), a reply to Revs. J. M. Sturtevant, Edward Beecher, and John P. Gulliver, who had accused the "Boston Abolitionists" of dividing their denunciations equally between "Southern slavery and evangelical Christianity"; "Mr. [George] Peabody and the South" (*Ind.* Aug. 19, 1869), elicited by Mr. Peabody's expressing his "cordial esteem for the high honor, integrity, and heroism of the Southern people," and "Honored beyond his Deserts [George Peabody]" (*Ind.* Feb. 10, 1870); "Mistaking the Product for the Germinating Power" (*Ind.* Oct. 9, 1873), in reply to an assertion that the anti-slavery agitators "made little impression upon the public mind"; "False and Invidious Comparisons," by Revs. F. H. Hedge and E. E. Hale, at the Memorial Service to Dr. S. G. Howe (Boston *Journal*, Feb. 10, 1876, signed "Fiat Justitia"); Reply to W. H. Ward's aspersions of W. L. G. and the abolitionists in a eulogistic sketch of Joshua Leavitt (*Ind.* Nov. 17, 1870).

2 "The truth is, in writing his History, he has failed to show the vital difference between genuine and sectarian abolitionism, but tried to play the amiable all round the circle; finding no fault with anything said or done by the sectarian seceders, but mildly deploring the acts of some of the old abolitionists — as in the case of Foster and Beach" (MS. Jan. 23, 1872, W. L. G. to Samuel May, Jr.).

hand after Mr. Wilson's death, was even more open to criticism in its treatment of the churches and their relation to the struggle. To Mr. May, who had just given his anti-slavery library to Cornell University, Mr. Garrison wrote as follows:

CHAP. IX. — 1868–76.

W. L. Garrison to S. J. May.

ROXBURY, Feb. 9, 1871.

MS.

MY DEARLY BELOVED FRIEND: I heartily thank you for your letter, enclosing a very interesting and justly appreciative one from Prof. Fiske of Cornell University, which I herewith return, in accordance with your request. His retrospective view of the anti-slavery struggle, and of the peculiar characteristics of the abolitionists, is very happily expressed; yet none but those who were called to endure the heat and burden of those times of fiery trial can fully realize what qualities of head and heart were needed to ensure uncompromising fidelity to the end. Some who early enlisted ran well for a time, and then fell by the way; in most instances, I think, because of their religious exclusiveness and intolerance. I am struck with the keen observation evinced by Prof. Fiske where he says —

Willard Fiske.

"It is strange to see how all the players in the drama appear just when they are wanted; how one scene of action follows another; how the *dramatis personæ* become constantly more numerous, until they embrace half a nation; how the fool and the knave of the play (the slaveholder) always comes forward, when the action lags, with some hideous piece of folly or equally hideous crime, which is suddenly seized and turned to advantage by his assailants."

Drawn to the life! I always marvelled, at the time, at the manner in which our co-laborers appeared or disappeared, according to the shaping of events. It would be unreasonable to say that our noble cause was not retarded by any defection that took place from our ranks; nevertheless, almost every event seemed to conspire, in some way or other, to give an impetus to it, so that, for more than thirty years, there was no lull in the excitement, no truce between the opposing parties. What the slaveholders were driven to do, in support of their "peculiar institution," was necessarily so base and cruel, often so diabolical, as powerfully to react in favor of those whom they so desperately but impotently endeavored to crush.

In giving your valuable collection of anti-slavery books and pamphlets to Cornell University, you have chosen an important

CHAP. IX. 1868-76. depository, through which the truth of history may be more intelligently ascertained and correctly illustrated. Your own excellent work, 'Anti-Slavery Recollections,' will be among the number that will be read with the deepest interest, inspiring many a student to enter the broad and illimitable field of philanthropy and reform.

Our old co-workers are fast disappearing from this earthly stage, and, in accordance with the laws of mortality, we must follow them at no distant day. How unspeakably pleasant it will be to greet them, and to be greeted by them, on the other side of the line! The longer I live, the longer I desire to live, and the more I see the desirableness of living; yet certainly not in this frail body, but just as it shall please the dear Father of us all. "It is sown a natural body; it is raised a spiritual body. It is sown in corruption; it is raised in incorruption. It is sown in dishonor; it is raised in glory. It is sown in weakness; it is raised in power." What a blessed exchange, and how magnificent!

You have doubtless heard of the translation of our dear and venerated friend and coadjutor, Thomas Garrett of Wilmington, Delaware. He was one of the grandest men of the ages.

The "translation" of Thomas Garrett was soon followed *July* 1, 1871. by that of the beloved and saintly pastor of Syracuse himself, and Mr. Garrison journeyed to Central New *July* 6. York to attend the obsequies of this "brother beloved incomparably beyond all blood relationship," to whom he felicitously applied Wordsworth's description of the "Happy Warrior." For many years the duties of ministers at large to the "come-outers" of the anti-slavery host had devolved upon Mr. Garrison and Mr. Phillips, and one or both of them were called to officiate or speak at many a funeral (and doubtless would have been asked to perform many a marriage ceremony, had they possessed the legal right to do so). Their services in this direction naturally became more and more in request as the veterans in the cause passed in quick succession from the stage. Notable among these occasions was the funeral of Henry C. Wright, at Pawtucket, R. I., in the sum- *Aug.* 19. mer of 1870, at which Mr. Garrison delivered an admirable *H. Wilson.* address, and Mr. Phillips and Senator Wilson spoke impressively.[1] In the following letter two more instances are recorded: CHAP. IX. 1868–76.

W. L. Garrison to Oliver Johnson.

ROXBURY, Dec. 28, 1873. *MS.*

Last Friday, I attended the funeral of our old anti-slavery co-laborer, Charles Lenox Remond, at Greenwood. He had been wasting in consumption for the last eighteen months. John T. Sargent, Wendell Phillips, and myself conducted the *Dec. 26. Mass.*

[1] On the death of Henry C. Wright, the conduct of his funeral and the decision as to the place of interment devolved upon Garrison and Phillips as his nearest friends. While they knew that Mr. Wright fully shared their own views as to the unimportance of the fate of the body after death, there was still a question, as he had lacked a home of his own for many years, in which of three or four places that were suggested—Newbury, Danvers, Roxbury, Providence—the burial should be made. Temporarily, the body was placed in the receiving tomb at Swan Point Cemetery, between Providence and Pawtucket, R. I., in which latter town Mr. Wright had died. Mr. Garrison, however, being in poor health at the time, and dangerously ill a fortnight later, the responsibility of determining the matter worried him more than it otherwise would have done. On Sept. 7, 1870, he consulted in Boston a "healing medium" in whom he had confidence, solely for a diagnosis of his own case. After that had been given him, the medium described Henry C. Wright as present and wishing to communicate with him. The impersonating spirit accordingly at once assumed control of the medium, and began to speak of his funeral, saying that he perceived his friend was troubled about the disposition of his body. "You know my views on that subject," he continued, and, suggesting that it would be simplest to inter the remains in the cemetery where they then lay, declared that there was a triangular lot, just large enough for a single grave, in the northwest part of the grounds, at the intersection of two roads; and a small tree which stood on it would serve the purpose of a monument.

Mr. Garrison went to Providence a few days afterwards, for medical treatment, and promptly visited the cemetery. As the Superintendent was absent, he asked his assistant to take him to the northwest portion. He failed, however, to recognize any such lot as had been described, and his conductor told him that they had no lots with single graves for sale, inasmuch as these were always bought up as soon as laid out. Through another medium whom he happened to meet during his stay in Providence, the existence of such a lot was reaffirmed, and he again visited the cemetery. The Superintendent corroborated his assistant's statement, but did not refuse to accompany Mr. Garrison and his brother-in-law, Mr. Henry Anthony, to the locality indicated. On the way, he suddenly remembered an unsold lot there. Lot and tree, in fact, were quickly recognized by Mr. Anthony, as they approached the spot, and the purchase was at once made and the body subsequently transferred to its final resting-place. It transpired that the Superintendent's assistant had, by mistake, led Mr. Garrison to the *western* instead of the northwestern part of the cemetery.

CHAP. IX. — 1868–76. services. A number of white and colored friends from Salem and Boston were present.

Dec. 27, 1873. Mass. Yesterday forenoon, I was present, with many others, at the funeral obsequies of our departed friend and aged saint, Sarah M. Grimké, at Hyde Park. We all felt the tenderness of heart and warm appreciation growing out of the attachments, labors, and perils of the past, in a common struggle to break the yoke of bondage and let the oppressed go free. She was the impersonation and incarnation of Divine Love; and, though bowed and wasted by bodily decrepitude, as fresh in her spirit as though but twenty instead of eighty-one years of age. There was no phase of reform or progress in which she did not take a heartfelt interest. She was singularly beloved and venerated by all who knew her. In addition to the services usual on such an occasion, tributes to the character and labors of the deceased were paid by our dear Theodore D. Weld, Lucy Stone, and myself. Theodore spoke with thrilling pathos and power, yet weeping like a child, and almost choking at times with the thoughts and words to which he tried to give utterance. Dear Angelina was very deeply affected.[1]

Angelina Grimké Wild.

Ever generous in panegyric to those who had passed from their earthly labors, Mr. Garrison was no less given to rehearsing the praises of his old coadjutors who still remained. He constantly took occasion, if writing them on other themes, to express his exalted regard for them. He was even repeatedly at pains to write a kindly word to some of his former antagonists in the anti-slavery ranks, recognizing the services they had rendered in the day of small things, and rejoicing with them in the triumph of freedom. One of these was Lewis Tappan, from whom a letter touching his brother Arthur elicited the following reply:

Lewis Tappan to W. L. Garrison.

MS. BROOKLYN, N. Y., Jan. 29, 1870.

MY DEAR SIR: It would be sheer affectation in me not to acknowledge the gratification your letter has given me. I greet

[1] Other funerals at which Mr. Garrison spoke were those of Joseph and Thankful Southwick, James Brown Yerrinton, William Adams, Bourne Spooner and wife, Mary Ann W. Johnson, William C. Nell, James Miller McKim, Edmund Jackson, Abby May Alcott, Charles C. Burleigh, and as

and congratulate you on your bodily and mental vigor, and the fruition of [our] hopes in the emancipation of our colored fellow-men. And as John Quincy Adams wrote to me on the deliverance of the *Amistad* Africans, so I can unite with you in saying, "Not unto us, not unto us," etc.

Ante, 2:326.

Yes, it is forty years since I first saw you, conducted you to my brother's desk, and introduced you to him. I seem to see now your open countenance and elastic step.

Arthur Tappan.

Francis Todd was a customer of mine in Boston, and I remember his sharp look and fox-like demeanor. How unlike John Peabody and Arthur Gilman of that day.

Ante, 1: 165-167.

After much importunity, I have prepared a sketch of the life of my brother Arthur, and in the chapter on Anti-Slavery agitation have endeavored to do justice to you and your labors. I have also introduced your letter to my brother, and to his daughters. I have tried, while I justified the withdrawal of my brother and those affiliating with him from associated labors with other abolitionists, not to say anything impeaching their love of the cause, or their adherence to what they believed was right principle. I remembered that I was not writing a history of the anti-slavery agitation, but of A. T.'s personal efforts in the cause, and on behalf of moral reform generally. While sketching my brother's activities I have wished for an opportunity to read the chapter referred to, in your hearing; and, should opportunity occur, it would give me satisfaction to do so.

My unpretending volume will contain some three hundred or more pages, and may be printed in the course of two or three months.[1]

Henry Wilson and Joshua Leavitt have each in hand a history of the cause. I have heard that you have also. I could wish that a history might be written to embody the views of all parties, or at least not to be unjust to any party. Our differences should, as far as principle allows, be swallowed up in principles and measures that, under God, led to victory.

Should you have kept any of my brother's letters, I shall be glad to peruse them, or, if you can state any facts illustrating

many more not named. His tributes to Richard D. Webb, James Haughton, Charles Sumner, David Lee Child, Gerrit Smith, and Henry Wilson will be found in the N. Y. *Christian Union*, April 9, 1873, *Independent*, March 19, 1874, Jan. 7, 1875, and Boston *Journal*, Nov. 29, 1875.

[1] 'The Life of Arthur Tappan.' New York: Hurd & Houghton. 1870. 12mo, pp. 432. With portrait.

CHAP. IX. 1868–76.

his character, that are probably unknown to me, I shall be pleased to receive them.

Very truly yours, LEWIS TAPPAN.[1]

Edmund Quincy received his laurel wreath with characteristic lightness and jest.

Edmund Quincy to W. L. Garrison.

MS. DEDHAM, Aug. 26, 1875.

I am much obliged to you for your appreciation of my services and sacrifices in the Anti-Slavery cause. I hope the services may have been somewhere near your valuation of them; but I claim no credit for the sacrifices. For, really, I made none that were not a hundred-fold compensated for by the satisfaction attending my course and the friendships I obtained by it — chief among which was that with yourself.

At the time I came into the cause, and all the time I was engaged in it, it never seemed to me that there was anything else for a man who wished to take some part in public affairs to do. I had no turn for the law, and politics seemed to me beneath the notice of a gentleman. Anti-Slavery was the only national and historical movement on foot — besides its humanitarian aspects. As for the *cold shoulders* and petty social ostracisms, I really cared nothing about them — and there was not much of it that was forced upon my notice. I knew I was abused behind my back, but people were always civil enough to my face. And I never made the slightest show of having done anything I was ashamed of. Quite the contrary.

The only gems which I claim for my celestial crown were the Meetings and Picnics at which I had to preside. These became almost intolerable bores to me, and even yet I feel a sensation of satisfaction, at the times and seasons when they used to occur, to think that I have not to go to them. I told John Sargent the other day that I wished they[2] could have kept on abolishing Slavery for the rest of their natural lives, it was such a pleasure to me to know they were at it, and I having nothing to

Rev. John T. Sargent.

[1] See Mr. Garrison's reply on p. 424 of A. Tappan's Life.

[2] That is, the American and Massachusetts Anti-Slavery Societies after 1865, of which latter Mr. Sargent was President. In this capacity he expressed the hope that Quincy would freely visit the Anti-Slavery Office, as of old, before the separation. "Thank you," answered the wit; "I'm afraid of ghosts."

Edmund Quincy

do with it. There is certainly no reason why they should not have continued as well as before. . . .

I am always, my dear Garrison, affectionately yours,

EDMUND QUINCY.

In March, 1873, Mr. Garrison was earnestly besought to write his autobiography, and an appeal to that end, inspired by Oliver Johnson, was addressed to him by many of his old associates.

Edmund Quincy and Others to W. L. Garrison.

March 10, 1873.

DEAR SIR: We take the liberty, as your personal friends of many years' standing, and your fellow-laborers in the Anti-Slavery movement, to address you on a matter which we have very much at heart. We mean the preparation of the history of your life by yourself. We venture to make this suggestion both on public and private considerations. The part which you had in the most important passage of our history makes it essential, as it appears to us, to the full understanding of its facts and its philosophy, that they should be set down by your own authentic pen. Such a narrative would furnish the most valuable material possible, as to the matters of which it would treat, for the future historian of this country. But, besides its public value, we are sure that your autobiography would be a very entertaining work, from the varieties of your career and the many interesting persons on both sides of the Atlantic with whom it has brought you in contact, besides affording a most instructive example, never more needed than now, of the genuine happiness and true success of a life devoted to a great and unselfish purpose.

Assured that you will take our application in good part, and hoping most earnestly that you will see fit to comply with the request it contains, we are, dear Mr. Garrison, most respectfully and affectionately, your friends.

The signatures to this letter included the familiar names of Quincy, Sewall, Chapman, Weston, Whittier, Mott, McKim, May, Smith, Weld, Grimké, Grew, and Burleigh, with those of Henry Wilson, Henry Ward Beecher, Mrs. Stowe, James Freeman Clarke, and others. But the labor

CHAP. IX. 1868-76.

asked of him seemed scarcely less formidable to Mr. Garrison than the still unwritten history of the anti-slavery movement, and he preferred discussing the topics of the day to recording his life-experiences for posterity. Referring to the ill-health which had in part deterred him from attempting the larger work, he said, in replying to these friends:

Mar. 17, 1873.

"It is extremely problematical, therefore, whether I shall yet be strengthened to depict, even on a limited scale, the most noteworthy moral and political struggle in the annals of civilization. Covering as it did a period of nearly forty years, and rending the nation by the antagonistic elements which it aroused, to portray it in all its multitudinous phases, without exaggeration or abatement, exceeds my ability, notwithstanding your encouraging voices. Moreover, my connection with it, from its commencement to its close, was so close and peculiar that a sense of delicacy almost precludes me from trying to record my views and recollections of it. So far as I am personally concerned, I feel no interest in any history of it that may be written. It is enough for me that every yoke is broken and every bondman set free. Yet there are lessons to be drawn from it that cannot fail to be serviceable to posterity. The millennial state, if it ever come on earth, is yet in the far distant future. There are innumerable battles yet to be fought for the right, many wrongs to be redressed, many evil customs abolished, many usurpations overthrown, many deliverances wrought; and those who shall hereafter go forth to defend the righteous cause, no matter at what cost or with what disparity of numbers, cannot fail to derive strength and inspiration from an intelligent acquaintance with the means and methods used in the Anti-Slavery movement."

NATIONAL POLITICS.—In the three Presidential campaigns which followed the civil war, Mr. Garrison naturally took a deep interest, being ever apprehensive that a Democratic triumph would lead to a negation of the civil and political rights of the freedmen. During the perplexing and anxious decade of "reconstruction," at first under the hostile Administration of Andrew Johnson, it is enough to say here that Mr. Garrison was in general accord with the measures adopted by Congress to thwart the reactionary designs of the Executive, and to maintain Republican control of the States lately in rebellion — not a *party* control, in his eyes. The failure to impeach President Johnson was a great disappointment to him. In the Presidential campaign of 1868 (when General Grant and Horatio Seymour were the rival candidates), the terrorism rampant at the South, and the Southern hopes of Democratic restoration, furnished themes for several of his articles in the *Independent;* but he refused to preside at a Republican ratification meeting in Faneuil Hall, or, at the request of Horace Greeley, to write an address to the freedmen, urging them to vote for Grant — believing himself too little known to the beneficiaries of his life-long endeavors in behalf of freedom.

Aug. 13, *Oct.* 1, 15, 22, 29, 1868.

MS. July 23, 1868. *Greeley to O. Johnson.*

He was not found, either, among the partisans of President Grant when the latter, in 1870-71, was bent on annexing San Domingo to the United States. He both sustained Mr. Sumner's opposition to the measure, and protested against the Senator's consequent removal from the head of the Committee on Foreign Relations.

Ind. June 23, *Dec.* 22, 1870; *Apr.* 13, 27, 1871.

Ind. Mar. 16, 1871.

Charles Sumner to W. L. Garrison.

WASHINGTON, 29th Dec., 1870. *MS.*

DEAR MR. GARRISON: Your letter is cheering, and reminded me of other days. I find now that same old heartlessness and violence which prevailed against Kansas — showing how, when people embark in such a policy, they act and speak accordingly.

When you read my speech, you will see that it was strictly to the point, discussing the subject-matter and avoiding all allusion to the President, except where the case positively required.

The Haytian minister had been to me full of emotion at the message of the President as "trampling his country under foot." I could not refer to despatches or documents. Therefore, I was driven to take up the message and draw from that as much as I could.

I was in earnest, and determined if possible to arrest this sacrifice. The only answer was a flood of personalities. Nothing

Boston Daily Advertiser. has been baser than the *Advertiser*. Its allegation was absolutely false. At the West I am generally sustained. In Boston — you know.

There is a menace to displace me from the Committee on Foreign Relations, of which I have been chairman ten years. This is a sop to Cerberus. It is founded on my difference with the Administration on this question, and the character of my speech. You will receive the speech soon, and I commend it to your perusal. Consider, if you please, that documentary evidence known to me could not be used.

Wendell Phillips. Gerrit Smith writes as you do. What will W. P. say?

Ever sincerely yours,

CHARLES SUMNER.

Mr. Garrison had to take issue with his friend in the following year, when the Democracy made a final rally under Horace Greeley, and Sumner (for personal reasons and general considerations of public policy) joined a portion of the reform element in the Republican Party in opposing Grant's reëlection at all hazards. A long *Aug.* 3, 1872. letter by Mr. Garrison, in confutation of Sumner's letter to the colored voters of Washington on behalf of Greeley, was very widely copied by the press, and presumably had *Sept.* 5. its effect. In another letter, addressed to the Boston *Sept.* 6. *Journal* (to which he contributed frequently during the campaign, both editorially and in his own name), Mr. Garrison replied at length to Mr. Sumner's last appeal for Greeley on the eve of departing for Europe.

Of Mr. Greeley's course in consenting to stand as the *Ind. Sept.* 12, *Oct.* 3, 24, 31, *Dec.* 15, 1872. candidate of the Democratic Party, he wrote with great plainness and severity, though the opinion of him which he now expressed was one he had long entertained, namely, *Ind. Oct.* 24, 1872. that the editor of the *Tribune* was "the worst of all counsellors, the most unsteady of all leaders, the most pliant of all compromisers in times of great public emergency" — *Century Magazine, June*, 1888, *p.* 291. a judgment since strikingly confirmed by the publication of Greeley's extraordinary letter to President Lincoln after the battle of Bull Run.

When, after Mr. Sumner's death in 1874, there was a deadlock in the Massachusetts Legislature over the election of his successor, Mr. Garrison was approached by one of the Republican leaders to know if he would accept the position, and replied:

CHAP. IX. 1868–76.

"Your friendly and complimentary letter of inquiry causes me very great surprise, because, although we have lived to see many strange occurrences in our day, I deem it scarcely more supposable that, under any fortuitous combination of circumstances or rallying of forces, I should be chosen successor of Charles Sumner in the U. S. Senate by the Legislature of Massachusetts, than that 'Birnam wood will come to Dunsinane.' What, therefore, is utterly out of the question cannot be with me a matter of grave consideration. Besides, if, by any possible 'change of base,' such a choice should happen to be made as a *dernier ressort*, I have some conscientious difficulties, particularly as respects the war provisions of the Constitution of the United States, that would prevent my qualifying under that instrument."

MS. Mar. 28, 1874, to Edward Atkinson.

In the latter years of the reconstruction period, when one after another of the Southern States was wrested from the control of the so-called "carpet-bag governments," Mr. Garrison saw in the violent uprising of the whites not so much a revolt against thieving and corrupt adventurers who were sustaining themselves in office by the aid of the colored vote on the one hand, and the military support of the Federal Government on the other, as a determined effort to rob the freedmen of the ballot and make them again a subject race. If he had no adequate conception of the financial misrule under some of these governments, he knew accurately the still unquenched spirit of slavery, and that nothing which was alleged against it was impossible. And in truth there was, especially in communities in which black voters were in the ascendency, enough of genuine outrage and calculated terrorism practised (under the general name of Kukluxism) to make exaggeration or invention of them for political effect unnecessary. These and worse he anticipated if the restraining Federal arm should be withdrawn, with iniquitous and oppressive legislation directed against the disfranchised blacks (such as is to be found in most of the

CHAP. IX. 1868–76. Southern statute-books to-day). He could not see that any Constitutional obstacle existed to maintaining with Federal troops the governments in South Carolina and Louisiana — the last that remained to be artificially held up in this manner — so long as the legally constituted State Governments invoked their aid. He therefore viewed with foreboding President Grant's admission, towards the close of his second term, that the military administration could no longer be maintained at the South; and entered an earnest protest against President Hayes's retirement of the troops directly after the latter assumed office in 1877.

FREE TRADE.— In January, 1869, Mr. Garrison was elected a Vice-President of the American Free Trade League, of New York, and actively assisted in the formation of a Revenue Reform League in Boston, the following April, making one of the principal speeches at the Boston meeting. In justification of his part in it he said: *April 20, 1869.*

Boston Journal, April 21, 1869.

"This is a meeting with special reference to business interests, in their most substantial form. In a technical sense, I am not a business man, and have nothing more at stake in matters of commerce or manufactures than others whose pursuits lie in another direction. Yet, perhaps, no man has had more to do with the business of the country — at least as a disturbing force — for the last forty years than I have; and, certainly, the industrial elements have had a good deal to do with me, in an antagonizing way, during the same period. Happily, we are no longer at variance for any such cause.

"As to mere details and statistics respecting free trade on the one hand, and the protective policy (so-called) on the other, I am but a novice; but as to those principles which underlie all national prosperity, and determine the legitimate scope of legislation in regard to international reciprocity and interchange of commodities, I profess to be considerably enlightened. . . .

"For the cause of human liberty covers and includes all possible forms of human industry, and best determines how the productions thereof may be exchanged at home and abroad to mutual advantage. Though never handling a tool, nor manufacturing a bale of cotton or wool, nor selling a yard of cloth or a pound of sugar, he is the most sagacious political economist who contends for the highest justice, the most far-reaching equality, a close adherence to natural laws, and the removal of all those restrictions which foster national pride and selfishness. The mysteries of government are only the juggles of usurpers and demagogues. There is nothing intricate in freedom, free labor, free institutions, the law of interchange, the measure of reciprocity. It is the legerdemain of class legislation, disregarding the common interests of the people, that creates confusion, sophisticates the judgment, and dazzles to betray. The law of gravitation needs no legislative props or safeguards to make its operations more effective or more beneficent. . . .

"It is to be supposed — other things being equal — that those whose lives are devoted to business affairs and financial matters will have a clearer perception of what concerns their interests than those whose pursuits are simply professional or philanthropic. Other things being equal, I say — that is a very important qualification! Alas! they are often most unequal, because of a profligate disregard of principle; and then follow incongruity, entanglement, loss of vision, impaired judgment, desperate expedients, calamitous results. This was strikingly illustrated in the insane conduct of the business men of the nation, of all classes, in burning incense and servilely bowing the knee to the Southern Moloch for a period of threescore years and ten, animated by the belief that it was a paying business investment! What came of it, we have all had bitter occasion to know. . . .

"Believing that the interests of the American people in no wise materially differ from those of the people of any other country, and denying the rectitude or feasibility of building ourselves up at their expense by an exclusive policy, obstructing the natural flow of material exchanges, I avow myself to be a radical free trader, even to the extent of desiring the abolition of all custom-houses, as now constituted, throughout the world. That event is far distant, undoubtedly, but I believe it will come with the freedom and enlightenment of mankind. My faith is absolute that it will prove advantageous to every branch of human industry, whether at home or abroad. Its advocacy, however, will not be the object of the proposed Reform League. That object has been stated to you to be the procurement of a simple, moderate, and effective tariff, for revenue purposes exclusively, with the least possible interference with the industrial pursuits of the people; opposition to

CHAP. IX. 1868–76.

all special legislation intended to foster private or class interest; the negotiation of treaties of reciprocity with all States upon the continent of North America; the abatement of some of the most onerous taxes imposed under the existing tariff; the restoration of the specie standard of value at as early a day as practicable; and, finally, to promote reform in the civil service, and the appointment of all Government officers upon the sole ground of fitness and ability to discharge the duties of their respective offices. I trust it will meet the hearty approval of this assembly, and at no distant day that of the people of Massachusetts and of the whole country. . . .

"Gentlemen, the object which has brought us together is neither partisan nor geographical, but patriotic and all-comprehensive; not for any one interest in special, but for all interests; not for Massachusetts alone, but for the whole country. Its realization cannot fail to bring great and signal blessings along with it, and to foster a more noble and expansive spirit of human brotherhood, through which at last all the nations of the earth shall strike hands in amity and peace."[1]

In an article in the *Independent* on "Protection *vs.* Free Trade," he declared, "There is not a more deceptive and at the same time more plausible word in popular use than 'protection.'"

Ind. May 20, 1869.

"'The protection of American labor' has a taking sound; but it really means the restriction and taxation of that labor. Protection against what? Have we not the best educated and most intelligent population on earth? And does not this imply industry, thrift, skill, enterprise, invention, capital, beyond any other forty millions of people? Have we not muscles as well as

[1] Mr. Garrison having alluded, in the course of his speech, to the immense market opened up by the abolition of slavery for a multitude of the appliances of civilization unknown to the slaves and now demanded by the freedmen, a correspondent wrote him: "I beg to afford you an incident in this connection, sustaining your sensible application of your principles to the workings of trade. I was informed by a wholesale stove dealer at Wheeling, W. Va., last June, that he was then engaged in sending $100,000 worth of cooking stoves, per Ohio River steamers and those connecting with them, to Louisiana, to supply a pressing demand then existing for them by the emancipated negroes. What a volume of wants and traffic unprecedented in amount and profit is opened up to the mind's eye, through the entire length and breadth of the Ohio and Mississippi valleys, from this source in the future!" (MS. April 27, 1869, I. L. Hodsdon, ex-Adjt.-Gen. of Maine, to W. L. G.)

brains? Have we not a country unrivalled in the variety and abundance of its natural productions, and the abounding riches of its mineral resources? What more need we to claim, or ought we to have? If, in an open field, we cannot successfully compete with 'the cheap and pauperized labor of Europe,' in all that is necessary to our comfort, or even to our luxury, then let us go to the wall! Was the slave labor of the South at all a match for the free labor of the North? In which section of the Union was industry best protected or wealth most augmented? Is it not ludicrous to read what piteous calls are made for the protection of the strong against the weak, of the intelligent against the ignorant, of the well-fed against the half-starving, of our free republican nation against the effete governments of the Old World, in all that relates to the welfare of the people? With all that God has done for us in giving us such a goodly heritage, cannot we contrive to live and flourish without erecting barriers against the freest intercourse with all nations? Must we guard our ports against the free importation of hemp, iron, broadcloth, silk, coal, etc., etc., as though it were a question of quarantine for the smallpox or the Asiatic cholera? Refusing to do so, will the natural consequences be 'vacant factories, furnaces standing idle, the shops of manufacturing industry closed, labor begging and starving for the want of employment,' and all the other fearful results that are so confidently predicted by the advocates of the protective policy, falsely so-called? Similar predictions were made by the defenders of Southern slavery in regard to the abolition of that nefarious system, and in order to subject to popular odium those who demanded the immediate and unconditional emancipation of the oppressed. Freedom, as well as Wisdom, is justified of her children; and in proportion as she bears sway will it go well with any people."

On the 10th of December, 1875, Mr. Garrison celebrated at once his 70th birthday and the fiftieth anniversary of his graduation from the *Herald* office, by going to Newburyport and again taking up the composing-stick in the familiar place. Selecting Whittier's beautiful poem, "My Psalm," he set it with almost his old-time rapidity and expertness; and though the type was small, and the "case" not over well supplied with it, not an error was found in the seventeen verses when the first proof was

Joseph B. Morss.

pulled. While he was at work, an old fellow-apprentice came in to greet him, and though, from the latter's indifference to the anti-slavery movement, there had been little sympathy and intercourse between them in the intervening half century, they now fraternized and found common ground in reminiscences of their boyhood days, and in unexpected sympathy of views on other topics. Very fitting, therefore, seemed the closing verses of the poem, when the veteran printer and agitator, turning once more to his task, put them in type:

"Enough

"That care and trial seem at last,
Through Memory's sunset air,
Like mountain-ranges, overpast,
In purple distance fair,—

"That all the jarring notes of life
Seem blending in a psalm,
And all the angles of its strife
Slow rounding into calm.

"And so the shadows fall apart,
And so the west winds play;
And all the windows of my heart
I open to the day."

CHAPTER X.

Death of Mrs. Garrison.— Final Visit to England. 1876, 1877.

IN January, 1876, the heaviest bereavement of his life befell Mr. Garrison in the loss of his wife, who was taken from him, after a short and sharp attack of pneumonia, on the 25th of that month. It had been evident for several weeks that her health was seriously impaired, but the event, when it came, was unexpected, and Mr. Garrison, himself suffering from a severe cold and worn by care and watching, was so prostrated by it that grave anxiety was felt for a time as to his own recovery.[1] During his weeks of convalescence he found solace in preparing a memorial sketch of Mrs. Garrison, which was printed, with the addresses at the funeral and many tributes from friends, in a small volume for private presentation.[2]

Chap. X. 1876–77.

In June he visited Pennsylvania, and attended, for the last time, the Progressive Friends' Meetings at Longwood, with his usual active participation. He subsequently devoted several days to the Centennial Exhibition in Philadelphia, but the resultant fatigue crippled him for

1876.

1 He was unable to be present at the funeral services, which were held at Rockledge, and conducted by the Rev. Samuel May, assisted by Wendell Phillips, Lucy Stone, and the Rev. George Putnam. Mr. Phillips's tribute was an exquisite portrayal of Mrs. Garrison's character.

2 'Helen Eliza Garrison. A Memorial.' 1876. "While writing it, my head and heart were heavily oppressed, and in my enfeebled condition the task was as laborious as it was delicate. I hope it will not seem to indicate anything of mental weakness to those into whose hands it will be put" (MS. March 30, 1876, W. L. G. to W. P. G.). The volume contains an excellent photograph of Mrs. Garrison.

CHAP. X. 1876–77. weeks, and the summer, as a whole, was a quiet and sober one for him. "What a solitude is the house!" he wrote to his absent daughter, and his letters repeatedly reflected his sense of loneliness. Nevertheless, he wrote and read much, received and visited many friends, and contributed *Hayes-Tilden.* two or three letters to the Presidential campaign. In June he received a note from Harriet Martineau, acknowledging the Memorial of Mrs. Garrison, and this was swiftly *June 27, 1876.* followed by the announcement of her own death, which it foreshadowed. He was deeply interested in the advance *Maria W. Chapman.* proofs of her Autobiography, which Mrs. Chapman sent him, and as to which she frequently conferred with him during that autumn.

Harriet Martineau to W. L. Garrison.

MS. AMBLESIDE, May 30, 1876.

MY DEAR FRIEND: When you kindly sent me the memorial card announcing your precious wife's departure and burial, I asked our dear Mrs. Chapman to thank you on my behalf; and her latest letter brings me your response. With it comes the Memoir — the picture of her beautiful life and death. I wish I could convey to you any idea of the emotion excited in my household by the reading of this narrative; but I have strength for no more than a bare acknowledgment of your valued gift, and assurance of sympathy under the pain of your bereavement. What a woman she was! I am thankful to have been *Ante, 2:27, 28.* in Boston at the crisis which proved that she was worthy of the honor of being your wife.

I can say no more. My departure is evidently near, and I hold the pen with difficulty.

Accept the sympathy and reverent blessing of your old friend,

HARRIET MARTINEAU.

W. L. Garrison to Maria W. Chapman.

MS. ROXBURY, Jan. 18, 1877.

DEAR MRS. CHAPMAN: I have forwarded by the Weymouth *Harriet Martineau.* Express, to-day, H. M.'s Autobiography and your supplemental volume, hoping I have not put you to any inconvenience by not returning them at an earlier date, and proffering you many thanks for so kindly allowing me to peruse them in advance of their publication.

The result is a higher appreciation, if possible, of the intellectual strength, solid understanding, conscientious integrity, fearless independence of thought and expression, courageous "heretical" non-conformity, far-reaching humanity, intuitional grasp, varied knowledge, and literary fertility of that extraordinary woman. I was not aware of the extent of her writings, or the wide range of her investigations pertaining to political economy, statesmanship, government, mental and moral philosophy, psychology, history, biography, international law, philanthropy, well-founded reform, etc., etc. It is not doing any injustice to the eminent women of the world to place her at the head, in comprehensiveness of mind and devotion to the general welfare, working through numerous channels, and discussing with masterly ability questions and measures which for ages have been exclusively assigned to the male sex. Then, privately and socially, how admirable her characteristics!—But all this is superfluous to you.

I had high expectations as to your portion of the forthcoming work, but these have been transcended by the manner in which you have discharged so delicate and responsible a task. Your appreciation of H. M. is in no instance exaggerated; and you evince excellent judgment, rare critical acumen, profound philosophic insight, united with personal and historical fidelity. It was fortunate for you that you had such a trust committed to you, and fortunate for H. M. that she selected you to complete that portion of her life not contained in her Autobiography. I congratulate you on the successful achievement of a most arduous performance.

I am profoundly grateful to you for the kind and generous manner in which reference is made to myself and my anti-slavery labors in the closing volume. The thought has never come into my mind how I should or might be estimated in my own day or generation, or by those coming after me, if remembered at all; but it is none the less gratifying to me to be recognized by two such women as H. M. and M. W. C. as entitled to their esteem and approbation, and the favorable judgment of all true friends of liberty and equal rights.

I am pleased to see my letter to Miss Jane Martineau printed with others, especially those from H. M.'s maid-servants, paying a just and sincere tribute to the memory of the deceased.

CHAP. X. — 1876–77. Of course, that portion of the work which relates to H. M.'s views of theology and a future life will elicit more or less invective and traducement from a sectarian religious press; but the best answer to it all will be —

> "For modes of faith let graceless zealots fight;
> His can't be wrong whose life is in the right."

Judging by this test, H. M. is surely entitled to a conspicuous place in "the household of saints." Anyhow, "it is a small thing to be judged of man's judgment."

Though, through much overworking and years of bodily prostration, I think she seemed to covet at last "the sleep that knows no waking," my faith is absolute that she "still lives," with all her faculties unimpaired, and there as here eager to know and serve the true and the right.

With kindest regards to you all,

WM. LLOYD GARRISON.

The winter of 1876–77 was a very trying one to Mr. Garrison, and his health became so much impaired that he finally yielded to the urgent solicitation of his physician and children that he should try a transatlantic trip. His friends in England, who hailed with delight the prospect of another visit from him, were warned that public meetings and receptions were out of the question, and that they must permit him to move among them quietly and obtain all the rest possible. He was doubly afflicted, on the eve of his departure, by the death of a beloved daughter-in-law, who was to have accompanied him on his voyage, and, a few days later, by that of his dear friend, Edmund Quincy, whose funeral he was unable to attend, being already in New York and about to embark when the news reached him.

May 11, 1877. *Lucy McKim Garrison.* *May* 17.

His companion, as on his previous visit to England, was his youngest son. Leaving New York on the 23d of May, in the steamer *Algeria*, they arrived in Liverpool on the 3d of June, in good condition for the twelve weeks of delightful travel and social intercourse which followed, and of which it is difficult to give any adequate conception in this brief narrative.

F. J. G.

Obeying the injunctions which had been reiteratedly sent them, Mr. Garrison's friends endeavored, with a fair degree of success, to abstain from precipitating meetings and receptions upon him; but the desire to see and hear him was so strong that they could not resist the temptation to fill their parlors with invited guests, when he came among them, and to ask him to tell them about his early life, his anti-slavery experiences, and his views on one or another question of morals and reform. Young and old thus gathered to listen to his discourse on slavery, war, intemperance, non-resistance, and the rights of women, and to gather inspiration from his clear and simple exposition of fundamental principles. To his companion, who had been familiar from childhood with the facts he narrated, and his habitual phraseology in discussing these themes, it was a constant surprise to note the freshness with which he invested, and the vigor with which he presented them, and to find himself listening as to a new rather than an oft-told tale. As to the effect on Mr. Garrison's auditors generally, who listened with riveted attention as to one indeed "having authority," the evidence does not rest on filial testimony. Expressions as to the influence thus exerted and the deep impression made came to him from many sources. "For three days we have heard the gospel preached," said one of the most admirable and intellectual women in the kingdom, after spending that length of time in Mr. Garrison's company, and conversing with him on a wide range of topics; and a cultivated gentleman who met him for the first time, and entertained him for a single night in his charming country home, wrote subsequently, "He came among us like a perfected spirit, bearing testimony."

Helen Bright Clark.

Herbert New.

Evesham.

The first person whom Mr. Garrison sought, on his arrival in Liverpool, was Mrs. Josephine E. Butler, whom he had wished to meet ever since her inauguration of the movement for the repeal of the Contagious Diseases Acts had become known to him. The high opinion he had formed of her from her writings was more than confirmed

Ante, p. 248.

CHAP. X. 1876-77. by personal acquaintance, and she on her part received his expressions of sympathy and support with the deepest gratitude and encouragement. He spent an evening in informal discourse to a number of gentlemen whom she convened at her house, with what effect she subsequently wrote him:

Josephine E. Butler to W. L. Garrison.

MS. LIVERPOOL, June 10, 1877.

I wished one more word in reply to your most kind and encouraging letter — it is this, that if you should have the opportunity again — and you will — to speak to friends as you did at our house, I wish most earnestly that you should exactly do as you did here; you can and will, thereby, wonderfully serve the different sacred movements of reform going on here. I mean, that it seems to me and my husband the very best thing possible that you should relate that wonderful narrative of your labors — or some portion of your labors — with all its deep and suggestive lessons, enforced in a few words, as you can enforce them, and *then*, having quite won your hearers, speak at the end a few grave and earnest words concerning the struggles going on here — our own great conflict for justice and purity, the temperance movement, etc. You won *several* at our house, and you can do us thus *immense* service with, I trust, not too much effort yourself, and without any *public* meetings at all.

You perhaps scarcely realize the gladness imparted by your visit to England to all of us, and we are *many now*, who have to fight so sacred a battle against great odds — a battle which in some of its essential features resembles the great and marvellous anti-slavery struggle.

To another, Mrs. Butler wrote of Mr. Garrison:

MS. June 26, 1877, to F. J. G. "I think he has a peculiar gift for awakening the conscience, and for making us all feel to what extent we have severally failed to see, or to *live up to*, the principles we profess or love. To me, his influence is that of a visit to a fortifying mountain-top where a strong, pure breeze is blowing, and where mists are cleared away and one gets above the strife of earth for a moment, though still, and more widely, beholding all that strife."

Mr. and Mrs. Wm. Crosfield. From Liverpool, where he passed pleasant hours with his friends, the Crosfields, Mr. Garrison went to Manchester for five days, enjoying the society of his hosts, Dr. Louis Borchardt and family, and of the Steinthals, and other friends. Thence he made a trip through Derbyshire, visiting Chatsworth and Edensor, and spending a day or two amid the lovely scenery about Mayfield and Ashbourne, and at Dovedale, the favorite haunt of Izaak Walton, whither his friend and host, Joseph Simpson, drove him. At Oxford he was too late to see the throngs of graduation week, but enjoyed all the more the summer quiet of the fine old town, to which this was his first visit. He declined the urgent invitation of Prof. Jowett, who was just starting for London, to occupy his apartments at Balliol College, but accepted the services of his secretary as guide through the several colleges, and subsequently spent an agreeable hour with Prof. Jowett in London. He had the privilege of meeting that modest scholar and public-spirited citizen, Thomas H. Green, whose early death was such a loss to the town and to every good movement with which he had identified himself, and of becoming still better acquainted with that genial and charming gentleman, Prof. George Rolleston, Linnæan Professor of Anatomy and Physiology at Oxford, who gave a dinner party in his honor, and listened with approval to his guest's testimony in favor of total abstinence.[1]

June 6–11, 1877. *Rev. S. A. Steinthal.* *June* 11. *June* 12, 13. *June* 14–16. *Benjamin Jowett.* *June* 17. *June* 15.

Two weeks were devoted to London, every day of which was fully occupied. The Chessons, Ashursts, and Stansfelds were the first to welcome their old friend, and social

June 16–30.

[1] It was naturally elicited by Mr. Garrison's refusal to take any of the wines offered, which the host, though himself an abstainer, felt obliged to provide for his guests. "We have talked and thought a good deal about you since you left," he wrote, two days later (MS. June 17, 1877, Rolleston to F. J. G.). "Very sorry am I to have heard so little of your father's words, 'which make a man feel strong in hearing truth.' I do hope we shall see him again. May he prolong his days, and may the work of goodness prosper in his hand. But he did me real good, of a kind which I wanted, at a moment when the detestable spirit of the *Pall Mall Gazette* [then a Jingo organ] appears to have wholly entered into and entirely filled up the minds of so many Englishmen. We are just now in a very unwholesome state, and I fear nothing short of some national calamity is likely to shake us out of it."

June 21, 25, 1877. gatherings were given by the first two in his honor. He
June 24. spent an evening also at Jacob Bright's, and an hour or
June 19. two in the lobby of the House of Commons, one afternoon,
exchanging greetings with his friends in the House,—
John and Jacob Bright, Sir Wilfred Lawson, Joseph
Cowen, Samuel Morley, Henry Richards, Duncan McLaren,
Benjamin Whitworth, and Sir Thomas Bazley. One day
June 18. was given to Kew, Twickenham, Hampton Court, and
June 22. Richmond, and another to the Händel Triennial Festival
at the Crystal Palace. Mr. Garrison attended and spoke
June 21. briefly at the annual meeting of the National Woman
Suffrage Association; and at a meeting in behalf of the
June 25. London School of Medicine for Women he listened to
James Stansfeld, Henry Fawcett. Sophia Jex Blake. speeches by the Earl of Shaftesbury, Mr. Stansfeld, Mrs.
Westlake, Prof. Fawcett, Miss Jex Blake, and Dr. Garrett-Anderson. He also heard a liberal discourse by Dean
June 24. Stanley at St. Stephen's. One of his pleasantest mornings
was spent at Argyll Lodge, in Kensington, where he break-
June 23. fasted with the Duke and Duchess of Argyll and their
daughters,—John Bright, Hon. Charles Howard, and Hon.
Lyulph Stanley being the other guests; and he had a cheer-
June 28. ful interview also with Lord Houghton, who was just then
confined to his room by a painful accident, but who insisted
on seeing him, though other callers were turned away.

The British and Foreign Anti-Slavery Society would not consent to Mr. Garrison's leaving London without receiving some mark of attention from them. Among
June 26. the fifty gentlemen present at the breakfast which they tendered him, at the Devonshire House Hotel, there were over a dozen members of Parliament, including William E. Forster, Evelyn Ashley, and Sir George Campbell, who all spoke. The guest of the occasion had understood that it would be entirely informal, and was unprepared for any speech-making, but he complied with the request of the President (Edmund Sturge) that he would give some account of the progress of the colored people in the South since emancipation, and spoke with ease and fluency to deeply interested auditors.

One more meeting awaited him, at which, with no expectation on his part, he was the principal figure, and his speech the chief feature of the occasion. This was a general Conference, held the day before he left London, of the various Associations for the repeal of the Contagious Diseases Acts, representatives from all parts of the kingdom being present. The slow and painful fight with legalized vice and iniquity had now been going on for eight years, and the small number of faithful women and men who had borne the heat and the burden of this battle for the protection of womanhood, and the honor and dignity of manhood, for social purity and the equal accountability of the sexes to the moral law, met to take counsel together. The discouragements and reverses had been many. The clergy as a body had hesitated to take up a question presenting so many revolting aspects, and from the very mention and discussion of which timid and sensitive natures shrank; the press, especially the large dailies, treated it with deliberate and systematic silence; and Parliament steadily refused to repeal the law. Meetings held now and then in different cities and towns, but usually unreported; tracts and documents, petitions and appeals, scattered broadcast, seemed to produce little impression on the public, and still less on Parliament, which appointed Royal Commissions of Inquiry, but went no further. A deep seriousness pervaded the hundred earnest men and women who now came together, and an almost overpowering sense of the magnitude of their task and the formidable obstacles yet to be overcome seemed to rest upon them.

CHAP. X.

1876–77.

June 29.

William Shaen,[1] a long-time friend of Mr. Garrison, presided, and, after giving a clear and able summary of their past labors and the present position of the movement, and introducing Professor James Stuart and Sir Harcourt Johnstone (the latter the Parliamentary leader

[1] An eminent solicitor, who received his legal training under Wm. H. Ashurst. No man in London was more active in every philanthropic movement.

Chap. X. 1876–77.

for repeal of the Acts) to make their reports, he asked for a few words of encouragement from their American guest, the thought of whose career ought to relieve any momentary depression on their part. Especially did he invite him to give an account of his early labors and sufferings; but Mr. Garrison, on rising, brushed aside, with a smile, those "light afflictions" which "were but for a moment and were hardly worth talking about," and indulged instead in an account of the labors and sacrifices of George Thompson in America, as an introduction to the reasons why his own participation with them in the present struggle was not improper.

The Shield, London, July 7, 1877.

"I have heard of your doings," he said, "when on the other side of the Atlantic, and my heart went out to you. I felt myself one with you in spirit, one with you in your aim. I often said,— you did not hear me, but I said it in my heart, many times,— with my heart's voice I said, 'God bless the noble men and women now striving to cleanse the land of England from the foul pollution implied by such atrocious laws as they are working to abolish.' Generally, where I stand up to speak, I am 'native and to the manner born,' but here I am a foreigner, standing on foreign soil; and I ask myself, 'What right have I to be here, an intermeddler, an agitator, if you will?' . . . But I have in my own mind long come to this conclusion, that 'the earth is the Lord's'; and wherever on His footstool I may be placed, if iniquity is to be arraigned, and immorality is to be confronted, I claim my right before God to denounce it. And so I feel at home here, and that I have a perfect right to speak; and I do denounce the iniquitous and infamous Acts as disgraceful to Great Britain and the Government thereof. (Loud applause.) I bid you God-speed; and if I were to continue here I would try whether I could help you in any way whatsoever, however feebly; and whatever I could do, I would be very sure to do. Your cause is righteous. This question of pollution — what! not to be confronted! not to be talked about! Men and women to be separate when they talk about it! Why separate? If they are virtuous, shall they not speak of that which is not virtuous and denounce it in common? It struck me as rather singular when I heard . . . [of] certain gentlemen so exceedingly virtuous, so exceedingly afraid of anything indelicate in the presence of ladies, that they cannot discuss this matter. . . . I have no respect for virtue which will not have pollution brought forward into the very light of the sun, so that, being seen, it may be abhorred and forever put away. And this is not a matter of statistics. Your Government sanctions pollution; and you say pollution is not to be sanctioned. You are bound to confront it as a great immorality, an impiety against God; and statistics cannot but show (if they are correctly compiled) that immorality does and will work evil in every direction. For God does not make it possible that that which in itself is immoral and iniquitous shall be good anyhow, at any time, or under any circumstances. And thus it is that I would have you take up this matter, and press it home. Let every man and every woman make it a moral test of purity; but let not any men dare to assume that they are the advocates of virtue while they are saying, 'Let us have a class of women set apart for infamous purposes, and so regulate them that men may go on in a lustful course with impunity, as far as that is possible.' No, friends, we must not have any squeamishness about this; we must speak out plainly — call things by their right names; and, especially, we must say, 'It is immoral, it is unclean, it is an offence against the Divine Law, and therefore it must be put down.' (Applause.)

"I am very sorry indeed that one to whom reference has been made this afternoon, is not here — I mean Mrs. Josephine Butler. I have, on the other side of the Atlantic, felt the force of her moral magnetism, and the uplifting power of her influence, and I have desired for a long time to be able to see her, to make her personal acquaintance. I cannot express to you the estimation in which I hold her, so well balanced as she is in intellect, in mind, in soul: such purity, such completeness of character, such judgment, such circumspection, everything to make up a noble and complete character; such feeling, such firmness, such courage, to dare to stand up and grapple with the nation! (Loud applause.) . . . Oh, she is a worthy leader. And I honor the women as well as the men who are working with her, also doing nobly, and striving to do all that she is striving to do, and has done so well — I honor you all. But the work, as a matter of justice, belongs to ourselves; *to us, who are men.* It is the men who have wrought this evil. It is the men who have done this wrong. It is the men who are responsible for it — the women did not pass the law. Had there been one single woman in Parliament, do you suppose that there would have been any one man audacious enough,

CHAP. X. 1876–77.

indecent enough, to have dared to stand up and advocate such a measure? But I believe this thing was born in darkness; it was carried through nobody knew how. It had the very stamp of unrighteousness about it. All in the dark these Contagious Diseases Acts were passed. How very innocent in name, and yet how thoroughly iniquitous and polluting in intention, while making the best professions—regard for sanitary measures, and so forth, and so forth, and so forth!

"Well, friends, you will go on, of course. (Applause.) Not one of you will think of retreating. Why, it is the best investment for the soul's welfare possible, to take hold of something which is righteous but unpopular. (Hear, hear.) *Righteous* but unpopular, for men may get hold of an unpopular cause which deserves to be unpopular and is not righteous. But it invigorates and strengthens us to work in a righteous but unpopular cause; it teaches us to know ourselves, to know what it is we are relying on—whether we love the praise of men or the praise of God. As for me, I think I should not know how to take part in a popular movement—it would seem so weakening, so enervating. Everybody is there, and there is nothing to be done, excepting to shout. Let others do that if they like; but while this world remains as it is, while so much has yet to be *done* to make the world better, God grant that while I live I may be connected still, as far as possible, with causes which, being righteous, are unpopular, and struggling, in God's name, *against* wind and tide. Living and dying I will give my support to such, and look to God for His blessing in the end."

The effect produced by this little speech, delivered, as the report betrays, without premeditation, was wonderfully inspiring.[1] To Mr. Garrison's companion it remains one of the three most impressive incidents and memories of that fortnight in London. The second was the interview between Mr. Garrison and John Bright, which was marked by great tenderness of feeling and mutual affection. Meeting first in the lobby of the House of Commons,

June 19.

1 "Mr. Butler would tell you of the pleasant meeting we had on Friday afternoon. He could not tell you how much we missed you and longed for you amongst us. But he could say what a grand speech we had from Mr. Garrison, so sympathetic and encouraging that it made one feel almost ashamed of ever having felt, even for a passing moment, disheartened at the apathy which we sometimes have to meet" (MS. July 1, 1877, R. F. Martineau to Josephine E. Butler).

where, withdrawn from the throng of members, and sitting together in a retired corner, they discussed the events and changes of the last ten years, they subsequently went into the Library of the House and stood by one of the windows looking out upon the Thames, with its multitudinous craft passing to and fro in the bright sunlight of the June afternoon. The conversation turned on war and the recent imminence of complications between England and Russia. "The danger is past," said Mr. Bright, "for fortunately we have now no allies." "How would it do," said Mr. Garrison, "to place this interrogation above the door of the House of Commons?—'Shall the throne of iniquity have fellowship with thee, which frameth mischief by a law?'" "I used to quote that in the Anti-Corn Law Days," replied Mr. Bright, with a smile. Then he alluded to Lewis Morris's recent poem, "The Epic of Hades," which had greatly impressed him, and repeated, with exquisite feeling, Whittier's beautiful apostrophe to his sister in "Snow Bound." Descending next to the river terrace, the two friends talked of the future life, and Mr. Garrison narrated the curious circumstance of Henry C. Wright's post-mortem suggestions about his burial-place. The story greatly interested Mr. Bright, who had known the author of 'A Kiss for a Blow' thirty years before, and he speedily repeated it to others.

Psalm xciv. 20.

Ante, p. 253.

The third memorable incident, which an artist might well have depicted on canvas, was when, during a quiet stroll through the aisles of Westminster Abbey, one afternoon when the proceedings in the House of Commons had ceased to interest, and it was a relief to escape to the cool seclusion of the old sanctuary, Mr. Garrison paused before the admirable statue of Wilberforce, and, leaning backwards upon his cane, long contemplated the face and figure, and read the elaborate inscription which covers the front of the pedestal.

June 29.

The last night in London was spent in listening to the closing debate on the County Franchise Bill in the House of Commons. The Liberals were then in a minority and

CHAP. X. 1876–77. occupying the Opposition benches; but with two exceptions they mustered their entire strength in favor of the measure, which was defeated by fifty-six majority.

In spite of all the labor and excitement, Mr. Garrison gained perceptibly in health during his stay in London. Besides the friends already named, he met many others with whom he enjoyed a renewal of intercourse — among them, Henry Vincent, Madame Emilie Ashurst Venturi, Mrs. Priscilla Bright McLaren, Mrs. Fawcett, Miss Helen Taylor, Thomas Hughes, Professor James Bryce, Justin McCarthy, and George J. Holyoake. But he was glad at last to leave the great metropolis for the rural quiet and beauty of Somersetshire, whither he now went to visit Mr. Bright's daughter, Mrs. Helen Bright Clark, and her *William S. Clark.* husband. With them he spent a delightful Sunday in *July 1.* their home at Street, near Glastonbury and its ruined *July 2.* Abbey. Thence he drove with them by way of Wells (whose cathedral, with its Bishop's Garden and ancient moat and wall, he greatly admired) and Cheddar to Sidcot, where he enjoyed the hospitality of Mrs. Margaret A. Tanner, a staunch supporter of Mrs. Butler, in her beautiful home overlooking the Bristol Channel and Welsh hills. In Bristol he was to have been the guest of the well-known philanthropist, Miss Mary Carpenter, but her *June 14.* letter making the arrangements for his coming had reached *June 16.* him at Oxford simultaneously with the public announcement of her sudden death the very night after she had *July 3–5.* written to him. His two days in that neighborhood were spent at Clifton with Miss Mary A. Estlin,[1] who was unwearied in her attentions to him and his companion. *July 5.* With her they visited Tintern Abbey and the lovely valley of the Wye, which they saw under peculiarly favorable conditions of weather and sky. At Evesham, where they *July 5.* spent a night under the hospitable roof of Mr. Herbert

[1] The daughter of his old friend, Dr. J. B. Estlin, and one of the most steadfast of the English supporters of the American abolitionists. Miss Estlin had visited the United States in 1868, in company with Richard D. Webb and his daughter.

New, they had a glimpse of the quiet rural scenery along the Avon, and from Leamington they drove to Warwick *July* 6, 1877. and Kenilworth Castles, which Mr. Garrison had never before found time to visit.

In Birmingham he again bore testimony in behalf of Mrs. Butler's movement to a private gathering of friends at the house of his host, Mr. Robert F. Martineau, and *July* 7. responded to an address presented to him on the occasion by the Committee of the Repeal Associations.[1] He also visited the grave of Harriet Martineau, in one of the *July* 8. Birmingham cemeteries. At Sheffield he paused only long enough for an hour's call on his venerable friend, *July* 9. Mrs. Rawson, at Wincobank Hall, after an interval of *Ante*, 2:395. thirty-one years since his previous visit to her, and then hastened to Leeds to spend a week with Mr. and Mrs. *July* 9–15. Joseph Lupton, and to be near George Thompson; for, in the ten years since they had last met, Mr. Thompson had taken up his residence in Leeds, and was now hopelessly shattered in health and barely able to walk. The meeting between the old friends was most affecting, the invalid dropping his head on Mr. Garrison's shoulder as he embraced him, too overcome for speech. Indeed, paralysis had so far affected his utterance that conversation was difficult, but he rallied his powers after a time, and showed his unabated interest in public and personal matters. Mr. Garrison, whose heart was wrung by his sadly altered appearance, devoted as many hours as possible to him each day during his stay. When the final parting came, *July* 15. Mr. Thompson sobbed aloud as he gave his brother beloved the last fervent embrace, and watched his retreating form till it was out of sight.

This was the only sorrowful experience in Mr. Garrison's English visit. From Leeds he made delightful excursions to Bolton Abbey and Wharfedale, to Ripon *July* 10.

[1] The Midland Electoral Union for the Repeal of the Contagious Diseases Acts. The address and a subsequent written reply of Mr. Garrison's were published in the (London) *Shield* of Sept. 8, and (Boston) *Woman's Journal* of Nov. 17, 1877.

July 13, 1877. and Fountains Abbey, and to Scarborough, where he saw a typical English watering-place, and was handsomely July 16. entertained by Sir Harcourt Johnstone, who gave a supper in his honor at the Royal Hotel. About fifty prominent residents of the town were present, and Mr. Garrison spoke with much felicity on the marked progress made in the various reformatory movements in England since his previous visit. After touching upon temperance, education, the extension of the franchise, municipal suffrage for women, and the Contagious Diseases Acts, he enlarged, by request, upon the duty of the State to provide secular education only, not knowing at the time that several of his hearers were unsettled on the question, which was then being discussed, and that his utterances were helping to clear their minds.

A drive with Sir Harcourt Johnstone through his fine estate,[1] with its model farmhouse and stables, and its ancient church dating back eight or nine centuries, was July 17. only one of the experiences of the following day, which included glimpses of York Minster and Durham Cathedral on the journey to Newcastle-on-Tyne. John Mawson was Ante, pp. 219, 235. no longer living to welcome him to the latter city, but his beautiful home at Gateshead remained, and the hospitality July 17–21. of his family was unstinted during the four days of Mr. Garrison's visit. The evenings witnessed successive gatherings of friends to meet him, and a semi-public July 20. breakfast was tendered him in Newcastle by Mrs. Butler's supporters, to which he consented only because of their earnest assurance that his endorsement would greatly help their cause in the North of England.

Twenty days were allotted to Scotland, the first seven July 21–28. of which were spent in Edinburgh, with Elizabeth Pease Nichol. Very precious and happy days they were, for Huntly Lodge was like a second home to Mr. Garrison, and communion with its dear and honored mistress one of his greatest delights. Thither came, during the week,

[1] Hackness Hall, six miles from Scarborough. The place is one of great natural beauty.

many friends to greet and converse with him — Dr. John Brown [1] and Thomas Constable among them, and Alfred Webb,[2] who came from Dublin for the purpose. These social reunions, with frequent drives and excursions in the neighborhood, made the week pass all too quickly, but happily Mrs. Nichol was able to accompany him and his son to Glasgow, where they were all the guests of Prof. John Nichol, at the University. The four days there were also full, one day being occupied by a trip to Largs, on the coast, with superb views on the journey to and fro, of Wemyss and Rothesay Bays and of the mountains from Arran to Ben Lomond. Mr. Garrison spent as many hours as possible with the Patons and Smeals,[3] and, by invitation of the Town Council of Glasgow, accompanied that body in their annual inspection of the four public parks of the city — a significant honor, in view of the Southern proclivities of Glasgow during the slaveholders' rebellion. By a pleasant coincidence, it occurred on the first day of August, and Mr. Garrison, in his after-dinner speech at the Council Chambers, did not forget to allude to the anniversary of West India Emancipation.

July 24, 1877.

July 28–Aug. 1.

Three days sufficed for a most enjoyable trip through the Highlands, which embraced the sail up the coast to Oban and Ballachulish, the stage-ride through the Pass of Glencoe, a sail and row on Loch Lomond at sunset, and Loch Katrine, the Trosachs and Callander as the return route to Edinburgh. One more excursion was made — to Newport,[4] opposite Dundee — before the concluding visit at Huntly Lodge, whose hospitable door never opened

Aug. 2–4. *Aug. 2.* *Aug. 3.* *Aug. 4.* *Aug. 7–10.*

[1] The author of 'Rab and His Friends' was greatly impressed by Mr. Garrison's seemingly unabated vigor and animation, after ten years, and said to a friend: "What a beautiful face he has! It's really wonderful."

[2] A son of Richard D. Webb. He had visited "Rockledge" in 1872.

[3] Both Andrew Paton and William Smeal were living, and the latter seemed remarkably bright and vigorous when Mr. Garrison spent his last evening with him. He died suddenly, a fortnight later, at the ripe age of 84.

[4] Mr. Garrison was entertained at Newport by Mr. and Mrs. Edward Parker, who gave a reception in his honor. The newly completed, but ill-fated, Tay Bridge greatly excited his wonder and admiration.

more reluctantly for a departing guest. A brief tour *Aug. 10–15, 1877.* through the English Lake District followed, the region being new to Mr. Garrison, who thoroughly appreciated its beauty, and enjoyed rowing, successively, on the placid waters of Derwentwater, Windermere, and Ullswater. *Aug. 12.* At Ambleside he visited "The Knoll," Harriet Martineau's late home, and rejoiced to find the house occupied by *Mr. and Mrs. W. H. Hills.* sympathizing friends, who welcomed him with especial cordiality.

Little leisure remained for him in the few days that now intervened before his departure for America. He spent a *Aug. 15.* night at Worsley, and two days at Lymm (near Warring- *Aug. 17.* ton), where a banquet was tendered him by his old friend, William Robson. At Chester he saw the antiquities of the *Aug. 18.* town under the delightful guidance of Rev. Charles Wick- *Aug. 19.* steed, with whom he spent more time the following day at his home in St. Asaph, Wales. This was the region where Mrs. Hemans had lived, and it inspired in Mr. Garrison lively reminiscences of his youthful ardor and extravagant admiration for the poetess. He took the fine *Aug. 20.* railroad ride along the north coast of Wales to Bangor and Llanberis, to see the bridges over the Menai Straits, and Conway and Carnarvon Castles, and, after a farewell *Aug. 21–23.* visit to Manchester, he hastened to spend his last two days among his Liverpool friends. Mrs. Butler convened a *Aug. 23.* special meeting of adherents at her house to bid him farewell, and to present him with the following Address, written by herself and signed by eighteen representative women in different parts of the kingdom. This, beautifully engrossed and illuminated, Mr. Garrison had carefully framed on his return home, and it is doubtful if he left any heirloom to his children in which he took greater pride and pleasure.

Woman's Journal, Nov. 17, 1877.

To William Lloyd Garrison of Boston, U. S. A.

DEAR AND HONORED FRIEND: We, the undersigned, members of the Executive Committee of the Ladies' National Association for the Abolition of the State Regulation of Vice, desire, before you leave this country, to tender to you the expression of our deep gratitude for the invaluable service you have rendered the sacred cause of Liberty and of Social Purity, by the repeated public expression of your sympathy with and approval of the principles and labors of the Repeal Association.

We desire also to express our acknowledgment of the strength and hope we have derived from personal intercourse with you, or from reading your encouraging words — words which derive an extraordinary force and vitality from the fact of your own noble life-work for the redemption of the slave.

As women, especially,— and in the name of hundreds of women of the Association we represent, as well as our own,— we thank you, from the depths of our hearts, for the stand you have made in America, throughout your life, for the principle of the absolute equality of all human beings; and, more lately, in our own land, for the application of that principle as between men and women, in presence of the moral law.[1]

Another farewell reception was given at the house of William Crosfield, Jr., on the evening of the 24th of August, and on the following day Mr. Garrison and his son began their homeward voyage in the *Bothnia*, landing in New York ten days later.[2] *Sept. 4, 1877.*

"Now that our transatlantic tour has been consummated," he wrote to his daughter, on returning to Rockledge, "it seems almost like a delicious dream; and yet, from beginning to end, nothing could be more realistic. We did not pass an idle hour, whether in England, Scotland, or Wales, but were busily engaged either in sight-seeing or receiving or making calls, or participating in social parties drawn together to give us a most cordial reception. . . . Nothing could exceed the courtesies and kindnesses showered upon us by our multitudinous *MS. Sept. 10, 1877.*

[1] Thanks to the untiring efforts of Mrs. Butler and her noble host of supporters, and to the splendid leadership in the House of Commons of the Right Hon. James Stansfeld, Jr., the revolting features of the Contagious Diseases Acts were finally repealed in April, 1886.

[2] The tedium of the days at sea was beguiled not a little by the perusal of Edmund Quincy's letters of many years to Richard D. Webb, which the latter's son had entrusted to Mr. Garrison, and from which we have extracted somewhat freely in the third volume of this biography.

MS. Sept. 14, 1877, to S. May, Jr.

friends, whose respect and affection are in value beyond all price." And to his friend May he wrote: "From the time of our departure from New York to our leaving Liverpool, everything went auspiciously with us. Our good angels seemed to be ever at our side. We lost no appointment, met with no accident, and had our cup of enjoyment filled to overflowing."

CHAPTER XI.

LAST YEARS.—1877–79.

IF his summer in Great Britain did not materially check the progress of the disease which had for years been undermining Mr. Garrison's health, it certainly must be credited with the fresh vigor and spirit which he manifested during the brief remainder of his life. In reviewing his movements and undertakings in the succeeding year and a half, it is difficult to realize how much debility and weakness he really experienced, or how steadily his vital powers were being sapped.

CHAP. XI.

1877–79.

His undiminished interest in public affairs, and his deep solicitude as to the fate of the colored population of the South, now practically denied all the political representation, influence, and power to which they were numerically and legally entitled, were manifested soon after his return from England. In a letter to the New York *Times* he condemned the Southern policy of President Hayes as "totally at variance with all his fair-spoken words and pledges, a deplorable betrayal of a most sacred trust, a discount upon inflexible loyalty, and a bounty upon rebellious usurpation"; and in January, 1878, he returned to the theme in another letter, which was widely circulated.

Oct. 30, 1877.

Jan. 21, *to W. E. Chandler.*

The social enjoyments of the fall and winter were many, between the frequent intercourse with old friends, and the numerous lectures and concerts which continued to attract him. An affectionate interchange of letters took place between himself and Whittier in December, when the latter's seventieth birthday was celebrated; and to the many public tributes paid the poet, Mr. Garrison

1877–78.

MSS. Dec. 18, 20, 1877.

contributed a friendly and critical estimate in blank
Dec. 1, 1877. verse, through the columns of the Boston *Literary World.*

A new friendship, which he greatly enjoyed, was formed in the spring of 1878, when he became acquainted, through Mrs. Child, with the gifted sculptress, Miss Anne Whitney of Boston, and was invited by her to sit for his portrait bust. During the months of March, April, and May he made frequent visits to her studio, and gave her full opportunity to study his features and character. His mobility of expression in animated conversation revealed to her the difficulty of her task—a difficulty enhanced, in respect to the eyes, by the fact that spectacles cannot well be reproduced in sculpture.[1] She succeeded admirably, however, and the bust, when completed, received the emphatic and unanimous approval of Mr. Garrison's children and friends. With no abatement of strength and dignity, it happily portrays his sweet and serene expression, and the firm repose of his later years.[2]

[1] Mr. Phillips held that as the spectacles were not literally part of the face, a portrait for posterity should be painted without them, and he accordingly commissioned a Boston artist to make one of Mr. Garrison with the glasses omitted. The result was a picture which Mrs. Garrison failed to recognize as even intended for her husband, and Mr. Phillips consigned it to his garret. Two other busts of Mr. Garrison had been made before Miss Whitney executed hers,—one by S. V. Clevenger (in 1841), and the other by John A. Jackson (in 1858), neither of great excellence. In writing of the conflicting opinions of friends about the latter, Mr. Garrison said: "One thing is certain—for some reason or other, I have one of the most difficult faces in the world to take (owing, probably, to its changeableness of expression); all artists, at home or abroad, having failed to get a likeness generally satisfactory to my personal friends. . . Jackson acknowledges that he has never had one sit to him whose living expression it has been so difficult to catch as in my own case; nor has he ever had one sit to him so many times, or for whom he has exerted himself so laboriously to achieve success. Besides, there is an inherent difficulty with which he has had to contend, and which it is not possible for even genius to surmount, in making a bust of me. My spectacles are a part of my face,—few ever see me for a moment without them,—and they greatly modify the appearance of my eyes, and my general expression of countenance. In fact, when I lay them aside, I am almost another man" (MS. May 1, 1858, to Oliver Johnson).

[2] A marble copy of the bust was cut in Italy, and was received in Boston in March, 1879, shortly before Mr. Garrison left home for the last time.

He had spent the Christmas holidays of 1877 with his children in New York, and was with them again in May, for a fortnight. The greater part of July, August, and September, 1878, he passed with his daughter and her family at Tarrytown, on the Hudson, a region appealing strongly to his love of the beautiful and romantic in nature. There he rested quietly for weeks, enjoying the lovely outlook upon the Hudson and Tappan Zee, playing at ninepins with his grandchildren, driving to Sleepy Hollow and other places in the vicinity, and making excursions up the river to the Military Academy at West Point, and to Vassar College at Poughkeepsie, by way of contrast. He also spent a few days at Osterville, on Cape Cod, and in September went to Philadelphia to see Lucretia Mott and other friends.

CHAP. XI. — 1877–79.

Aug. 2, 8, 1878. *Aug.* 13. *Aug.* 15–20.

In June he had been summoned to Florence, Mass., to speak at the funeral of Charles C. Burleigh,[1] and early in

June 16.

"It is admirably executed," he wrote to his daughter, "and the marble is of the purest white. . . . I do not think a more accurate 'counterfeit presentment' of your father's features could possibly be made; and I am particularly pleased that it has been achieved by a woman" (MS. Mar. 28, 1879, W. L. G. to F. G. V.). The bust, which is now (1889) at Rockledge, stands on a pedestal which brings it exactly to Mr. Garrison's height (5 feet 8½ in.). An engraving of it forms the frontispiece of this work.

[1] Mr. Burleigh came to a premature death through injuries received from a passing railroad train. "For more than forty years," wrote Mr. Garrison of him, "he was almost constantly in the lecturing field, during which period he travelled many thousands of miles, addressed hundreds of thousands of hearers, cheerfully encountering every hardship, serenely confronting mobocratic violence, shrinking from no peril, heedless of unescapable ridicule (stimulated and intensified by the non-conformity of the outward man in the matter of dress, the wearing of the hair and beard); yet evincing such a mastery of his subject, such powers of argument and persuasion, such force of intellect and breadth of mind, such copiousness of speech and fertility of illustration on every question discussed, as made it an easy task for him to confound and vanquish all opponents. Indeed, he never found 'a foeman worthy of his steel.' . . . He never lost his balance. Whoever else, in the heat and conflict of reform, might be led into extravagance of speech, or bitterness of invective, or error of reasoning, his self-control was absolute, his presentation of the case singularly dispassionate, his accusations and impeachments within the truth, his supreme effort not to 'bring down the house' but to enlighten and convert it. At the bar, before a jury, he would hardly have found his peer; on the judicial bench he would have been chief" (MS. written for publication, but not used).

October he was apprised by cable that George Thompson *Oct. 7, 1878.* had passed away. He at once prepared a long biographical sketch of his old coadjutor for the New York and Boston papers,[1] rehearsing his labors and achievements, and paying a fervent tribute to his memory.

1878. The 13th of October was the sixtieth anniversary of Mr. Garrison's apprenticeship to the printing business, and by way of celebrating the event he visited Newbury- *Saturday.* port on the morning of the 12th, and once more essayed the task of setting type in the office of the *Herald.* It proved to be the last time he ever visited his birthplace or handled the composing-stick. For "copy" he took *Ante, 1:179; 2:432, 433.* three of his own sonnets,—the "Freedom of the Mind," that on "Liberty," and the one written on his thirty-fifth *Newburyport Herald, Oct. 14, 1878.* birthday,—and he set them, the editor of the *Herald* testified, "in a time which many a younger printer might emulate." The type "was a little formidable to look at, *Speech at Franklin Club Dinner, Oct. 14.* if one might describe it so," said Mr. Garrison; "it was nonpareil type, and that for seventy-three years was rather a task, but nevertheless I was able to achieve it; I did not squabble a line, and, on taking a proof of what I had set, there was not a single error."

The sonnets were printed in the *Herald* of the 14th, and on the evening of the same day a dinner in honor of his anniversary was tendered to Mr. Garrison by the New England Franklin Club, an association of printers, at Young's Hotel in Boston. Mr. Henry O. Houghton, the founder of the Riverside Press, presided, and the leading printers of Boston, as well as some from New York, were present. Mr. Garrison's address was wholly extemporaneous and colloquial, but spoken with unusual ease and charm of manner. Naturally reminiscent and biographical, in the main, as he recounted his early expe-

[1] N. Y. *Times*, Boston *Journal* and *Transcript*, Oct. 14, 1878. Mr. Garrison also wrote a briefer sketch to accompany a portrait of Mr. Thompson in *Harper's Weekly* (Dec. 21, 1878), and sent a heliotype copy of the daguerreotype taken in 1851—the same from which the engraving in Vol. I. of this work was made—to nearly a hundred of his friends in England and America.

riences in the printing-office, and described his various editorial experiments until he established the *Liberator*,[1] he closed in this cheerful and inspiriting strain:

CHAP. XI. 1877-79.

"Now, of course, I am here to look you in the face as brother printers, as members of the same craft; and this welcome is extended to me in view of our relations in that matter, not as an endorsement of my anti-slavery labors, certainly, for that question will stand by itself. But, however we may have differed in opinion in regard to the *modus operandi* in seeking the abolition of slavery, I am quite sure of one thing at this hour, that there is but one feeling on this question, and that is one of thankfulness to God that chattel slavery no longer curses our land. And if there is anything in my career that is suggestive, that may be of use to those who may hereafter come into conflict with great and colossal wrong, it will be that by not compromising with the wrong, by speaking the truth and applying it boldly to the conscience of the people, there is no need of despairing of the final result. Nobody ought to despair whose cause is just. Nobody is justified in despairing if he has a righteous cause to uphold. It may not be given to him to see it triumph, but that is only a question of time. . . . None can ever defeat it in the end. God himself is pledged to its final victory.

Boston Traveller, Oct. 15, 1878.

"I need not say, Mr. President, how mighty an instrumentality the press is in regard to the progress of mankind. Ours is 'the art preservative of all arts,' and it stands at the head of all. Every craft is honorable [if] it is useful, but the printing craft is that which takes hold of the mind and intellect and soul. It is the power to move the world, and it is moving it. Some one has wittily said that the greatest stand in behalf of civilization is the inkstand, but I would add that it is the printer's stand, with a well-assorted case, and a compositor at that case with active brains and active hands putting

'Thoughts that breathe and words that burn'

into type to help the age onward and upward.

"It is a grand era in which we are living. We must not despair of anything in regard to the final triumph of right. A great many people are troubled in their minds as to what is to befall this nation, and there are many evil signs, and many dark clouds. What then? Is this republic to go down after

[1] We have already borrowed freely from this address in our narrative of Mr. Garrison's early life (*ante*, 1 : 36, 40, 140, 158).

CHAP. XI. — 1877–79. having succeeded in abolishing slavery, which was its deadliest curse? Delivered from that, is it still doomed to perish? No; as long as we have a free press, free speech, free inquiry, and free schools, we shall never go down, Mr. President. We shall go upward and onward—Excelsior to the end. And so we are to have the great battle of the world fought out on our soil for all mankind. Thank God for our boundless domains, broad enough to take in the whole of the population of the globe; and all mankind are coming to us in samples and specimens, and large samples and specimens. And for the first time in the history of the world all races of men on our soil are looking each other in the face and asking the question whether they can dwell together in unity, whether they cannot stand by one another in regard to their rights and liberties. And thus far the experiment has mightily succeeded. For, whatever may be our political and party differences on the day of election, we do not find that nationalities are divided here, but issues pertaining to our own soil and our own institutions are the dividing lines, and we blend together in one mighty mass, though differing in our notions. I therefore say that it is the sublimest spectacle on earth that is now being presented to the gaze of mankind, and my hope is boundless as to the future."

Rev. E. W. Allen, a son of the old proprietor of the *Herald*, was present, and described in glowing phrase the apprentice boy who had lived in his father's house and won the affection of the whole family; and Mr. Frank W. Miller, son of Mr. Garrison's fellow-workman in those days, followed. Not the least interesting feature of this altogether delightful occasion was the confession by Mr. George C. Rand[1] that he, as a printer's apprentice, had helped print and distribute the incendiary handbill which precipitated the mob of 1835.[2]

Ante, 1:55.

Rev. T. H. Miller; ante, 1:41.

Ante, 2:9, 10, 11, 35.

[1] Mr. Rand left a sick bed to attend the dinner, and died two months later. He was the first printer of 'Uncle Tom's Cabin.'

[2] "It was a very gratifying and handsome reception extended to me by the Franklin Club, and I am sure you would have greatly enjoyed the occasion, as all present manifestly did. My connection with the printer's craft is to me a source of unspeakable pride and delight, and it had everything to do with shaping my career, and literally putting into my hands the great instrumentalities for the final overthrow of the slave system. Had I not been a practical printer—an expert compositor and able to work at the press—there had been no *Liberator*" (MS. Oct. 23, 1878, W. L. G. to George W. Stacy).

One week later, the forty-third anniversary of the Mob was celebrated by an impromptu gathering of the surviving veterans of the cause, at the rooms of the New England Women's Club, and, considering the shortness of the notice, a surprising number of them came together. Mr. Garrison, though suffering from a severe cold, spoke for upwards of an hour, recounting the history of the Mob, and reading the confession of its chief instigator, James L. Homer, given in a previous volume. Of the eye-witnesses of the affair who were present, Wendell Phillips, James N. Buffum, and A. Bronson Alcott gave their recollections, and the occasion was one of rare interest and pleasure.

Oct. 21, 1878.

4 Park St., Boston.

Ante, 2:10.

The following frank note which Mr. Garrison wrote to Mr. Phillips at the close of this eventful month, had reference to a financial tract which the latter had written, and to his strange support of General Butler as a candidate for the gubernatorial chair of Massachusetts.

Benj. F. Butler.

W. L. Garrison to Wendell Phillips.

ROXBURY, Oct. 30, 1878. *MS. copy.*

MY DEAR PHILLIPS: . . . Thanks for your tract on the money question — a question which I do not profess to have mastered in all its bearings, though I do not deem it a difficult matter to discriminate between that which carries intrinsic value with it, and that which possesses no such value; in other words, between gold and a paper promise which may or may not be redeemed. With me, however, it is a very subordinate question, although it is assumed to be one of paramount importance at the present hour. While the freedmen at the South are, on "the Mississippi plan" and by "the shotgun policy," ruthlessly deprived of their rights as American citizens, and no protection is extended them by the Federal Government on the ground of impotency, the old anti-slavery issue is still (and must be persistently insisted [on] as constituting) the paramount issue before the country.

I cannot endorse your estimate of Gen. Butler. Indeed, your praise of him is so lavish as to surprise me. He was re-elected with a virtual understanding and expectation that he, of all

Chap. XI. — 1877–79.

others in Congress, would be the man to champion the cause of the outraged colored people at the South as against such haughty usurpers as Ben Hill, Gordon, and the rest; but on no occasion has he since, on the floor of the House, made any such issue, or protested against "bulldozing" the loyal colored voters, or arraigned Hayes's "conciliatory policy." Besides, he is sustained by the worst elements in the Commonwealth, and opposed by the best. I hope for his defeat.

Yours for the triumph of the right,
Wm. Lloyd Garrison.

Dec. 10, 1878.

In December, Mr. Garrison completed his 73d year, and his letters in reply to the congratulations sent him by his absent children betrayed a feeling that his earthly career was approaching its limit, and a cheerful readiness for the inevitable change, whenever it might come.

W. L. Garrison to W. P. Garrison.

MS.

Roxbury, Dec. 12, 1878.

Thanks for your congratulatory letter, with its filial remembrance of the day, which certainly completes at least seventy-three years of my earthly pilgrimage. Notwithstanding this advanced period of life, to which so few comparatively attain, you propose for me additional "length of days," even to a centennial climax! However that may be, while it will be hard for me at any stage to part with my beloved children and grandchildren, I trust to be ready for the summons to "go hence," come when they may. The matter of death, regarding it as I do as simply an exchange of spheres for the better, grows more and more insignificant as I advance; and what may be a painful separation from loved ones here will, I doubt not, prove a joyful reunion with loved ones gone before. I shall not object to being permitted to see myself enrolled on the list of great-grandfathers; but I could hope that I might pass on before my faculties are essentially impaired, or the body bowed down with hopeless infirmities. The first two I desire to meet on "the other side of Jordan" are your fond mother and my own. It is something curious that, while my mother was only forty-seven years old when she died, and I am now seventy-three, I feel my filial impulses bounding within me as though I were again a child, whenever I think of the possibility of coming into her presence; and though our ages are reversed according to earthly dates, there still seems to be the same relative distance between us, as to the point of time, that existed when she was here in the body. CHAP. XI. — 1877–79.

The Christmas holidays were again spent by him in New York, and he came back apparently much brightened and refreshed by the week with his children and grandchildren there. 1878. Both in December and January he plied his pen busily. 1878–79. The suppression of the colored vote at the South, and the helplessness of the blacks under the new régime, constantly engaged his thoughts, and four letters from him on the subject were printed during January.[1] In these he urged that the cry of "the bloody shirt," that "awful symbol (yet but faintly expressive) of the gory tragedies that have been performed at the sacrifice of a hecatomb of loyal white and colored victims," be made the rallying cry of the Republican party in the next Presidential campaign. *Boston Advertiser, Jan.* 13, 1879.

"The time has come to make this device return to 'plague the inventors,' by furnishing the occasion for such a fresh

[1] N. Y. *Tribune*, Jan. 4 and 25, 1879; Boston *Advertiser*, Jan. 13; Boston *Traveller*, Jan. 27. In the last of these Mr. Garrison quoted the testimony to him of a Northern lady, who, with her husband, was driven from South Carolina after the overthrow of the Chamberlain State Government. "In attempting to give you a faint outline of our experiences I am helpless. The truth cannot be told in many pages, and it almost exceeds belief. It does not seem possible in this age, in this land of boasted freedom. I could tell you of the horrors of the Hamburg massacre, which have never yet been made public; of the eight hundred poor creatures driven into noisome swamps, and there fired into as if they had been wild beasts; of women in the pangs of maternity while standing to their knees in the slimy waters of the swamp; of a poor deaf and dumb boy riddled with bullets because he did not answer these 'chivalric gentlemen' (!) when they rode up and demanded the whereabouts of his parents and friends" (MS. Jan. 11, 1879, Elizabeth L. Palmer to W. L. G.). A description of the bulldozing tactics of the South Carolina whites in the campaign of 1876 followed. "The two Senators from South Carolina, at Washington, Hampton and Butler," wrote Mr. Garrison in his letter on the "Exodus" (April 22, 1879), "are occupying seats to which they were not honestly elected, and their faces should become crimson every time they enter the Senate Chamber. If they had their deserts, instead of presenting their brazen visages in the Capitol, Hampton would be in the penitentiary, and 'Hamburg massacre' Butler be lying in a grave of infamy, according as crimes are adjudged and punished in a civilized community" (Boston *Traveller*, April 24, 1879).

CHAP. XI. 1877-79. elucidation of the fundamental principles of popular government, and such an exposure of the terrible wrongs perpetrated with impunity at the South, as shall enlighten, electrify, consolidate and render invincible a liberty-loving and liberty-upholding North in the possession and administration of the national government."

On the evening of the 3d of February, 1879, the colored people of Boston held a Memorial meeting in honor of George Thompson, in one of their churches, and at the close of a long and admirable commemorative address by George W. Putnam, Mr. Thompson's secretary during his second visit to the United States, Mr. Garrison was called upon to speak. The hour was late, but the reminiscences of the thrilling scenes of 1835, which the orator of the occasion had graphically described, and the tribute to his dear English coadjutor, had greatly stirred him; and as he rose in the pulpit, a fine color suffused his face, his eyes were bright, his form erect, and he spoke with a clear, ringing voice which surprised his hearers. He seemed, *Rev. R. C. Waterston.* indeed, as one of the subsequent speakers remarked, to have renewed his youth. It was the last flash of fire in the fading flame. He spoke but once again in public, and *Feb. 14, 1879.* that was a last plea for the enfranchisement of women, before a hostile legislative committee, at the State House.

On the same day that he was thus vindicating human rights by advocating the equality of the sexes, Senators Blaine and Conkling, rival aspirants for the Republican nomination for the Presidency, were making their respective bids for the support of the Pacific coast by advocating, in the Senate at Washington, a bill to restrict Chinese emigration, in defiance of existing treaty obligations. The moral sense of the country was shocked by this wanton disregard of a solemn contract between nations, and startled by the recreancy to the fundamental theories of the republic manifested by party leaders of such eminence. The better newspapers of both parties (save those on the Pacific slope) opposed the bill, and commented freely upon the transparent motives of the ambitious

Senator from Maine. Mr. Garrison lost no time in denouncing, in an earnest letter to the New York *Tribune*, this base and demagogical action as adding " a fresh stain of caste proscription to the many that have sullied our national character," and calling for " the indignant protest of every lover of his country, every friend of the whole human race." After ridiculing the provision, in the proposed bill, that no vessel should bring more than fifteen immigrants at a time,—as if a sixteenth would be fatal to the safety of the republic,— and characterizing the Senate debate as, " with one or two honorable exceptions, most disgraceful to all who participated in it," he warned the Republican party against advocating such " utterly indefensible proscription," and continued:

Feb. 15, 1879.

" The reasons advanced by Mr. Blaine in opposition to the Chinese were unworthy of his head and heart, and therefore unworthy of the least consideration, being based on contempt of race, a low selfishness, a blind and cowardly fear of consequences, and the gratification for party purposes of a local hatred (in its climax reaching to the diabolical) against a helpless, unoffending, industrious, frugal, and temperate class of inhabitants. They are such reasons as were formerly urged by some against allowing the Irish to emigrate to this country; and against emancipating the Southern slave population; and against labor-saving machinery, as reducing the wages of the laborer, etc., etc. They are not born of reason, or justice, or historical experience."

N. Y. Tribune, Feb. 17, 1879.

Mr. Blaine betrayed his sensitiveness to this censure by a labored reply, which was sent broadcast over the country by the Associated Press, and in which he endeavored to break the force of it, and becloud the issue, by declaring that there had been no voluntary Chinese immigration to America, but only cooly importation; that the entire Chinese population of the Pacific coast were horribly vicious and depraved, and breeders of pestilence; that unless checked, the tide of Chinese immigration would overwhelm the western slope, reducing the white laborers to starvation; that having the power, the

N. Y. Tribune, Feb. 24, 1879.

CHAP. XI. 1877–79. United States Government had the right to abrogate its treaties at any time; and that the conversion of the Chinese to Christianity was an impossibility.

Feb. 25. N. Y. Tribune, Feb. 27, 1879. Mr. Garrison's rejoinder was prompt and emphatic. Recurring to Mr. Blaine's speech as going far, by its "vulgar assumption of superiority of race on the one hand, and a demagogical cropping out on the other, . . . to sap the foundation of personal confidence and respect," and as embodying, "in its spirit and special pleadings, whatever of contempt and proscription of race has been fostered and exemplified in the world, from the earliest period of history," he declared his elaborate letter to be "simply a repetition of the irrelevant allegations and empty fallacies contained in his Senatorial rodomontade, but more consecutively arranged under ten distinct heads. Of these ten there is but one that touches the real question at issue; the other nine are mere padding and clap-trap, ignobly resorted to to inflame race passions and prejudices." The one relevant point as to whether the Chinese Government had observed or violated the treaty was next considered, and the former affirmed; the "damning atrocities" perpetrated against the unoffending Chinese were rehearsed in indignant terms, and the letter concluded with an earnestness and solemnity befitting the theme and the writer:

N. Y. Tribune, Feb. 27, 1879. "Mr. Blaine shows that he is not sincere — if that is too harsh a term, certainly not consistent — in basing his opposition to the treaty on the ground that we are having, or at least have had, under it, nothing but a profligate, cunningly devised cooly immigration from China. What he wants is virtual non-intercourse with that country. It is not simply a lot of degraded Chinese — duped and enthralled by contract — that he objects to; he despises the entire population of the Celestial Kingdom, and (oh, foolish pride!) vaunts himself on the superiority of his own stock! He says: 'California is capable of maintaining a vast population of Anglo-Saxon freemen, if we do not surrender it to Chinese coolies.' Again: 'The only question we have to regard is, whether on the whole we will devote that interesting and important section of the United States to be the home and the refuge of our own people and our own blood, or whether we will continue to leave it open, not to the competition of other nations like ourselves [a sop to Irishmen, Germans, etc.], but to those who, degraded themselves, will inevitably degrade us.' There is nothing reasonable or manly, or even plausible, in this; it is narrow, conceited, selfish, anti-human, anti-Christian.

"Against this hateful spirit of caste I have earnestly protested for the last fifty years, wherever it has developed itself, especially in the case of another class, for many generations still more contemned, degraded, and oppressed; and the time has fully come to deal with it as an offence to God, and a curse to the world wherever it seeks to bear sway. The Chinese are our fellow-men, and are entitled to every consideration that our common humanity may justly claim. In numbers they constitute one-third of mankind. Of existing kingdoms theirs is the oldest, the most peaceable, and apparently the most stable. Education is widely diffused among them, and they are a remarkably ingenious, industrious, thrifty, and well-behaved people. Such of them as are seeking to better their condition, being among the poorer classes, by coming to these shores, we should receive with hospitality and kindness. If properly treated, they cannot fail to be serviceable to ourselves or to improve their own condition. It is for them to determine what they shall eat, what they shall drink, and wherewithal they shall be clothed; to adhere to their own customs and follow their own tastes as they shall choose; to make their own contracts and maintain their own rights; to worship God according to the dictates of their own consciences, or their ideas of religious duty. Such of them as may be in a filthy and squalid state we must endeavor to assist to a higher plane; and if we would see them become converts to Christianity, we must show them its purifying and elevating power by our dealings with them. To assert that they are incapable of being converted is as much at variance with facts as to limit the saving power of our religion to those of 'our own blood,' as Mr. Blaine egotistically terms it. The same assertion was formerly made in disparagement of our colored population. But it was false in their case, and it is not less false in the other.

"It is pitiable to see how determined Mr. Blaine is to depict the Chinese immigrants as so utterly vile in their habits and morals as to be incapable of reformation, and too loathsome to be endured. He knows that there is a large portion of them who are neat in their persons, courteous in their deportment,

CHAP. XI. — 1877–79.

excellent in character, and trustworthy in an eminent degree, but he makes no exceptions. And if there were none to be made, still the Christian obligation would rest upon us to try to extricate them from the miry pit, to the extent of the means that we happily possess. Evidently no such thought enters into the mind of Mr. Blaine, and he would leave them to their miserable fate as unconcernedly as though they belonged to the brute creation. And as the climax of his speech, and also of his assurance, he declares: 'We have this day to choose whether we will have for the Pacific coast the civilization of Christ or the civilization of Confucius.' Has he forgotten that, long before the advent of Christ, it was from the lips of Confucius came that Golden Rule which we are taught in the Gospel to follow as the rule of life in all our dealings with our fellow-men, and which, carried into practice, will insure peace, happiness, and prosperity not only to the dwellers of the Pacific Coast, but to all peoples on the face of the whole earth?

"This is not a personal controversy with Mr. Blaine, but a plea for human brotherhood as against all caste assumptions and clannish distinctions; and I take my leave of him, earnestly hoping that he may be led to see and regret the great mistake of his public career."

W. L. Garrison to his Daughter.

MS.

ROXBURY, Feb. 20, 1879.

Feb. 15.

Ever since Saturday I have been confined to the house by the worst cold I have had since the death of your mother. The catarrh in my head has made great confusion of the brain, . . . and my throat has been so sore and inflamed as to make any attempt to swallow even liquids very painful. It has seemed as though it might be a case of incipient diphtheria, but I am somewhat relieved to-day. My other chronic ailments have also been very troublesome, which, with nightly loss of sleep, have made me "good for nothing" indeed. All these are the natural indications, at my period of life, that the "outward man," being less and less capable of resisting exposure and disease, is steadily tending towards that dissolution which in every such case is wisely decreed.

Sick and miserable as I was on Saturday, I was so morally incensed at Senator Blaine's demagogical speech in the U. S. Senate, in favor of excluding Chinese immigration to these shores, and indecently discarding the Burlingame treaty, that I was nerved to write the letter which appeared in the *Tribune*, and which has already been very widely approved. An abstract of it will appear in very many of the newspapers, and so its purport will become known to a great number of readers in various sections of the country. Of course, I am prepared to receive some hot denunciations from California, as I used to from the South for my anti-slavery articles. As far as I can learn, the press, here at the North, without distinction of party, is strong in its rebuke of the action of the Senate. The Boston *Journal* says that all the Republican newspapers on its exchange-list are united in condemning it. It is particularly noteworthy, too, that the Legislature of Connecticut has unanimously expressed its reprobation of the disgraceful proceeding.[1] I wish I could believe (though I do hope) that President Hayes will interpose his veto; but what he will do remains to be seen.

To his son Wendell he wrote:

MS. Mar. 4, 1879. H. Villard.

"I was much gratified to receive a letter from Harry yesterday, warmly commending my rejoinder to Mr. Blaine in the *Tribune*. Indeed, I am equally pleased and surprised to see how favorably it is regarded by the press generally. I am receiving on all hands the strongest expressions of satisfaction in regard to it.[2] I need not say that your cordial approval was fully ap-

[1] Mr. Garrison tried to prod the Massachusetts Legislature to similar action, but without success.

[2] The Chinese Minister at Washington was one of the first to send his thanks. Among the many letters received by Mr. Garrison was one from Wong Ar Chong, an intelligent Chinaman (MS. Feb. 28), closely dissecting and answering Blaine's charges, and another from W. H. Besse, a New Bedford sea-captain, who testified warmly in favor of the Chinese, from thirty years' knowledge of them (MS. Feb. 27). From San Francisco came an unexpected letter from John A. Collins *(ante*, 2 : 277), from whom Mr. Garrison had heard nothing directly or indirectly for many years, and a pleasant correspondence and interchange of photographs followed. To his friend A. J. Grover of Chicago, Mr. Garrison wrote (MS. March 7): "It is essentially the old anti-slavery issue in another form — whether one portion of mankind may rightfully claim superiority over another on account of birth, descent, or nativity, or for any other reason, and deny to them those rights and interests which pertain to our common humanity. After the successful struggle to emancipate the Southern bondmen from their chattelized condition and to elevate them to the plane of American citizenship, I did not imagine that any occasion could arise on our soil for the persecution of any other class, because 'not to the manner born.' . . . The paradoxes of human nature are as grotesque as they are inscrutable." The colored people of New York protested, in public meeting, against the proscription of the Chinese, having known themselves "what it was to belong to a despised and persecuted race."

CHAP. XI. — 1877–79. *President Hayes.*

preciated. I am much obliged to you for sending me the printed comments upon my replication contained in your last letter. I wish the President's veto had been more emphatic and less technical, but, nevertheless, am thankful it has saved us from disgrace."[1]

The correspondence resulting from this discussion occupied and enlivened the early days of March, and helped to divert Mr. Garrison's mind to some extent from the bodily ailments which were increasingly trying and tormenting. Only his children knew how serious these had become; and the vigor of his writing, as well as of his daily conversation, made it difficult even for them to think that the culmination was near. An attack of sciatica prevented his attending the debate in the Massachusetts Senate (March 19), on the bill conferring school suffrage on women, but he was made happy by its passage a few days later. In spite of colds and frequent debility, he went often to the city, and was certainly less prudent in this respect than he should have been. "I have got to be quite a chicken in my old age, in the matter of exposure to the weather," he wrote to his daughter, "my chronic catarrh growing worse and worse, and making me more and more susceptible. There is a final remedy for all human ailments." When obliged to keep to the house, he still wrote constantly; and letters commending a newly-invented anti-fraud ballot-box, expressing his hearty interest in the formation of the Kansas Historical Society, and in response to an invitation to a Channing Memorial meeting at Newport, R. I., followed in quick succession.

MS. Mar. 28, 1879.

Mar. 18.

Mar. 25.

Boston Journal, Apr. 8, 1879.

In April the country was stirred by the sudden and

1 "Our common interest in the Chinese question leads me to report what was told me yesterday by a gentleman who had a talk with the President a few days since: that the President expressed great satisfaction with your discussion of the question, describing your letter as admirable and conclusive, but expressing the fear that the question was by no means settled, but was likely to be agitated again with the view of passing a new bill aimed at the same result. It is pleasant, I think, to find Mr. Hayes sound on this question, though he did put his veto on the narrowest possible ground, omitting altogether the broad ground on which you put it, and on which it really rests" (MS. March 9, 1879, D. H. Chamberlain to W. L. G.).

extraordinary exodus of indigent colored people from Louisiana and Mississippi, who fled en masse to Kansas as a promised land in which they could find work at fair wages, and the protection in their legal and political rights denied them in their old homes. Thousands obtained transportation by river as far as St. Louis, and thence made their way to Kansas, aided by the contributions which the reports of their utter destitution elicited from many quarters. An announcement by Mr. Garrison in the Boston papers that he would receive and forward any sums for these unfortunate people until a committee should be formed for the purpose, brought him numerous offerings from old anti-slavery friends, and again increased his correspondence in a pleasant manner. Several hundred dollars were acknowledged and transmitted by him to the efficient committee in St. Louis before Boston moved in the matter. He was too unwell to attend the meeting held in Faneuil Hall on the 24th of the month, and the letter which he addressed to this and to a similar meeting in New York was his last published utterance:

CHAP. XI. 1877-79.

April, 1879.

"The spectacle of thousands of half-naked, empty-handed, despairing men, women, and children fleeing as for their lives from one part of the country to another, and preferring to risk starvation and death by the way rather than remain where they naturally belong, is one calculated to move pitying Heaven, and to awaken all that is sympathetic and generous in the human breast. Their claims for immediate charitable relief are equally just and imperative; and it is most gratifying to perceive a disposition in various directions to minister to the wants of these poor outcasts. By nothing that they have done, on the score of idleness, dissipation, or disorderly conduct, have they brought this suffering and exposure upon themselves. On the contrary, they have been the only industrious, unoffending, law-abiding, and loyal portion of the population in that quarter, with but few exceptions; and yet their safety is only in flight!

Boston Traveller, *Apr.* 24, 1879.

"While, therefore, grave, exciting, and relatively important as the present exodus of a few thousands of colored refugees from Mississippi and Louisiana may be, it is only an incident of the hour, demanding succor and aid in various forms until they have time to select their dwelling-places. But what of the four millions of colored people in the entire South? Their exilement is a question not to be seriously entertained for a moment, either as a desirable or possible event. The American Government is but a mockery, and deserves to be overthrown, if they are to be left without protection, as sheep in the midst of wolves. If the nation, having decreed their emancipation, and invested them under the Constitution with all the rights of citizenship, can neither devise nor find a way to vindicate their manhood, then its acts have been farcical, and the local usurpation of a contemptible body of aristocratic factionists is more than a match for the loyalty and strength of the American people; and it is the latter who are as effectually 'bulldozed' and ruled by the 'shotgun' policy as the colored people themselves. . . .

"It is clear, therefore, that the battle of liberty and equal rights is to be fought over again, not in a party sense in the ordinary use of that term, but by the uprising and consolidating of a loyal, freedom-loving North, overwhelming in numbers, resolute in purpose, invincible in action, and supreme in patriotism based upon impartial justice and all-embracing citizenship.

"Let the edict go forth, trumpet-tongued, that there shall be a speedy end put to all this bloody misrule; that no disorganizing Southern theory of State rights shall defiantly dominate the Federal Government to the subversion of the Constitution; that the millions of loyal colored citizens at the South, now under ban and virtually disfranchised, shall be put in the safe enjoyment of their rights — shall freely vote and be fairly represented — just where they are located. And let the rallying-cry be heard, from the Atlantic to the Pacific coast, 'Liberty and equal rights for each, for all, and forever, wherever the lot of man is cast within our broad domains!'"

Yielding to the entreaties of his daughter, who visited Rockledge in April with her children, Mr. Garrison consented to follow her back to New York and place himself under the care of her family physician. He arrived at the Westmoreland apartment house (Union Square), where she resided, on the afternoon of Monday, April 28, much exhausted, and the treatment began a day or two later, with immediate promise of good results; but the disease (an affection of the kidneys) was too deep-seated for any remedy. "I feel as if the machinery were giving way," he said, and on the 10th of May he took to his bed, completely prostrated. His children were with him constantly, by turns, and when, on Tuesday, May 20, the symptoms became unmistakably alarming, they all hastened to his bedside and remained with him to the end.

CHAP. XI. 1877–79.

The final changes proceeded slowly, and the death-struggle did not set in till half-past ten o'clock on the evening of Friday. Up to that time Mr. Garrison, though disinclined to talk unless spoken to, or to indicate his wants, retained all his faculties, and recognized his children and grandchildren by voice and sight. His thoughtfulness for them and for others, his desire not to give trouble, and his affection, were repeatedly manifested. His illness had been in many respects a distressing one, even in comparison with the wretched months that preceded it; but the prevailing sense was of weariness — frequently expressed in a desire to "go home" — rather than in acute bodily pain, though that was not wanting. Once, in a wandering moment, he asked: "Am I in England?" his mind evidently reverting to his last happy visit there. "What do you want, Mr. Garrison?" said his physician to him on the morning of the 23d. "To finish it up!" was the reply. The wish was not long denied. That evening his children sang for him the old hymns of which he was so fond,— "Ward," "Hebron," "Amsterdam," "Christmas," "Lenox" (the last three especial favorites), "Denmark," "Portuguese Hymn," "Coronation," "Confidence," and "Old Hundred." He could no longer speak, but he manifested his pleasure and consciousness by beating time both with his hands and feet, and was evidently happy in listening to the familiar words of spiritual cheer. An hour or two later the great change began; but so strong was his vitality that he lingered, unconscious, for twenty-four hours, and expired peacefully at a few minutes past eleven on Saturday evening, May 24, 1879.

May 23, 1879.

A post-mortem examination having been made on Monday, Mr. Garrison's remains were taken on the same

CHAP. XI. — 1877-79. *Unitarian.*

night to Roxbury, where the funeral services were held on the afternoon of Wednesday, May 28. The spacious church of the First Religious Society, on Eliot Square, near Rockledge, was kindly placed at the disposal of the family and the public, and was thronged by the multitude who came to take a last look at the face of their old friend and leader. The gathering was remarkable for the number of his surviving co-laborers in the anti-slavery and kindred reformatory movements,[1] and with these were present many of the race to whose redemption he had consecrated his life, and others who, formerly indifferent or hostile to the cause he advocated, now came to pay their tribute of respect. In accordance with Mr. Garrison's views of death, everything was done to avoid the appearance of mourning or of gloom. The blinds were opened to admit the cheerful light of the perfect spring day, the pulpit was tastefully decorated with flowers, and his favorite hymns were sung by a quartette of colored friends.

The services were conducted by the Rev. Samuel May, who read some of the passages from Old and New Testaments so often quoted by Mr. Garrison in anti-slavery days, and spoke briefly and with deep feeling. He was followed by Mrs. Lucy Stone, who acknowledged the debt which women owed to the deceased; the Rev. Samuel Johnson (who read a poem written by Whittier for the occasion); and Theodore D. Weld, whose emotions almost overpowered his utterance; after which Wendell Phillips delivered an address masterly in its analysis and characterization, and tender in its concluding words of farewell and benediction to his beloved comrade.[2]

[1] The pall-bearers were Wendell Phillips, Samuel May, Samuel E. Sewall, Robert F. Wallcut, Theodore D. Weld, Oliver Johnson, Lewis Hayden, and Charles L. Mitchell.

[2] The proceedings were subsequently published in a small volume, 'Tributes to William Lloyd Garrison at the Funeral Services, May 28, 1879.' Mr. Phillips's address is also printed in the Appendix to Oliver Johnson's 'William Lloyd Garrison and his Times.' See a striking article from him on "Garrison" in the *North American Review* for August, 1879.

The closing scene took place at sunset, when the body was interred beside that of Mrs. Garrison in the beautiful cemetery at Forest Hills, in the presence of a large number of friends, and with no other service or ceremony than the singing of an appropriate selection by the quartette.

The flags of the city and State were at half-mast on the day of the funeral. The Governor of the State, in his order respecting Decoration Day, invoked special honor to the "great citizen whose name will be forever associated with the cause and the triumph of the contest." In various Northern and Southern cities the colored people met in memory of their illustrious champion. The leading papers of the United States and Great Britain contained long editorial and biographical articles on the founder of the anti-slavery movement, which were, with rare exceptions, appreciative and eulogistic. Even the very sheets which had formerly caricatured and reviled him, joined in the general panegyric, and it was one of the bitterest of these which confessed, the morning after his death, that the life just ended "was lived with a simplicity, singleness of purpose, and unflinching devotion to a self-imposed task rare in the annals of any time or any land."

Thomas Talbot. May 30.

Boston, Philadelphia, Washington, Cincinnati, Raleigh, Atlanta.

N. Y. World, May 25, 1879.

CHAPTER XII.

INNER TRAITS.

CHAP. XII.

TO the hand which began this narrative has been allotted the vastly more difficult task of concluding it in the pages which are to follow. It has not seemed to me hard to stand off and view, and accordingly depict, my father as an historical personage. Critics must decide how far this objective treatment has been successful; yet, given the materials for this biography, in print and in manuscript, ours, I would fain hope, is the portrait that would be drawn by any seeker after the truth. To attempt, on the other hand, to exhibit my father from the side of his private and domestic life, or in the light of a psychological analysis, fills me first of all with a sense of insufficiency, and imposes a restraint quite different from that exacted by the foregoing documentary narrative. In another place and connection I might, giving a free rein to filial feeling, strive to convey an adequate impression of what my father was in his home to wife and children, and in common intercourse with friend and fellow-man. Some glimpses of this have been already incidentally afforded, and much has been able to be inferred as to the absolute consistency of his public and private behavior — a uniform simplicity, humility, self-abnegation, sympathy with all suffering, detestation of all forms of cruelty and oppression, active benevolence, charitable toleration, endless patience in adversity, indomitable courage, perennial cheerfulness. Something, too, has been observable of the magnetic power to charm and move others which displayed itself both on and off the public stage. These scattered threads I will now draw together in such fashion as I can.

The lineaments of the boy were, as ordinarily happens, partly preserved and partly effaced in the man. My father's childish love of out-door sports naturally succumbed *Ante*, 1:28, 314. to the stern requirements of his twofold struggle for existence and for the cause which he founded. I recall his indulging in quoits while at the water-cure near *Ante*, 3:228. Northampton, a game in which he was fairly skilful, as if by virtue of that balanced judgment which showed itself in so many other ways; and in later years he was fond of croquet. His love of skating utterly died out from *Ante*, 1:28. disuse, but, what is perhaps surprising, his passion for swimming equally became a mere reminiscence, though his *Ante*, 1:28, 29. home was always by tide-water. Among indoor games, he enjoyed checkers as long as his children were interested in it; and to us he seemed a good player, but not an expert. In the evening of his life, whist afforded him solace for his failing eyesight; but in this he remained a tyro, and his naïve revelations of the quality of his hand were most amusing.

I never saw my father draw even a diagram, and he had had not the least training in drawing; yet his penmanship was handsome, and wonderfully persistent in its uniformity. *Ante*, 1:28; 3:397. It was always, however, very labored and inflexible, and latterly he wrote much in pencil, having begun with quills, then taken to steel nibs, and sometimes used a gold pen. Greater suppleness in this art would have made writing much less abhorrent to him, and resulted in a far more copious editorial productiveness. But this was as much a matter of temperament as of manual proficiency. He had an innate love of thoroughness, which was developed in the printing-office and was fostered *Ante*, 1:40. by his experience of bad "copy." His own manuscript was flawless, punctilious to the last degree, and as legible as the print itself. He seldom, except on grave occasions, resorted to a rough draft, but wrote almost without correction, his afterthought coming so quickly

CHAP. XII. that his finger could generally blot out the faulty word while the ink was still wet. He had a habit of gently tapping the paper with his pen-hand while deliberating for a phrase. The psychical and moral side of this was an extreme scrupulousness, that weighed every word and uttered nothing at random. It is seldom that anything like abandon is found in his private correspondence, despite the haste in which he commonly wrote. In his letters, as in his speeches, he had always first in mind justness and aptness of expression, not the pleasure of the reader or listener, least of all the effect (how will it sound?), as gratifying his own vanity or sense of rhetorical power. He thus lacked both the ease and versatility and the perfect sympathy which are combined in the great letter-writers. His tact, however, was remarkable, and his letters were highly prized by the recipients, especially when of a consolatory nature. In controversy or in exhortation they partook of the best qualities of his public style; and I cannot imagine, for example, that such an appeal as his to Dr. Channing in 1834 could have been read without a thrill.

Ante, 1:464.

His domestic correspondence did not escape the general stiffness of his epistolary manner. A man so much in the glare of public censure could not shake off the consciousness of the scrutiny to which his most trivial and private utterances might be subjected. Even when addressing his wife, especially if he was absent on a lecturing tour, he either wrote so that extracts might be made for the *Liberator* as a *quasi*-report, or in view of the necessity of the letter being shown to the abolition circle for their information. When any of the children were away from home, it was our mother chiefly who kept us supplied with the family news. On the whole, the volume of my father's private correspondence was large enough to be a monument to his resolute grappling with the mechanical impediment, even if not to be compared with that of purely literary men. As for his editorial writing, that could doubtless be claimed for it which Edmund Quincy once

Hope for the American Slaves.

I.

Ye who in bondage pine,
Shut out from light divine,
Bereft of hope;
Whose limbs are worn with chains,
Whose tears bedew our plains,
Whose blood our glory stains,
In gloom who grope:—

II.

Shout! for the hour draws nigh,
That gives you liberty!
And from the dust,
So long your vile embrace,
Uprising, take your place
Among earth's equal race—
'Tis right and just.

II.

Proposals

for

Publishing a weekly periodical in Washington City, to be entitle

the

Public Liberator,

and

Journal of the Times.

The primary object of this publication will be the abolition of slavery, and the moral and intellectual elevation of our colored population. The Capital of our Union is obviously the most eligible spot whereon to build this mighty enterprise:—first, because (through Congress and the Supreme Court) it is the head of the body politic, and the soul of the national system; and secondly, because the District of Columbia is the first citadel to be carried.

On this subject, I imagine my views and feelings are too well known to render an elaborate exposition necessary. In its investigation, I shall use *great plainness of speech*—believing that *truth can never conduce to mischief, and is best discovered by plain words.* I shall assume, as self evident truths, that the liberty of a people is the gift of God and nature:—That liberty consists in an independency upon the will of another:—That by the name of slave, we un-

IV.

Mrs. George H. Quincy:

Dear Madam—Your letter has been forwarded to me, by one of my sons, to this city (New York), where I am on a temporary visit. Your kind donation of $15 enclosed in it, in aid of the poor homeless colored refugees

I. Autographic copy of Garrison's own lyric, "Ye who in bondage pine," probably made for the programme of some out-door anti-slavery meeting in the forties or fifties.

II.-III. Autographic original draft of the "Proposals," etc., 1830. See Vol. I., p. 199.

IV. The last letter (unfinished) penned by Garrison, 1879.

asserted of his own journalistic total — that it was equal to the sum of Voltaire's works. He never had a study, and seldom a "den," in which to write in quiet. The guest-room was his refuge when he could not bear or forget the ordinary distractions about him. CHAP. XII.

My father's hand — not to relax quite yet my grasp on this sympathetic member — was more mechanical than his mind. His unsatisfactory experiments in cobbling and in cabinet-making proved this, showing that tools had no attraction for him. Printing, of course, is a mechanic art, and this he mastered; but it is of a simple sort, making but a small demand on ingenuity. His ambidextrousness abided with him to the end: he shaved himself with great facility, using either hand; at table he held his knife in his left. He was what would be called a handy man about the house, though not fertile in contrivances. He hung the window-shades and the pictures — the latter with a good eye to symmetry, squareness, and general effect. He *helped* in everything.

Ante, 1:31, 34.

Ante, 1:28.

The town boy was quickly absorbed in the citizen, and my father, once a Bostonian, never coveted a return to rural life, though he enjoyed his suburban residence at Rockledge. Revisiting Brooklyn, Conn., in the summer of 1854, after an absence of fourteen years, he wrote to his Aunt Newell of the fine landscape, but added: "I could not long, however, be contented with the quietude of the country, unless I had withdrawn from public life." Yet a broad prospect was ever a delight to him, and to mark eligible house-sites as if for himself was his customary way of praising the scene before him. He had neither a scientific nor, strictly speaking, a poetic love of nature. He had no botanical knowledge whatever, and small cognizance of the varieties of trees or flowers.[1] A solitary walk in the country could hardly have been congenial to him, at least as an habitual diversion. Though as a walker not easily fatigued, he is not to be described as a

MS. Aug. 19, 1854.

Cf. ante, 1:72.

[1] The elm-tree near the gate at Rockledge was planted by W. L. G. and his son Frank in May, 1868.

CHAP. XII. pedestrian in the sense of one who made excursions for pleasure. Time and opportunity were here desiderata.

Ante, 1: 30; 2: 47, 48. My father's love of pets never forsook him—or, rather, of cats: towards dogs he had an aversion. With my mother the opposite was the case, though she yielded sweetly to his preference. When away from home, he thought of the well-being of puss as much as of that of any member of the family. "Remembrances to Mary Ann [the one maid-servant]. My good-will to the cat. Love to all the friends"—seemed the natural order of affectionate solici- *MS. Oct.* 28. tude in writing to his wife in 1858. And again to my *MS. Feb.* 8, 1857. mother from Albany: "I need not ask George to look after the cat during my absence, for he is my natural successor in that line—only he must not give her too much at a meal." "See that pussy is put down cellar," he *MS. Feb.* 21, 1878, *to F. J. G.* wrote on a memorandum slip to one of us returning home after bedtime; "you will find plenty of milk for her and for yourself." I remember one cat who attached himself unbidden to the family (and was therefore distrusted as not having been bred from kittenhood), who used to mount my father's shoulders while carving at table. My father did not quite share a cat's local attachments. For *Ante*, 1: 467. his birthplace—meaning Newburyport and not the little *Ante*, 1: 79; 2: 407. house on School Street—for Boston, he had a deep and undying attachment; towards this or that house of the *Ante*, 2: 51. many which successively became his home, he evinced no special sentiment. He was, on the contrary, rather fond of moving into *new* houses—of being the first occupant. Such were those in Pine Street, in Suffolk Street, in Concord Street.

Ante, 1: 29, 78. The love of a pretty face was inextinguishable in my father. It pleased him, as it does many a man, more than any other beautiful thing in nature. His æsthetic sense in general was uncultivated, but it would have repaid cultivating. He had a great fondness for pictures, with but little artistic discrimination, his modest purchases being often dictated by pure sentiment. His visit to the Louvre gave him pleasure, in spite of much that seemed

CHAP. XII.

to him rubbish, while the acres of gory battle canvases at Versailles offended his moral sensibilities. He took real delight and lingered long in the art section of the Paris Exposition of 1867, of which he especially enjoyed the statuary where the intent was chaste. It fell to his lot to befriend artists among other struggling and impecunious fellow-beings, and his charity to them was undoubtedly reënforced by his love of art. *Ante*, p. 191.

To music he was attuned from infancy, and he never ceased to sing. He had a correct ear, and his vocalization was always agreeable, though time had robbed his voice of its youthful capacity. Excessive public speaking, and that bronchial deterioration which the east wind of the New England coast works in almost every inhabitant, told inevitably upon my father. Sacred music was particularly dear to him, and struck a responsive chord even in his last conscious moments. He liked nothing better than to join with two or three friends — with Francis Jackson, or Henry C. Wright, or Samuel May, Jr., or Oliver Johnson — in singing hymns in his own parlor, or wherever they were met together.[1] At the anti-slavery grove meetings he always took a leading part in the singing. He did not conceal his fondness for martial music, and, when taxed with this as a non-resistant, would reply: "It is just as valuable for the moral warfare." His taste for instrumental performances grew with his opportunities, and these in Boston were at first furnished by the Germania orchestra. He could not immediately appreciate the great classical productions, but in the end he took a complete satisfaction in listening to the best concerts of the day. He heard most of the famous *prime donne*, from Jenny Lind to Parepa-Rosa, and these afforded him the greatest *Ante*, 1:29, 30. *Ante*, 1:29. *Ante*, 1:30; 4:305.

[1] "Adjourned from the stormiest meeting, where hot debate had roused all his powers as near to anger as his nature ever let him come, the music of a dozen voices — even of those who had just opposed him — or a piano, if the house held one, changed his mood in an instant, and made the hour laugh with more than content; unless, indeed, a baby and playing with it proved metal even more attractive" (Wendell Phillips, 'Tributes to W. L. G. at the Funeral Services,' p. 48).

CHAP. XII. delight. At home, he drew unfailing enjoyment from the piano, both indirectly profiting by the musical education of his children, and performing himself in a rude way with one hand, while spelling out his psalm-tunes, accompanying the notes with his voice as he went along. An "æolian attachment" to his daughter's instrument gave an organ effect and support which somewhat smoothed the imperfections of the exercise, while calling up the associations of church and congregation.

Ante, 1:30.

Ante, 1:42, 56.

The reading habit of his boyhood could not be maintained by my father amid the unremitting cares and occupations of his life-work. The list of authors already mentioned as his early favorites cannot be greatly extended; but in prose, Algernon Sydney and Jonathan Dymond; in poetry, Shakespeare, Milton, Cowper, Coleridge, Shelley, Montgomery (to say nothing of Whittier), should be added. About the year 1850, certain publishers began with some regularity to send books to the *Liberator* for review; and it is pathetic to observe the scrupulous acknowledgment of them, generally with a notice, however brief, when the readers of the paper might have grudged both the space used in this way, and the diversion from much more urgent editorial writing. The books in question were, as a rule, of a rather poor grade, on religious or reformatory topics; yet it must have been a pastime to read them under a sense of discharging one duty by way of exemption from another. The value of the criticism depended very much upon the material. That of the Life of Channing, cited above, will rank as a specimen of the best; the reflections suggested by the writings of Thomas Paine are in the same category. Very frequently the review had to be controversial.

Ante, 1:42.

Ante, 3:239.

Ante, 3:145.

A college education would have been likely to confirm my father's evident literary bias from the start. He made an ineffectual effort to unite literature and polemics in the original scheme of the *Liberator*, but he soon found he could do no more than make selections, and that

Ante, 1:219.

neither freshly nor systematically. His poetical talent had a better chance for expression, but it too was conditioned by the reformer's needs, and took on a quite different development from what might have been the case had the higher education, pecuniary ease, and leisure for letters been his. The total product was considerable in amount, the lyrical portion being relatively small, though it could boast some successes as being singable and often sung. A lack of imagination is perceptible here, among other limitations; and nearly every piece bore the stamp of the moralist. The sonnet proved attractive above all other forms of verses, suiting well my father's habit of condensation.[1] Some of this variety found immediate recognition. The sonnet on "The Free Mind," composed in Baltimore jail, was reprinted in at least two literary collections, one being 'The Boston Book' (Boston: Geo. W. Light, 1841, p. 272), the other as thus related by the Rev. Jacob M. Manning, who called it "the immortal sonnet." "It may not be uninteresting to you to know," he wrote to my father in 1860, "that the circumstance which first settled me in my abhorrence of slavery, was learning and declaiming, while a school-boy in Western New York, a sonnet entitled *The Free Mind*, written by you while in a Southern prison. I found the piece in Dr. Cheever's 'Commonplace Book of Poetry.'"

CHAP. XII.

Ante, 1:330; 3:42.

Ante, 1:179.

MS. Apr. 13.

Geo. B. Cheever.

This sonnet maintains its place in the anthologies of more recent years — either alone, as in 'The Cambridge Book of Poetry and Song' (New York, 1882), or with other examples, as in the 'Library of Religious Poetry' (New York, 1885), and in 'Harper's Cyclopædia of British and American Poetry' (New York, 1881). To the numerous collections of this sort which my father owned and enjoyed reading, he purposed adding one of his own,

1 Speaking of his resolutions at the twenty-fifth anniversary of the American Anti-Slavery Society, he said: "—— in which, by a sort of hydraulic pressure, I have endeavored to concentrate my thoughts, feelings, and ideas as pertaining to our struggle generally, and in regard to its particular aspects during the past year" (*Lib.* 28 : 82).

CHAP. XII. consisting of reformatory pieces, and virtually did get it together. But his standard of admission was the moralist's. His *Liberator* column of poetical selections and contributions exhibits his indulgence for mediocre original verse in view of its reformatory motive — "and it will please the writer," he used to add apologetically.

Ante, 1:56. The boy's fondness for declaiming did not betoken the natural orator. My father had, at the outset, to overcome much diffidence in appearing before an audience, being conscious that his strength lay in his pen. In this respect *Wendell Phillips.* he was the exact opposite of the incomparable Phillips. He lacked the latter's memorizing power which enabled him to block out a discourse and partly formulate it in advance; and, in fact, he generally had no time for such preparation. When he had, he wrote out his speeches; but he was so far rid of this practice, in my recollection, that I never heard him read any but a lecture such as he delivered in the intervals of the weekly issues of the *Liberator*, and which he might have repeated forty times, I believe, without feeling free to dispense with his manuscript. His custom was, for anti-slavery meetings, to fortify himself with notes; and, in pursuit of his main object — to persuade — he was also commonly provided with newspaper clippings (choice extracts from or for the "Refuge of Oppression") with which to intersperse his remarks. This, of course, was destructive of finished *Ante*, 3:19. oratory, to which he seldom rose except under extraordinary inspiration. Then, indeed, in respect of weight, fervor, or diction, he might justly claim the name of orator. In general, it may be said, he revised but little the stenographic report of his speeches, again in marked contrast *Ante*, *p.* 39. to his friend Phillips.[1]

[1] Compare, for an example of felicitous improvement, the leading epigraph following the title-page of our Vol. I. (the passage is also repeated at 3:14) with the verbatim report, viz.: "The truth is, they who start any reform which at last grows into one of surprising magnitude, are always ill-judged and unfairly treated at the outset. They are looked upon with utter contempt, and are treated in the most opprobrious manner, which is unfair and unjust. In due season the cause grows and expands and advances to

Some disinterested testimony is here admissible. Quincy, humorously describing in the N. Y. *Tribune* the abolition celebration of Forefathers' Day at Plymouth, Dec. 21, 1856, wrote thus of my father:

CHAP. XII.

"His expression is rather mild than otherwise, until he kindles with his subject, when one can detect the fire which has had such incendiary results. His head, which is very bald, is what I suppose phrenologists would call a full one, and his eye is remarkably good. Indeed, if one could divest one's self of the associations connected with his name, he would pass for a very well-looking man, indeed. . . . His style of speaking is earnest and forcible, deriving its power from the substance of what he says, rather than from the rhetorical pains he takes to say it. . . . And he has a very unpleasant[1] way of producing proofs of the charges he makes. . . ."

Lib. 27:2.

And Oliver Johnson records, in his Life of my father:

"He was not, in the usual sense of the word, an orator; nevertheless, he was one of the most impressive and forcible public speakers to whom it has ever been my good fortune to listen. In early life, he was a complete slave to his pen; he could not trust himself to make a speech without carefully writing it out beforehand. He grew tired of this sort of slavery after a while, and resolved to emancipate himself, which he did *immediately* and triumphantly. He found, upon trial, that thoughts and words on his favorite themes flowed freely. He was so thoroughly alive to his subject, and so intensely in earnest, that he never failed to command the sympathy and attention of his audience. His personal presence disarmed prejudice and inspired confidence, and his constant identification of himself, in thought, principle, and feeling, with 'those in bonds as bound with them,' the clear moral insight that enabled him to comprehend principles and penetrate every disguise of sophistry and false pretence, and his strong appeals to reason and conscience, gave him great power over men, both in public

W. L. G. and his Times, p. 395.

its sure triumph; and in proportion as it nears the goal, in that proportion does praise and panegyric fall to the lot of him who may have suffered somewhat in the course of the struggle. The praise on the one hand and the defamation on the other are both unmerited; and in the sober judgment of a distant posterity, if the thing . . ." (here the fragment breaks off).

[1] *I. e.*, for his opponents, as the omitted context shows.

CHAP. XII. speech and private intercourse. If he lacked the resources which a classical culture alone can furnish, he possessed others of the very highest importance, and which such a culture often fails to supply. If he did not please the imagination or tickle the fancy of his hearers, he did what was better — he enlightened their minds, stirred their consciences, and swayed their judgments. No cause, in his hands, was ever put to shame by any hasty or ill-considered word. In dealing with opponents, his tact was unfailing. Thoughtful people especially heard him with delight, and the largest audiences felt the power of his logic and the magnetism of his voice and presence."

May 29, 1884.

Hist. of the Rebellion, Book I., § 99.

The Rev. Dr. Joseph F. Tuttle, President of Wabash College, wrote in the N. Y. *Independent:* "In [1844] I first saw Wm. L. Garrison and Wendell Phillips in Broadway Tabernacle. Mr. Garrison's eloquence was like to that which Clarendon attributes to Sir Thomas Coventry: 'He had, in the plain way of speaking and delivery, without much ornament of elocution, *a strange power of making himself believed — the only justifiable design of eloquence.*'" Finally (and it is praise from Sir Hubert Stanley), James Russell Lowell testifies: "It may interest you to know that I thought Mr. Garrison the most effective speaker among anti-slavery orators." Whatever judgment may be arrived at on this point, there can be no question that, next after the doctrine of immediatism and anti-colonization, what most distinguished my father from Lundy and all his anti-slavery predecessors was his oratorical capacity. Without it we can hardly conceive of his having created the anti-slavery organization.

MS. Nov. 17, 1885, to F. J. G.

No speaker on the anti-slavery platform cared to follow Mr. Phillips, and he was commonly reserved for the very close of an evening session. But this place also frequently fell to my father, especially after stormy debates and roused or despondent feelings, when his function was to soothe and to cheer. "It was, besides, getting quite late," wrote N. P. Rogers in January, 1842, of the anti-slavery meeting at the State House, "and we felt that the meeting needed a winding-up from Garrison."

Lib. 12:26.

There were, I think, few set occasions for testing my father's ability as a close debater. Certainly he was not to be compared with Charles Burleigh, who, in this respect, was easily first of all the abolition orators. In repartee, especially with a mob, my father was quick and effective, as witness the Rynders mob. His speeches were, though often severe and "radical" in the extreme, impersonal and not calculated to excite combativeness in his hearers. His whole appearance was placid and peaceful. The impression he made on the prejudiced who heard him for the first time was the more favorable because his mild and benevolent aspect, the manner and the matter of his discourse, were so opposed to his evil reputation.[1] He was sparing of gesture, though using more than the more graceful Phillips; and a familiar attitude on rising was with his right hand thrust in his bosom (as in the portrait at p. 358 of Vol. III.). He stood very erect, and presented a good figure.[2] His voice was strong and sonorous, his enunciation and delivery good. He could easily sway an audience in the right mood.

CHAP. XII.

Ante, p. 289.

Ante, 3:298.

Ante, 3:19.

Of my father's beauty in youth and early manhood I cannot doubt, and I may be permitted to repeat here the description of him by an artist companion in Newburyport, the late Thomas B. Lawson, already cited: "His hair a rich dark brown; his forehead high and *very* white; his cheeks decidedly roseate; his lips full, sensitive, and ruddy; his eyes intent — wide open, of a yellowish hazel; with fine teeth, rather larger than the average, and a complexion more fair, more silvery white, than I ever saw upon

Ante, 1:55, 56.

Ante, 1:xv.

[1] Sarah Pugh noted in her diary for Dec. 6, 1853: "Spent at the [A. S.] fair [in Philadelphia]. Garrison's speech in the evening pleased every one. An orthodox Friend who came from curiosity to see and hear '*the monster,*' was perfectly fascinated. 'Never heard a more impressive and solemn speech;' begged to be introduced to him, to express his great satisfaction with what he had heard" ('Memorial of Sarah Pugh,' p. 89).

[2] In his prime, my father may have measured five feet nine to ten. His limbs were straight and shapely, his trunk perhaps slightly longer than his legs, so that he seemed in sitting a taller man than he was. His head was set well forward on his shoulders, which grew rounded with bending over the printer's form, and with age; but he was never bowed.

CHAP. XII. a man." Baldness set in early; and as my father always shaved, he presented a uniform appearance throughout his adult life. His complexion always retained traces of the red that originally adorned it, and which is said to have been heightened by his blushing when spoken to. The remnant of his hair was slow to gray. Mary Grew, who saw him first in Hartford in 1830, found him to tally with a friend's description of him as "a young man with a very black beard, which he shaved very close, giving the lower part of his face a bluish appearance." When let grow, however, his beard, with a parental reminiscence, was of a sandy or light brown color; and I think my father liked it none the better for that. A man of singularly few prejudices, he never freed himself from the public opinion in which he grew up as regards beards, which were, even till Kossuth came over and broke the fashion, associated with men of no reputation — just as the conventional stage villain was bearded. He fostered independence in his children,[1] but almost rated it a moral delinquency that his sons, one and all, eschewed the razor.[2]

R. Purvis to W. P G., Feb., 1881.

Ante, 1: 13.

My father's eye was known to the public only in combination with his glasses, which were always kept on except for reading or writing; nor was it to his family so pleasing when the glasses were removed. None of his children can remember the full lips of which the early portraits bear unmistakable evidence, as late as that daguerreotype of 1846 which serves as frontispiece to the third volume. When he fell into the hands of the

1 "If I give my children no other precept," he wrote in the *Liberator* (16 : 18), "if I leave them no other example, it shall be a fearless, impartial, thorough investigation of every subject to which their attention may be called, whether those principles agree or conflict with my own, or with those of any other person."

2 Here may belong an anecdote related to me by Oliver Johnson. A good abolitionist in the rural districts of Massachusetts, who went down to Boston to annual meetings and conventions, was filled with a great admiration for Charles Burleigh, concerning whom he carried back glowing reports to his family. In the fulness of time he arranged a lecture in his own town for Burleigh, and was sorely troubled when the one stage arrival brought not the expected guest. An hour after, a knock was heard at the

dentist, its shapeliness was lost forever. This feature he derived from the Palmer side of his ancestry, and it was a mouth of extraordinary mobility, the despair of photographer, painter, and sculptor. Of the Jocelyn engraved likeness, a relative wrote (some fifty years after): "The features I believe to be nearly perfect, yet to me there is something lacking in it — the want of an expression which he always bore on his countenance when I knew him — an expression of sympathy or commiseration manifested by his lips in some way, doubtless better understood by you than I should be able to describe." Nothing could be truer than this suggestion of what was, in fact, indescribable. To this expression of the mouth,[1] in harmony with the beaming eye, was due the wonderful benevolence and geniality of aspect which made my father so attractive — so bewitching, as he seemed to Miss Martineau. There were two other faces akin to his in the anti-slavery group — that of Samuel J. May, well called a benediction, and the brimming, soulful, angelic countenance of Mrs. Follen. To say that my father was worthy to be classed with either of these spiritual presences is to make a large, but not too large, claim for him.

Chap. XII.

Ante, 1:344.

MS. Sept. 27, 1880, Wm. A. Garrison to W. P. G.

Circa 1840.

Ante, 2:69-71.

His head was imposing not from its size, for it was very compact, but from its balanced parts, culminating in the bump — a visible bump — of firmness, humorously commemorated by Lowell, which was the opposite pole of the benignity residing in his face. Quincy has just

Ante, 3:178.

door, and the curious children scrambled pell-mell to answer it. There stood a tall figure with long beard and ringlets, dusty with foot-travel, and carrying a pack of anti-slavery publications slung at the end of a rough staff resting on his shoulder. The first child to catch sight of him rushed back to the sitting-room, crying: "Oh, mother, mother! the Devil has come!" "And no wonder," said Garrison, when told the story; "hair 'em scare 'em." It is worth remarking, by the way, since Burleigh was an available model of Christ for artists, that the fashionable abhorrence of beards prevailed in spite of the conventional representations of the great Exemplar.

[1] See, for the nearest approach to it ever made in portraiture, the frontispiece to the present volume.

Ante, p. 317. Mrs. E. D. Cheney in the Open Court newspaper, p. 1143.

called it, phrenologically speaking, a "full" one; and Bronson Alcott, in his Boston "conversations" on Representative Men, in 1851, characterized my father in one masterly stroke as a "phrenological head illuminated."

My father inherited an enviably strong constitution, as was proved both by his longevity and by his exceptional recuperative powers when prostrated by illness. His digestion was perfect, and he used to say that he never knew what it was to have a stomach. He was wholly unfastidious about his food, bringing to whatever was set before him a good appetite, and abstaining from only one or two easily dispensable articles. The home table was plainly but abundantly supplied, my mother being an excellent housekeeper. My father was a good sleeper, of which I can give no better token than the fact that he could fall asleep directly after his return from a speech in the evening. He dreamed habitually except in sickness, and I have heard him remark on the singular experience that, despite his daily contemplation of the horrors of slavery, and the not infrequent apprehensions concerning his own safety, he had almost never in his sleep been troubled with images of either. The advent of the hot weather usually found him run down in health, and needing to get away from the printing-office and the city. The most serious illness of his life was the attack of Western fever in Cleveland in 1847, from which his system never recovered. It affected his brain periodically, and was, I presume, the cause of that spinal inflammation and weakness which from time to time disabled him, and made him exclaim against his paradoxical "want of backbone." In following his life day by day in the ample records available to us, I have been struck with the total amount of his ailing (particularly after 1847), as compared with our childish recollection of his physical condition. I attribute this to the fact that he never dwelt upon his distresses and sufferings, but maintained a cheerful mien and conversation. Low spirits, like dyspepsia, were unknown to him.

Ante, 3:206. MS. July 20, 1858, W. L. G. to S. J. May.

First and last he certainly took a good deal of medicine, largely by his own prescription. CHAP. XII.

"He is quite ignorant of physiology," wrote Quincy to Webb in 1853, "and has no belief in hygiene, or in anything pertaining to the body except *quack medicines*. That he has survived all he has taken is proof of an excellent constitution. . . . You remember his puff of Dr. C——'s Anti-Scrofulous Panacea, . . . in which he said that he felt it 'permeating the whole system in the most delightful manner.' 'Permeating the system!' said Hervey Weston, with the malice of a regular practitioner; 'why, it was the first time he had taken a glass of grog, and [he] did n't know how good it was!'— some sort of spirits being the basis of all these sort of quackeries." *MS. Jan. 13.*

The want of physiological instruction combined with my father's acquired distrust of authority, creeds, and schools to make him a thorough eclectic in matters medical. His first experiment was with Thomsonian remedies, and for these he retained a fondness to the last, and regarded their inventor as a benefactor and a martyr to innovation.[1] I fancy that the pungent or at least positive taste of some of these gave him an idea of their efficacy. He thought himself a poor subject for homœopathy, whereas my mother was noticeably susceptible to this treatment, which was also provided for the children from the time of making Dr. Wesselhoeft's acquaintance. Hence they were, to their lasting gratitude, saved from the nauseous doses of the old school, and knew not the meaning of blue pill or castor oil. The hydropathic treatment was agreeable to my father, and was applied by him to his children in case of cold or fever; but it had the disadvantage of sometimes being awkward for family use. For himself, he bought a great variety of patent medicines of whose potency the advertised testimonials (owing to his spontaneous trust in human nature) had persuaded him; and often, as would appear, rather

MS. Mar. 4, 1879, W. L. G. to W. P. G.

Ante, 3: 82.

Ante, 1: 37.

[1] See Thomson's own account of his being imprisoned Nov. 10, 1809, on a charge of murder brought by a rival practitioner of the old school. The place of confinement was the Newburyport jail, the condition of which was loathsome in the extreme, and the whole management barbarous.

CHAP. XII. against a rainy day than for present need, for they remained unopened in his closet. Or, if not unopened, their contents were frequently very slightly diminished, for my father carried his *immediatism* into medicine: it was instant relief he sought, and he was impatient of gradual recovery. A few doses determined him. In

MS. May 5. May, 1836, he wrote to my mother from Providence, of being about to visit a botanical doctor, "having more willingness to try a new medicine than faith in its efficacy." "It may do me good," he added; "it certainly will not if I do not try it." There was in this experimenting a trace of both the Yankee and the reformer, and I class it with my father's fondness for labor-saving inventions, which he indulged, in a spirit of domestic benevolence, as freely as his means would permit.

The name of gentleman, like that of Christian, is sadly abused; but if my father did not deserve to bear both the one and the other, there is no reason why the world should cherish either. The root of gentlemanliness, as of Christianity, is in the preferment of others to self, and I cannot believe that any human being ever lived in whom this affection was more innate, more constant, or more gracious,

Ante, 3:438. than in this "infidel of a most degraded class." There was no creature wearing God's image to whom he had to condescend, none before whom he felt abashed because of wealth or station. A simple dignity, free from self-consciousness, marked his carriage in any society — and abroad he was received with respect by all classes. At home, he saved his wife and the one maid-of-all-work the heavier burdens of lifting and carrying, taking water and wood to the upper stories of the house, attending to the furnace till his children could relieve him, and the like. Had he a guest, he would black his shoes for him with the same readiness that he would show him about the city. In short, he performed as a part of his religion those

Diary of J. Q. Adams, 5:10. menial services which Calhoun, in a famous conversation with J. Q. Adams, drew the line at, as impossible for white men without degradation (in distinction from mere mechanic employment).[1] He did it, too, without forfeiting the respect or respectful demeanor of servants, not one of whom, I am sure, ever failed to feel (as they seldom failed to manifest) esteem for my father's goodness of heart. And here let me cite the testimony of one who worked with him at the "case" for many years, besides (in the capacity of official reporter to the Massachusetts Anti-Slavery Society) preserving his speeches stenographically, with admirable fidelity — Mr. J. M. W. Yerrinton. He prefaces the following lines by saying: "They are not what I could wish, but it is hard for me to write of your father without feeling that others, who did not know him so well, may think the picture too highly colored — which it would be impossible for me to make it, or, as I think, any other man, in respect of the qualities of which I speak":

MS. July 5, 1888, to F. J. G.

"Mr. Garrison's presence in the printing-office was 'like sunshine in a shady place.' The 'art preservative of all the arts' is not commonly attended by many of the æsthetic graces, and the *Liberator* office was no exception to the general rule. Lowell's description of it in his early days as 'dark, unfurnitured, and mean' fitly characterized it until its removal to the Washington Building [on Washington, opposite Franklin Street], in 1860, when, for the first time, even the cheap luxury of gas was enjoyed. But the poor and dingy surroundings were little heeded by those who served under its editor, who, from the master-workman to the office-boy, felt 'e'en drudgery divine' in such service, and daily labor became a daily delight. So uniformly cheerful was he, so patient, so careless of his own ease, and so considerate of the feelings and comfort of others,

Ante, 1: 245.

[1] Mrs. J. G. Swisshelm relates, in her 'Half a Century,' p. 60 *(circa* 1838): "To a white woman in Louisville, work was a dire disgrace, and one Sabbath four of us sat suffering from thirst, with the pump across the street, when I learned that for me to go for a pitcher of water would be so great a disgrace to the house as to demand my instant expulsion" *(Cf. Niles' Register*, 41: 131). "Mrs. Trollope says a Virginia gentleman told her that ever since he had been married he had been accustomed to have a negro girl sleep in the same chamber with himself and wife, and that, being asked why he had this nocturnal attendant, he replied: 'Good Heaven, if I wanted a glass of water during the night, what would become of me!'" *(Lib.* 2 : 107).

CHAP. XII. — that he won the admiration, respect, and affection of all connected, in any capacity, with the paper.[1] The many annoyances, almost inevitable in every printing-office, never disturbed his serenity. The worst 'proof,' though studded with dark spots as the Milky Way with light, never called forth an impatient, still less a harsh or reproachful, word. An excellent printer and careful proof-reader, he took great pride in the 'make-up' and typographical accuracy of the paper, and often 'made up' and corrected the 'forms' with his own hands. On the evening preceding publication day he would frequently insist on the printers going home, while he remained until a late hour, or came down to the office at daylight the next morning, to prepare the paper for the press. And thus in very many ways his sweet and gracious spirit, his self-abnegation, and his thoughtfulness for others were made manifest; and thus it was that he endeared himself to all."

Ante, 2:329; 3:84. Oliver Johnson, more than once an inmate of our family, and as intimate a visitor as could be named, has this to say:

W. L. G. and his Times, *p.* 397. "Of Mr. Garrison's private, domestic, and social life I hardly dare trust myself to speak. A man of more spotless excellence in every relation of life I have never known. As a husband, father, and friend he was indeed a model, and his home was ever the abode of love and peace. His wife . . . was a noble woman and a true helpmate. Mr. Garrison's devotion as a husband and father was one of his most beautiful characteristics. He never made his public relations an excuse for neglecting his family. Did one of the children cry in the night, it was in his arms that it was caressed and comforted. In every possible way, in the care of the children and in all household matters, he sought to lighten the cares of his wife, taking upon himself burdens which most husbands and fathers shun. In short, he made his home a heaven, into which it was a delight to enter. He was never so happy as when surrounded by his wife and children and a few favored guests. Under such circumstances, he was at his best — happy as a bird, genial, witty, and full of a generous hospitality."

Tributes to W. L. Garrison at the Funeral Services, *p.* 47. Wendell Phillips said at his funeral:

"His was the happiest life I ever saw. . . . No man gathered into his bosom a fuller sheaf of blessing, delight, and

[1] See the poetical tribute of one of his apprentices on the *Journal of the Times* on the occasion of his departure from that paper (*Lib.* 1 : 56).

joy. In his seventy years, there were not arrows enough in the whole quiver of the Church or State to wound him. As Guizot once said from the tribune, 'Gentlemen, you cannot get high enough to reach the level of my contempt,' so Garrison, from the serene level of his daily life, from the faith that never faltered, was able to say to American hate, 'You cannot reach up to the level of my home mood, my daily existence.' I have seen him intimately for thirty years, while raining on his head was the hate of the community, when, by every possible form of expression, malignity let him know that it wished him all sorts of harm. I never saw him unhappy; I never saw the moment that serene, abounding faith in the rectitude of his motive, the soundness of his method, and the certainty of his success did not lift him above all possibility of being reached by any clamor about him."

And Mr. Johnson again:

"He was always courageous and hopeful. Never in a single instance did I see him in a discouraged mood. His faith in the goodness of his cause and in the overruling Providence of God was so absolute that he was calm and cheerful alike under clear or cloudy skies. I have seen him again and again when the expenses of the *Liberator* were running far beyond its receipts, and he did not know whence the money was to come to supply the wants of his family; but never once did any shadow fall upon his spirits on this account. He had given himself and all his powers to a cause that he believed had the favor and support of Heaven, and he did not doubt that in some way he would be taken care of. And help always *did* come — sometimes in unexpected and surprising ways. His unselfish devotion to his work touched and opened the hearts of all who witnessed it, disposing them to stay up his hands and relieve him of pecuniary embarrassment. If in his greatest extremity he had been absolutely certain that he could make his paper profitable by the slightest dereliction of principle, by trimming a little on this side or that, or by the suppression of unpopular truth, he never would have yielded to the temptation."[1]

W. L. G. and his Times, p. 396.

Ante, 3:464.

The hospitality proffered by my parents and imposed upon them greatly augmented their expenses. Apart

[1] So far was he from this, that he admitted articles from correspondents whose views or whose modes of expression he knew would cost him the support of his more narrow-minded subscribers. This sacrifice he made in the interest of free thought.

CHAP. XII. from my father's leadership and editorship, the peculiar circumstances of the anti-slavery circle in Boston caused our home to be singled out as a hostelry; and besides native guests there was a large foreign contingent, whose sojourn was often prolonged. In anniversary and convention times, invitations were always freely extended at the meetings to come to dinner, when the table was stretched to its utmost capacity, and the flow of conversation—often in continuation of the morning's debates—was inexhaustible. "My house is a semi-hotel, with the numerous anti-slavery friends and visitors whom I am called to entertain, and whose presence is ever welcome," wrote my father to Mr. Johnson in 1857, with reference to the difficulty he had in making both ends meet. "I am never so far in funds as to have a spare dollar by me, using what economy I can," he said in the same letter; and to my mother (writing from Ohio the next year), he spoke of "being all the time pressed pecuniarily to keep out of debt—for debt is my dread, and yours not less." The more, by the way, he went afield as a lecturer, the greater the obligations of hospitality he incurred.

MS. Apr. 16.

MS. Oct. 14, 1858.

Ante, 3:478.

Helen E. Garrison, a Memorial, p. 40.

One guest above all others had the freedom of our home. "I shall never forget," said Wendell Phillips at my mother's funeral, "the deep feeling—his voice almost breaking to tears—with which Henry C. Wright told me of the debt his desolate life owed to this home. And who shall say how much that served the great cause?" Mr. Wright wrote to my parents in 1858—just after the financial panic: "I have nowhere to take my things but to your own home, which has so long been the centre of my life so far as a *Home* is concerned. . . . Your love and kindness to me have been the joy and life of my life. My heart and my grateful tears often bless you for the home feeling you have permitted me to cherish with you and yours. . . . Well I know your home is the hotel of anti-slavery mankind. I feel anxious and troubled lest, in these times, you are perplexed to meet your current family expenses."

MS. Jan. 19, 1858.

My mother's hospitality, like her kindliness of heart, did not fall behind my father's, though her extreme modesty, with perhaps a natural reserve, made her less expansive towards strangers. She accepted without a murmur of dissent, and in all cheerfulness, the obligation to receive the bidden and the unbidden guest, of all colors and conditions. Again, like the conventional housewife, she sometimes wished the shades drawn, to shield her carpets from the sun, but she never contested her husband's preference for abundance of light. "In the warmest days of summer," writes Mary Grew, "he would open window-blinds and draw aside curtains, and let the sunlight pour into the parlors regardless of the heat. He said that the Crystal Palace was not too light nor too large to suit him for a residence. Yet how readily he could accommodate himself to any house which he occupied!" The hygienic maxim that where the sun does not enter the physician will, had less to do with this practice than had my father's aversion to gloom, physical or mental, and his sense of the identity of light and life and energy.[1] As a result, our home made the impression of being lived in in every part, with nothing formal, or kept for show, or too good for daily use.

MS. Dec. 4, 1888, to F. J. G.

Along with this, in my father's domain, there was naturally some disorder, against which my mother strove incessantly and patiently. Seated in one corner of the sofa, he would strew the floor with his exchanges, or he would leave table or desk covered with heaps of clippings and manuscripts. She could easily have escaped detection if she had destroyed the older piles, whose con-

[1] After hearing his neighbor, the Rev. Dr. George Putnam's Thanksgiving discourse in 1866, my father wrote him a complimentary note about it, but added a remonstrance against the sepulchral darkness of the church (amply provided with windows, which were carefully blinded and curtained), which he said was enough to prevent his going often to hear the Doctor, even if the latter had "the eloquence of Paul, the zeal of Peter, and the love of John." The Doctor acknowledged that his people closed more blinds than was necessary, and seemed to prefer a "dim religious light"; "but," he added, with a playful allusion to the skylight over his pulpit, "you know I get my light *from above!*"

tents her husband had well forgot; but they were somehow mostly saved, if even in barrels in the cellar, and were a part of the Penates moved from house to house in our family wanderings. To her forbearance we owe a large measure of the manuscript material preserved to become available for this biography. My father rarely came up from the *Liberator* office without a roll of exchanges under his arm, which had their interest for his boys, as a source both of reading and of pocket-money, being salable in the stores for wrapping-paper. On Saturday evenings he brought the proofs of the first and last pages of the *Liberator*, and his jocose inquiry after supper—"Come, boys! who wants to get the *Liberator* in advance of the mail?"—was the invitation for one of us to "follow copy" while he read aloud from the proof-slip and corrected the typographical errors, which were apt to be pretty numerous. He often groaned in spirit (and audibly to us) over these, but he never said anything at the office that savored of complaint or fault-finding. On Wednesdays, when the inside pages were made ready for the press, he seldom came home to dinner, but went without, making a long day at the office, and returning thoroughly fatigued from the culmination of the week's work. The next day his wife would try—often with success—to take him off with her for an excursion into the suburbs or a round of calls.

Ante, p. 326.

At the office, as at home, being the most accessible of men, he was often interrupted by callers—dear friends whom he was glad to see and converse with—or bores and cranks whom he tolerated and allowed to consume his precious time, or beggars to whose more or less plausible and deserving cases he never refused to listen. If he was wont to give to these last more generously than he could afford, he nevertheless did not give hastily or impulsively; and I was often struck by the singular expression in his face of sympathetic and respectful attention, while listening to their stories, and of reserve and caution withal, as he would occasionally cross-question the applicant (not very severely). One day he was detained from the dinner-table by a man who begged for a pair of trousers; and, thinking he might as well give him the pair he had on, and don a new pair he had lately purchased, he went up-stairs and made the change. He was somewhat dashed, on coming to the table and explaining matters, by my mother's exclamation: "If you gave him the pair you had on, you gave him your *new* trousers!" But he laughed and said: "Well, he has a good pair, anyhow." If my mother sometimes chided him for his excess of generosity, she was not less prone to give freely to those who needed it; and not only did she part with her own things, but she would unshrinkingly assume the far harder, and, to her, particularly disagreeable, task of soliciting aid from others. On one occasion she went from store to store the whole length of Washington Street, selling the pamphlet narrative of a French political refugee who had escaped from Cayenne, until she had disposed of four hundred copies and thus made a hundred dollars for him. *Ante*, 3:464.

Of necessity, my father was a great wanderer on both continents, and he never wearied of seeing new faces and new types of mankind, and making new friends. Yet, like Wordsworth's "Happy Warrior," his was

> "A soul whose master-bias leans
> To home-felt pleasures and to gentle scenes."

I cannot recall his ever coming home in other than a bright and joyous mood, bringing with him the "eternal sunshine of the spotless mind." Had he arrived distraught or depressed, I think the mere sight of wife and children would have gladdened him. The brunt of domestic discipline generally falls on the mother, and ours, in sheer fatigue, sometimes laid the day's naughtiness before her husband for his moral support of her censure; but the offence was too remote, and the child-nature too near, to evoke the proper warmth of reproof from him. Both our parents appealed to us as reasonable and affectionate beings, never using violence and seldom force with toler-

CHAP. XII. ably unruly subjects. He played with us either romping games when small, or games of skill when older. He could not assist us much in our studies, but encouraged us in competitions in penmanship, he being the umpire. Rarely he read aloud to us, but he frequently recited favorite verses, like Derzhavin's "Ode to the Deity," in Bowring's translation, Byron's apostrophe to the Ocean in "Childe Harold," Cowper's "I would not have a slave," or Campbell's "Hohenlinden"— with stock repetitions of "My name is Norval"; or sang (with dance accompaniment)

> "Of all the little boys [girls] I know,
> There is none like my ——y."

At table, his hands prepared the food for us, and later for his grandchildren — our mother's broken arm excusing her; and when urged by her to satisfy his own hunger, he would protest: "I must scratch gravel for my little chickens first." When we were sick, he provided the invalid meal, with the instinct and tenderness of a nurse. His daughter has her first distinct remembrance of him as he came to kiss her good-night in her little crib, and said: "How glad I am that my darling has such a nice warm bed and kind parents to love her. The poor little slave child is torn away from its mother's arms. How good my darling ought to be, and how we must pity the poor slaves!" She once asked him if she had ever been baptized (having had the question put to her at school). He promptly responded: "No, my darling, you have had a good bath every morning, and that is a great deal better," — which being reported by the little girl to her inquirers, "Oh yes!" they cried, "you are the daughter of an infidel."

Ante, 3: 84.

The childish age had a peculiar fascination for my father, who often told his wife that if there was one thing he was fitted for, it was to tend babies. "I found several babies at Longwood," he wrote to her in 1870, "and so have not been wholly disconsolate on account of the absence of the dear little ones at Rockledge and Linwood

Ante, 2: 115, 118.

MS. June 6.

Street." "I can stand being a grandfather to an indefinite extent," he wrote after he had become one. "Instead of feeling older, I shall feel all the younger for it." Other people's infants, like his own, came to him without fear and of their own motion. Seldom indeed was it that a sick, tired, or fractious child, once held in his strong and sympathetic embrace, did not become soothed and yield to his singing of "Olmütz" or the "Portuguese Hymn." Once, when a two-year-old granddaughter was ill with brain fever, and would no longer go to his comforting arms, he could not refrain from tears. He liked a smiling infant, and was disturbed by the gravity of one of his grandchildren, who developed, however, a very merry disposition. *MS. Mar. 5, 1867, to F. J. G.*

The *vocal* animation which he lent the household was remarked by all visitors. When the family were taking a summer recreation in New Hampshire in 1860, Miss Caroline Putnam, left in friendly occupancy of the house in Dix Place, wrote to my mother: "Dick [the canary] seems to share in the feeling of your absence, and is dispirited — as Miss Coffin declares — because he is not cheered by Mr. Garrison's voice. . . . At breakfast there was one assent when Miss Holley said: 'How we *do* miss Mr. Garrison's pleasant voice!'" At table, where the gravest topics were in place,— the atmosphere of the home being surcharged with moral ideas and considerations connected with the great cause of human rights,— his conversation was enlivened with puns. These were not always repressed on public occasions, where his pleasantry helped to make him the good presiding officer that Quincy — the best of judges — pronounced him. His humor was, in fact, the great preserving quality of my father's mind as a reformer: it saved him both from compromising his dignity and from undue sensitiveness to abuse and ridicule; it enabled him to see men and things as they were; it was anti-sectarian. He derived much innocent amusement from the idiosyncrasies of his co-laborers,— as they were free to do from his,— and he contributed his full

Ante, 3: 132. *MS. Aug. 1.* *Charlotte G. Coffin.* *Sallie Holley.* *Ante, 2: 125; 3: 381.* *Ante, 3: 91.* *Ante, 3: 82-84, 91, 156, 198; 4: 323.*

CHAP. XII. share to the flow of wit in those choice gatherings where Thompson, Phillips, and Quincy vied with each other. There was, however, a limitation to this humor: "On anything that he deems a serious subject, he won't bear a jest," wrote Quincy to Webb in 1843. *MS. Nov. 27.*

Mrs. Stowe has borne witness to my father's singular tact in conversation, adapting himself unconsciously to his auditor. *Ante, 3:401.* As he had a very poor memory for past events even in his own experience, he seldom indulged in reminiscence.[1] His life was strictly from day to day, his thoughts projected into the future—shall we say, like a sailor's, like his father's?

A. H. Clough.

"Where lies the land to which the ship would go?
Far, far ahead, is all her seamen know;
And where the land she travels from? Away,
Far, far behind, is all that they can say."

Had he been otherwise fitted for an historian, it is certain that he would have been as punctilious as his penmanship, as just and accurate as his habitual expression. His letters are noticeably minute as chronicles, and free from blunders as to dates. The *Liberator* may be searched in vain for his being called to account for any serious misrepresentation as the result of carelessness: of deliberate misrepresentation he was as incapable as of vindictiveness.

My father's goodness was so transparent that to be *known* by the good was equivalent to his being loved. His friendships in both hemispheres were numerous and very wide, and of a kind to do honor to any man; his companionships more restricted, and of very different degrees of intimacy. Quincy, who proclaimed my father's friendship one of the chief pleasures and honors of his life, was less often seen at our home than Phillips (being, to be *Lib. 20:152; cf. ante, p. 256.*

[1] The only autobiographical sketch known to have been drafted by him was (on request) for Oliver Johnson's use in preparing the article Garrison in Appletons' 'New American Cyclopædia,' in 1859. This MS. is probably still in existence, but its whereabouts is unknown.

sure, a suburban resident of Boston), or Hovey, or Francis Jackson, or Samuel May, Jr., for example; another group of closer attachments consisted of S. J. May, Oliver Johnson, and H. C. Wright. But, taking one degree of nearness with another, the one man who stood next to my father in a bond of warm and romantic friendship, was unquestionably George Thompson. This more than any other pairing suggested David and Jonathan; and the days of their intercourse were to my father, I am sure, the very happiest of his life. The affinity for N. P. Rogers was of course very strong, and was in a fair way to be confirmed when the unhappy separation took place; but it lacked the parity of age and the historic roots which the attraction for Thompson had. It can be said that my father never forsook or cast off a friend, and was ever ready to forgive and to be reconciled to one who had broken with him. In four conspicuous instances his fidelity and magnanimity were put to the proof by the changed and even hostile feelings of old, familiar, and beloved associates. The test was severe, but it was met.

Ante, 3:120.

Ante, 2:322; 3:37, 125; 4:156, 238.

I speak with diffidence of my father's relation to his immediate colleagues in the cause, but I think no one who survived the sectarian division in 1840 ever chafed under his primacy, which was held unobtrusively, with invariable deference to others, and by common consent, while it involved a deal of unshared labor. In the counsels of the Massachusetts Society and of the Executive Committee of the American Anti-Slavery Society after its transfer to Boston, his was commonly the initiative in devising practical measures, and he was expected to prepare the address, the petition, the call, the appeal. In conventions, when he was present, his place was always on the Business Committee, usually at the head of it, and to him fell the task of drafting the resolutions. The amount of drudgery thus performed was enormous. He was entirely tolerant of criticism, not a stickler for phraseology, and disposed to keep in the background

Ante, 2:333.

Ante, 3:91.

Ante, 1:400; 3:127.

CHAP. XII. when others were ready to take the floor. Confidence in his judgment was universal, and I cannot do better than quote the words of John Bishop Estlin, in a letter to Crabb Robinson in 1847:

Oct. 27.

Diary of H. C. Robinson, 3:301.

"I am very glad to learn from you Dr. Boott's opinion upon the slavery question. In the *infallibility* of Mr. Garrison's judgment I certainly do not place full confidence, but *unlimited* in his singleness of purpose, his noble disinterestedness, and his indefatigable zeal in the anti-slavery cause. I am, however, compelled to confess that, as regards *judgment* on his subject, what he has effected by his fifteen years of labor ought to plead for his wisdom; and those friends who have longest and most minutely watched his course, are very accordant in their decision that his views have evidenced a prophetic sagacity."

My father's theological evolution has been already sufficiently indicated. It would not be easy to name the *exact* dates of his relinquishing his belief in the supernatural sanction of the Bible or in the divine nature and atoning mission of Jesus. This radical change made no difference in his regard for the Scriptures, or in his use of them, as a moral engine, and he never failed to urge the reading of them upon his children. We were encouraged also to go to Sunday-school, at the Warren-Street Chapel and afterwards with Theodore Parker's congregation; and Sunday (in the forties, at least) had a certain staidness, not to call it solemnity, in our home that did not wholly proceed from a civil respect for the scruples of neighbors. Long before my father had quite freed himself from the trammels of orthodoxy, he was loosening the fetters of others. At the twenty-seventh anniversary of the American Anti-Slavery Society, Mrs. Elizabeth Cady Stanton remarked: "My own experience is, no doubt, that of many others. In the darkness and gloom of a false theology, I was slowly sawing off the chains of my spiritual bondage when, for the first time, I met Garrison in London. A few bold strokes from the hammer of his truth, I was free! . . . To Garrison we owe,

Cf. ante, 3: 18, 95, 145.

May 8, 9, 1860.

Lib. 30:78.

Ante, 2:383.

more than to any other one man of our day, all that we have of religious freedom." CHAP. XII.

It is small wonder that the clergy were reluctant even to baptize any namesake of my father's. Nor was there anything peculiar in their ferocious attacks on him for the heresies he ventilated while still in full accord with them as to the authority of the Scriptures — attacks parallel at all points with those of the Slave Power on political abolitionists who acknowledged the binding force of the Constitutional compromises, while proposing nothing unconstitutional. On the other hand, it took him some time to recover from the shock which he sustained on being repelled or neglected by the clergy in his first ingenuous appeals to them; and if he never ceased to hold them rigidly accountable as moral teachers and professors, he came to see that neither they nor the body of our church members were separable from the average morality of the age. There was something ludicrous in the contrast between his simple and childlike character, his absolute blamelessness as a citizen, with the clergy's holy horror and denunciation of him as, in one aspect, an arch-conspirator against the very frame-work of society; in another, a wretch for whom the penitentiary was too good. The more he used the Scriptures in his agitation, the more he appeared to them a poacher on their preserves; and his secular movement was a standing irritation to them as an obvious work of Christian charity conducted without the aid and direction of the cloth. But they never could succeed in organizing a clerical anti-slavery society having any vitality, whereas, in our war time, we saw the U. S. Sanitary Commission call a U. S. Christian Commission into existence. His identifying his peace doctrine with the Saviour capped the climax of his audacity and their indignation. Probably they will never forgive his succeeding without their patronage or permission (as an organized body), nor allow that slavery went under in any but "God's good time" and way.

MS. Jan. 2, 1866.

Ante, 1: 204, 211, 215, 464, 465.

Ante, 1: 469; 2: 306.

CHAP. XII. My father's standing with the clergy was not improved by his belief in the reality of the so-called spiritual manifestations — *i. e.*, in proofs of the future existence not resting solely on human aspiration or on the Bible. Some hints have already been given of his attitude towards these phenomena, and little need be added here. A letter written in 1871 well portrays it:

Ante, 3: 375.

MS. Jan. 31, 1871, to J. S. Adams.

"In reply to your letter, inquiring what are my views of Spiritualism, I will state for your private information that, after long and close investigation of the subject, I have had sufficient evidence, again and again, to convince me that it is more or less practicable for those who have left the body to hold communion with relatives and friends still in the flesh, and to make known their presence by signs and tokens in the shape of what are called 'manifestations.' I believe that this has been true in all ages and in all countries of the world, but only to a limited extent; whereas, in our own times, mediumship is multiplied indefinitely, and the number of believers in direct communication with the departed may be safely reckoned as legion, embracing persons of all ranks and conditions, from the most cultivated and refined to the most rude and ignorant. The Old and New Testaments abound with analogous manifestations; and these we are taught from childhood to regard as unquestionable, simply because they are recorded in that particular volume — for there are no living witnesses to authenticate any of them. And it is a noticeable fact, that those who are the most credulous in regard to ancient spirit intercourse, are the most sceptical in regard to similar intercourse in their own day, though the latter is vouched for by multitudes of living and reliable witnesses.

"Personally, I give very little time or attention to this matter, needing no further evidence, and having had my curiosity fully gratified. There is no reason why you should not investigate it, exercising all possible caution, and receiving nothing as true that does not commend itself to your reason and judgment. There are many weak-minded and deluded Spiritualists, who are easily imposed upon by unprincipled 'mediums,' and who foolishly waste a great deal of time in gratifying a morbid love for the marvellous; and the greater proportion of spirit-literature is utterly worthless. But this is no more to the disparagement of Spiritualism itself than the follies and ex-

Ante, 3: 375, 376.

travagances of professed Christians are to Christianity, or the unprincipled acts of Democratic partisans are to genuine Democracy. 'Beloved, believe not every spirit, but try the spirits whether they be of God,' is as needful advice to-day as it was in the Apostolic age."

In the following year he wrote thus to Edward M. Davis of a certain adventuress:

"Mrs. —— thinks 'there is no more thoughtless and irrational conclusion than that people acting under *Spirit guidance* are less to be trusted, and less personally trustworthy, than those acting under other guidances.' But this is to beg the question; for it assumes, first, that when any persons claim to be 'acting under Spirit guidance,' their word is not to be questioned; and secondly, that conceding that they are thus influenced (which certainly I do not doubt), it is not to be supposed that they are not wisely led. Now this is a sieve that will not hold water. . . . Hers is not the first case of Spirit hallucination which has come under my notice; and in every instance it has seemed to me to border closely upon lunacy. Certainly, immense credulity attends it." *MS. Jan.* 4, 1872.

It must be freely admitted that my father was himself too credulous in regard to marvels, such as the "spirit photographs," which have been thoroughly exposed as sheer imposition. Partly he was misled by his assumption of integrity in every human being with whom he came in contact, but partly also by the fact that if you say A in any class of spiritual phenomena, there is no reason why you should not say B. For example, if a bell is lifted from the table by the unseen agency, it is not past belief that the table itself may in turn be lifted from the floor; and so on through the whole round of physical manifestations. He witnessed, as he says above, a very great variety of manifestations in daylight and in dark, at the houses of friends, at the rooms of mediums, in his own home, both with and without mediums. As to this class he wrote to Mrs. Child in 1857: "I do not greatly wonder at your 'distrust of professional *paid* mediums'; and yet, is it unreasonable, if I ask a person to give me his time, his

Ante, 3:375, 408; 4:253.

MS. Feb. 6.

 room, etc., for him to require some remuneration, especially when (as is generally the case) he is very poor? Beyond a doubt, some mediums are base impostors, and are pursuing the business merely as selfish adventurers."

MS. Feb. 17, 1857, W. L. G. to H. E. G. My mother did not look kindly on Spiritualism, not envying my father's realizing sense of the actual presence of the departed; and he was not inconsiderate of her repugnance. Such differences only revealed their perfect union. *Ante*, 1:423. His estimate of her at the end of the first year of their marriage held true to the hour of their final separation. She supplied a needful element of repose, a useful example of punctuality and executive efficiency; added no care to his life (so long as she was in health), and warded off many. She steadily combated the procrastinating habit which was probably inborn in my father, and which journalism easily fostered. She reminded him of editorial writing to be done, of letters to be answered. Her order and system were in such sharp contrast with his lack of these qualities that another kind of temperament than hers would have been worn with chafing. Happily, if my father was slow to begin, he was not inefficient; *Ante*, 3:87. and if, for example, he habitually left himself too little time to reach the depot without "running for dear life," he seldom missed a train or an appointment. All her energy and self-denial were employed in keeping the family out of debt; and her constant concern in this regard was a wholesome correction of her husband's trust in Providence, which in turn lightened her own spirits. In her despondency, he would put his arm round her and lead her up and down the parlor, while he sang his favorite air,

Ante, 3:22. "In the days when we went gypsying"

till the cloud was lifted.

She was ever solicitous for the respectable appearance of her children, as well as for their moral purity and their enlightenment. His own want of early training made my father underrate the value of education; but, while her schooling had been much more narrow than her parents' circumstances might have afforded at a period when, to be sure, the higher education was withheld from women, she all the more was ambitious for her children. She encouraged and stimulated us in our studies, and, according to our respective love of them, would have had us advance as long and as far as her self-sacrifice could maintain us.

"If any man," wrote my father to Elizabeth Pease in 1846, "was ever blessed with an affectionate and loving wife, I am that man; and if ever children had a watchful, assiduous, devoted mother, mine have. I tell Helen that the only fear I have is, that her attachment for me is carried to an undue extent. She always feels my absence so keenly that I never leave home without great reluctance, though she never wishes me to forego the discharge of any duty to please her. May I ever prove worthy of one so confiding, faithful, and loving!" *MS. Nov. 15.*

Most anxious hours my mother certainly passed in these absences, if one considers only her responsibility for the health of a large family. But her husband's health also caused solicitude, and when he left her, in stormy times, to attend the anniversaries in New York, with the certainty of violent disturbance from the mob, her forebodings were natural and most poignant. They often arose over the daily delays in my father's arriving home from the printing-office, he being exposed even in Boston to personal attack, and in frequent receipt of menaces through the mails.

My mother's paralysis devolved the care of her — and it was a very great care at night — upon her husband and only daughter, who repaid to the full all the tenderness and affection she had lavished upon them. For an extremely active person reduced to sudden dependence, she bore her fate with singular fortitude. "If I needed to learn a lesson of patience and resignation, the example of your invalid mother would be most instructive," wrote my father to his absent son, in 1874. "How closely in her waking hours, during the long period of eleven years, has she been confined to her chair at the window, with- *MS. Dec. 14, to W. P. G.*

CHAP. XII. out a murmur at her hard lot!" She was inexpressibly grateful for all the attentions she now received, and made heroic exertions to diminish them as far as lay in her power. I remember one instance in which she toiled up the long flight from the sitting-room to the chamber above, holding her skirt in her teeth, and dragging the useless limb from stair to stair, rather than call her daughter, who was putting her baby to sleep, to bring down the forgotten handkerchief. And during all these years of weary waiting for release from the thraldom of the flesh, she was ever thinking and planning for the welfare of each member of the family. "Outwardly and inwardly, she was loveliness itself," wrote my father just after the grave had closed over her. "No choice could have been a more fortunate one for me, and our married life was fraught with such blessings and enjoyments as have seldom been realized in a state of wedlock."

MS. Feb. 27, 1876, to W. P. G.

END OF THE FOURTH AND LAST VOLUME.

CORRIGENDA AND ADDENDA.

Volume I.

Postscript, following p. xiv. In the last sentence of the second paragraph, too much borrowing is implied. For "passage" read "sentence," and *dele* "etc."

Page 3, line 13 from bottom. Old Town was part of Newbury, Mass.

Page 4, line 13. *Dele* both commas.

Page 12, note 3. The record reads, conformably to our guess, "*and* here with her Child."

Page 14, line 5. Read, "Kinsale, County *Cork*, Munster."

Page 78, line 12, and page 98, line 10. For "Malcolm" read "Malcom."

Page 87, line 17. For "Handwich" read "Hardwick."

Page 132. The passage quoted in the second paragraph is from Fisher Ames.

Page 161, line 5 from bottom. For "1858" read "1848."

Page 289, last sentence of note 1. It was Isaac Winslow (not Nathan) who lived for a time at Danvers, Mass.

Page 301, line 4 from bottom. Supply an apostrophe after Thoughts.

Page 332, last paragraph; and page 401, first paragraph. Whittier's poem to W. L. G. was composed early in 1832 and published at once (not in 1833, as stated).

Page 349, line 9 from bottom. *Dele* "his first experience." See *ante,* 1: 343.

Page 354, line 15. For "Wesleyan" read "Baptist."

Page 388. The poetical extract is from Campbell's Stanzas to the memory of the Spanish Patriots.

Page 397, note 3. The name of Orson S. Murray should have been inserted.

Page 449, note. The Mr. Breckinridge mentioned was the Rev. Robert J. Breckinridge.

Page 453, note 1, line 3. For "Crowley" read "Cowley."

Page 501, line 1. For "Mayor" read "ex-Mayor."

Volume II.

Page 35, note 1. Mr. Edward L. Pierce thinks that Mr. Ellis Ames's reminiscence was unjust to Mr. Sumner, and we are inclined to the same opinion.

Page 98, note 1. As Mr. Stephen Higginson died in 1834, and never owned a pew in Dr. Channing's church, Mrs. Chapman's memory was clearly at fault. The *incident*, however, really occurred, as the following letter (which has been placed in our hands since Vol. 2 was published) shows:

BOSTON, May 17, 1836.

DEAR SIR: Mrs. Higginson requests me to say that she will soon want the whole of her pew for some friends and relatives recently come to town. Will you be good enough to accommodate yourself elsewhere as soon as may be convenient?—Yours very truly,

HENRY HIGGINSON.

HENRY CHAPMAN, jr., Esqre.

The writer was a brother of the late Mr. Stephen Higginson. The letter is endorsed in Mrs. Chapman's handwriting: "The Sabbath preceding this date [May 15], Garrison and May sat in our pew." The discourse alluded to by Mr. Garrison on page 98 was given two months before this.

Page 103, lines 10, 11. *Teste* Dr. H. I. Bowditch, Mr. Ward lived in Salem (not in Danvers).

Page 142, line 6 from bottom. For "1832" read "1831."

Pages 236, 237. Both letters are from the MSS.

Page 247, last sentence of first paragraph. Senator Davis denied having heard Preston's threat (being either engaged or absent). See *Lib.* 12 : 177.

Page 315. The writer of the letter of Nov. 14, 1839, was the Rev. L. D. Butts (*Lib.* 17 : 24).

Page 360, line 4 from bottom. The denial concerning Mr. Child is not quite accurate. See *post*, 3 : 20, note 2, and 49, 83, 101.

Page 395, second paragraph. For "*Quarterly Review*" read "*Edinburgh Review.*"

VOLUME III.

Page 354, note 2. To show the difficulty of attempting to write history with entire accuracy, we remark that Mr. Phillips, in 1851, called "the West India interest" in Parliament "some fifty or sixty strong." To keep within bounds, he would claim no more than "fifty votes." In 1879 (?) he wrote to F. J. G. of this incident: "Yes, Buxton told me the story, and O'Connell has himself told it in one of his later speeches. But it was twenty-seven votes, not sixty, they promised him. You will tell Lizzy Pease this."

VOLUME IV.

Page 113, last line but one. *Dele* the comma after "coming." Though it occurs in the original MS., it perhaps implies that Mr. Thompson accompanied Mr. Garrison to Baltimore, which was not the case. His coming was expected.

Page 166, note 2, last line but one. For "Washburne" read "Washburn."

Page 176, line 2. It is literally incorrect to say that the Massachusetts A. S. Society continued the *Standard*. This paper remained the organ of the *American* A. S. Society after the schism of 1865. Nevertheless, as previously, the main support of the paper (through the Subscription Festival and otherwise) came from the Massachusetts organization, or what was left of it.

Page 324, second paragraph. In reading our remarks about our father's title to be called a Christian, Mr. Oliver Johnson reminds us of the following passage on p. 366 of his Life of W. L. G.:

"Several years since, a clergyman, bearing a name of great eminence throughout the Christian world, said to me in substance: 'I should not dare to call Mr. Garrison an infidel, for fear of bringing Christianity itself into reproach. For, if a man can live such a life as he has lived and do what he has done,—if he can stand up for God's law of purity and justice in the face of a frowning world, and when even the professed ministers of Christ are recreant,—if he can devote himself to the redemption of an outraged and plundered race and be pelted with the vilest epithets for a whole generation, without flinching or faltering, and yet be an infidel, men may well ask what is the value of Christianity. No, no; I must believe that Mr. Garrison is a Christian, who has his walk with God, or he never could have had strength and courage to go through the fiery trials to which he has been exposed.'"

INDEX.

INDEX

TO THE

FOUR VOLUMES.

THE DE VINNE PRESS.

www.ingramcontent.com/pod-product-compliance
Lightning Source LLC
LaVergne TN
LVHW010529100826
845148LV00001B/133

* 9 7 8 1 4 2 5 5 7 3 5 0 8 *